Spiritual Classics
Series

World Wisdom
The Library of Perennial Philosophy

The Library of Perennial Philosophy is dedicated to the exposition of the timeless Truth underlying the diverse religions. This Truth, often referred to as the *Sophia Perennis*—or Perennial Wisdom—finds its expression in the revealed Scriptures as well as the writings of the great sages and the artistic creations of the traditional worlds.

The Perennial Philosophy provides the intellectual principles capable of explaining both the formal contradictions and the transcendent unity of the great religions.

Ranging from the writings of the great sages of the past, to the perennialist authors of our time, each series of our Library has a different focus. As a whole, they express the inner unanimity, transforming radiance, and irreplaceable values of the great spiritual traditions.

The Path of Muhammad (s.a.w.s): A Book on Islamic Morals and Ethics appears as one of our selections in the Spiritual Classics series.

Spiritual Classics series

This series includes seminal, but often neglected, works of unique spiritual insight from leading religious authors of both the East and West. Ranging from books composed in ancient India to forgotten jewels of our time, these important classics feature new introductions which place them in the perennialist context.

Cover Art: Turkish miniature depicting the Holy Prophet
receiving his first revelation from the Archangel Gabriel

THE PATH OF MUHAMMAD ^(ﷺ)

(AL-TARIQAH AL-MUHAMMADIYYAH)

A BOOK ON ISLAMIC MORALS AND ETHICS

&

THE LAST WILL AND TESTAMENT

(VASIYYETNAME)

by

IMAM BIRGIVI

A 16th Century Islamic Mystic

Interpreted by
Shaykh Tosun Bayrak al-Jerrahi al-Halveti

Foreword by
Shaykh Abdul Mabud

Introduction by
Vincent J. Cornell

World Wisdom

The Path of Muhammad (s.a.w.s): A Book on Islamic Morals and Ethics
© 2005 World Wisdom, Inc.

All rights reserved.
No part of this book may be used or reproduced
in any manner without written permission,
except in critical articles and reviews.

Library of Congress Cataloging-in-Publication Data

Birgīvi Mehmet Efendi, ca. 1522-1573.
  [Ṭarīqah al-Muḥammadīyah]
  The path of Muhammad : a book on Islamic morals and ethics / by Imam Birgīvi ;
interpreted by Shaykh Tosun Bayrak al-Jerrahi al-Halveti ; foreword by Shaykh Abdul
Mabud ; introduction by Vincent J. Cornell.
     p. cm. – (Spiritual classics series)
  Includes bibliographical references.
  ISBN 0-941532-68-2 (pbk. : alk. paper) 1. Religious life–Islam. 2.
Muslims–Conduct of life. 3. Islamic ethics. I. Bayrak, Tosun. II. Title. III. Series.
  BP188.B56 2005
  297.5–dc22

                                                                    2004028733

Printed on acid-free paper in Canada

For information address World Wisdom, Inc.
P.O. Box 2682, Bloomington, Indiana 47402-2682

www.worldwisdom.com

I dedicate this book to my spiritual children, the Jerrahi Dervishes of America and to my children and grandchildren from my loins. May they read, understand and follow my last will and testament and this book of guidance. The words are from us, the persuasion is from Allah.

*

I wish to acknowledge my gratitude to my dervishes Hajja Rabia Harris who reviewed and edited the manuscript, Hajja Zinnur Doganata who typed it with careful attention to important details, and to Adel Y. al-Akel who checked the Arabic transliterations. May Allah be pleased with them.

CONTENTS

LIST OF ILLUSTRATIONS
(English translations of Arabic calligraphy only)

NOTE ON ABBREVIATIONS

i. s.a.w.s.—*salla Allahu 'alayhi wa sallim* ("May God's peace and blessings be upon him"): a blessing reserved for the Prophet Muhammad.

ii. a.s.—*'alayhi as-salam* ("Peace be upon him"): a blessing reserved for prophets and archangels.

iii. r.a.—*radiya Allahu 'anhu* (or *'anha*) ("May God be pleased with him/her"): a blessing reserved for the family and companions of the Prophet Muhammad.

iv. q.s.—*qaddusa Allahu sirrahu* (or *sirraha*) ("May God sanctify his/her secret"): a blessing reserved for saints.

FOREWORD

"O Prophet—behold, We [Allah] have sent thee as a witness [to the truth], and as a herald of glad tidings and a warner, and as one who summons [all men] to Allah by His leave, and as a light-giving beacon" (Qur'an 33:45-46).

Prophet Muhammad (s.a.w.s.), the last and the greatest of Allah's messengers said, "None of you has real faith unless I am dearer unto him than his father and his child and all mankind" (Bukhari and Muslim). An ostentatious affection for the blessed Prophet can do little to create an authentic affinity with him. Real love between us and the Prophet is established when we follow the actions of his life: actions that made his life truly the Last Messenger's life and a life that is worthy of imitation for all people until the end of the world. Following the Prophet's *sunnah* is to submit to Allah, and to efface one's ego. In its comprehensive sense, *sunnah* is not just following the Prophet in one particular act, but adopting the way of the Prophet in the pursuit of meritorious acts and supererogatory practices and habits.

Al-Tariqah al-Muhammadiyyah of Imam Birgivi (r.a.), translated and interpreted by Shaykh Tosun Bayrak, has combined in itself the expositions of both the law (*shari'ah*) and the way (*minhaj*) as exemplified in the life of Prophet Muhammad (s.a.w.s.). Written in clear, lucid language and replete with verses from the Qur'an and *hadith*, this book presents Islam as practised by the Prophet. Through his interpretative translation, Shaykh Tosun Bayrak has indeed rendered a great service to those English-speaking readers who are interested in learning the essentials of Islamic faith and practices. It discusses the inner meaning of religious injunctions and how to purify our inner selves so as to gain closer proximity to Allah.

Allah created human beings pure and perfect, with no original sin. Sinners destroy this perfection with their own hands. Believers strive to preserve this perfection with their dedicated obedience. Ever since Adam (a.s.) received revelation from his Lord, human beings, over the generations, have been guided through a chain of Divine Messages. The Qur'an revealed to the Prophet is the culmination and end of all prophetic revelations. For all humanity, Allah has ordained a law and a way in conformity with His universal divine plan. Our Prophet was sent down as the epitome of this plan, a human model that we should all aspire to. He was the imam of all the prophets during the night journey (*mi'raj*) and was endowed with the unique honor of crossing the farthest limit of the realm of creation and of conversing with the Lord of the Worlds in the very presence of His Throne.

The Prophet's life shows that there is a supplication (*du'a*) for every action—from waking up in the morning and for every action that ensues throughout the day until bedtime. He turned to Allah in every situation—whether in calamities or in happiness. When suffering befell him, he reacted with calmness and a readiness to accept that whatever happens, comes from Allah. When his prayers were answered, he wept for the love of Allah and His almighty mercy. Thus was his life permeated with the remembrance of Allah.

The path of Prophet Muhammad (s.a.w.s.) encompasses the whole of human life. Undeterred by any worldly power, unmoved by any offer of worldly gain, he proclaimed the glory of Allah. When his uncle, Abu Talib asked him to desist from his mission, he said, "Uncle, should they give me the sun in my right hand and the moon in my left hand in return for abandoning my call, I would not do so until Allah has brought this message to triumph or until I have perished." All who come after Prophet Muhammad (s.a.w.s.) should endeavor to pursue this stoic frame of mind. He was indubitably a trustworthy recipient of Allah's message. In him, there was no question of changing or hiding the revealed word, even when it contained his divine admonition. Nor did he preach that which went against the word of Allah in order to satisfy his own desires. He only conveyed the word that Allah revealed to him. So, his words were law.

The sublime state in which man has been created can be maintained only through the love, and ultimately the gnosis of Allah, but our recognition of Allah is only to the extent that He has revealed himself to us, both in the world of manifestation and within the deepest recesses of our souls. Man's greatest achievement is in possessing those qualities that make him truly human. These qualities are enshrined in the eternal names of Allah, the greatest manifestations of which are to be seen in Prophet Muhammad (s.a.w.s.). This is why the Prophet told us that he was sent to complete the excellence of character. A believer can hope to attain some of the sweet qualities of the Prophet by following him in both the physical acts (the exoteric aspects) of the *sunnah* as well as the spiritual acts (the esoteric aspects) of the *sunnah*. His *sunnah* is the only means of drawing near to Allah. Prophetic qualities cannot be imbibed, save through the emulation (*ittiba'*) of the Prophet, and this emulation is the precondition of the love of Allah: "If you love Allah, follow me, then Allah will love you" (Qur'an 3:31). By emulating every act of the Prophet, every living moment of a believer becomes significant, every action full of meaning.

To comprehend the entire spiritual status of the Prophet, to whom Allah revealed some of the ultimate truths of His creation, is beyond any mortal, but the moral and spiritual teachings of the Prophet are a living reality in the lives of millions of Muslims today. By following his moral and spiritual teachings, they follow the best of human examples. There are no virtues other than the virtues of Prophet Muhammad (s.a.w.s.); all virtues are subsumed under the virtues of the Prophet.

Let us pray that Imam Birgivi's *al-Tariqah al-Muhammadiyyah*, translated and interpreted by Shaykh Tosun Bayrak, proves to be an invaluable companion to both the novice and the advanced in the path, as well as common believers in their spiritual journey to meet their Lord. May Allah guide us to Him by means of his chosen prophet, Hadrat Muhammad (s.a.w.s.) and may He bless our beloved Prophet Muhammad (s.a.w.s.), and his family and companions and give them peace.

Shaykh Abdul Mabud
Director General
The Islamic Academy
Cambridge, U.K.

INTRODUCTION

This long-awaited classic of Islamic spirituality fulfills important needs in scholarship on the history of Sufism and in the contemporary search for spiritual direction in today's troubled world. Imam Birgivi's manual of ethical conduct and spiritual practice details the "Path of Muhammad" (*al-Tariqah al-Muhammadiyyah*), a Sufi method created in late fifteenth-century Morocco and disseminated as far as India and beyond through the mediation of Ottoman Sufi masters. This path seeks to instill the *sunnah* of Muhammad not only through imitation of the Prophet's outward behavior, but more importantly, by teaching one to assimilate the Prophet's inner spiritual states. In this way, the seeker becomes empowered to find a personal solution to the challenges of the times without merely repeating the answers of the past.

Shaykh Tosun Bayrak's lucid and at times lyrical translation of Imam Birgivi's text gives new life to this work and makes the reader believe it was written yesterday, not five centuries ago. In an era of rampant fundamentalism and simplistic and politicized responses to the world's problems, this work reminds us that the greater struggle is within ourselves, and that the life of the body cannot be improved without the transformation of the soul.

The term, *al-Tariqah al-Muhammadiyyah*, appears to have been used for the first time by the Moroccan Sufi 'Abdallah al-Ghazwani (d. 1528-9). A Bedouin by origin, Ghazwani is one of the famous "Seven Saints" of Marrakech and is known locally as *Mul al-Qusur* (Master of Palaces). In his works, Ghazwani also refers to the Path of Muhammad as the "Method of the Muhammadan Sunnah" (*Madhhab al-Sunnah al-Muhammadiyyah*) and the "Technique of Archetypal Perception" (*Suluk al-Nazrah al-Azaliyyah*).[1] The link between this Moroccan Sufi and Imam Birgivi's teachers may have been the Egyptian jurist, Sufi, and Qur'an commentator Muhammad al-Laqani (d. 1528-9), who corresponded extensively with Ghazwani about the details of *al-Tariqah al-Muhammadiyyah*. Sufis of the Qadiriyyah Sufi order ultimately passed on these doctrines throughout the Ottoman Empire and South Asia.

In Ghazwani's version of the Path of Muhammad, the key figure is the "Bell Saint" (*al-Jaras*), the axial Sufi teacher of his time, who can hear

---

[1] On 'Abdallah al-Ghazwani and the origins of the "Path of Muhammad," see Vincent J. Cornell, *Realm of the Saint: Power and Authority in Moroccan Sufism* (Austin: University of Texas Press, 1998), pp. 155-229.

the "pealing" or reverberation of the divine archetypes on the verge of their actualization into forms. The ability of the Bell Saint to teach his followers to perceive these reverberations is based on his assumption of the Prophetic Inheritance (*al-wirathah al-nabawiyyah*), which comes about through the assimilation of the Prophet's inner *sunnah* or spiritual consciousness. Ghazwani's concept of the Bell Saint comes from a famous tradition, found in the *hadith* collections of Bukhari, Tirmidhi, and Nasa'i, where the Prophet describes the sound of divine revelation as like the clanging of a bell. In the words of Ahmad al-Buni (d. 1225), an earlier Sufi who used this metaphor, "The bell tolls for each man. He who listens to it is elevated and is taken from the world for union with Allah, which is the goal of prayer."

'Abdallah al-Ghazwani was the third major shaykh of the Jazuliyyah Sufi order, which dominated Morocco in the fifteenth and sixteenth centuries. This brotherhood, which combined the teachings of the Shadhiliyyah and Qadiriyyah Sufi traditions, was founded by Muhammad ibn Sulayman al-Jazuli (d. 1465). Imam Jazuli is famous throughout the Muslim world as the author of *Dala'il al-Khayrat* (Tokens of Goodness), the best known and most widely disseminated book of prayers on the Prophet Muhammad. The complete assimilation of the Prophet's *sunnah*, both outwardly and inwardly, was a hallmark of the Jazuli method. The invocations of *Dala'il al-Khayrat* were used to supplement the formal practice of learning the Prophet's outward behaviors, and provided a balance between the outer form of the Islamic *shari'ah* and the spiritual consciousness that lies behind the *shari'ah*. Jazuli's idea of assimilating the Prophet's spiritual consciousness drew upon Ibn 'Arabi's (d. 1240) concept of the Muhammadan Reality (*al-haqiqah al-Muhammadiyyah*) and 'Abd al-Karim al-Jili's (d. 1402-3) concept of the Muhammadan Image (*al-surah al-Muhammadiyyah*). Both concepts were fundamental teachings of the Qadiriyyah Sufi tradition during Jazuli's lifetime.

The Path of Muhammad by Imam Birgivi is a handbook of spiritual practice in the tradition of Imam Jazuli and his followers. In fact, it is so close to the tradition of the Jazuliyyah that it may be taken as a replacement for Jazuli's own treatise on Sufi practice, which is now lost. In addition, those who choose to use this work for their personal spiritual development may want to supplement its teachings with the recitation of Jazuli's *Dala'il al-Khayrat*, which can be found in numerous editions across the Muslim world. Tosun Bayrak, a shaykh of the Halveti-Jerrahi order based in Istanbul, worked ten years to complete this translation of *The Path of Muhammad.* In its original language, Imam Birgivi's masterwork is still used as a text in the most important faculties of theology in the universities of many Muslim countries. Nureddin Jerrahi, the seventeenth-century founder of the Halveti-Jerrahi Sufi order, declared that to study this work was sufficient for the moral education of his followers. This is because *The Path of Muhammad* is not just a handbook of rules and regulations. Instead, it is a study guide for the spiritual life, which takes the reader step by step toward understanding the moral and spiritual consciousness of the Prophet Muhammad. Shaykh Tosun Bayrak's translation of this work has done more than simply bring a Sufi classic to a wider audience; it has opened the door for the revival of an important Sufi tradition that bridges the continents of Asia, Africa, and Europe, and which will again bring spiritual nourishment to a barren and confused world.

Vincent J. Cornell
Professor of History and Director
King Fahd Center for Middle East and Islamic Studies
Chair of Studies, Program in Religious Studies
University of Arkansas

THE LAST WILL AND TESTAMENT

(*Vasiyyetname*)

by

Imam Birgivi

Interpreted by

Shaykh Tosun Bayrak al-Jerrahi al-Halveti

This is our last will and testament, and supplication to the seekers of Truth: In the name of God, the Merciful and the Compassionate: All thanks, praise, and glory be to God, who has brought us, the faithful, to Islam—to submission to Him and who has given us His Beloved, Hadrat Muhammad, may God's peace and blessings be upon him, as our prophet, guide, and example, intercessor of our wrongs and His mercy upon the world, and who made us one nation, one family under him.

May our Lord's mercy, His angels' prayers for our deliverance, and the prayers and praise of His true servants be upon all the Prophets and Messengers and their blessed companions. And may God forgive this humblest of His servants, and my parents, and my children, and my brothers and sisters in Islam who are in desperate need of His mercy and the forgiveness of our sins. We have attempted, for our own deliverance and for those whom we love, to gather the little we know and to write in your language, so that you understand it, our Last Will and Testament. May it remind you of your own departure from this world, and help in your salvation.

ON ALLAH (MAY HE BE GLORIFIED AND EXALTED)

First, I beseech all Muslims to believe, say, and confirm this with their hearts: there is no god but God worthy and deserving to be worshiped, obeyed, and loved.

He has no partner, nor is anything like Him. He eats not, drinks not, sleeps not, begets not, nor is He begotten. He does not have a wife, son, or daughter. He exists neither in a place nor at a time. He is neither on earth nor in heaven, on your right or your left, under or above. He has no shape or form or color, nor face, hands or feet. He fears not, hurts not, is saddened not, changes not, and is free of all defects. He is other than all we know or can imagine.

He has no age. He was before always, and will be after the after, forever. He is self-existent, and does not depend on anything. His essence is only His. It is unknown to anyone but He, and is constant. He has priority over everything. He created all from nothing and can turn all into nothing. Nothing has the power to resist Him, and there is no difficulty for Him. For Him to create seven heavens and seven earths is the same as creating a fly.

No one can influence, dominate, or judge Him, and He governs all and everything. He needs no one, and all are in need of Him. No good or harm can come to Him from anywhere or anyone, even if all the faithless kept faith with Him or if all the sinners became obedient. All the worship directed to Him, from the beginning of time until the end, confers no benefit upon Him. If no one ever believed in Him, it would not harm Him at all.

He is One, Only, and Unique. He is Ever-Living, All-Knowing, Aware of all that is in heaven and earth, whether it is observed by or hidden from humanity. He has the accounting of all the leaves on the trees, the number of wheat kernels, and the grains of sand. Nothing is unknown to Him. He knows the parts of every whole, and the past, present, and future of every existence. He knows what you do, what you say, think, and feel, what you show and what you hide. He knows all that is visible and invisible, what there is and what is yet to come. He cannot be mistaken, nor miss or forget anything that He knows. His knowledge existed before there was anything to know: it is uncreated, like Him.

God is All-Seeing and All-Hearing. He sees the tiny black ant walking on a black stone in the darkest of nights, and hears its footsteps. If you whisper in someone's ear and neither he nor even you hear your voice, know that God hears your voice loud and clear. He has no eyes, no ears, yet He hears and sees without any senses.

All will is His. He does what He wills. Nothing happens or exists without His will. He has no needs or wishes. No one's wishes, no matter how strong, can influence His will and make Him do things. Every atom in the universe exists because He willed it to be. Both good and evil are His will. If He willed not, the faithful could not have believed and obeyed Him by their will. He is the one who wills the faithlessness of the faithless, and the sin of the sinner. If He did not, there would be neither sin nor evil. Not a fly can move its wing without His will. What man does, God makes him do. If He willed, all people would have been pious. If He willed, all people would have been evil. Then why did He not will everyone to be devout, but made some sinners? The answer is that no one has the right to question Him. He is absolute, one, unique in His will and in His actions.

Yet there is a divine reason and wisdom in what He does that human beings cannot understand. There is always an advantage for all. Even if you cannot know, believe that there is a multitude of good hidden in the existence of poisonous snakes, scorpions, vermin and bugs, and all other things we associate with suffering and misfortune. It is an obligation for all faithful ones to believe this, and to believe that it has always been so, and always will be.

God's will is eternal as He is, not created. God is All-Powerful: All power belongs to Him. His power is only conditional upon one thing: His will. Only what He makes, comes to exist; only what He does, happens. There is nothing He cannot do. He has brought the dead back to life, made stones and trees talk and walk, made stars disappear and reappear, turned earth to gold and gold to earth, made rivers flow uphill, raised those He loved above the seven heavens and brought them back, transported them from the eastern end of the world to its western end in an instant. He is the one who does everything with His power, which is eternal like Himself, though created afterwards, and which is inexhaustible.

Every word, every sound, all that is said and heard are His. His commands, His ordinances and judgments that apply to His creation, are in His words. These are contained in the last divine book, the Holy Qur'an, which includes all the other preceding holy books. The Qur'an is His final word, whose meaning is infinite and eternal.

God's word is soundless. It does not need a tongue or lips to pronounce it, nor does it need ears to be heard, nor does it need letters to be written or eyes to be read.

God is the creator of all and everything. There is no other who created but He. He is the one who created the eye and what it sees, the hand and what it does, the tongue and what it says. He is the one who created us and our deeds—the whole, the parts, the essence and the attributes of men and *jinn*. The worlds and the heavens, devils, beasts, plants, rocks and jewels, all that can be seen, felt and imagined, and the invisible and unimaginable, are created by Him from nothing. Only He existed before anything existed. He created the creation, not because He needed it, but to manifest His Love, His Will, His Wisdom, His Power, and His Compassion.

So: He is before the before. He did not become; He always was. He is after the after, eternal: He always will be. He is one, only and unique, without partner. He is the cause of all and everything. All are in need of Him, while He needs no one and nothing. He said "Be" and all became. Everything will be gone when He says "Be gone." He is the creator, bearing no resemblance to what He created. He is the self-existent, independent, without any needs.

These are the essential things that human beings can understand about the perfection of their Sustainer, whom they should believe, love, and obey.

ON THE ANGELS

And know that God has created angels. Some of them live in God's spiritual kingdom in the heavens, and some on earth among us. They eat not, drink not, nor are they male or female. They cannot be seen or heard, but they see and hear us. They are the ones who bring God's words to us and ours to Him. They each are given a duty, which they perform obediently. One of them sits on our left shoulder to record our wrongs, and one on our right shoulder to count our good deeds. But by the grace of God the Compassionate, the one who records our sins is charged not to do so immediately, but to wait and see if we repent. And when we repent our sins are annulled, and our repentance is recorded as a good deed.

5

Among them are four archangels. Gabriel is the greatest of them all. His size is larger than the whole distance the eye can see. His power is such that a single feather of his wings could flatten a mountain. But he appeared to our Prophet as a gentle beautiful young man and brought him the Qur'an from God, word by word, over 23 years. He was God's messenger to all the prophets. That is the purpose of his creation: to bring God's words to humankind.

Michael's divine duty is to take charge of all natural phenomena in the universe, from building the paths that stars and planets follow, to governing the winds and rains and the growth of grains on earth.

Azra`il is the angel of death whose duty is to separate men's souls from their bodies. When Israfil blows his trumpet, Azra`il will kill all that was created in an instant. He is the last one to die on Doomsday.

Israfil is charged with the Hereafter. With the first sound of his trumpet everything will die and disappear and all will become void. Then the Lord will bring him back from death, and he will blow his trumpet for the second time. Then all the dead will be raised to give their accounting on the Judgment Day.

All the prophets and the holy books God has sent say that angels exist, even if people cannot see them. In the material universe there are so many things we neither see nor know: Be persuaded of angelic existence by the discovery today of a thing you did not know existed yesterday.

You cannot deny the existence of a thing you do not see. Do you deny that you have an intelligence, conscience, and soul, although you cannot see them? You may say, "But we see their effects." Then know and believe that all the order in the universe and our world, from the heavens to the smallest atom, all of that is maintained due to the vast number of angels working under their Lord. Likewise you, all people, and the whole of creation are under the scrutiny and control of these invisible servants of God.

ON THE REVEALED SCRIPTURES

And know that our Lord has sent 104 or 144 holy books to His prophets, brought by His archangel Gabriel, that are known to humanity. Some of them are lost, some of them have changed, for it has been thousands of years since they were revealed.

The greatest of them are the Torah revealed to Prophet Moses, the Psalms revealed to Prophet David, the Gospel revealed to Prophet Jesus, and the last, the Qur'an, which contains the essence of all holy books, revealed bit by bit over 23 years to the last and the seal of the prophets, Muhammad, may God's peace and blessings be upon him and upon all of them.

All the messages of our Lord prior to the Holy Qur'an have been lost, abrogated, or altered, but not the Qur'an. Not a single letter has been changed nor will it be, until the end of time, since God Himself has forbidden it and made it impossible. God says,

We have, without doubt, sent down the Message, and We will assuredly guard it (from corruption). (*Hijr*, 9)

As these holy books contain God's will, orders, and prohibitions for humanity to follow for their own salvation in this world and the Hereafter, it is an obligation for all to believe in their truth, respect them, and follow them.

ON THE PROPHETS (MAY GOD'S PEACE BE ON THEM)
And know that God has sent prophets at different times to different peoples. God chooses prophets among perfect human beings who are spiritually, morally, intellectually, and physically superior to all others. All of them had the following characteristics:

They were beautiful in appearance: all the senses of the ones who saw them were enchanted. They looked beautiful, their voices were soft and melodic; their smell, touch, and taste delighted those who came close to them. Their minds were all-encompassing. They commited no error or mistake in their impressions, thoughts, and judgments. In their character they were truthful. They obeyed their Lord totally and taught all that was revealed to them, without changing or hiding a single word, out of fear and consideration of the consequences. They were perfectly just, honest, faithful, and trustworthy. They were faultless, blameless, and innocent of all human error, sin, and frailty. They were fearless: they feared nothing and nobody except their Lord.

The fear of God is of two sorts. Ordinary people fear God's wrath and punishment in this world and in the Hereafter. That is not the fear known to God's prophets. Theirs is the awe of God's almightiness, majesty, and greatness. That fear is felt only by those who know the perfection of God.

God has sent 124,000 or 224,000 prophets between Adam, the first prophet, and Muhammad the last and the seal of prophethood, God's peace and blessings upon all of them. The prophets mentioned in the Holy Qur'an are Adam, Noah, Hud, Idris, Salih, Abraham, Ishmael, Isaac, Jacob, Joseph, Moses, Aaron, Shu`ayb, Zachariah, John the Baptist, Jesus, David, Solomon, Elias, Elijah, Dhul-Kifl, Job, Jonah, Lot, and Muhammad. Dhul-Qarnayn, Ezra, Luqman, Tubba' and Khidr are also mentioned in the Qur'an, but whether they were prophets or saints is debatable. Although all these prophets are men, it is believed by some that blessed women, such as Eve the wife of Adam, the mother of Moses, Virgin Mary, Asiya the wife of Pharoah, Sarah, and Hagar were also prophets. The greatest chosen ones among all the prophets are five: Muhammad, Jesus, Moses, Abraham, and Noah, God's peace and blessings upon all of them.

ON THE PROPHET ADAM (A.S.)

Adam, peace be upon him, was the first human being God created and also the first prophet. When God intended to create a human being He had angels gather handfuls of earth from all parts of the world, high and low, black and white, mixed them with water, and made a wet clay. He made Adam's body on a Friday and dried it for 40 years in the air and over fire. Then He blew life into it from His own breath, and Adam woke up in the Garden of Eden. God taught Adam His beautiful Names, which also included the names of all and everything created, and asked Adam to teach what he knew to the angels. When the human being was thus esteemed higher than the angels, God ordered the angels to prostrate in respect to Adam's knowledge. All obeyed, but a *jinn* who was in heaven among the angels, ambitious for God's approval and excessive in devotion, refused to humble himself in front of Adam, judging himself better than Adam. God cursed Satan and threw him away from the Garden and His mercy. But God permitted the Devil and its many children to test Adam's children till the end of time.

Each human being has an accompanying devil that penetrates human nature as water penetrates a sponge. That devil whispers into the left ventricle of the human heart, inspiring fantasies, leading people into mischief and disobedience to their Lord. Satan is the archenemy of humanity—so recognize Satan as your enemy. If you do so, it will not have the power to steal your faith nor to lead you astray. But some say your ego, the desires of your carnality, make a devil 70 times more powerful than the Satan who is intent on destroying you.

ON THE HOLY PROPHET MUHAMMAD (S.A.W.S.)

And Muhammad, peace be upon him, is the last and the seal of all the prophets. All the others were sent to particular people at a certain time, but the Beloved of Allah, the best of all creation, was sent as God's mercy upon the universe, as the Prophet of all humanity until the end of time, and afterwards in the Hereafter. His prophethood preceded the creation of Adam, the first man and the first prophet, for he himself said:

I was a prophet when Adam was between water and clay. (Bukhari, Abu Naeem)

God created the Light of Muhammad, his soul, as His first creation. He created all and everything from the Light of Muhammad. Thus the essence of all prophethood was always present in his first-created soul, but he declared his prophethood in the body at the age of 40. It is wrong to think that he became a prophet at the age of 40.

His Miracles

Since miracles are not ordinary but supernatural, God has given them to prophets to convince ordinary people of their superiority. For Prophet Salih, God made a camel from a block of stone. For Prophet Abraham, He made the fire into which Nimrod threw him turn into a fragrant rose garden. He made the staff of Prophet Moses turn into a dragon as he cast it to the ground, and made sweet water pour from twelve corners of a rock to quench the thirst of his people. God made iron soft for Prophet David, and from it he molded armor to wear against his enemies; He placed mountains and birds under his orders, and they sang the praises of God with him. He made the *jinn*, birds, beasts, and winds obedient to Prophet Solomon, and taught him their language, so that he could command the wind to carry him a month's distance in a day. His Lord caused Jesus to give life to a bird made out of clay, to make the blind see, to cure leprosy, and to revive the dead.

Just as John the Baptist and Christ had done before him, the Prophet Muhammad spoke as soon as he was born. He made prostration, and people heard him begging his Lord: "O my people, O my people, Lord save my people!" and then he said: "I bear witness there is no god but God and that I am the Messenger of God." By the permission of God he split the full moon in half to convince the faithless in Mecca—but in vain. Trees and rocks spoke and saluted him, and bore witness to his prophethood. When on many occasions there was no water to drink and wash, water poured from between his blessed fingers, enough to quench the thirst of hundreds of his people.

But the greatest of all miracles was the Prophet Muhammad's Night Journey to meet his Lord. He went in an awakened state, in the company of the archangel Gabriel, from the Holy Mosque in Mecca to the Aqsa Mosque in Jerusalem. There he led the souls of all the prophets in prayer before traversing the seven heavens and passing the Lotus Tree that marks the furthest limit of creation. Passing beyond, he met his Lord in a realm that no other human being or angel has ever entered. He spoke ninety thousand words with God. Then he returned to this world. The bed he had left was still warm, and a leaf he had brushed on arising was still moving.

No one before ever saw God in life, nor will anyone else but our Prophet ever see Him. Although it is promised to the faithful in Paradise to see God as clearly as the full moon, only God knows if it is with the eyes in the head that we shall see, or with the eyes of the heart.

Yet a greater miracle even than this was the Holy Qur'an, the word of God, which came from the blessed lips of the Holy Prophet. No one before its revelation, and no one until the end of time, could write a single verse equaling its meaning and beauty. Its meaning is so deep and vast that if all the oceans were ink and all the heavens were paper, and all of them were employed in writing out its mysteries, they would be exhausted before the meaning of the Qur'an was exhausted. All knowledge of the visible and invisible realms, of the world and Hereafter, of things past and things to come, all the cures for all human ills are in it. And it is constant: not a word or a letter has changed since its revelation, nor will it change until the end of time.

It is an obligation upon everyone to accept the prophethood of Muhammad, God's peace and blessings be upon him, and also to know about his life.

His Birth

Muhammad, peace and blessings be upon him, was a human being who came into this world through a father, `Abdullah, and a mother, Aminah. He was born in the city of Mecca in Arabia, during the earlier hours of the forenoon on a Monday, the 12$^{th}$ of *Rabi` ul-Awwal* in the Year of the Elephant [570 A.D.], 52 days after the armies of Abraha, who had intended to destroy the Ka`bah with his elephants, were defeated.

He was from the family of Bani Hashim of the tribe of Quraysh, and a descendant of Prophet Ishmael, the son of Prophet Abraham, through the tribe of Bani Kinana. He grew up as an orphan. His father died before he was born and his mother died when he was a young child. Thus instead of calling on his parents when he was in need, he called upon his Lord.

He was unlettered. He never had a man as a teacher, yet he was the wisest of men, for he had the Lord as his teacher.

O Allah, for as long as day turns to night and night recedes into day, for as long as the ages succeed one another, as day and night unceasingly follow upon each other and as the glowing stars remain suspended in the firmament, we beg that You bestow Your grace and favors upon our master Muhammad, and that You transmit unto his blessed soul and unto the souls of the people of his house our greetings and our respect, and that You bestow upon him Your peace and blessings in great abundance!

So may Allah bestow His peace and blessings upon our master Muhammad and upon all the prophets and messengers; upon the saints and the righteous servants; upon the angels and upon those who reside by the Throne of Grace; and upon the obedient and vigilant servants among the people of the earth and those of the skies. And may Allah most High be pleased with His Prophet and with all his companions and people. *Amin.*

His Spiritual State

Allah Most High, in His mercy, sent His Beloved as a mercy upon the universe. Muhammad, peace and blessings be upon him, was the one whose soul was Allah's first creation, created from the Light of Allah, as he himself confirmed, saying to us:

> The first creation that Allah created was the light of your prophet from His Light. (Bayhaqi, Jabir ibn Abdullah)

And he was the first of all prophets as he said:

> I was a prophet when Adam was between water and clay. (Bukhari, Abu Naeem)

He was also the last of all prophets, as he said:

> I was the first of prophets in creation, and the last of them in Resurrection. (Abu Hurayrah, Naeem)

Such is the one about whom Allah says,

> Certainly a messenger has come to you from among yourselves, grievous to him is your falling into distress, most solicitous for you, merciful to the believers ... (*Bara'at*, 128)

May Allah inspire our hearts with the love of our Master above anything else we love, for he said:

> As long as you do not love me more than anything else, your faith is not complete. (Bukhari, Anas ibn Malik)

We must realize that to love is not within our will, nor can we be forced to love. But one can wish to love someone, and it helps to know the person whom one wishes to love.

His Nature

His physical appearance. He was neither tall and lanky nor short and stocky. He was slightly taller than medium height. He had broad shoulders and a broad high chest. He was strongly built; his chest and stomach were flat and firm. No part of his flesh was loose. On his back, between his shoulders, was the Seal of Prophethood. His bones were heavy and his wrists were long. His thighs were lean. His complexion was white tinged with reddishness, like a flower. His skin was soft. When he took his shirt off of his shoulders, the color of his body was like cast silver. Fine hair covered the line from mid-chest to navel. He had no hair on his chest, but his arms and shoulders were hairy.

He had a large head and a round face. He had large black eyes, the lids of which seemed to be outlined, and he had long lashes. The whites of his eyes were slightly pink. He had wonderful eyesight. He could see in the dark as well as he could see in daytime.

He had a high forehead and thick eyebrows separated in the center, where there was a visible vein. It used to swell when he got angry, and his temples would turn red.

His hair was jet black, with about twenty white hairs. It was neither curly nor straight, but moderately wavy. He braided his hair. When he let it loose, its length would not pass his earlobes. He would part it in the middle.

He had long sideburns and a thick beard and moustache, which he shaped by clipping and thinning it, keeping his moustache above his lips. He would wash his beard often, and perfume it with musk. He used often to gently hold his beard when he was sad and pensive.

His face was not plump, his cheeks were not round. He had a straight nose and a rather large mouth. His neck was like a column of silver. His teeth were perfectly white and even, with a slight space between them. When he smiled delicately, they shone like pearls, and one could see his eyeteeth. When he laughed he used to put his hand in front of his mouth.

When he was happy, his face shone like the moon, and when he spoke, it seemed as if a light emanated from between his teeth. He had big but beautiful hands and feet. The palms of his hands and the soles of his feet were firmly padded. He had no hair on his feet. When he washed them, the water didn't stay on them.

He walked with a firm gait, slightly leaning forward as if he were holding a staff, and without any evident effort, as if striding downhill. He walked very fast. People would run behind him, and could not keep pace with him. When people who were weak were his companions, he slowed down or made them ride animals of burden and let them follow behind, and he prayed for them.

He did not look to the side, and never turned to look behind him. Even when his robe would get caught in a bush he would not turn and look. Others who saw it would come and free it. He insisted that his companions walk in front of him rather than behind him. His face was the most beautiful of human faces. His form was the most beautiful to be found among men; so was his character.

His manner. He was the most generous, the most valorous, the gentlest. He cast his eyes down more often than up, and appeared shyer than a well-sheltered young girl. When someone came to him with a happy face, he would take his hand.

When gifts were brought to him, he would ask if they were alms or gifts. He would accept the gifts and decline the alms. Yet the gifts did not stay in his hand or his house for very long. He would give them away.

He used to take off his shoes when he sat down, and bend and gather the skirt of his robe. He would always sit on the floor with his knees pulled up to his chest.

He would stay silent for long periods and laugh little, yet he had a sense of humor and liked to see others smile. When he met with his people he would first give them the greeting of peace and blessings and then embrace them. Caressing them, he would pray for them. When he was with other people he would not leave their company until they left, and when he took someone's hand, he wouldn't withdraw his hand until the other person released it. When someone whispered into his ear something that he did not want others to hear, he would not pull his face away until the other did.

He was very compassionate and loving, especially to women and children. When he promised something to someone, he would fulfill his promise without fail at the first opportunity.

When he sat with his people, they sat around him in a circle, and in love and fascination they would be so quiet and still that if a bird had sat on their heads, it would not have flown away.

As he spoke, he often lifted his eyes to the heavens. When something that greatly pleased him was announced to him, he would immediately prostrate as a gesture of thankfulness to Allah, and his face would shine like the full moon. When he began speaking he would always smile.

In all his relationships he never caused two people to be angry at each other or to have to defend themselves. Whenever he was asked for something, he would give it if he had it. If he did not have it, he would not refuse, but would not respond. He never said no. When he was asked to do something, if it was possible he would say yes. If it was not possible, he would keep silent. He did not approach nor listen to people from whom he expected to hear bad talk, and he did not accept people's talking against each other.

He spoke very clearly, separating each word, so that one could easily count each word if one cared to. When he spoke publicly he would repeat each sentence three times to make sure that it was well understood, but he would not repeat it again.

He did not like people who were loud and rude. He preferred people who spoke softly. He also did not like people who asked too many questions.

He smelled beautiful. From his perfume, which would precede him, people knew that he was coming. Since his perfume lingered, people would know when he had been in a place.

His displeasure. When he knew of something bad someone had done, he wouldn't give the person away by mentioning his name, saying "Why is so-and-so doing this?" Instead he would say, "Why do people do this?"

When he was not pleased it became evident on his face. He would lift his face to the heavens and pray *subhanal-lahil-`Azim. Ya Hayyu ya Qayyumu bi-rahmatika astaghithu*, "God the Majestic is exalted beyond this. O Living and Ever-Transcendent One, by Your mercy: I seek help."

He was terrifying to the enemies of Islam.

What he hated most was lying. Even in his own household, if someone told the slightest untruth, he would not speak with that person until he or she repented.

When he was angered his temples would become flushed and the vein between his eyebrows would swell, and he would sweat. To appease his wrath he would sit if he had been standing, lie down if he had been sitting, get up and make two cycles of prayer, and his anger would pass.

When, rarely, he was really wrathful, no one would dare to come close to him except his son-in-law, Hadrat `Ali (r.a.). Yet to the worst of his people he appeared loving and gentle in his words and his being, and so gained their hearts.

When he did not see one of his people for three days, he would ask after that person, and if absent people could not come, he would go to them. When he did not know the name of one of his people he would address him as "O son of Allah's servant." When he would take someone's hand to say farewell, he would not withdraw his hand before the other withdrew his, and he would pray, "I entrust you to Allah's care, you and your faith and your trust and your deeds and your end." When he was about to leave a gathering, he would say *astaghfirullah* ("I seek God's forgiveness") aloud twenty times, and lift himself up, supporting himself with one arm.

His dressing. Whatever he did, he did well.

He liked to wear a simple robe, the skirt of which was down to his heels, and the sleeves down to his fingers. He would gather his robe so that it hung in front, but lifted it behind when he walked so that it would not drag.

He washed and mended his own clothes.

He would cover his head and most of his face. He would wear a white cap, and sometimes wrap a turban around it so that the end of the turban would hang down his neck between his shoulders.

He was very careful of the cloth that was used in his robes. If it contained silk, he would discard it. He liked wool. He had a woolen robe that he wore on Fridays and holy days. The robe he liked most was made from colored Yemeni cloth. The colors he liked best were green and yellow.

When he had a new dress made, he would give it a name and wear it on Fridays. When he wore anything new, he would praise Allah and make two cycles of prayer in thankfulness, and immediately give his old dress to a poor person.

When groups of foreigners came to visit him, he would wear his best clothes, and ask his companions to do the same.

He wore treated leather sandals with a thong between the toes, which he liked to be the size of his feet, not larger. He wore silver rings on both his right and left hand, and interchanged them. Sometimes they would have a carnelian set in them.

When he dressed and washed and combed himself, in fact in all his doings, he liked to start from the right. When he put on his sandals and robe he would dress his right foot and right arm first. In taking them off, he would remove the left foot and left arm first.

He disliked bad smells.

He bathed on Fridays with five buckets of water. Sometimes he and one of his wives would share the same tub and the same water. He used depilatory every month on the genital area, each time washing it thrice, and then would depilate his armpits. He would cut his fingernails every two weeks. He fumigated himself with incense. He liked to use the *miswak*, a stick of wood beaten into fibers at one end, as a toothbrush. He carried it with him, and used it to clean his teeth very often. He wouldn't enter the houses of his wives, nor go to bed, without brushing his teeth.

He used to sweat a lot, but his sweat smelled of roses. He would perfume and oil his hair and beard with musk. When someone offered him perfume he would never refuse, and would apply it. Sometimes he would go into his wives' rooms and look for perfume.

When he used perfume he poured it into his left hand and first applied it to his brow, then around his eyes, then to his head. He liked best the smell of the balsam flower.

His eating and drinking. He liked to drink cool and sweet drinks, and among these he liked best water sweetened with honey. He also liked milk. When he drank he would breathe before swallowing, and say *bismi Llah ir-Rahman ir-Rahim,* "In the Name of Allah, the Beneficent, the Compassionate." After each swallow he would say *al-hamdu li-Llah,* "Praise is due to Allah." He would take only two or three swallows in this way.

He had a glass cup from which he drank. He liked to drink water from its source. Sometimes he would send people to particular springs, wells, and fountains where there was good water, and he would pray for the people who brought the water to him. He would drink *Zamzam* water each time he went to Mecca; he would carry it himself or ask his people to bring it to him.

He liked to sit and watch running water and greenery.

He kept his water in covered containers.

He ate little, and if he ate in the evening he wouldn't eat in the morning. He ate only when he was hungry, and stopped eating before he was full.

He fasted often. In addition to the month of *Ramadan*, the month in which he fasted the most was *Sha`ban*. The ninth of *Dhul-Hijjah*, the day of `Ashurah*, the first three days and the first Monday of each month he passed fasting. It was rare if he did not fast on Fridays.

Sometimes to appease his hunger pangs he would tie a flat stone against his stomach. Sometimes he would fast for days without breaking the fast, but he would forbid others to do that.

He never kept anything for tomorrow. Sometimes neither he nor his family had anything to eat for days. They often ate barley bread.

When he broke his fast at sunset, he would first eat a date or two or drink water before he made his sunset prayer.

When he ate, he sat on the floor and set his food on the floor; he never leaned on anything while he ate. He washed his hands well before and after eating. He started the meal by saying *bismi Llah*, "in the name of God." He ate with the three fingers of his right hand. He ate what was on his side of the plate; he never reached for a morsel in the middle of the plate, and did not approve when other people who ate with him from the same plate did it. He did not start eating a warm dish until it cooled. In fact, he did not like warm dishes. He said, "Eat cold food, because it has the blessing of abundance. If you are heedful you will see how much more you must eat when you eat warm food ..."

He never blew on his food to cool it, nor did he blow into his cup when he drank. He liked to break his fast with fresh dates or something fire had not touched.

He liked dates: he liked to hold them in his hands attached to their branches in bunches and eat them one by one. He ate them with bread, with watermelon, with cucumber, with cream, and he would say, "What a blessed fruit!" Even when there was a worm in a date, he wouldn't throw it away; he would clean the worm out and eat the date. He started his meals with dates and finished them with dates.

He liked sweet things. He liked honey, and *halwa* (a sweet made with cereals, sesame oil, and syrup), and raisins.

He ate meat. The meat he preferred was the front part of the sheep, especially the shanks of the front legs. He disliked eating the internal organs of the animal. He refused to eat the kidneys, although he did not forbid others to eat them.

Among vegetables he liked squash and cucumbers. He disliked onions, garlic, leeks and such things as leave a smell on the breath, for he spoke with angels, and did not like to offend other people in congregations.

He accepted all invitations to dinner, even from a slave, where he may have eaten stale animal fat with old barley bread. He ate everything that was offered to him if he was hungry. He started eating only after others started. After each meal he said *al-hamdu li-Llah*, "praise is due to Allah," and prayed for his host and the ones who had shared the meal.

His sleeping. He went to bed after the night prayer, awoke in the middle of the night to pray, and slept again until before the morning prayer. He liked to take an afternoon nap. His eyes slept but his heart did not sleep.

His bed was a piece of felt. Sometimes he used a straw mat thrown on the hard floor, which marked his blessed side when he lay upon it. The mat was not bigger than the size of a grave.

Before he went to bed, he would always recite *Suratul-Kafirun* and one or more of the following: *Suratul- Mulk, Suratus-Sajdah, Surat Bani Isra`il,* and *Suratuz-Zumar.* He would not go to bed without taking an ablution and cleaning his teeth. He kept his *miswak* (toothbrush stick) next to his bed and would use it when he woke up.

He slept with his head turned in the direction of the Ka`bah. He slept on his right side and used his right hand as a pillow, placing his palm under his cheek. Before he fell asleep, he would pray:

O my Sustainer, I live with Your name; I die with Your name. (Bukhari, Al-Bara')

He then would repeat three times:

On the day of Resurrection, save me from Your wrath. (Bukhari, Hudzaifa)

He breathed heavily when he slept.

His family relations. He loved and cherished his wives. Whether they were young or old, beautiful or less beautiful, he treated them equally. When he got married or performed a wedding ceremony, he distributed dates to the wedding guests. He liked to give gifts, and advised his people to do the same. He would say that giving gifts brought people together.

He smiled when he spoke, and showed care and compassion to the members of his household. He did not touch even the hand of a woman from outside his family. He would talk to, amuse, and play with his wives. He would show them affection, kiss and caress them even when he was fasting. He did not consider his ablution lost as a result, and would make his prayers without renewing his ablution.

He divided his time equally among his wives. He was able to visit all of them in a day or a night and satisfy them all. He would send word to the wife whom he intended to visit.

He had a yellow bedsheet, dyed with saffron, which was always kept proper and clean. He took this with him to sleep on with his wives. The wife with whom he spent the night would wash and fold it for him. He would take ablution and say *bismi Llah*, "in the name of God," when he came close to his wives; he asked them to recite *subhan Allah* ("God is exalted above everything"), *al-hamdu li-Llah* ("praise is due to God"), and *Allahu akbar* ("God is greater") thirty-three times each. When they made love, they were careful to keep their sexual parts chastely covered. During intercourse he usually stood on his knees. They took a total ablution immediately afterwards; rarely, in dire conditions of cold and fatigue, he delayed ablution and slept until before prayer time. He would not sleep with his wives when they had their periods, but he would still show them physical affection.

He helped with the household chores. He cleaned, washed, mended, and milked the sheep. No work was beneath his dignity. He took his wives out, and brought them and his children to special holiday prayers. When he traveled or left for battle, he would not choose one of his wives to accompany him; rather he would let those who wished to go draw lots to decide who would accompany him.

When his wives became ill, he took care of them and cooked soup for them saying, "Drink! This will cleanse the pain and sadness in the heart of the sick as water cleanses the dirt of a person's body."

He would pray for them when they were ill, reciting *Surah Falaq* and *Surah Nas* three times. When one of his wives was sick with an infectious disease, especially of the eye, he would not go close to her, fearing to infect others.

When his wives wanted something, he never said no, but brought them what they wanted as soon as he could. If he was worried about forgetting it, he would tie a string to his little finger or to his ring. He would pray for his wives and sacrifice sheep for them. When they were annoyed, he would be gentle with them. Once when Hadrat `A'ishah (r.a.) was annoyed, he gently caressed the tip of her nose and called her "my little `A'ishah," and asked her to pray so that her anger would subside.

He was wonderful with children. He saluted them like grown-ups, talked to them, caressed their heads, and hugged them. He would stand up, the gesture of respect, when his daughter Hadrat Fatimah (r.a.) came to see him, and he would kiss the top of her head. He always wanted children around him during prayer time in the mosque. His grandchildren would climb on his back while he prayed and he did not mind. He loved all of his people, but he loved the very young and the very old most of all.

His possessions. He possessed little, did not keep things long, and gave them away. He liked to give names to his belongings. He had a mirror he called *Mudillah* ("Misleader"), and a pair of scissors he called *Jami`* ("Uniter"). He had a water pitcher called *Mamshuq* ("Thin and Tall") and a sleeping mat called *Quzz* ("Shunner of impurity"). He had a glass cup and two *kohl* containers. He used to put *kohl* on his eyelids every evening three times from each container. He had a wooden perfume bottle. He always had one new robe, which he wore on Fridays. He had one towel. He had a heavy iron basin that it took four people to lift, called *`Unarah* ("Well built"), and an iron cooking pot with four rings as handles.

He kept a maid named Hadirah. When he addressed her, he would ask her "What would you like?" He never complained about the service of the ones who served him.

He had a donkey named *Ya`fur* ("Gazelle") that he often rode without a saddle. He had two horses, a roan named *Murtajaz* ("Spontaneous") and a black named *Sakb* ("Swift"). He had a mule, *Duldul* ("Vacillating") and a she-camel, *Kaswa* ("Split ears"). He loved and cared for his animals. When he left this world, *Kaswa* ran away into the desert. Every night she would come to the mosque looking for him, crying and hitting her head on the stone steps. One night she killed herself by hitting her head on the stone walls of the mosque.

He had a sword called *Dhul-Fiqar* ("Double-pointed") with a decorated silver handle with a silver ring. He had a bow called *Dhus-Sadad* ("Mark hitter") and a quiver for his arrows called *Dhul-Tamam* ("Always full"). He had a short spear called *Nab'ah* ("Arrowwood") and a shield called *Zaqan* ("the Beard").

His devotions. He had two *muezzin*s who called the prayer five times a day, Hadrat Bilal and Ibn Maktum, who was blind.

What he liked best in this world was *salat*, the ritual prayer. He made his prayers seeing his Lord. That is why he asked his people to do their prayers as they saw him do them, not as he did them. It would have been impossible for anyone to pray as he did. The people whom he liked most were the people who were constant in their devotion. When he led the prayer, he made it short and easy. When he prayed alone, he made it long. He would stand at prayer all night until his blessed feet were swollen.

When the weather was cold, he prayed early. In the heat of the summer, he delayed his prayers. When he sent someone to a place as governor or *imam*, he would warn them:

> Speak not long. Long talk has the effect of a sorcerer's spell. Make your preaching short and make things easy for people, not difficult. Give them good tidings, not threats of punishment. (Bukhari, Abu Burda)

He performed his ablution before every prayer. When he made ablution he would try to conserve water. He would put aside a little and sprinkle it on the place where he would put his head in prostration. When he washed his hands, he would move his rings so that water got under them. When he washed his lower arms up to the elbows, he rubbed well up above them. He would wash and rub his earlobes and then take a handful of water, put it under his chin, rub his beard well and comb it with his fingers. When he washed his feet, he rubbed between his toes with his little finger. He liked to dry his hands and arms after ablution by air and rubbing, rather than by drying them with a towel. After the ablution was completed he used to make two cycles of private prayer before he did his prayers in congregation. He did not permit anyone to assist him when he performed his ablution. He would not let them pour water or even hand him a towel. Neither did he like to ask people to serve him.

When he prayed, his color would change: sometimes he would grow pale, sometimes he would flush. At the time of the morning prayer, the maids of the people of Medina would come to the mosque with water pitchers: he would dip his fingers in the pitchers and bless them. After finishing the morning prayer, he would sit and offer private prayers with his face turned toward the Ka`bah until sunrise. Then he would turn to the congregation and say:

> If anyone is sick, let me go and visit him. If anyone is dead, let me assist at his funeral. If anyone has dreamed, let him come and tell me his dream.

When he stood up to pray, he would raise his hands, open his fingers with palms facing forward and say *Allahu akbar,* "God is greater." Then he would lower his hands and hold his left hand with his right hand. When he bent from the waist in prayer, he would place his hands with open fingers right above his knees; his back would be so straight that if you poured water on it, it would remain there and not run off.

Nothing prevented him from praying, nor from doing so at the proper time. When he traveled, however, he would make the *salat* of noon and afternoon together at the time of afternoon prayer, and he made the evening and night *salat* together at the time of night prayer. In fact he was in constant prayer, for he never forgot Allah, but remembered Him at each breath.

He liked to pray in gardens and open spaces. He usually prayed on a treated sheepskin or a straw mat. He usually took off his shoes when he prayed, but sometimes he kept them on. He would make extra prayers between the afternoon and evening times, but forbade others to do so. He would do two cycles of private prayer before the noon congregational prayer and two cycles afterwards, two cycles before afternoon prayer, two cycles after evening prayer, and two cycles after night prayer.

Sometimes during the prayer it would appear that he was looking around him out of the corners of his eyes. Indeed he sometimes saw what was happening behind him as if it were in front of him. When he led prayers, men stood in rows behind him; behind them stood the children, and behind the children stood the women.

Sometimes he remained so long in prostration that he momentarily fell asleep from fatigue. He would get up and continue his prayers. Although sleep breaks an ablution, his eyes slept, but his heart did not sleep.

He kept the fingers of his hands spread apart when he raised them at the beginning of the *salat*, and when he placed them on his knees, when he bent from the waist, and when he sat on his knees, but he held them tightly together when he pressed them on the floor next to his face during prostration. He raised his elbows so high so that one could see the white of his armpits.

At the end of the formal prayers, during his private supplications, he prayed first for himself, and then for those who were in urgent need. When he prayed for someone, his prayer affected not only that person, but his family, children, and grandchildren as well. When he made his supplications, he opened his hands with palms facing his face; sometimes he raised them high toward the heavens. When he finished supplicating, he wiped his palms over his face.

On Friday, when he got up to preach at congregational prayers, he greeted people near him. When he climbed the pulpit he turned his face to the congregation and saluted them. When he preached, he leaned over his staff. His face flushed, his eyes reddened, he raised his voice. He appeared wrathful, as if he were warning about imminent danger from an army, or as if he were ordering an army to attack the enemy. He would say, "Your night has turned into day!" When he spoke to his warriors during battle, he leaned over his sword.

When revelations came to him, he would bow his head low, as if a heavy load were on his neck. He would appear crushed. Once he received a revelation while mounted on a camel: the knees of the camel gave out. Even when it was cold, drops of sweat like pearls would roll down his forehead. The color of his face would change; a strange sound like the buzzing of many bees would emanate from around his face. He would have terrible headaches. They would put *henna* on his head to alleviate the pain.

His acts of remembrance. When he encountered something pleasing to him he said *al-hamdu li-Llah illadhi bi-ni`matihi tatimmus-salihat*: "Praise is due to Allah through whose grace good tidings are brought to earth." When he encountered something unpleasant he said *al-hamdu li-Llahi `ala kulli hal*:

"Praise is due to Allah under all circumstances." When he swore an oath he often said *la-walladhi nafsu Abil Qasimi bi-yadihi*: "By Him who holds the life of Abu al-Qasim in His hands."

When he would lie down to sleep he would put his hand under his cheek and say *bismika Allahumma ahya' wa bismika amut*: "In Your name, O Allah, I live and in Your name I die." When he used to go to bed, he would say *bismi Llahi wada`tu janbi. Allahumm ighfir li-dhanbi wa akhsi shaytani wa fukka rihani wa thaqqil mizani waj`alni fin-nadiyy il-a`la*: "In the name of Allah I lie down upon my side. O Allah, forgive my sins, and drive away my personal devil. Redeem my pledge and make my good deeds weigh heavy in the scale, and set me in the Highest Assembly."

When he sent someone to work and fight for Allah's sake, he would say *istawda` Allahu dinakum wa amanatakum wa khawatima 'amalikum*: "Unto Allah I commend your religion, your trust, and the completion of your work."

On starting a trip he would say *Allahumma bika asulu wa bika ahulu wa bika asiru*: "O Allah, with You I go to battle, with You I depart, and with You I travel."

When he prayed for rain, he said *Allahummasqi `ibadaka wanshur rahmata-ka wa ahyi baladakal mayyit; Allahumma anzil fi ardina barakataha wa zinataha wa sakanaha warzuqna wa anta khayr ur-raziqin*: "O Allah, give Your servants drink, shower all with Your mercy, and bring to life Your dead land," and "O Allah, bestow blessings, adornments, and dwellings in this land, and provide our sustenance, You are the best of sustainers."

When the north wind blew hard, he would say *Allahumma inni a`udhu bika min sharri ma arsalta fiha*: "O Allah, I seek refuge in You from the evil of what You have sent therein."

When he became ill, the Archangel Gabriel would come to him and pray for him saying *Bismi Llahi yabrika min kulli da'in yushfika min sharri hasidin idha hasad wa sharri kulli dhi `ayn*: "In the name of Allah. He recovers you from every malady. He cures you from the evil of the envious when he envies you, and from the evil of those who cast the evil eye."

When he was saddened he would say *Hasbi ar-rabbu min `ibadah. Hasbi al-khaliqu min al-makhluqin. Hasbi ar-raziqu min al-marzuqin. Hasbi alladhi huwa hasbi. Hasbi Allahu wa ni`m al-wakil. Hasbi Allahu la ilaha illa huwa `alayhi tawakkaltu wa huwa rabb ul-`arsh il-`azim*: "The Lord is not in need of worship. The Creator is not in need of the creation. The Sustainer is not in need of the sustained. Sufficient unto me is He Who is sufficient unto me. Allah is sufficient unto me, and how excellent a guardian is He! Allah is sufficient unto me; there is not god but He. On Him I rely, and He is the Lord of the glorious throne."

Every morning and every evening he prayed *Allahumma inni as'aluka min faj'at il-khayri wa a`udhu bika min faj'at ish sharr. Fa innal-`abda la yadri ma yafja'ahu idha asbaha wa idha amsa*: "O Allah, I ask You to surprise me with good tidings, and I seek refuge in You from sudden evil, for the servant has no knowledge of what may unexpectedly occur in the morning or the evening."

As he woke up in the mornings and as the sun set he would say *Asbahna `ala fitrat il-islami wa kalimat il-ikhlasi wa dini nabiyyina Muhammad sallallahu `alayhi wa sallam wa `ala millati abina Ibrahima hanifan musliman wa ma kana min al-mushrikin*: "We entered upon the morning as followers of the religion of Islam, of the doctrine of the unity of Allah, of the religion of our Prophet Muhammad (s.a.w.s.), and of the creed of our father Abraham, who was upright and was not among those who set equals to God."

When he broke his fast he would say *Allahumma laka sumtu wa `ala rizqika aftartu wa taqabbal mini innaka antas sami` ul-`alim*: "My Lord, it is for Your sake that I fasted, and with Your sustenance did I break the fast. Accept this fast from me; You are the All-Hearing, the All-Knowing," and *al-hamdu li-Llahi lladhi a'anani fa-sumtu wa razaqani fa-iftart*: "Praise be to Allah Who aided me to fast, and provided me with sustenance that I might break the fast." When he broke fast in someone's house he would say *aftara `indakum us-sa'imu wa sallat `alaykum ul-mala'ika*: "A fasting person has broken his fast in your home, and thus, the angels have invoked blessings upon you."

When he ate or he drank he said *al-hamdu li-Llah illadhi at`ama wa saqa wa sawwaghahu wa ja`ala lahu makhrajan*: "Praise be to Allah Who fed us and gave us to drink, made it agreeable to swallow, and made an outlet therefore."

As he entered his room he would say *al-hamdu li-Llah illadhi at`amana wa saqana wa kafana wa `awana fakam mimman la kafiya lahu wa la mua'wi*: "Praise be to Allah, Who gave us food and drink, provided us sufficiently, and gave us shelter. How many there are who have neither provider nor shelter!"

As he turned from one side to another in his bed, he would say *la ilaha illa Llah ul-wahid ul-qahhar rabb us-samawati wal-ard wa ma baynahum ul-`aziz ul-jabbar*: "There is no god but Allah, the One, the Ever-Dominant, the Lord of the heavens and the earth and whatever is between them, the Victorious, the All-Forgiving."

When some matter bothered him, he said *la ilaha illa Llah ul-halim ul-karim subhan Allahi rabb il-`arsh il-`azim al-hamdu li-Llahi rabb il-`alamin*: "There is no god but Allah, the Clement, the Generous. Glory be to Allah, the Lord of the glorious throne. Praise be to Allah, the Lord of the universe."

When he expected harm to come from his enemies, he prayed *Allahumma inna naj`aluka fi nuhurihim wa na`udhu bika min shururihim*: "O Allah, we place You in front of them and seek refuge in You from their mischief."

When he suspected a mischief directed against him, he would pray *Allahumma barik lahu wa la tadurrhu*: "O Allah bestow Your blessings on this and do not cause it harm."

When he left his house, he would pray *Bismi Llah. It-tikaluna `ala Llah. La hawla wa la quwwata illa bi-Llah*: "In the name of Allah. Reliance is on Allah. There is no power nor strength save in Allah." Or he would pray *Bismi Llah. Tawakkaltu `ala Llah. Allahumma inna na`udhu bika min an nazilla aw nazlima aw nuzlama aw najhala aw yujhala `alayna*: "In the name of Allah. Upon Allah I rely. O Allah, we seek refuge in You lest we slip, or wrong or be wronged, or act foolishly, or any one act foolishly with us." Or he would pray *Bismi Llahi rabbi. A`udhu bika min an azilla aw adilla aw azlima aw uzlama aw ajhala aw ujhala aw yujhala `alayya*: "In the name of Allah. My Lord, I seek refuge in Thee lest I slip, or lead someone astray, or wrong or be wronged, or act foolishly, or any one act foolishly with me." Or he would pray *Bismi Llah. Tawakkaltu `ala Llah. La hawla wa la quwwata illa billah. Allahumma inni a`udhu bika min an udilla aw udalla aw uzilla aw uzalla aw azlima aw uzlama aw ajhala aw ujhala aw yujhala `alayya aw abghiya aw yubgha `alayya*: "In the name of Allah. I rely upon Allah. There is not power nor strength, save in Allah. O Allah, I seek refuge in You lest I send any one astray, or go astray myself, or slip or cause some one else to slip, or wrong or be wronged, or act foolishly, or anyone act foolishly with me, or oppress or be oppressed."

When he entered a mosque he would pray *a`udhu bi-Llah il-`Azimi wa bi-wajhih il-karimi wa sultanih il-qadimi min ash-shaytan ir-rajim*: "I seek refuge in Allah the Magnificent, in His glorious Self, and in His eternal Dominion from the accursed Devil." (He also said that the one who recites this will be safe from the accursed Devil elsewhere.) Sometimes upon entering a mosque he also prayed *Bismi Llah. was-salamu `ala rasulillah. Allahumm ighfir li dhunubi waftah li abwaba rahmatik*: "In the name of Allah, Peace be upon the Messenger of Allah. O Allah, forgive me my sins and open unto me the gates of Your mercy." Sometimes he prayed *Bismi Llah. Was-salamu `ala rasuli Llah. Allahumm ighfir li dhunubi waftah li abwaba fadlik*: "In the name of Allah. Peace be upon the Messenger of Allah. O Allah, forgive me my sins and open unto me the gates of Your grace and favor." Alternatively he would say *Rabbi ighfir li dhunubi waftah li abwaba rahmatik*: "My Lord, forgive me my sins and open unto me the gates of Your mercy." Or he would say *Rabb ighfir li dhunubi waftah li abwaba fadlik*: "My Lord, forgive me my sins and open unto me the gates of Your grace and favor." Or he would say *Bismi Llah. Allahumma salli `ala Muhammad wa azwaji Muhammad*: "In the name of Allah. My Lord, blessings be upon Muhammad and the wives of Muhammad."

When he went to relieve himself, he would say *Bismi Llah. Allahumma inni a`udhu bika mi-al khabathi wal khaba'th*: "In the name of Allah. I seek refuge from obstruction and whatever gets obstructed." Or he would say *ya* *dhal jalal; Allahumma inni a`udhu bika min ar-rijsin njisil khabith il-mukhbath ish-shaytanir-rajim*: "O Lord of Majesty; O Allah, I seek refuge in You from the malicious filthy dirty accursed devil." Or else he would say *Al-hamdu li-Llah illadhi adhaqani ladhdhatahu wa abqa fiyya quwwatahu wa adhhaba `anni `adhahu*: "Praise be to Allah who made me appreciate this matter, who provided me with strength, and who removed its unpleasantness from me."

When he left the privy, he would say *ghufranak*: "Your pardon," or *al-hamdu li-Llah illadhi adhhaba `annil-adha wa `afani*: "Praise be to Allah Who relieved me from suffering and gave me health" or *al-hamdu li-Llah illadhi ahsana ilayya fi awwalihi wa fi akhirih*: "Praise be to Allah in the beginning of the matter and in its end."

When he entered a marketplace he would pray *Bismi Llah. Allahumma inni as'aluka min khayri hadhihis-suqi wa khayri ma fiha wa a`udhu bika min sharriha wa sharri ma fiha; Allahumma inni a`udhu bika an usiba fiha yaminan fajiratan aw saqatan khasira*: "In the name of Allah. O Allah, I ask of You the good of this market, and the good of that which is therein; and I seek refuge in Thee from the evil thereof, and the evil of that which is therein. O Allah, I seek refuge in You lest I strike a bargain herein incurring a loss, or meet with a false oath."

When he visited graveyards he addressed the graves, saying *as-salamu `alaykum ayyatuhal-arwah ul-faniyah wal-abdan ul-baliyah wal-'izam in-nakhir allati kharajat min ad-dunya wahiya mu'mina. Allahumma adkhil `alayhim ruhan minka wa salaman minna*: "Peace be upon you, O mortal souls with decayed flesh and rotten bones, who departed this world believing in Allah. O Allah, impart upon them a spirit from Thee and peace from us."

When he passed a graveyard he would say *as-salamu `alaykum ahlad-diyar min al-mu'minina wal-mu'minati wal-muslimina wal-muslimati was-salihina was-salihati wa inna insha'Allahu bikum lahiqun*: "Peace be upon you, O faithful, Muslim, and righteous men and women of these abodes. We, when Allah wills, shall be following in your footsteps."

When it rained he prayed *Allahumma sayyiban nafi`an*: "O Allah, make it a profitable downpour."

When he saw the new moon he prayed *Allahumma ahillhu `alayna bil yumni wal-amanati was-salamati wal islami. Rabbi wa rabbuk Allah*: "O Allah, let this new moon appear unto us with peace and faith, with safety and Islam. My Lord and thy Lord is Allah." Or he would say *Allahu akbar Allahu akbar. Al-hamdu li-Llah. La hawla wa la quwwata illa bi-Llah*: "Allah is greater, Allah is greater. Praise be to Allah. There is no strength nor power save in Allah." Or he would pray *Allahumma inni as'aluka min khayri hadhash-shahri wa `udhu bika min sharr il-qadari wa min sharri yawm il-mahshar*: "O Allah, I ask Thee to bestow upon me all that is good of this month, and I seek refuge in Thee from the misfortunes of destiny and the misfortunes of the Day of Judgment." Or he would pray *Allahumma ahhilhu `alayna bil-amni* *wal-imani was-salamati was-salami wat-tawfiqi li-ma tuhibbu wa tarda. Rabbuna wa rabbuk Allah; Allahumma ahhilhu `alayna bil-amni wal-imani was-salamati wal-islami was-sakinati wal-`afiyati war-rizq il hasan; hilala khayrin. Al-hamdu li-Llah illadhi dhahaba bi shahri kadha wa ata bi shahri kadha. As'aluka min khayri hadhash-shahri wa nurihi wa barakatihi wa hudahu wa zuhurihi wa mu`afatihi:* "May the new moon be a source of good. Praise be to Allah who took away the month of ... and brought forth the month of ... I ask for the best of this month, its light and its blessings, its guidance, its appearance, and its good effects." Or he would pray *Allahumm aj`'alhu hilala yumnin wa rushd. Amantu billadhi kalaqaka fa `addalak. Tabarak Allahu ahsan al-khaliqin:* "O Allah, let this new moon be a moon of prosperity and guidance! I believe in the One who has created you and balanced you. May Allah be praised! He is the best of Creators."

When something annoyed him he would say *Allah Allah rabbiy. La sharika lahu:* "Allah, Allah is my Sustainer. He has no partner."

He congratulated newly married men, saying, *Baraka Llahu laka wa baraka `alayka wa jama`a baynakuma bi-khayr:* "May Allah bless you and happily unite the two of you."

He would often raise his eyes to heaven and say *ya musarrif al-qulub thabbit qalbi `ala ta`atik:* "O Director of hearts, keep my heart in a state of obedience to You."

After meals he would pray *al-hamdu li Llahi kathiran tayyiban mubarakan fihi. Al-hamdu l-Llah illadhi kaffani wa `awani ghayri makfiyyin wa la makfurin wa la muwadda'in wa la mustaghnin `anhu rabbana:* "Much praise be to Allah, praise in which there are many blessings. Praise be to Allah who provided for me and sheltered me. He is our Lord without ceasing, irreplaceable, never-parting, and indispensable is He."

When he saw lightning or heard thunder he said *Allahumma la taqtulna bi-ghadabika wa tuhlikna bi `adhabika wa `afina qabla dhalik:* "O Allah, slay us not with Your wrath, and destroy us not with Your punishment, but preserve us before that."

When he drank he said *al-hamdu li Llah illadhi saqana `adhban furatan bi-rahmatihi wa lam yaj`alhu milhan ujajan bi dhunubina:* "Praise be to Allah who quenched our thirst through His mercy, with fresh sweet water. Praise be to Him for not making it salty with our sins."

Often, before he started his prayers, he would caress his head with his right hand and say *Bismi Llah illadhi la ilaha ghayruh ur-rahman ir-rahim. Allahumma adhhib `annil-hamma wal-huzn:* "In the name of Allah; there is no god but He, the All-Compassionate, the All-Merciful. O Allah, remove anxiety and grief from me."

When a storm was brewing he would pray *Allahumma inni as'aluka khayraha wa khayra ma fiha wa khayra ma ursilat bihi. Wa a'udhu bika min sharriha wa min sharri ma fiha wa sharri ma ursilat bihi:* "O Allah, I beg of You the good of this, and the good of that which has been sent therewith. I seek refuge in Thee from the evil of this and the evil of that which has been sent therewith."

When he sneezed he said *al-hamdu li-Llah*: "Praise be to Allah." When those around him responded *yarhamukallah*: "May Allah have mercy on you," he would reply *Yahdikumu Llahu wa yuhdi balakum*: "May Allah guide you and make you righteous."

When he went into battle he would say *Allahumma anta yadi wa anta nasiri wa bika uqatil*: "O Allah, You are my arm and my helper, and with Your help I do battle."

When his young wife `A'ishah (r.a.) would sometimes be annoyed, he would gently caress the tip of her nose and say *Ya 'Ulwaysh, quli Allahumma rabba Muhammadin salla Llahu `alayhi wa sallam, ighfir li dhanbi wa adhhib ghayza qalbi wa ajirni min mudillat il-fitan*: "O my little `A'ishah, why don't you pray and say, 'O Allah, the Lord of Muhammad (s.a.w.s), forgive me my sins, remove my anger, and protect me from evil leading to discord.'"

After meals he would pray *al-hamdu li-Llah illadhi at`amana wa saqana wa ja`alana muslimin, Allahumma lakal hamd. Saqayta wa ashba'ta wa arwayta falakal-hamdu ghayra makfiyyin wa la muwadda'in wa la mustaghnan `anka*: "Praise be to Allah who fed us and gave us drink and made us Muslims; O Allah, praise be to You. You fed us satisfying our hunger, gave us to drink quenching our thirst. Therefore, unceasing, never-parting, indispensable praise be to You." Or he would pray *Allahumma innaka at`amata wa saqayta wa aghnayta wa aqnayta wa hadayta waj tabayta. Allahumma fa-lakal-hamdu `ala ma a`tayta*: "O Allah, You fed us and gave us to drink. You bestowed riches upon us and guided us. O Allah, all praise belongs to You for what You have given and chosen."

When he returned from the pilgrimage or from battle, he would stand on a high spot and say three times *Allahu akbar*: "Allah is greater." Then he would say *La ilaha illa Llahu wahdahu la sharika lah. Lahul-mulku wa lahu-hamdu wa huwa `ala kulli shay'in qadir. Ayyibun ta'ibun `abidun sajidun li-rabbina hamidun. Saddaqa Llahu wa`dah wa nasara `abdah wa hazzamal-ahzaba wahdah*: "There is no god but God. He is alone. He has no partner. Unto Him belongs the Kingdom, and unto Him belongs all praise. He is All-Powerful. We turn toward Allah; penitents, worshipers, and prostrators unto our Lord, and His extollers. Allah fulfilled His promise, helped His servant, and alone routed the Clans."

Bowing and prostrating, he would say *Subhanaka wa bihamdik. Astaghfiruka wa atubu ilayk*: "Glory be to You. All praise be to You. I seek Your forgiveness and I turn unto You in repentance."

When he looked into a mirror he would say *al-hamdu li-Llah illadhi sawwa khalqi fa `addalahu wa karrama surata wajhi fa hassanaha wa ja`alani min al-*

muslimin: "Praise be to Allah Who has formed my person well, made it symmetric, fashioned it into my figure, finished it well, and set me among the Muslims." Sometimes he would say *al-hamdu li- Llah illadhi hasana khalqi wa khuluqi wa zana minni ma shana min ghayri*: "Praise be to Allah Who beautified my person and character, and adorned in me that which He made unsightly in other than me."

When the wind blew he turned toward it and knelt, stretched out his hands toward the wind and said *Allahumma inni as'aluka min khayri hadhi-hir-rihi wa khayri ma ursilat bihi. Wa a`udhu bika min sharriha wa sharri ma ursilat bihi. Allahumm aj'alha rahmatan wa la taj`alaha `adhaban. Allahumm aj`alaha rihanan wa la taj`alaha rihan*: "O Allah, we beg of You the good of this wind, and the good of that which has been sent therewith. And I seek refuge in You from the evil thereof, and the evil of that which is therein. O Allah let this wind be a merciful blessing, and let it not be a punishment. O Allah, let it be a blessed wind, and let it not be an accursed wind."

When they buried someone he said *Bismi-Llah. Bi-Llah. Wa fi sabili Llah. Wa `ala millati rasuli Llah*: "In the name of Allah, with Allah, and in the way of Allah. And following the creed of the Messenger of Allah."

When he made an oath he said *la wa musarrif al-qulub*: "No, by the Director of hearts!"

He often repeated this prayer: *ya muqallib al-qulub thabbit qalbi `ala dinik*: "O Changer of hearts, fix my heart on Your religion." He also often recited *Rabbana atina fid-dunya hasanatan wa fil-akhirati hasanatan wa qina `adhab an-nar*: "Our Lord, bestow upon us good in this world, and good in the Hereafter, and save us from the torment of the Fire."

When he left a place he always prayed *subhanak Allahumma rabbiy wa bihamdik. La ilaha illa anta astaghfiruka wa atubu ilayk*: "Glory be to You, O Allah, my Lord. All praise is to You. There is no god but You. I seek Your forgiveness and unto You I turn in repentance."

He often relieved his sadness by using this prayer: *La ilaha illa Llah ul-`aziz ul-halim. La ilaha illa Llahu rabb ul-`arsh il-`azim. La ilaha illa Llahu rabb us-samawatis-sab`i wa rabb ul-ardi wa rabb ul-`arsh il-`azim*: "There is no god but Allah, the Victorious, the Clement. There is no god but Allah, the Lord of the glorious Throne. There is no god but Allah, the Lord of the seven heavens, the Lord of the earth, and the Lord of the Mighty Throne."

He began all of his prayers by reciting *subhana rabbiy al-`aliyy il-a`la al-wahhab*: "Glory be to my Lord, the Exalted, the Most-High, the Giver."

He asked people to recite this prayer against malaria and other fevers: *Bismi Llah il-kabir. A`udhu bi-Llah il-`azimi min sharri kulli `irqin wa min sharri harr in-nar*: "In the name of Allah, the Great. I seek refuge in Allah the Glorious from the evil of all races and from the evil of the heat of the Fire."

His Passing

He left this world at the age of 63, in the city of Medina, to which he had migrated ten years earlier. His last words were *jalalu rabbir-rafi'. Faqad ballaght*: "The sublime majesty of my Lord! For I have fulfilled my mission," and then he gave up his blessed soul.

His last advice to us was:

> Do not ever abandon prayer. Do not ever abandon prayer. Do not ever abandon prayer. And fear Allah in your treatment of those under your control.

*

May the true and intended meaning of these words find its place in your hearts. May they paint an image in your hearts' eye that is of the best shape and form imaginable. May you feel as close to that image as a child to the most beneficent of fathers.

Yet this intimacy should not make us suppose that he is like us. Is a chip of stone the same as a diamond, even though they are both rocks? Are the sun and a candle the same because they both shed light?

May we see his real shape in this life, when our souls become light and soar to the heavens in our dreams. In following his path, in imitating his character, may we be worthy to gather under his banner on the Day of Judgment. May we receive the intercession of the one whom Allah sent as His mercy upon the universe. May we be blessed to love him and Allah more than everything else. May we find Allah's pleasure and grace and enter Paradise.

All blessings and salutations of Allah be upon His beloved Prophet Muhammad whose soul He has created from the divine light of His essence, whom He has made a mirror of His beautiful attributes, and whom He has sent as His mercy. And peace and blessings be upon the members of his household, his family and descendants, and his companions and helpers, and the saints of all times who carry his light.

ON THE RIGHTLY-GUIDED CALIPHS

After the Holy Prophet came the four righteous caliphs, all of them saintly men, companions and trusted friends of the Prophet: Abu Bakr, `Umar, `Uthman and `Ali, may God be pleased with them all. We believe in their sainthood, as they all had the character of those close to God. They feared God and were truthful. They followed God's prescriptions in the Holy Qur'an and the guidance of the Prophet word by word. They were compassionate, merciful, and generous. They were heedful and knew what they did; they were in continuous remembrance and adoration of their Lord. If they occasionally erred, they knew when they had done so and undid their

29

errors by repentance. They were in continuous awe and fear of the Day of Judgment and made an accounting of their actions every day. They loved for God's sake, and what they opposed they opposed for God's sake. They were patient with the trials of life and thankful for all God's blessings. They sacrificed themselves for the good of other people.

Hadrat Abu Bakr was the first leader of the Muslims after the Messenger of God, who said of him, "There is no man under the sun who is a better man than Abu Bakr, with the exception of God's prophets." He was the father-in-law of the Prophet, who married his daughter `A'ishah. He served for two and a half years as caliph.

After him came Hadrat `Umar. He was known as `Umar the Just. He was compassionate to the poor and needy, and hard on tyrants. Valorous but humble, he was victorious over the enemies of Islam: he conquered the Persian Empire and much of the land of the Christian Byzantines to the north. He became the father-in-law of the Prophet when he gave his daughter Hafsah to him in marriage. He ruled close to 10 years.

After `Umar came `Uthman, chosen by consensus of the Companions of the Prophet. He ruled for close to 12 years. He was a saintly man known for his gentleness and kindness. He was the one who had the Holy Qur'an organized and written down, as we know it today. Before his time the words of God were partially written, but not gathered together, although there were many who had memorized the whole of it. `Uthman had seven copies of the Qur'an written. He sent them to different provinces of the growing Islamic world. During his rule, more land was added to the expanding Islamic Empire. The Prophet wed his daughter Ruqqiya to `Uthman. When she died, he gave him the hand of his daughter Um Kulthum. When she also died, the Prophet said, "If I had another daughter, I would give her to `Uthman too." This indicates how much he loved and appreciated him.

After `Uthman was martyred, Hadrat `Ali became the fourth caliph. He was the husband of the beloved daughter of the Prophet, Hadrat Fatimah, and the father of Hadrat Hasan and Hadrat Husayn, whom the Prophet loved dearly. He ruled for six years, during which time Islam spread far and wide as a coherent, united, highly moral and powerful society, ruled justly, with consideration for all: an example to humanity till the end of time.

So know these facts, believe in them, take lessons from them, and love these men who were loved by God, who saw with God's eyes, who spoke with God's words and did God's deeds. Love them and follow their example, for the Prophet said, "My companions are like stars, if you follow any one of them you will find the right way."

ON THE END OF THE WORLD AND THE DAY OF JUDGMENT
And know that the end of this world will come, and that there is a Hereafter. There is a Day of Divine Judgment, and Paradise and Hell, where one will reside forever.

The signs of Doomsday are already here. Here are some mentioned by God and His prophets:

- Men will be devoid of real wisdom. The wise will be few; fools will dominate and rule the world. The ones who claim to be wise will be corrupt and tyrannical. Those who are made governors, judges, generals, teachers, and even religious leaders will be ignorant, not worthy of their positions. The lowest among people will be considered highest; their voices will be heard and the wise will be silenced.
- The deeds of the tyrants with power will be considered as right and the innocent tyrannized as wrong. No one will trust anyone as there will be none to trust. The ones who tell the truth will be ostracized and condemned. The gentle and the kind will be considered fools. The tyrants will be rewarded and rights will only be had through bribery.
- Children will revolt against their parents. Sanity will be lost to intoxication. Adultery and promiscuity will be prevalent. Murder, treachery, and thievery will be common and multiply. Men will dress like women and women will dress like men. Decency and morality will be considered to be abnormal and comical. Sinning will be the common way of life.
- Leaders among men will lead them astray; feelings of love and compassion will be lost forever; Islam will be only a name and the Qur'an only writing on paper.

Then *Dajjal*, the Antichrist, will be born in Khurasan, and seventy thousand Jews of Isphahan will join him. For forty days, whose first day will be as long as a year, the second day as a month, the third as a week, and the last 37 days like days of this earth, they will devastate the world. Then Christ will descend from the heavens and be joined by the *Mahdi* who shall be born from the progeny of blessed Fatimah, the daughter of the Prophet. They will destroy *Dajjal*. Peace, justice, and harmony will return to humanity to the extent that the lamb and the wolf will live together in peace. This state will last for forty years. Then there will be a night much longer than other nights, and in the morning the sun will rise from the West. All the faithless, in fear, will then believe in God, but it will be too late and in vain. God will send a wind and all the faithful will die. The world will be left to the infidels, who will destroy each other and live the life of hell.

The last of the signs of Doomsday is a fire that will rise from Arabia or from the bottom of the Sea of Aden and surround the faithless like a ring. The world will shake; the mountains will fly and strike each other in the sky. The sun will melt and pour from the heavens like hot oil. All things will then die and disappear, except perhaps God's Throne above the heavens, the Tablet of God's decrees and the Pen that inscribed it, Paradise and Hell, the soul and the "base of the spine" from which God will recreate humanity for the Last Judgment.

Then, on that day, God will recreate the earth. It will be as flat and white as silver. The seven heavens stretched above it will be as red as red gold. And God will resurrect all the dead. On that day, those who are close to God will ride on heavenly steeds; the simple faithful will walk in the shade of God's Throne. The nonbelievers will slide on their faces like worms, blind, dumb, and deaf. All will approach the great balance of justice, where good deeds will be weighed against sins.

Only the following seven kinds of believers will feel safe on that day:

1. Those who led and governed people in kindness and justice.
2. Those who passed their youth in decency and prayer.
3. Those who worshipped together in mosques and kept up prayer.
4. Those who loved and helped each other for God's sake.
5. Those who feared God and shied away from sinning when they were tempted.
6. Those whose left hand did not know when their right hand gave alms for God's sake.
7. Those who remembered God by themselves, hidden from others' eyes, and shed tears in yearning for love of God and fear of losing God's care.

But the faithless will suffer the terror of the unexpected. The sun will descend close above them. Their brains will melt in their skulls; they will drown in their own sweat. They will wait in that tortured state for 50,000 years—and a day of the Hereafter is worth a thousand worldly years.

Yet God judges His faithful servants in the time that one can milk a camel. Everyone will be asked these four questions:

1. How did you pass your youth?
2. To what did you devote your life?
3. How did you obtain what you called your property, and on what did you spend it?
4. What did you learn in your lifetime, and how did you use your knowledge?

Then according to our answers, to which all our organs will bear witness, we will either receive the record of our acts in our right hand, and be saved, or from the back or our left, and be doomed.

God sent Prophet Muhammad (s.a.w.s.) as His mercy upon the universe. He gave him the privilege of interceding for sinners who breathed their last breaths as believers. And indeed he will intercede for the sinners, and save multitudes from Hellfire.

The bridge stretched over Hell is thinner than a hair, sharper than a sword. The ones who are saved will cross it as fast as lightning. But it will take a thousand years for the sinners to cross, and many will slide into Hell.

The beautiful fragrance of Paradise spreads to a distance of five hundred years. Even a few people in this world can smell it. After the Judgment, the blessed will be led toward Paradise by that perfume. All of them will have become young and beautiful, devoid of any deficiency in their appearance or character. They will know no aging, hunger, pain, fatigue, worry, or sickness. In Paradise there is no hatred. Everyone loves everyone else. Those who reside there eat and drink, but not out of hunger or thirst: God gives them what they wish to taste. What they see is what they wish to see, what they hear is what they wish to hear. But none of these gifts can be imagined in our temporal life on this earth.

Paradise exists today and has always existed. The parent of all humanity, Prophet Adam (a.s.), originated there. Its earth is of musk, its stones are diamonds and rubies, its rivers are milk and honey, the homes of its inhabitants are built from bricks of gold and mortar of silver. And the sincere believers who have served their Lord selflessly will abide there forever.

The selfish, who set themselves up as God and thought of themselves as their own masters, will fall into Hell. Its depth is seven levels. Even those who believed in God but were afflicted with arrogance, thinking themselves better than others, who were envious, greedy, hypocritical, hiding who they really are, mean and tyrannical, loving no one but themselves and the false pleasures of this life, will temporarily abide in the upper regions of Hell. There, their faults will be cleansed. Then they will enter Paradise by the mercy of God and the intercession of the Prophet.

Those who deny God, the evil who have destroyed and never repented, will abide forever in fire, burning to ashes and being resurrected to be burnt again. They will always be hungry and thirsty, yet their food will be thorns and their drink boiling water. Whatever they see, hear, touch, and smell will be what they hated in their lives. Their suffering will never diminish, but only increase. May God in His mercy save us from this.

ON DESTINY

And know that all and everything existing, happening, felt, thought, and said, whether it is good or what seems to human beings to be bad, is willed by God, created by God, and was written as our destiny in the Secret Tablet before God ever created the heavens and the earths.

The faith of the faithful, the goodness of the good, the deeds and the service for God's sake of the ones who fear God, and the love and compassion of the ones who love God, are all predestined. And they are earned by those who are thus blessed by heeding the words of God and His

Messengers. God is pleased with them, and they are pleased with God. The faithless and their faithlessness, the vicious and their perversity, the false and their falsity, the tyrants and their tyranny, those who believe themselves to be gods and their idols—all these also exist by the will of God, for He is the only creator. Yet those who are rejected by God's mercy still earn their punishment by their own will and evil deeds. They deny their Lord and their Lord is displeased with them.

There are two kinds of destiny. The first is the inexorable decree of God, which is inevitable. Humanity cannot know its cause: therefore we cannot do anything but accept it. When this befalls, if we think of the results as bad, we should remember our own private experiences with good arising from what seemed to us to be bad. Water drowns, but is also the source of life. Fire burns, but it also warms. Poison for one is cure for another.

The other destiny hangs in suspense, uncertain. Whether or not it comes to pass depends on certain conditions, on causes. One kernel gives a hundred only if it is planted and watered. A child is born only if a woman and a man are united. Not all seeds that are planted grow, and a child is not born to every marriage. These things do not happen unless God wills. Yet they certainly will not happen if we do not undertake to act.

Whether it be inevitable or dependent upon our acts, do not ever question destiny. For God has the right to interrogate man, but man has no right to interrogate God.

Now you know. God willing, you have been able to taste a drop from the vast sweet ocean of faith. A drop is not the ocean; neither is it other than the ocean.

THE PILLARS OF FAITH
On Profession of Faith

So if you agree with what you know, and know that you can act upon it in your life, then say with your tongue and confirm in sincerity in your heart: "I believe that there is one God, and I believe in His angels, and in all His books, and in all His prophets, and in the Day of Judgment, and in Destiny, and that everything, good or bad, is from Him." And hope that you will be counted among the faithful. These are the conditions of faith. They are also the conditions of Islam. Faith and Islam are one and the same.

Now you have to add another phrase. Its meaning has to be known intimately, believed in certainty, said in sincerity, and confirmed by heart. God says:

And your God is one God: there is no god but He. He is the Beneficent and Merciful. (*Baqarah*, 163)

And:

> Allah! There is no god but He, the Ever-Living, the Self-Existent by whom all subsist. (*Al-i `Imran*, 2)

And He says:

> Muhammad is the Messenger of Allah (s.a.w.s) and the seal of prophets. (*Ahzab*, 40)

Addressing him, God said:

> We have not sent you save as a mercy upon the universe. (*Anbiya*, 107)

Muhammad's coming was announced both by Moses in the Torah and Christ in the Gospel, God's peace and blessings be upon them all. God says:

> And when Jesus son of Mary said: "O Children of Israel, surely I am the Messenger of Allah (s.a.w.s) to you, verifying that which is before me of the Torah and giving the good news of a messenger who will come after me, his name being Ahmad." (*Saf*, 6)

So say *la ilaha illa Llah, Muhammadun rasulu Llah*, "There is no god but God, and Muhammad is His Messenger," knowing what you are saying.

When you say "there is no god but God," it is necessary that you be totally aware and convinced that you, your mother, your father, all of humanity, all the universe and what it contains, from the smallest atom and living creature to the furthest of stars—all are created by Him. He is the owner of your body and mind, the air you breathe, the food you consume, and everything you own. But He entrusted all this, and things hidden from your eye, to you. You are to govern in His name. He made you His deputy in the universe, to rule in justice. He taught you how to do it by sending you His instructions in holy books, and He sent teachers and examples in His prophets and saints. He counts on you not to accept anyone else but Himself as your Lord, and to take no other guide except His prophets, and to follow no other rule except His divine words. When you fulfill what you were created for, He promises that He Himself and the invisible forces of His angels will be at your side to help.

Each human being and every living thing is dependent upon and in need of another, and that other is dependent upon a third. This chain of dependence goes on and on until it reaches the One God upon whom all depend. That is another fact we must realize in our faith in One God: no part of our existence, or the existence of all and everything, is independent of Him.

To say *la ilaha illa Llah* with this kind of conviction is to declare the unity of all and everything with its Creator, as God has ordained. Although the Creator bears no resemblance to His creation, yet His creation cannot be conceived of as separate from Him. The creation is the only manifestation of the Creator and the only means of knowing Him. Human beings may become conscious of being the supreme creation of God and containing traces of the attributes of God, inherited from the parent of humanity, the Prophet Adam (a.s.), into whose soul God breathed from His own soul, and whom He taught His beautiful Names. That makes us aware of our responsibility. The realization that the peace, happiness, and success of humanity depend on our obeying our Lord is a result of faith in One God. If all people realized this, it would be the cause of a perfect order and a united indomitable force, preventing any tyranny against the rights established by God.

The human being, whom God created as His deputy in the universe, possesses the qualities needed to assume this responsibility and duty. The infinite capacity of the human mind is capable of understanding that the cause, the reality, and the purpose of everything created is knowable only through the One God, the only Creator and the cause of all and everything, the unity and oneness of the whole creation. We should observe that everything is created in relation to human beings and for our benefit. Suns and stars and all the heavens and what they contain, the world and what is in it, all are given to humanity so that we may seek, learn, understand, use, enjoy, and take care of them all. All this is a gift from God, but it also establishes the right of God over humanity, for we have accepted it all as a trust.

This responsibility is the basis of human morality: heedfulness, equality of all humanity, respect for others' rights and freedom, conscience, kindness, care and generosity. It is peace and justice, love and compassion, tolerance and forgiveness, and thankfulness for God's gifts—of which time is the most valuable. It should not be spent in vain.

The person who is aware of One God, and of the unity and oneness of everything, enters his life as if entering God's house as a tenant. He will enjoy it as a home, but also assume its upkeep, cleanliness, and protection. Man, who was created as a watchman over the rest of creation, upon his departure from this world will be obliged to return that which was entrusted to him in a better state than it was when he received it. A person who accomplishes this task is called *zahid*; a good person as God meant all of us to be.

And when you say *Muhammadun rasulu Llah*, that you bear witness to Allah's Messenger, you must believe and be aware that all of God's creation, visible and invisible, can only be seen through the Light of Muhammad. For he himself said:

The first thing Allah created was my light. (Bayhaqi, Jabir ibn Abdullah)

You must also believe that all of God's attributes manifested in all and everything; what you hear and learn, what you think and feel, exist through the *haqiqah Muhammadiyyah*, the Truth of Muhammad. As he himself said:

With my light, Allah has created my soul, my mind, and the Pen with which everything is written.

And worship and love God, your Lord and the Creator of all. God says in a divine tradition:

I was a hidden treasure; I loved to be known, so I created the creation.

That Love is God's love for Himself: all creation is created from that Love. It is through that Love for Allah that His creation came to know Him. Thus our Creator loves us both for His own sake, and also for our sake. And He created us for Himself.

Allah's love for us manifests itself in His giving us the ability to know what kind of actions, what kind of life, will lead us to salvation and felicity; and how to save ourselves from things that are against our birthright, our nature, and our reason for being in this world.

The purpose of our creation is revealed in this verse from the Holy Qur'an:

I have not created *jinn* and men except that they should worship Me. (*Dhuriyat*, 56)

The Arabic word *ya`budun* means "to worship." But it can also be understood as "to serve," because the Arabic word `*abd* means servant. Thus it is clear that we are created both to praise God and to serve Him.

Our obligation to praise Him is a natural phenomenon. God says in the Holy Qur'an that:

The seven heavens and the earth and all beings therein praise Him. And there is not a single thing that does not glorify Him with His praise; but you do not understand how they declare His glory! Verily He is Oft-Forbearing, Most Forgiving! (*Bani Isra`il*, 44)

And:

Seest thou not that Allah is He who is glorified by all those who are in the heavens and the earth, and the birds with wings outspread? Each one knows its prayer and its praise. (*Nur*, 41)

Thus praise, glorification, and thankfulness, prayer to God, is a natural manifestation of existence from all that is created.

In the first verse, God Most High addresses "you" in plural to all mankind, saying "you do not understand." But in the second verse, when He says "seest thou not?" in the singular, He is addressing our master, the Holy Prophet. This means that we cannot see and understand this universal glorification without a great effort. In general we must believe in it blindly, though when He asks "seest thou not?" He indicates that the Prophet is able to see clearly.

Therefore to take our honored place within the creation—having been given the privilege of having a mind, a will, a conscience, and a human soul, delegated by our Lord to be His regent in the universe and to praise Him heedfully—the only path is to try to be like our master, His beloved Prophet Hadrat Muhammad Mustafa (s.a.w.s.).

God in His mercy has created His messengers, His prophets, in the shape of other human beings. Their blessed physical bodies were quite similar to ours, and our physical being is not much different from the animals. In fact in its structure the human body contains the same elements that are in plants and earth, water and air.

If all the visible universe is praising God (although people cannot hear it), then our physical being—our hands, our feet, our tongues—is also in a state of continuous prayer, though we are not aware of it. God says:

... on the Day (of Judgment) when their tongues and their feet and their hands will bear witness against them as to what they did. (*Nur*, 24)

For us, who possess a human soul blown into us by Allah from His own Soul, who possess intelligence and will, to praise Allah like a mineral or a vegetable is not sufficient. These divine gifts are given to us so that we can prove our worthiness of them. Otherwise we will lower our state below that of the animals. The animal, the plant, the rock—these will never revolt against their own natures, because they do not know anything except themselves and do not do anything except what they were created to do. They submit. They are better Muslims than many human beings.

God says in the Holy Qur'an:

And to Allah makes obeisance every living creature in the heavens and on the earth, even the angels, and they are not proud ... They do what they are commanded. (*Nahl*, 49-50)

But men are proud, and they do not know themselves. We are proud of what we are not, of that which our egos make us believe is real. Until we find out who we really are, our worship and devotion to God will be hypocritical—at best, an imitation.

One way to know ourselves is by comparison. We should not compare ourselves to other people, which would be comparing an unknown with an unknown. But we should compare our state, even our imaginary state tainted with pride, to what we are supposed to be, as God meant us to be.

God, as a clear manifestation of His love for us, has sent His holy books and His prophets—ideal human beings as examples to humankind—as the embodiment of all His wishes for us. But people kept distorting the messages and reshaping the Messengers in their own image. So Allah sent His final, unalterable message in the Qur'an, which contains the truth of all the divine messages. And He sent a Messenger as the seal of prophethood who contains the essence of all the prophets since Adam (a.s.): Hadrat Muhammad Mustafa (s.a.w.s.).

If we measure ourselves against the commands of God in the Qur'an, and if we compare our life to the life of the one whom He sent as His mercy upon the universe, we will perhaps be able to see our sad condition. Then perhaps our devotion, our worship, will be a little more sincere and true. Still it will be forced, tinted with the pain of self-disappointment, and selfish. We keep expecting a reward, even if the reward is forgiveness.

On Praying

Hadrat `Ali (r.a.) said that there are four kinds of worship. The lowest one, which is totally useless, is to go through the motions of prayer mechanically. When the Messenger of God said:

> There are some who fast and all that they get from it is hunger, and some who pray and all that they get from it is fatigue

he was describing this kind of prayer.

The second kind of prayer is that in which the devotee begs God to give him things: money, fame, health, and so forth. In a sense even the ones who ask for forgiveness of their sins and entrance into Paradise are included among these. Hadrat `Ali (r.a.) calls this not worship, but commerce, for this kind of devotee thinks his prayers can be payment for Allah's blessings. Allah says in a divine tradition:

> There are some who ask this world from Me in their prayers, and I give them this world, but they have no portion of the Hereafter. And some ask Me for the Hereafter, and I give them the Hereafter, but they have no

portion of this world. And some love only Me and ask for Me alone. And I give them Myself and this world and the Hereafter.

The third kind of worship is that which is done in thankfulness, not only for the infinite good that Allah pours over His creation, but also for the trials that test our love for Him. Although this is a very high form of praise of God's generosity, love, and compassion for His creatures, Hadrat `Ali (r.a.) calls it a selfish form of prayer.

The highest form of worship is the praise of the lover for the Beloved, out of pure love of Allah. Allah mentions those who pray like this in the Qur'an:

> ... a people whom He loves and who love Him ... (*Maidah*, 54)

Certainly our love for Him cannot possibly be like His love for us. The love of which we are capable is either natural love (which many of us, if not all, can feel) or spiritual love, which very few can understand and fewer still can experience. Spiritual love cannot be acquired. It is a gift, and to receive that gift we must be worthy of receiving it. The highest form of devotion is to praise the Beloved with both the natural love given to us and the spiritual love that must be won.

To receive the gift of spiritual love, we have "to know, to find, and to *be*." You cannot find a thing when you don't know what you are looking for, and you cannot find it if you don't know the way. We cannot *be* that thing if we do not leave ourselves behind. Allah says in a divine tradition:

> When my faithful servant comes close to Me with extra worship, I love him and he loves Me. And when I love him, I become his eyes with which he sees, his hands with which he holds, his feet with which he walks ...

That is when man knows, finds, and is with his Lord. But what is this "extra worship" that will bring us close to our Lord? It is service.

There are two levels of worship. One is the obligatory worship of five-times-daily prayer, fasting during the month of Ramadan, paying alms of one-fortieth of our liquid assets to poor Muslims, and going on the Pilgrimage once in a lifetime. Although Allah has set specific times for these formal devotions, in His mercy He has permitted us, in cases of necessity, to delay these obligations. If we miss a prayer, a fast, paying our dues, or going to Pilgrimage, we are permitted to make up for these later. The Holy Prophet (s.a.w.s) used to break his fast and make his followers break their fast when they were facing danger. Allah permits us to shorten our prayers and not to fast when we face difficulties of travel or sickness.

The second level of obligatory worship does not have specific times. These duties are to be done now and always. They are exercised as the occasion presents itself in daily life. Such are kindness, forgiveness, concern for others, helping, protecting, feeding, advising, building and not destroying. In Allah's view:

The best of people is the one who is good to others.

To stand guard for the safety of others one night is much better than thousand nights of standing in prayer.

The Muslim is he from whose tongue and hand others are safe.

The one Allah loves best is the one who does good deeds and makes others do them, and makes them love Allah and makes Allah love them.

Allah does not permit this form of obligatory worship to be delayed. You cannot say, "I will save him later, I have to do my prayers first" when someone is drowning. You cannot say "I will feed him tomorrow" when someone is hungry.

This second form of prayer through service is the "extra worship" that will bring us closer to our Lord. In fact, if we are given the occasions and are able to perform the worship of service, it is a sign that our formal devotions of daily prayers, fasting, and almsgiving are accepted. We must firmly believe that someone who is no good to himself, his family, his neighbors, his nation, the family of Islam, and all of humanity, but on the contrary does harm, will not enter Paradise even if he stands in prayer all night and fasts all day.

When someone has proven himself worthy to be a human being and a faithful servant of his Lord by serving selflessly in his Lord's name, he is called a *zahid*, a good person. That person may then be given the gift of spiritual love.

Know that the Beloved loved with spiritual love does not accept a partner. As Allah has no partner, love for Him also cannot be divided. Yet spiritual love includes the love of the Beloved for His sake as well as love for the lover's own sake, since it is a combination of the Beloved's love for the lover and the lover's love for the Beloved. On the other hand, the natural love that many people know is always for the sake of the lover alone. Both kinds of love wish to reach out and unite lover and beloved. Natural love, at its best if the love is mutual, reaches its peak when the lovers meet. Each may be enriched, but they will still be two together. In spiritual love, the lover becomes one with the Beloved.

When we are worthy to be in that state of unification, our prayers will become our actions, our entire life. Life itself could then be nothing other than the manifestation of Allah's divine attributes in us. That is the definition of an *'arif*, a perfect human being.

The worship of the *zahid* is through obedience. The one who knows, the `arif*, worships with pleasure. The *zahid* hopes for the Garden, the `arif* for Allah. The *zahid* is with his ego; the `arif* is with his Lord. The *zahid* remembers Allah with his tongue, while the `arif* remembers Him with his heart, with his life. The *zahid*'s heart is with the world of causes. The `arif*'s soul is with Allah.

The *mu'min*, the believer, at best sees with the light of Allah. The `arif* sees with the eyes of Allah. The believer holds onto the rope of Allah, the Qur'an; the `arif* holds onto Allah Himself.

We are attached to this world, to our desires, to our *nafs*, our ego; and the *nafs* is a prison. Behind the prison bars is the divine door.

The good person looks at the creation and people with the eyes of his *nafs* and is disillusioned, angry, and becomes the enemy of the creation. The `arif* sees the creation with its Creator and looks upon it with love and compassion, and is at peace.

The *zahid* walks, the `arif* flies. The `alim*, the person of knowledge, stands below what he talks about. The `arif* stands above knowledge. The `arif* does not divulge his wisdom except to the ones who know. His best words are silence. As he comes closer to Allah, he becomes more distant from people. He only needs what comes from Allah, therefore he does not ask from anyone else. Because he is lowly in front of his Lord, he is loved and respected by the creation. He is far from desire, he wishes nothing. His hands are empty, so he is free and at peace.

The path to Allah Most High certainly passes through the life of this world, then through the life of the Hereafter. The `arif* has passed through both this world and the Hereafter. The strength of the good man comes through eating and drinking. The strength of the `arif* comes from remembering Allah and from being with Him. The *qiblah*, the direction of prayer, of the heedless is gold and worldly glory; the *qiblah* of the `arif* is Allah's mercy.

So know why the most perfect of all men, our Prophet said "*salat* is the light of my eyes." He also esteemed the *salat*, the obligatory prayers done five times a day, as the *mi'raj*, the ascension, of the believer to the presence of his Lord. For *salat* is the vision of things beyond our sight, as our Prophet saw realms beyond our vision and closer to God, which permitted him to converse with Him.

God says:

Mention Me in remembrance and I will respond by remembering you. (*Baqarah*, 152)

Thus *salat* is a conversation between God and His servant. In a divine tradition He says:

I divided *salat* in half between Myself and My servant. Half of the worship belongs to Me and half to My servant and My servant will certainly receive that which he asks of Me.

All material things came into existence through motion. The motion that caused existence is found within the movements of the *salat.* These motions are three: vertical movement, upward; horizontal movement, forward; and the reverse movement, backward and downward.

The first, vertical movement, is in the position of *qiyam,* standing up. The second, horizontal movement, is in the position of *ruku`,* bent over. The third, reverse movement is in the *sajdah,* prostration. These three motions are also manifest in the three kingdoms of creation: the vertical in human beings, the horizontal in animals, and the prostration upon the earth, in earth itself. In the final movement of prostration, the worshiper becomes a receptive earth that does not move or do anything on its own, out of its own will, but only moves and does by the will of another. That is the state of the Beloved of Allah, who did not attribute anything he was or did or said to himself, but attributed all to his Lord. When he said "*salat* is the light of my eyes," he meant that it is neither his *salat* nor his eyes, but the Lord Himself seeing Himself in His Divine Light. Thus, in the *salat,* reality sees its realness, the truth sees nothing but the truth. That is why it is maleficent and forbidden by the Lord to care for anything else other than what is being done through you during the *salat.* Whenever the mind wanders in imagination, the Devil steals from the *salat* and prevents the lover from reaching the Beloved. The true lover seeks only the Beloved.

The direction of the Ka`bah is where the worshiper looks for the Beloved. Whatever distracts us leads us astray—away from the Beloved. The word *salat* in Arabic means to come behind those who are ahead, as proven in the words of our Prophet, *inna Llaha fi qiblat il-musalli*: "Allah is in the direction toward which the believer turns to pray."

That is why, as we prostrate during the *salat,* we are prostrating neither to the wall before us nor to the Ka`bah, but to Allah Most High. The prostration is the time and place where the believer is closest to Allah. Thus we should keep our eyes open during the prostration.

Before sunrise, just past noon, at midafternoon, after sunset, and at night, Muslims pray following the example of our Prophet. You stand clean, in a clean place, facing the direction of the Ka`bah, with a sincere intention to be with your Lord. You start your prayer by raising your hands above your shoulders, as if throwing your worldly cares behind you with the backs of your hands, and saying *Allahu akbar. Allahu akbar* means "God is greater"—greater and absolutely independent of all the creation, all the manifestations of His attributes in the beauty of His creation. And although all that exist are from Him, none is He, nor is any like Him.

Every cycle of the ritual prayer starts by reciting the opening *surah* of the Qur'an, the *Fatihah*. This is an obligation: without it the prayer is not valid. The one in prayer says, *bismi Llah ir-rahman ir-rahim*, "In the name of Allah, the most Beneficent and the most Merciful." The Lord responds: "My servant commended Me." When the servant says *al-hamdu li-Llahi rabb il-`alamin*, "all thanks and praise to the Lord of all creation," The Lord says: "My servant is thankful to Me." When the worshiper says *maliki yawm ad-din*, "the owner of the Day of Judgment," the Lord says: "My servant has submitted to Me and left his life in My hands." These first three verses of the opening chapter of the Holy Qur'an belong to God. The worshiper says *iyyaka na`budu wa iyyaka nasta`in*, "we belong only to You and we ask all we need from You." Then the Lord says "My servant is now with Me and he will have all that he wishes." This verse in the center of the chapter is like the *barzakh* or interspace, Purgatory, a state of abandonment of the self. Then the servant says *ihdinas-sirat al mustaqim*, "lead us to the straight path, the truth," *sirat alladhina an`amta `alayhim*, "the path of those who are close to You, whom You love," *ghayril-maghdubi `alayhim wa lad-dalin*, "not the path of the ones who meet Your wrath or who go astray." And Allah says: "That belongs to My servant and he will have all what he asks."

If you are able to cleanse yourself from your worldly cares at least momentarily, and if your intention to be with your Lord during prayer is pure, and if you are truly yearning for Truth, then know that whoever yearns for truth, obtains it. For Allah says:

I am with the one who calls on Me.

The one with eyes certainly should be able to see the One who is with him. But "those who are blind in this world of matter will be blind to the real reality of the other world." Whether or not we are with the truth while praying should let us know where we are and who we are. Whoever feels the presence of the Lord during prayer is an *imam*, the leader of a congregation, even when praying alone, because the Prophet of Allah said:

Whoever truly prays is certainly an *imam*, because there are angels praying behind him.

That true servant of the Lord is raised to represent his Lord, for, when he says *sami`a Llahu li-man hamidah*, "God hears those who praise and thank Him," he is repeating God's promised response to himself and to the angels behind him. And the angels respond *rabbana lakal-hamd*, "our Lord, all praise and thanks are due to You." All this is seen by those who can claim, like our Master, the Messenger of Allah, that "*salat* is the light of my eye."

The ones who do not see or feel their Lord, but at least believe that He sees and hears them, may not receive these blessings unless Allah, in His mercy, gives them protection from sinning and doing wrong. Allah says in the Holy Qur'an:

Salat protects man from things wrong and forbidden.

And:

Allah knows what you are doing.

So:

Worship Allah as if you see Him, and if you do not see Him, certainly He sees you. (Bukhari, Abu Hurayra)

On Fasting

And fast during the holy month of Ramadan, for God has made it an obligation. Fasting is the light of the heart. It is what wipes off the dust and dirt of egotism from the mirror of sacred secrets, it cures the heart from the love and ambition of this world. Allah Most High says in the Holy Qur'an:

Ya ayyuha lladhina amanu kutiba `alaykum us-siyamu ka-ma kutiba `ala lladhina min qablikum la`allakum tattaqun. (*Baqarah*, 183)

"In that known month I have made it an obligation for you to fast from before the time of morning prayer until after sunset, with the intention of doing this for Allah's sake as a sign of your faith in Him, and for no other purpose. You are to abstain from eating, drinking and sexual acts. Fasting was ordained to the followers of all the other prophets that I have sent before you, as it is ordained for you. Now with what you will receive in return for your efforts, you will be protected from what Allah has forbidden to you and be a true servant, close to Him."

Everything that Allah Most High orders us to do has an outer and an inner meaning. The outer meaning of fasting during Ramadan is not eating, drinking, or having sex from before sunrise until after sunset. But take heed: our being is not only our stomachs and sexual organs. Fasting is ordained for all our physical being. Therefore, as we abstain from taking nourishment and making love, we should also abstain from lying, gossiping, or pronouncing any words that might hurt the feelings of any human being. We must prevent our eyes from looking at anything around us heedlessly. We must prevent our ears from listening to anything that is forbidden by Allah. We must prevent our egos from their ambitions for this world and their lusts for its pleasures and from selfishness and arrogance.

The inner fasting is undertaken by the heart and the soul. The fast of the heart, which is Allah's house, is to empty it of worldly concerns. Thus it is lightened, lifted from the attraction of material things, and protected from the invasion of the desires of our flesh.

The fasting of the soul is to keep it from wanting even the beauties of Paradise and the eternal life of bliss. In this way the soul becomes blind to anything but truth.

If we could fast like this and taste what the fasting brings, then we might receive what the Prophet promises:

> When the fast is broken, what peace and joy the faithful receive! (Muslim, An-Nissai)

If we fast without knowing what we are doing and spend no more effort than simply not eating, we certainly will not obtain what Allah promises, nor be protected from what He forbids, nor come closer to Him. Fasting and praying may cause only hunger and fatigue, and nothing else, if we do not realize their true meanings and try to act accordingly. The ordinary hunger we may feel is not a sufficient effort to fulfill our obligation. At least we should seek out those who are not only hungry while fasting in Ramadan, but always, and endeavor to help them.

Fasting is a proof that all your physical body and spiritual being believes in Allah Most High. It is also a way toward the unification of all human beings through caring for each other. The one who fasts yet thinks only of himself and breaks the hearts of others is just torturing himself with hunger. He will receive nothing else.

Our beloved Prophet said:

> The one who fasts becomes beautified by the attributes of Allah Most High.

A human being contains the divine attributes, for our father Adam (a.s.) was given all the beautiful names of Allah. Fasting is an obligation for human beings, not for animals. Someone who does not care for others and who is able to hurt and break the hearts of others is not a human being. A human being does not destroy, he constructs.

A human being who fasts transforms his material being of coarse matter into the fine matter of his spirit. When he does that he becomes pure compassion, the manifestation of his Creator's *rahmah*, the divine beneficence and compassion. That is what Allah Most High means when He declares in a divine tradition:

> I love the smell of the breath of the one who fasts for My sake.

This is not the bad odor from the mouth of someone who is hungry. What He means is, "Whoever truly fasts, who truly transforms himself into My divine attributes, who shows My creation a love and compassion that recalls My love and compassion, each of his breaths contains the perfume of compassion. This breath is sweet to his Creator."

Allah Most High also says:

> All the work of a son of Adam belongs to him except fasting. It is only for Me, and only I will give its reward. (Muslim, Abu Hurayra)

All rewards for our worship and good deeds are given by Allah Most High. So what does this saying mean? On the Day of Judgment the sum of our sins will be deducted from our good deeds. Yet when it comes to our fasting for Allah's sake, no sin will be permitted to eliminate this good deed. Allah Most High will declare that He Himself will pay for the remainder of our sins, and His rewards for our fasting will not be touched.

On Poor Rate

And pay your *zakat*, the poor rate. It is an obligation for all Muslims to pay one-fortieth of their extra wealth, upon which they do not depend for their sustenance, to other Muslims who are in need. This is not only an issue of proper human interactions. When you pay the *zakat*, you are made aware that what you think you possess is not really yours. It belongs to God, and has been given to you by Him both for your needs and to share with others who are in need. If you are blessed with the opportunity to share with others, you become an instrument in the hands of the all-beneficent, total generosity: Almighty God.

For those who are afflicted with the horrible sickness of miserliness and stinginess, which is nothing less than the expression of their lack of faith and hope in God's generosity, *zakat* is a strong medication. It may cure them of depending on their miserable selves rather than counting on God, the sustainer and satisfier of all needs.

On Pilgrimage

God says:

> ... the pilgrimage to the Holy House is an obligation owed to Allah, for whoever has the ability to find his way to it. (*Al-i `Imran*, 96)

So work to enable yourself to find the means, the time, and the way to visit the Holy House in Mecca. The pilgrimage, once in a lifetime, becomes an obligation when these conditions are met.

Here are the duties we are required to perform during Hajj, the pilgrimage to the Holy House: Before you leave your home, try to bring yourself, in mind and spirit, to a state of humbleness and gentleness. Become soft-spoken, good-natured, and above all, patient. Just before you leave, make two cycles of prayer, and saying *bismi Llah, tawakkaltu 'ala Llah, wa la hawla wa la quwwata illa bi-Llah il-'ali il-'azim,* "In the name of God, I trust in God, and there is no strength nor power except with God, the Most High, the Most Great," take refuge in Allah and bid farewell to your family and friends.

When you arrive at a *miqat,* an indicated point of proximity to the sanctuary, you make a total ablution, cut your fingernails, mildly perfume yourself, and put on your *ihram.*

Ihram, an obligation of the Hajj, for males consists of two pieces of white cloth, one covering below the waist and the other thrown over the shoulders. Women's *ihram* consists of white robes, white socks, and white head cover. *Ihram* is a symbol of having left behind all that is worldly. The white cloth is like your shroud. It equalizes the king and the beggar. When you put it on, you put behind you fame, wealth, honor, pride, lust, and need. In *ihram,* you are as naked as when you were born, without anything belonging to you; you are as naked as you will be when you die, totally in the hand of Allah and your destiny.

Men's heads are uncovered. Women may not cover their faces. All are either barefoot or wearing sandals without backs. So dressed, you offer two cycles of prayer and make your intention for Hajj, saying *Allahumma inni uridul-hajj, fa-yassirli wa taqabbul minna,* "O Lord, I intend to perform the Pilgrimage, so make it easy for me and accept it from us." Then say thrice the *talbiyah: Labbayk Allahumma labbayk, labbayka la sharika laka labbayk, innal-hamda wal-ni'mata laka wal-mulk, la sharika lak,* "I am present, O Lord, at Your orders. You have no equal. I am here, O Lord, pure and loyal, accepting Your invitation. All comes from You, all praise is to You, the universe is Your kingdom. You have no equal."

From this moment on you must watch yourself carefully so as not to hurt anyone or anything by either your words or your actions. You must not alter your physical state by shaving yourself, cutting your fingernails, covering your head, or changing clothes. Husbands and wives must keep away from each other and all must control the desires of the flesh. You must make your ablution whenever it is needed. After each prayer, each time you meet a group of people, each time you go uphill or come downhill, you must repeat the *talbiyah* three times, aloud.

The *talbiyah* recited during Hajj is a condition and an obligation of Hajj in just the way that the opening *takbir,* the declaration *Allahu akbar,* "God is greater," is a condition for beginning your *salat.* Allah invites you to His house. The *talbiyah* is your pronouncing your acceptance of this invitation.

By the order of Allah, as soon as the Prophet Ibrahim (a.s.) finished building the Ka`bah, he cried *labbayk Allahumma labbayk*—"I am present my Lord, all of me, as You created me, I am here, now, at your orders." And Allah brought what He had then revealed to Hadrat Ibrahim (a.s.) in His own voice to the ears of the souls of the faithful gathered in the realm of souls. Your soul in this world of flesh remembers this moment when we face the material Ka`bah and cry, "I am present, I am here, now, and I submit and obey and give myself to You without any reserve and without any condition."

Enter the city of Mecca in a state of ablution. As you see the Ka`bah, repeat the *talbiyah*, *takbir* (*Allahu akbar*), *tahlil* (*la ilaha illa Llah*, "There is no god but God"), and *as-salatu was-salam* (*Allahumma salli `ala sayyidina Muhammadin wa `ala ali Muhammad*, "O Lord, bless our master Muhammad and the family of Muhammad"), and say *Allahumma zada baytaka tashrifan wa ta`ziman wa takriman wa barran muhabbat*—"O Lord, increase the blessings, honor, grace, and bounties proper to Your House."

Then stand with the Ka`bah at your left, at the corner of the Black Stone. Salute the Ka`bah and say *bismi Llahi Allahu akbar*, "In the name of God: God is greater," and start the *tawaf*, the circumambulation, counterclockwise. Make three circumambulations with short but quick steps. Each time you come to the corner of the Black Stone, salute it and if possible touch it or kiss it. The last four circumambulations should be done quietly and slowly, again saluting the Black Stone each time. During the circumambulations you can recite whatever prayers you know, such *as Rabbana atina fiddunya hasanatan wa fil-akhirati hasanatan wa qina adhab an-nar*, "Our Lord, grant us good in this world and good in the Next World and protect us from the torment of the Fire," as well as and other Qur'anic passages, the Profession of Faith, *as-salatu was-salam*, and so forth, but above all try to be in a state of awareness and presence.

At the end of the seventh circumambulation, come out at the corner of the Black Stone and make two cycles of prayer near the place of Hadrat Ibrahim (a.s.), finishing with your private prayers.

Circumambulation of the Ka`bah is the most important part of Hajj. It is performed at least three times: once at the beginning, on arrival at Mecca; once at the end, upon returning from the gathering on the plain of Arafat; and finally for taking leave, before departing from Mecca.

Allah Most High placed the Ka`bah on the face of this earth as a symbol of *al-`arsh al-ala*—His throne in the heavens. He ordered us to circumambulate it, likening His servants' devotions to those of His angels circumambulating His throne in the heavens. He considers the circumambulation of those who are able to cleanse their hearts from all that is other than Allah, and who can unify the words of praise within their hearts with their whole beings, to be better than the praises of His angels.

For a secret reason known to Allah He put four corners on His symbolic House. In divine reality the Ka`bah is a three-sided pyramid with three corners, each symbolizing one of the three divine remembrances of the human heart. The corner of the Black Stone where the circumambulation begins is the memory of the heart's divine origin. The next corner, the Yemeni corner, is the reminder of the heart's angelic origin, and the third corner is the reminder of the primal sacredness of humanity itself. At these three corners there is no memory of anything evil. The hearts of all the prophets of Allah have only these three memories. But in accordance with the nature of human beings in the lower world of matter, where Allah gives us our little will and the possibility to choose between good and evil, He added a fourth corner, the Iraqi corner. There we may remember the evil influences and our revolts, disobediences, wrongs and doubts, and repent. The Ka`bah with its four corners is in the shape of the human heart, which contains these four influences.

The Black Stone, which we believe to have come from Paradise, was originally pure white but turned black in this world of matter. It is like Hadrat Adam (a.s.) who erred in order to gain the honor of being the first of Allah's prophets and the father of humankind. His error became the cause of his being chosen as the *khalifah,* the deputy of Allah on earth. It is a reminder that Allah not only forgives a fault realized and repented, but transforms it into a good deed.

It is in the *rahmah,* the mercy of Allah, that we remember our covenant with Allah. Kissing and touching the Black Stone as a symbol brings the memory of our pledge to Allah, to all His prophets, and to our Prophet— the most beloved, the seal of all prophethood, peace and blessings be upon him.

After the first sevenfold circumambulation is finished, you walk to the nearby hill of Safa, to a point where you can see the Ka`bah. Then repeating the *takbir* and *tahlil* and *as-salatu was-salam,* you start walking toward Marwah. You must make this trip seven times, four times from Safa to Marwah and three times from Marwah to Safa, finishing at Marwah. Both in Safa and Marwah, stand at a place looking at the Ka`bah, as you did at the beginning, and repeat the same prayers you said on first coming to Safa. You must quicken your pace each time between the two marked points. As you do so, say *Allahumma ighfir warham wa tajawuz `amma ta`lam, antal-`ali ul-a`zam* —"O Lord forgive me, have mercy upon me, don't look upon my faults. You are the Highest and the Greatest." This ritual is complete at the end of the seventh walk, at Marwah.

On the eight of *Dhul-Hijjah,* all pilgrims leave Mecca for Mina on their way to the plain of Arafat, where they must arrive by noon of the fifth to pray and meditate. In Arafat, noon and afternoon prayers are joined together late in the day, and the evening and night prayers are said together at sunset, following the tradition of the Prophet. Then everyone moves to Muzdalifah to spend the rest of the night and to perform the morning prayers. During this trip the pilgrims are recommended to visit and pray at Masjid al-Hayf and Mash`ar as the Prophet did.

On the day of `Id al-Adha (the tenth of *Zulhijjah*) the pilgrims return to Mina to stone the Devil. You throw seven stones at each of three places, following the tradition of Hadrat Ibrahim and Hadrat Isma`il (a.s.). These seven stones represent the seven greater sins of pride in one's spiritual state, vanity of one's physical state, hypocrisy, envy, anger, love of worldly possessions, and ambition for recognition and fame. Then you sacrifice an animal and return to Mecca.

In Mecca you will come out of *ihram*, bathe, put on your best clothes, and perform the final circumambulation, walking once more seven times between Safa and Marwah. You will have your hair cut, and drink and wash with the blessed water from the well of *Zamzam*. And that is the end of your obligations in performing the Hajj.

After the Hajj, it is proper to visit the beatified tomb of our beloved Prophet in Medina. As he was closest of all the creation to Allah Most High, who created him from His own divine light, we may hope to come close to Allah through him. He is the greatest guide to Him. He is the one who was honored with carrying His divine words to us, to bring us the awareness of truth. He is the one on whom we depend to intercede for us. Blessed is he who will see his light there, who will feel the presence of Paradise in the space between his blessed tomb and the *minbar* where he preached. He himself said, "Whoever visits my tomb receives my intercession." He also said, "Whoever visits the House of Allah and does not visit me has given me pain."

On the way to Medina, the city of purity, you should recite many times *as-salatu was-salam* from the depths of your heart. When you arrive you should bathe and dress up in your best clothes and walk to his tomb with great reverence. As you enter the *masjid* make two cycles of prayer, if possible between the blessed tomb and the *minbar*, as *talbiyyat al-masjid*, your respects to the mosque. Follow this with another two cycles of prayer of thankfulness. Then proceed gently, facing him, your back turned to the direction of the Ka`bah.

Stand not nearer than four steps from his tomb, heedful, present, respectful, and loving. Salute him with salutations such as *as-salamu `alayka ayyuhan-nabiyyu wa rahmatu Llahi wa barakatuhu*: "peace be upon you, O Prophet, and the mercy and blessing of God"; *as-salamu `alayka ya sayyid al-awwalina wal-akhirin*, "peace be upon you, Master of the First and the Last"; *as-salamu `alayka ya rasula Llah, ya habiba Llah*, "peace be upon you, Messenger of God, Beloved of God," and so forth. Then with deep respect toward him, ask Allah for the good things that are dearest to your heart, hoping that he will say *Amin* to your prayers.

Two steps to your right you will be standing in the presence of Hadrat Abu Bakr as-Siddiq (r.a.). Greet him also with reverence. Salute him and offer prayers for his blessed soul. Another few steps to the right you are in the presence of Hadrat `Umar al-Faruq (r.a.). Offer him also your salutations and your prayers for his soul. Then continue walking toward your left around the corner, and you will be in front of the house of Hadrat Fatimah (r.a.). This is not her tomb, but a place where she lived with Hadrat `Ali and their children, the beloved Hasan and Husayn (r.a.). Remember that, recite *Fatihah*s for their souls, and ask for their intercession.

Afterwards you should spend as much time as possible every day in the *masjid*, praying and repenting. It is recommended to complete forty occasions of prayer during your visit to Medina.

Know that the form of any kind of worship is a means to find Truth. If Truth is not found through it, form has no meaning or purpose by itself.

A man came to take leave from Hadrat Shibli (q.s.). Shibli asked, "Where are you going?"

"To the Hajj."

"Take with you two big bags. Fill them with mercy there and bring them to us, so that we will have a share of it to give out to our friends and to offer our guests!"

The man took his leave, and departed upon the Hajj. When he returned he came to visit Hadrat Shibli, who asked, "Did you go to the Pilgrimage?"

"Yes."

"What did you do first?"

"I took a ritual total ablution, put on my pilgrim's garb, made two cycles of *salat*, started reciting the *talbiyah*, and made my intention and decision to make the Pilgrimage."

"With your intention and decision to make the Pilgrimage, were you able to cancel all decisions you had taken that were contrary to this decision since the day you were born?"

"No."

"Then you have not made your intention to make the Hajj. You say you took off your ordinary clothes and put on your pilgrim's garb. Did you denude yourself of all you had done in your ordinary life?"

"No."

"Then you neither took off your clothes nor put on your pilgrim's garb. When you washed yourself and made your ablution, did you cleanse yourself of all your ills and defects?"

"No."

"Then you did not make your ritual ablution. When you recited the *talbiyah* and said 'I am present, my Lord, I am here, at Your orders, I am here heedful, there is none like You, all grace is to You, all blessing is from You, all belongs to You, there is no partner with You,' did you receive an answer, a call from Allah?"

"No."

"Then you did not recite the *talbiyah*. Have you visited Mecca?"

"Yes."

"When you entered Mecca, did you feel that you received a different state from Allah?"

"No."

"Then you have not been in Mecca. Did you enter the Haram, the sacred grounds?"

"Yes."

"When you entered the Haram, did you vow to leave behind all that is unlawful?"

"No."

"Then you did not enter the Haram. Did you enter the Sacred Mosque?"

"Yes."

"Did you feel closer to Allah in the Sacred Mosque?"

"No."

Then you did not enter the Sacred Mosque. Have you seen the Ka`bah?"

"Yes."

"In seeing the Ka`bah, did you achieve the goal for which you came?"

"No."

"Then you have not seen the Ka`bah. Have you circumambulated the Ka`bah three times quickly and four times slowly?"

"Yes."

"In running three times around the Ka`bah, did you run away from everything accompanying you, and in walking four times around it, did you reach salvation and security and thankfulness?"

"No."

"Then you have not left your old self, nor your worldly load; nor have you come closer to your Lord. You have not made your circumambulation. Did you touch and salute the Black Stone?"

"Yes."

"Pity upon you! It is said that whoever touches the Black Stone touches the Truth. The one who touches the Truth is in the securest peace. Did you feel this security?"

"No."

"Then you have not touched the Black Stone. Did you make two cycles of *salat* afterwards at the place of Hadrat Ibrahim?"

"Yes."

"In doing so, did you stand in front of your Lord and show Him your intention?"

"No."

"Then you did not make your *salat* there. Did you stand on the hill of Safa?"

"Yes."

"What did you do there?"

"I recited the *takbir*. I declared the greatness of Allah."

"As you stood there, did your soul find purity (*safa'*)? Did your heart find joy (*sa'ada*)? As you said *Allahu akbar*, did the world and worldly become smaller?"

"No."

"Then you neither stood on the top of Safa nor did you declare Allah's greatness. As you ran between Safa and Marwah, did you run from His majesty to His beauty?"

"No."

"Then you did not travel seven times between Safa and Marwah. Did you stand on the top of the hill of Marwah?"

"Yes."

"As you stood there, did you feel the peace and tranquility descend upon you?"

"No."

"Then you have not been there, either. Did you go to Mina from Mecca?"

"Yes."

"Did you receive your wish?"

"No."

"Then you have not been to Mina. Did you enter the Masjid-al-Hayf?"

"Yes."

"When you entered the Masjid-al-Hayf, was the fear of Allah refreshed in your heart?"

"No."

"Then you did not enter the Masjid al-Hayf. Did you go up to the Mountain of Mercy in the plain of `Arafat?"

"Yes."

"Did you come to know how and why you were created, and where you are going to go? Did you come to know who is your Lord, that Lord whom you deny? Has Allah shown you a sign that you are one of the chosen?"

"No."

"Then you have not been to `Arafat. Have you been to Al-Mash'ar Al-Haram?"

"Yes."

"Did you remember Allah at Al-Mash'ar Al-Haram in such a way that you forgot everything else? Did you come to understand there how we are addressed and how our prayers are answered?"

"No."

"Then you have not been to Al-Mash'ar Al-Haram. Have you sacrificed an animal?"

"Yes."

"Have you sacrificed your own desires and self-will for Allah's sake?"

"No."

"You have not sacrificed anything. Did you stone the Devil at Mina?"

"Yes."

"Did you throw away your ignorance? Have you received wisdom in its place?"

"No."

"You have not thrown stones at the Devil. Did you visit the Ka`bah, the Sacred House, after descending from `Arafat?

"Yes."

"What gifts did you receive from the Master of that House? For the Prophet said, 'The pilgrims are Allah's visitors'. It is right that a host should show honor and give presents to the guests."

"I have not received any gifts."

"Then you have not performed that visitation. Have you satiated yourself drinking the water of *Zamzam*?"

"Yes."

"Did the taste of *Zamzam* make you swear not to taste anything unlawful, ever again?"

"No."

"Then you have not drunk *Zamzam* water. Did you make the circumambulation of farewell at the Ka`bah?"

"Yes."

"Did you leave all your ego and all of your existence behind?"

"No."

"Then you have not made your farewell. Nor have you made your Pilgrimage. If you wish, you may return and make your Pilgrimage again. If you do, do it the way I told you."

Now you know the conditions of faith. Faith is surety, security, confirmation of teachings brought by the Messenger of God from God, believing them in your heart and expressing them with your tongue, your behavior, and your actions. Faith and Islam are one and the same. Every believer is a Muslim and every Muslim is a believer.

According to some it is sufficient to believe in God and His Messenger and in what they command. If one is remiss in doing what God commands and recommends, and in imitating what His Prophet did, one is still a believer, but a sinning one. According to others, if a person's faith exists only in words, but not in actions, that person is neither a Muslim nor a believer. According to most dependable sources, knowledge, sincerity, fear and hope in God, honesty, good character and behavior, and good deeds are part of faith and an indication of the perfection of faith. If we sometimes fail in acting upon our faith, we are not faithless, but our faith is weak. God and His prophets are merciful and forgiving. God's mercy far surpasses His wrath.

Shari`ah, orthodoxy, the canon law in Islam, literally means the source. It is an obligation for every Muslim to know what to do, how to behave, how to lead his life, even if he does not know or consider why. According to the canons an imitator of right behavior is a firm believer, yet in our times there have appeared a great many innovations, diluting, annulling, or exaggerating and adding to the original codes of Islam at the time of the Prophet. The believer who in all sincerity imitates this kind of behavior is certainly sinning nonetheless. It is no excuse that we do not know the reason, the source, the causes and effects of what we are asked to do. Therefore, although an imitator is still considered to be a believer, whoever follows the *shari`ah* blindly is held to be remiss, for he has not made an effort to know the reason, the cause, and the source of what he is doing. Left to themselves, such Muslims may fall into doubt and may claim as right things that which have been asserted by God to be wrong, or even forbidden. This is the cause of losing one's faith in Islam. May Allah protect us from such an eventuality.

So read this book and ponder, and follow what is said in it. This is what I wish, hope, and pray for all of us: that we may pass through the trials of this life as truly faithful, relying on God and the intercession of His Prophet, and attain peace and felicity in this world and the world to come.

THE PATH OF MUHAMMAD
(*al-Tariqah al-Muhammadiyyah*)
A Book on Islamic Morals and Ethics

by

Imam Birgivi

Interpreted by

Shaykh Tosun Bayrak al-Jerrahi al-Halveti

"Say 'I believe in God,' then be upright."

CHAPTER 1

ON HOLDING FIRM TO THE HOLY BOOK AND
THE TRADITIONS OF THE PROPHET (S.A.W.S.)

ON THE QUR'AN
From the Holy Qur'an:

Alif Lam Mim. This is the Book, in it is guidance sure, without doubt, for those who fear and love Allah. (*Baqarah*, 1, 2)

And hold fast, all together, by the rope which Allah (stretches out for you), and be not divided among yourselves. (*Al-i 'Imran*, 103)

Indeed there has come to you from Allah a (new) light and a clear book whereby Allah guides those who follow His good pleasure to a way of peace and safety, and leads them out of darkness into the light, by His will, and guides them thus to the right path. (*Ma'idah*, 17, 18)

And this is a Book which We revealed full of blessings, so follow it and be righteous, that you may receive mercy. (*An'am*, 155)

O mankind! There has come to you a direction from your Lord and a healing for the (diseases in) your hearts, and for those who believe, a guidance and a mercy. (*Yunus*, 57)

... and We have revealed to thee the Book explaining all things, a guide, a mercy, and glad tidings to those who submit. (*Nahl*, 89)

Surely this Qur'an guides to that which is most upright and gives good news to the believers who do good. Theirs is a great reward. (*Bani Isra'il*, 9)

We send down (stage by stage) in the Qur'an that which is a healing and a mercy to those who believe. To the unjust it causes nothing but loss after loss. (*Bani Isra'il*, 82)

And is it not enough for them that We have sent down to you the Book which is recited to them? Surely in it is mercy and a reminder to those who believe. ('*Ankabut*, 51)

Allah has revealed the most beautiful message in the form of a Book, consistent with itself (yet) repeating (its teaching in various aspects). The skin of those who fear and love their Lord trembles thereat, then their skin and their hearts soften to the celebration of Allah's praise. Such is the guidance of Allah. He guides therewith whom He pleases, but such as Allah leaves in error, there is no guide for him. (*Zumar*, 23)

... and indeed it is a Book of exalted power. No falsehood can approach it from before or behind it. It is sent down by One full of wisdom, worthy of praise. (*Ha Mim*, 41, 42)

From the Sayings of the Prophet:

Abu Shurah (r.a.) reports:

The Messenger of Allah came upon us and said, "Do you not witness that there is none other than Allah worthy of worship, and that I am His Messenger?"

All the Companions answered, "We do, O Messenger of Allah."

He said, "Then, truly: one end of this Qur'an is in the total power of Allah Most High, and the other end is in your hands. Hold firm to it with great care so that you will not go astray, neither will you perish." (Tabarani)

Jabir (r.a.) reports:

The Messenger of Allah (s.a.w.s) said, "The Qur'an is an intercessor. Its intercession is accepted. It is your champion, with an unconquerable power of eloquence, and approved and supported by Allah. Whoever follows it as a guide will be led to Paradise. Whoever leaves it behind and does not follow it, it leaves him to Hell." (Ibn Hibban)

Sahl ibn Mu`adh (r.a.) reports:

The Prophet of Prophets said, "If someone reads the Qur'an and acts according to it, on the Day of Judgment he will place upon the heads of his mother and father a crown whose brilliance is more beautiful than the sunlight upon the face of this earth. Just imagine the state of those who live according to it!" (Abu Dawud)

`Abdullah ibn Mas`ud (r.a.) reports:

The Prophet said, "Indeed, this Qur'an is a feast of Allah. Accept His invitation and partake of it in accordance with your appetite. There is no doubt that this Qur'an is a rope in Allah's hand, a rope that can never break. It is a clear light. It is a most beneficial cure. It is a total protection for the one who holds firm to it. It is a way to salvation for the one who follows it. No fault can be found in it for which it might be blamed, for it is only the truth. It never needs straightening, for it never bends. There is no end to its wonders and its secrets. It does not wear out by repeatedly rereading it. So, you, read the Qur'an. Allah will give you ten beautiful rewards for each letter you read, and I do not say that *Alif Lam Mim* is a single letter. Perhaps *Alif* is a letter, *Lam* is a letter and *Mim* is a letter." (Hakim)

Harith ibn A`war (r.a.) relates:

As I was passing by the mosque I saw a crowd gathered and heard a discussion underway. I went to Hadrat `Ali (r.a.) and informed him of it. He asked me to confirm this, saying, "Are things as you say?" I said, "Yes." He said:

"I heard the Prophet say, 'Be heedful, there will soon be mischief-makers spreading sedition.'

"When I asked him, 'O Messenger of Allah, what is the way to prevent such intrigue?' he answered, 'Hold onto the Book of Allah Most High. In it there is the account of the ones before you and the news of the ones after you. All the decrees to settle your differences are in it. It separates the truth from falsehood. It eliminates the unnecessary and the frivolous.

"'If someone abandons the Book because of hardheartedness, Allah Most High expels him from His mercy and destroys him. If someone seeks a guide other than the Holy Book, Allah leads him astray.

"'It is the unbreakable lifeline in the hand of Allah. It is full of the wisest of counsel. It is the shortest and the straightest way to truth. Indeed it is such a Book that even people perverted by the lowly desires of their egos, if they hold onto it, will not be able to wish other than the truth.

"'No other language resembles its language. The ones who seek knowledge will never come to the end of it. It never wears by being reread. Its wonders are inexhaustible. It is a Book of such wisdom that even the ethereal *jinn*s with their mischievous spirit could not but believe in it.

> ... They said: Surely we have heard a wonderful Qur'an guiding to the right way, and we believe in it ... (*Jinn*, 1-2)

"'Whoever gives its words as his proof and bases his words upon it has his words confirmed by all. Whoever lives by it, in time will be rewarded. Whoever rules by it has rendered justice. Whoever invites others to it brings salvation.'"

Ibn `Abbas (r.a.) relates:

On the Farewell Pilgrimage, before he left this world, the Messenger of Allah (s.a.w.s) addressed the congregation, saying, "The Devil has given up hope of being worshiped anymore in your land. He is satisfied that you follow him with your little errors, things that you consider trivial. Beware of following him. I have left you something to hold onto to save yourselves from him, and if you hold firm, you will never go astray. That is the Book of Allah and the tradition of His Prophet." (Hakim)

Hadrat `Ali (r.a.) relates:

The Messenger of Allah said, "Whoever reads the Qur'an, keeps it in his memory, denies himself what it says is unlawful and prefers what it says is lawful—Allah admits him to His Paradise and permits him to intercede for ten among those close to him."

ON THE TRADITIONS OF THE PROPHET
From the Holy Qur'an:
Say: "If you love Allah, follow me, Allah will love you and forgive you your sins, for Allah is oft-forgiving, most merciful." Say: "Obey Allah and His Messenger." But if they turn back, Allah does not love those who reject faith. (*Al-i 'Imran*, 30-31)

And obey Allah and the Messenger that you may be shown mercy. (*Al-i 'Imran*, 132)

Allah conferred a great favor on the believers when He sent among them a Messenger from amongst themselves, reciting unto them the signs of Allah, purifying them, and instructing them in the Book and wisdom, while before that, they had been in manifest error. (*Al-i 'Imran*, 164)

O you who believe! Obey Allah and the Messenger and those charged with authority among you. If you differ in anything among yourselves, refer it to Allah and His Messenger; if you believe in Allah and the Last Day that is best and most suitable for final determination. (*Nisa'*, 59)

But no, by your Lord, they can have no (real) faith until they make you judge in all disputes between them, and find in their souls no resistance against your decisions but accept them with the fullest conviction. (*Nisa'*, 65)

All who obey Allah and the Messenger are in the company of those on whom is the grace of Allah—of the prophets (who teach), the sincere (lovers of Truth), the witnesses (who testify), and the righteous (who do good): ah, what a beautiful fellowship! (*Nisa'*, 69)

Whoever obeys the Messenger obeys Allah. (*Nisa'*, 80)

... and My mercy encompasses all things. That (mercy) I shall ordain for those who do right and practice regular charity and those who believe in Our signs. Those who follow the Messenger, the unlettered Prophet, whom they find mentioned in their own (scriptures), in the Law and the Gospel, for he commands them what is just and forbids them what is evil, he allows them as lawful what is good (and pure) and prohibits them from what is bad (and impure), he releases them from their heavy burdens and from their shackles. So it is those who believe in him, honor him, help him, and follow the light which is sent down with him. It is they who will prosper. (*A 'raf,* 157)

Say: "O Mankind, I am sent unto you all as the Messenger of Allah (s.a.w.s) to Whom belongs the kingdom of the heavens and the earth. There is no god but He. It is He who gives life and causes death. So believe in Allah and His Messenger, the unlettered Prophet, who believes in Allah and His words. Follow him so that you may be guided aright." (*A 'raf,* 158)

And we have not sent thee but as a mercy to the whole of the universe. (*Anbiya',* 107)

... so let those beware who go against the Messenger's order, lest some trial befall them or a grievous chastisement be inflicted on them. (*Nur,* 63)

You have indeed in the Messenger of Allah (s.a.w.s) a beautiful pattern (of conduct) for anyone whose hope is in Allah and the Final Day, and who engages much in the remembrance of Allah. (*Ahzab,* 21)

O Prophet! Truly We have sent you as a witness, a bearer of glad tidings and a warner, and as one who invites to Allah's (grace) by His leave and as a torch spreading light. (*Ahzab,* 45)

... He that obeys Allah and His Messenger has already attained the highest achievement. (*Ahzab,* 71)

From the Sayings of the Prophet:
Irbaz ibn Sariyah relates:

One day the Messenger of Allah (s.a.w.s) led us in prayer, then turned to us and talked with such clarity that tears came to our eyes. Hearts trembled with the fear of Allah. A man said, "O Messenger of Allah, your speech is like that of someone who is giving his last preaching before leaving us. What would be your last advice?"
   "Fear and love Allah as He is worthy to be feared and loved, and obey and follow your leader even if he be an Abyssinian slave. Those among you who will survive me will encounter many conflicts at times of disagreement. Hold onto my traditions and follow my well-guided deputies [the first four caliphs]. Persist and show patience. Beware of and avoid innovations, because everything that does not follow our tradition is a

deviation, and every deviation is a perversion, a heresy, and the place for all perversion is Hell." (Abu Dawud)

Miqdad ibn Aswad (r.a.) relates that the Messenger of Allah (s.a.w.s) said:

Let it be known: I have been given the Book, and with it, as much more. Beware. Soon some well-fed arrogant person will sit on his throne and tell you, "All you need for your salvation is just this Qur'an. Know as right whatever you find in it as right. Know as wrong whatever you find in it as wrong."
Have no doubt: The things that the Messenger of Allah (s.a.w.s) has rendered unlawful are unlawful, as things that Allah has declared unlawful are unlawful.
Let it be known that it is not lawful for you to partake of donkey meat, or the meat of carnivorous beasts, or anything that belongs to a non-Muslim with whom we are at peace unless he has no need for it and has thrown it away. When a guest comes to a household, that guest must be treated with respect and distinction, while the guest should return the same favor to the householder. (Abu Dawud, Tirmidhi)

Abu Rafi` (r.a.) relates that the Messenger of Allah (s.a.w.s) has said:

I will not see among you one who would hear of what I have ordered or forbidden to be done and then would sit proudly and say, "I do not care about this, we follow whatever we have found in the Book of Allah." (Abu Dawud, Tirmidhi)

Irbaz ibn Sariyah relates:

The Messenger of Allah was among us. He stood up and said, "Does anyone among you proudly think that Allah rendered unlawful only the things mentioned in this Qur'an? Know that I ordered you, advised you, and forbade you to do many things—as much as what is contained in the Qur'an, even more. Allah Most High did not give you the right to enter without their permission the houses of the People of the Book [Christians and Jews] as long as they abide by the law and pay their taxes; did not give you the right to mistreat their women; did not give you the right to eat the fruits of their orchards." (Abu Dawud)

Jabir ibn `Abdullah (r.a.) relates:

Often the Messenger of Allah (s.a.w.s) would raise his voice. He would become wrathful. His eyes would become red while he addressed us as if to warn us of an enemy that would attack us at any moment, an army that would invade us. He would raise his hand, separating his middle finger from his index finger and say, "I and the end of the world and the Last Judgment are sent together like this."

In one of his addresses he said, "Surely the best word is the Book of Allah, the best path guiding to good is the Way of Muhammad. The worst of acts are invented deviations. Any innovation in the religion is a heresy and every heresy is a perversion." (Muslim)

Abu Hurayrah (r.a.) reports:

The Prophet said, "All of my people will enter Paradise with the exception of those who refuse to enter."

Someone asked, "Who would refuse?"

He answered, "The one who obeys me will enter Paradise. The one who refuses to obey me has refused to enter Paradise." (Tirmidhi)

Abu Sa`id al-Khudri (r.a.) reports that the Prophet said:

"The one who sustains himself lawfully with the best of food, who lives within the limits of the Traditions of the Prophet, and from whose hands people suffer no pain or cruelty, has entered Paradise."

Some of the Companions said, "At present there are many like this among your people."

"There will be still others among the people who come after me," he said. (Hakim)

Ibn `Abbas (r.a.) reports:

The Prophet has said, "When there will be sedition and intrigue among my people, the one who holds firm to my tradition will receive the reward of a hundred martyrs." (Bayhaki)

Zayd ibn Milhad (r.a.) relates that the Prophet said:

Indeed this religion was started by people who were lonely and poor. It will be brought back by poor and lonely people. Let this be good news for the meek, who will repair and correct my traditions when people have changed and distorted them after I have gone. (Tirmidhi)

Rafi` ibn Hudhayj reports that that Messenger of Allah said:

You know the affairs of this world better than I. When I order you something from your religion, learn it and take it. (Muslim)

`Abdullah ibn `Umar reports that the Prophet said:

If your worldly desires are not adapted to the divine orders sent through me, your faith is incomplete. (Muslim)

It is also reported by `Abdullah ibn `Umar:

The Prophet said, "I vow upon Allah who has sent me: The same misfortune (of sedition and intrigue) that befell the Children of Israel will also fall upon my people, as the horseshoe fits the hoof of the horse, up to the extreme. If among the Children of Israel there were people who openly had sexual intercourse with their mothers, there will be among my people too. Without doubt the Israelites were divided into 72 tribes. My people will be divided into 73 nations. With the exception of one, they are all for the Hellfire."

Someone asked, "Which nation is it which is the exception?" The Prophet answered, "The one which will follow our religion as I and my companions practice now." (Bukhari and Muslim)

Enes ibn Malik relates that the Prophet addressed him when he was a child,

O my little son, listen. If you could pass the day into night and the night into day with your heart clean of any feeling of enmity or vengeance against anyone, be so, for this is how I feel always. And anyone who likes to be like me, certainly must love me. And whoever loves me is with me in this world and in Paradise and in the Hereafter. (Tirmidhi)

Jabir relates:

Hadrat `Umar came to the Prophet and asked, "We hear some traditions from the Jews that we like. Could we write some of them down?" And the Prophet responded, "You know how the Jews and the Christians have been led to confusion and doubt. Do you also wish to be led into confusion? Allah is my witness, instead of those words you seem to like, I have brought you pure, fresh, clear words that you may understand. If Moses was alive today, he could not but follow our path." (Bazzar, Abu Dawud)

Mujahid relates:

We were traveling with Ibn `Umar. As we were approaching a place, he took a different path. When we asked him what he was doing, he said that he saw the Messenger of Allah (s.a.w.s) doing what he did. (Bazzar)

Ibn `Umar often made an effort to go some distance to a tree on the way between Mecca and Medina and rest in its shade in the middle of the day simply because the Prophet used to take a rest under that tree in mid day.
Enes ibn Malik reports that the Prophet said,

The one who does not follow my way and try to imitate what I do is not doing right and may not be one of us. (Muslim)

Abdullah ibn `Umar reports that the Prophet said,

Everything one achieves is a result of a strong desire, a wish, a choice and an effort, and at the end one needs to relax. If the relaxation is to gather strength to do yet another thing after having done a thing following my path, then that person has found salvation. But if he is resting for any other reason, he will be lost. (Ibn Hibban)

Hadrat `A'ishah relates that the Messenger of Allah (s.a.w.s) said,

There are six kinds of people that I curse, and Allah curses them and all the prophets whose prayers are accepted curse them. They are those who add to Allah's words, words which he has never said; those who deny destiny and Allah's will; those who are arrogant tyrants who molest my people, who try to abase those whom Allah has elevated and elevate the ones whom Allah has abased; those who esteem acceptance that which Allah forbade; those who think that it is permissible for my family and progeny that which is forbidden to others and those who abandon us. (Taberani)

Enes ibn Malik reports that the Prophet said,

As long as any of you do not love and esteem me more than your mothers and fathers and your own children or anyone else, your faith in Allah is imperfect and incomplete. (Bukhari)

CHAPTER 2

ON PERNICIOUS INNOVATIONS

Our Mother Hadrat `A'ishah (r.a.) reports that the Messenger of Allah (s.a.w.s) said, "In our religion, to invent and produce something that is not from it is unacceptable."
According to another report:

Any action outside of the frame of our religion and tradition is unacceptable. (Bukhari, Muslim)

Zuhri relates:

I went to see Anas ibn Malik (r.a.) and found him crying. "What is it that makes you shed tears?" I asked.
    Ibn Malik said, "Of the things I knew at the time of the Messenger of Allah (s.a.w.s) , I do not see any that have remained unchanged. Only the ritual prayer has stayed, and even that has suffered loss." (Bukhari)

Ghudayf ibn Harith reports that the Prophet said:

Any people that has invented something (in its religion) after its prophets has surely lost an equal part from its religion. (Tabarani)

Anas ibn Malik (r.a.) reports that the Messenger of Allah (s.a.w.s) said:

Certainly the heretic who follows innovations is prevented from repenting. Allah hides the thought of repenting from him until he stops, until he abandons following innovations. (Tabarani)

Ibn `Abbas (r.a.) reports that the Messenger of Allah (s.a.w.s) said:

Allah Most High does not like to accept the good deed of one who follows innovations (in the religion) until he stops following these innovations. (Ibn Maja)

Hudhayfah al-Yamani reports that the Messenger of Allah (s.a.w.s) said:

Allah Most High accepts from the heretic neither his fast nor his Pilgrimage nor his visit to holy places nor his struggle in the way of Allah, nor his extra prayers, nor his repentance, nor his just and kind actions towards others. As easily as a hair can be pulled out of dough, the heretic is pulled out of Islam. (Irbaz ibn Sariyah, Jabir)

One might ask, How can you reconcile the words of the Prophet when he said, "All innovations are perversities, a straying away from the right path," with the words of the experts in canonic law, who say that innovations are sometimes permissible in harmless everyday occurrences—for instance, the use of a sifter, or eating wheat cleansed of its bran (things which were not done at the time of the Prophet)?

Further, sometimes innovations are considered desirable—for instance, the building of minarets for mosques, or the building of schools for the teaching of theology and sciences, or the production of books, etc. Sometimes such an innovation becomes an obligation—for instance, the gathering of worldly proofs to refute the views of atheists.

Our answer would refer to the literal meaning of the word *bid'ah*, which means simply something that appears afterwards, whether it be a custom that appears after another custom or a fashion of worship that appears after another way of worship. The word *bid'ah*—"innovation"—is derived from the word *ibtida'*—the origin, the first appearance of a thing, and simply means that which comes after the original.

The general meaning of *bid'ah* as that which comes afterwards has permitted canonic lawyers to form different legal opinions about things that appeared after the time of the Prophet and his Companions (r.a.), depending upon whether these things are to be considered qualitatively as bad or good.

Strictly speaking, the religious meaning of innovation is the addition to, or subtraction from, the religion as it was at the time of the Prophet and his Companions, especially when these changes cannot be substantiated by anything said or done by the originator of the religion. The concept of innovation within its strictly religious context can only apply to forms of worship, but not to everyday life and customs.

The saying of the Prophet that "all innovations are perversions" makes use of the religious sense of the word *bid'ah*, and applies only to pernicious religious innovations, as these further words of the Prophet indicate:

Abide with my teaching and the teaching of my deputies who are well guided and guide you to the truth.

And:

You know the affairs of this world better than I.

And:

In our religion, everything that is not from it but is invented by man should be rejected.

INNOVATIONS WITHIN THE CREED
When one speaks about heresy—innovations to satisfy egotistical desires—and the acts of those who seek the pleasures of their lower selves, the first that comes to mind is true heresy within the creed.

Some innovations in faith are considered to be acts of infidelity. Some, which are not considered infidelity, are considered greater sins than all the other great sins, greater even than murder and adultery. Therefore there is nothing worse than heresy in faith except total disbelief or infidelity. This is true to such an extent that there is no acceptable excuse for an error in creed and conviction, while if one erroneously commits a heretical act, it may be excused.

The convictions of Sunnis who strictly follow the rules laid down by the Qur'an and by the habits and words of the Prophet may be compared against those of people who are afflicted by pernicious innovations in faith.

Innovations in the acts of worship are less pernicious than innovations in faith, yet the act is also a perversion and unlawful, especially when it contradicts a supererogatory act of worship seldom omitted by the Prophet Muhammad (s.a.w.s).

The practice which leads to the right path, a practice of worship which the Prophet sometimes omitted and which he did not reprimand those who omitted them is against innovation in the acts of worship.

To introduce innovations into the customs of Muslim daily life—such as using spoons and forks instead of eating with one's hand, or using newly invented utensils such as the strainer—is not wrong, although it is better not to use such devices if they are useless.

On the other hand, there are some customs that the Prophet practiced that serve to keep one heedful and should be maintained, such as starting to do something good by beginning with one's right hand and right foot, or starting to do something unpleasant but necessary by beginning with one's left hand or left foot.

Thus, generally speaking, innovations can be divided into three classes in accordance with their degrees of undesirability.

Yet it must be understood that there also are and will be innovations that are permissible, and may even, according to circumstances, become obligatory, despite the fact that they did not exist at the time of the Prophet. Such are building minarets so that the call to prayer can be heard from further places, opening schools and producing books to spread and facilitate the acquisition of knowledge, and gathering proofs to refute the innovations of heretics and to forbid unlawful things that some might wish to make lawful for their own purposes.

That such things did not exist or occur at the time of the Prophet is probably due to the absence of necessity or conditions or means, or the existence of more important things that had to be given priority. In fact, one will certainly be able to find signs or directions within the actions and sayings of the establisher of this religion to indicate that he would have approved of these good innovations.

One should also realize that, leaving aside these good innovations, the following of pernicious innovations is more harmful than not following the way of the Prophet at all. The experts in canonic law have concluded, "When there is some doubt whether a thing is in accordance with the way of the Prophet or is an innovation, it is best to abandon it altogether."

Then what should you do if you are in doubt whether something is incumbent upon you as a Muslim or is an innovation? Is it worse to abandon that which one thinks of as an obligation or to do something that one suspects is an innovation? This is a difficult situation, yet if one is hesitant whether a thing is a religious duty or an innovation, it is best to do it.

In a book called *Hulasa* (Summary), the writer, considering this subject, suggests: When someone does not remember if he has done one of the day's five obligatory prayers, if it is still the time for that prayer he should immediately do it. If he cannot remember whether or not he has performed a prayer after the time of that prayer is past, he need not do anything. There is, however, this exception: If the prayer in question is the afternoon prayer, when he makes the four obligatory cycles he should recite the verses after the first and the third cycle, not, as is normally done, during the first two cycles. For it is doubtful whether what is being performed is an obligation or an extra act of worship, and any extra prayer between the afternoon and sunset prayers is canonically held detestable and would be considered a pernicious innovation.

Thus it is only possible to reconcile a situation that might be a pernicious innovation (to pray between afternoon and sunset prayers) and a hesitation as to whether one has performed that which is religiously obligatory, by considering that the doubtful obligation supersedes the pernicious innovation. Allah Most High knows best.

If one holds that the necessity of depending upon the Holy Book and the Traditions of the Prophet—with which we have been concerned so far—means that it is also sufficient to depend on these two sources, then anything that is not approved by these two sources would be innovation and perversion. If that is so, how can we accept as true the claim of the experts in canonical law, that an act is religiously correct if it is supported by four religious proofs—the Book, the Traditions of the Prophet, the general concurrence of the legalists (*ijma`*), and their drawing conclusions through analogy (*qiyas*)?

Our response will be that in order to be valid, the general concurrence of the legalists must be supported in meaning and state by a proof from the Book or the traditions. In the case of analogy, it must again be based on an indication in the Book or the traditions. An analogy can only explain a judgment, it cannot prove that it is right. To prove a decree one needs a foundation; therefore, the sources of all decrees and the proofs of all judgments in reality are only two—the divine ordinances coming from the Holy Book, and the Traditions of the Prophet.

In our time, some who claim to be mystics appear to be doing certain things that are not in accordance with religious law and custom. When they meet opposition, they claim that their opponents base their opinions on the knowledge of laws that judge exterior circumstances only, while they themselves possess inner qualities and inner knowledge. They claim that the unlawful is lawful according to their inner knowledge. They claim that while their opponents judge by the Book, they receive their justifications directly from the Owner of the Book, the Prophet. When their opponents are not convinced even by that, they turn to Allah Most High for justification. They claim that in their special states, under the direction of their *shaykhs*, they reach Allah and receive knowledge through inspiration. Therefore they need neither to study under a teacher nor to obey the prescriptions of the Book. They say that to reach their state of closeness to Allah one must abandon all knowledge that depends upon and judges according to exterior circumstances—indeed, even the religious law.

They say that if they were wrong, they could not be in such a beatified state, surrounded by divine light, conversant with prophets, and possessing incredible miracles. They say that even if something unlawful and undesirable occurs through them, they are warned in their dreams and are made aware of what is right and what is wrong through those dreams. They say that even if their opponents call some of the things they do unlawful, if they themselves are not warned or forbidden in their dreams they will consider those things to be right.

All these and other such ridiculous claims have no relation to the truth. They are all falsehoods and perversions. Such claims are not only in opposition to religious law, the Holy Book and the Traditions of the Prophet, but they are open insults to them. Unfortunately, those who disregard the Holy Book and the traditions claim that they contain untruths. Such insanities exist. We take refuge in Allah from them. Whoever hears such claims and does not absolutely and totally believe that these are lies and oppose and deny them must be considered to be one of their proponents, and must be judged a heretic.

The ones who know have decreed that inspiration is not one of the causes of knowledge. Neither are dreams in one's state of sleep, especially if what comes through them is in opposition to the Book of Allah—which covers all knowledge—and the tradition of the Prophet Muhammad (s.a.w.s).

The head of the Sufis, the leader of the mystic path leading to truth, Junayd al-Baghdadi (q.s.) said:

All paths lead nowhere except the road of the Messenger of Allah. No one should follow someone who does not memorize the Holy Qur'an and who does not write the Traditions of the Prophet.

Indeed, this is our belief and all of our knowledge is tied to the Book and to the traditions.

Another Sufi, Sari al-Saqati (q.s.) says:

Our path is the total of these meanings:
1. The divine light of the wisdom and knowledge of Allah possessed by the true Sufi, which at no time puts out the wish to avoid that which is doubtful and to gather all virtues.
2. A sense that neither judges nor speaks in accordance with any knowledge that violates a divine instruction contained in the Holy Book.
3. A miraculous state that never induces one to tear the veils of things that Allah has made unlawful.

Abu Yazid al-Bistami (q.s.) once took his students on a first visit to a man who was famous as a saint, loved by many, and considered to be devout and pious. They saw him coming out of his house, and followed him in the crowd until they came to the mosque. As the man was about to enter the mosque, he spat in the direction of the *qiblah.* Abu Yazid gathered his students and left without even a greeting. He said to his students, "This man is not worthy of trust, because he has not acted in accordance with the behavior of the Prophet. How can we trust him in the things that he claims he possesses? Do not be fooled even by someone who can perform miracles, though he is sitting cross-legged in midair. See if he behaves in accordance with what Allah has ordered and what He has forbidden, whether he is sincere in guarding himself within the borders of the religion, whether he follows unfalteringly the religious law."

Abu Sulayman al-Darani said, "Often a wisdom belonging to the Sufis wanders in my mind for days until I accept or reject it, when the two just witnesses of the Holy Book and the traditions decide."

Dhul-Nun al-Misri said, "The sign of the love and attachment to Allah Most High is to follow Muhammad (s.a.w.s), the Beloved of Allah, in one's morals, character, behavior, state, and actions."

Bishr al-Hafi said that he saw the Prophet in his dream. When he asked him, "O Bishr, do you know why Allah Most High has raised you above others?" he said that he did not know. Then the Messenger of Allah (s.a.w.s) said, "He raised you among the good because you followed me, and because you served the righteous, because you gave good advice to your brothers, and because you love my progeny and my Companions."

Abu Sa`id al-Kharraz said, "Everything inner that is in opposition to what is outer is a falsehood."

Muhammad ibn al-Fadl said,

Four things are responsible for causing Islam to lose its brilliance:
1. Many Muslims do not live in accordance with what they know.
2. They live in accordance with what they do not know.
3. When they do not know the basis of their actions, they do not try to learn from those who know.
4. They prevent each other from knowing by distracting each other, either by attractive things or by things that are fearful.

All these great men among the seekers of truth, the wise men in the mystic path, honor and follow the religious law and base their inner knowledge upon the foundation of the principles of the Prophet.

Let none be fooled by the genial pretensions and excesses of those who claim to be pious without wisdom or knowledge, for they have left the straight avenue of the religion, the road of knowledge, the path of the true mystic guides. They have gone astray and led others astray. They are lost. Woe to them and to those who are drawn to them, and even those who consider them, for they are the ones who block the path of the seekers. They are the ones who inject falsehood into the truth. Indeed, they knowingly and purposefully hide the truth.

CHAPTER 3

ON ECONOMY IN DEEDS

... Allah desires ease for you, He desires not hardship for you ... (*Baqarah*, 185)

Allah desires to make light your burdens, and man is created weak. (*Nisa'*, 28)

O you who believe, forbid not the good things which Allah has made lawful for you, and exceed not the limits; surely Allah loves not those who exceed the limits. (*Ma'idah*, 87)

Say: Who has forbidden the beautiful (gifts) of Allah which He has produced for His servants, and the things clean and pure (which He has provided) for sustenance? Say: They are in the life of this world for those who believe, (and) purely for them on the Day of Judgment. Thus do we explain the signs in detail for those who understand. (*A'raf*, 32)

Ta Ha. We have not sent down the Qur'an to you to be an occasion for your distress. (*Ta Ha*, 1, 2)

... He has chosen you and has imposed no difficulties on you in religion ... (*Hajj*, 78)

Anas ibn Malik (r.a.) reports:

Some people came to the house of the wives of the Prophet to ask about the extent of the Prophet's worship. When they were given information about this, some appeared to think that it was less than they imagined, and (trying to justify) they said things like, "Who are we and who is our Master the Messenger of Allah? We cannot compare ourselves to him because all that he has done in the past and all that he will do is forgiven."
 One of them said, "I will pass the nights of all my life in prayer."
 Another said, "I will fast the whole year."
 Yet another said, "I separate myself from all women. I will never marry."
 As they were talking, the Messenger of Allah (s.a.w.s) came among them and said, "Are you the ones who say such-and-such? I swear I fear Allah more than you do, and I am more attached to Him, yet I fast and I eat, I pray at night and I also sleep, and I do marry. Know that whoever turns his back on my way and abandons doing what I do, is not one of us." (Bukhari, Muslim)

Our blessed mother `A'ishah (r.a.) reports:

The Messenger of Allah did something, prepared something very tasty, and permitted the others to do it too, yet one of the tribes would not do it. The Prophet was told about it. Then he delivered a sermon. After praising Allah he said, "How can one explain the conduct of those tribes who are so scrupulous that they hesitate to do what I do and they draw back from us? I swear that I know Allah better than they do and fear Him more." (Bukhari, Muslim)

Abu Juhayfah (r.a.) reports:

The Prophet declared Salman and Abu Darda' as brothers in religion. When Salman went to visit Abu Darda' he saw his mother in shabby old clothes, and he could not resist asking, "What is this state? What has happened to you?"

The poor woman answered, "What can I do? Your brother Abu Darda' behaves as if he has no need of this world."

Then Abu Darda' entered with food and offered it to them, saying "Please eat, I am fasting." Salman insisted that he would not eat unless his brother ate also. Abu Darda' broke his fast out of respect for his guest. When night came and it was time to sleep, Abu Darda' stood at prayer, as was his custom. Salman asked him to sleep, and he obeyed. After awhile he stood up to pray again and Salman insisted that he should go back to bed, and he slept. Toward the end of the night Salman woke him up, and they prayed together. Then Salman said to Abu Darda', "Indeed your Lord has His right over you, your self has a right over you, your family has a right over you. Therefore you have to give their rights to all those who have rights over you."

After this incident, Abu Darda' went to the Prophet and told him about it. The Messenger of Allah said, "Salman has told the truth." (Bukhari, Abu Dawud)

Anas ibn Malik (r.a.) reports:

When the Messenger of Allah (s.a.w.s) entered the mosque he saw a rope strung between two columns and he asked, "What is this for?"

They said, "It belongs to Zaynab"—for Zaynab (r.a.), when she became tired making her prayers, would hold onto it to get up and to sit.

The Prophet said, "No, no, it should not be done like this. Untie this rope right now. When one among you (wishes to make extra prayers), let him pray to the extent he pleases. When he gets tired, let him sit down." (Bukhari, Muslim, Nesahi)

Anas ibn Malik reports:

The Messenger of Allah said, "Don't distress yourselves (with heavy and tiresome deeds). If you do, then Allah will leave you in your weariness. A nation was led into hardship because of doing this. In our day you still see the leftovers of this in their churches and in their temples and in their homes. These asceticisms and austerities of the monks are things that they have invented themselves. Allah did not make such deeds obligatory for them." (Abu Dawud)

Abu Hurayrah (r.a.) reports:

The Messenger of Allah said, "Truly this religion is facility. There is no one who can overexert himself in exercising his religion (with the intention of not lacking anything in good deeds) and finally not find out that the religion still overpowers him. Therefore follow the median way and come close (to Allah). I give you the good news of success if you do this. Profit from your voyages in the mornings and in the evenings and as you walk at night."

In another report about the same tradition, it is said:

"Be economical in your efforts so that you will reach your goal." (Bukhari, Muslim)

Ibn `Abbas (r.a.) reports:

The Messenger of Allah said, "As Allah requires certain things to be done, He also requires that you observe the dispensations He has granted for the lightening of your religious duties." (Bazzar, Tabarani, Ibn Hibban)

Ibn `Umar (r.a.) reports that the Prophet said:

Just as Allah Most High is displeased with your being tempted by sins, small or large, He also wishes you to enjoy the dispensations that He has accorded you. (Ahmad, Tabarani, Bazzar, Ibn Khuzaymah)

Through the chain of Abu Darda' (r.a.) and Wasilah ibn `Asqa', Anas (r.a.) reports:

The Prophet said, "As the good servant of Allah wishes and seeks Allah's mercy and forgiveness, Allah wishes the dispensations He has permitted to lighten His servants' duties to be observed." (Tabarani)

`Abdullah ibn `Amir reports:

I said, "I swear that as long as I live, I will spend the days fasting and the nights praying."

This was reported to the Messenger of Allah. He asked me, "Are you the one who said this?"

"Yes, O Messenger of Allah—may my father and mother be sacrificed for you!" I replied.

"You don't have the power to do that," he said. "Fast and then eat, sleep and then get up and work. Fast three days each month, for all good deeds are multiplied by ten; thus it is like fasting the whole year."

"But I can do better than that."

"Then fast one day and eat two days."

"I can do more than that."

"In that case, fast one day and eat the next. This is the way the Prophet David fasted, and it is the most just."

"I have the capability of doing even better than that!" I protested.

"No, there is nothing better than that," said the Prophet. "Know that your body has rights over you, your family has rights over you, your guests have rights over you."

According to another version,

The Prophet said to Ibn `Amir: "Have I not been informed that you intend to spend the entire year fasting and to read the whole Qur'an every night?"

"Yes, O Messenger of Allah," he answered, "but I only wished good in that."

Then the Messenger of Allah (s.a.w.s) said, "It is sufficient if you read the Qur'an from beginning to end once a month."

"I can do more than that."

"In that case, finish reading it once a week, and not more than that."

Ibn `Amir also reports:

Because I pressed myself hard, I suffered many a hardship. The Prophet had told me, "I suspect that your life will be lengthened," and indeed what he said, happened. As I became older, I regretted that I had not accepted the dispensations that He permitted me.

There are other versions of this that need not be included here.

THE OPINIONS OF THE EXPERTS ON RELIGIOUS LAW
ON ECONOMY IN DEEDS

In the book called *Ihtiyar* it is stated:

The austerity of imposing upon oneself hunger and sleeplessness to the extent that one is too weak to perform one's obligatory prayers and duties is not right. The Messenger of Allah has said, "Indeed your body is your animal of burden upon which you ride. Have pity on it and treat it with compassion." To leave it hungry, to weaken it, does not fit the gentleness and compassion with which it should be treated. As it is not lawful to abandon prayer, a thing which may become a cause of abandoning prayer is also unlawful.

Earning one's living has many categories. To work to support oneself and one's family and to pay one's debts is a religious obligation. After having secured that, it is permissible to abandon effort for further gain. Yet it is lawful to gain more than one needs in order to build a reserve for oneself and one's dependents, because as reported by reliable sources, the Prophet stocked food sufficient for a year for his dependents.

It is also approved, even recommended, that one should increase one's gain over what is obligatory, to enable one to help people in need and those who are close to one, and to brighten their day, because to be useful and to serve others is much more worthy than to withdraw oneself from society and to occupy oneself with excessive worship. The reason for working for gain is not for the benefit of oneself only, but also for others. For the Prophet says, "The best of men is the one who is good to others."

In the book called *Tatarkhaniyyah* it is stated:

It is a thing disliked when a group, a congregation, is gathered, forbidding themselves to partake in and benefit from good and lawful things and dedicating themselves solely to worshiping Allah Most High. It is better to live and work in the midst of people, gaining one's livelihood lawfully, attending congregational prayers, and gathering in mosques with other people on Fridays.

If this statement appears to be contrary to the reported practice of some of our pious predecessors—who were ascetics who spent whole years fasting and nights praying, not partaking of anything appetizing even if it was clean and lawful, reading the Qur'an continuously and completing it in a day or two, spending all their effort and energy in prayer and meditation—our answer is that there can be no contradiction between Allah's revelations and all else. Only what is mentioned in Allah's Book and the traditions of His Prophet, and what is in concordance with these, can be taken and applied with confidence. Furthermore, suspicions can attach to the veracity of these reports about the predecessors because of the lack of strict verification and research in these reports. Many of them lack documentation, while there is no doubt in the Book of Allah and in the true Traditions of the Prophet. Then how should the two have to be reconciled, and how can one even consider the lack of concordance between the two?

Two further reasons prevent one's taking on difficulties and hardships in one's worship. The first is *a priori*: Unnecessary hardship brings one to destruction and prevents one from rendering the rights due to others. It may, at the end, lead one to interrupt one's worship, and may even cause one to stop worshiping altogether. The second is *a posteriori*: Our Master the Prophet was sent as Allah's mercy upon the universe. This is confirmed by Allah. If he is unable (rather made by Allah to appear to be unable) to do certain things, then no one of his followers can be able to do them. Certainly he loved Allah, feared Him, knew Him, more than anyone else. Then who would dare, how could one, associate with him ignorance, weakness, laziness, looseness, and the abandoning of divine prescriptions? If there were any other way, better and more beneficial, to come close to Allah Most High, and if there were a better way of worshiping than the one he was following, certainly the Prophet would have chosen that and led and encouraged his people in that way. Therefore, his way is better and more beneficial than any other way to know Allah Most High and to obtain His approval and pleasure.

Therefore, one must interpret the asceticism of the predecessors as being their attempt to cure their particular spiritual ills, or else suppose that asceticism for them became a habit, a second nature, a delicious spiritual food from which they could not hold back.

Whatever the case, there is no allegation, neither a creed, which claims that either their way or their state or what they said is better than that of the Master of all humanity, our Prophet, for he reached the highest level of perfection.

This level meant that, while his pure heart was in continuous communication with the truth that he spread to the world, he was not prevented from eating and drinking and sleeping or coming close to his wives. On such a level, to intermix with the people or to be in seclusion away from them is one and the same thing. If he appeared to be satisfied with certain specific exterior manifestations of worship because this was best both for himself and for his followers, still the contact of our Master (s.a.w.s) with the divine realms was continuous. It did not occur only during his visible acts of worship.

Some of the Sufi masters have been lifted onto levels in accordance with their lot. At these levels they admitted, "If someone saw me now, he would become a doubter, while when people saw me before, they became saintly." For when one reaches higher states, (although one's heart is viewing the divine realms) one appears as a common man—eating, drinking, sleeping, and performing just the necessary worship like everyone else. Yet while striving to reach that level, one spends all one's effort and energy and time withdrawing from the world and the worldly. Thus people who saw such a person in the earlier state and followed his example could indeed become saintly, while if one saw him returning to the world and performing strictly minimal worship, one might disavow all this effort, the mystic way, even the religion. We fear that one might even be led to denial.

We have no doubt that the predecessors were free from any lack of consideration or disrespect of the way of the Prophet, nor that they thought their efforts superior to what the Prophet practiced and proclaimed. We believe that we have tried to explain their attitude. Therefore one should be careful to be neither remiss nor excessive about the attitudes of these predecessors. It is best to be reconciliatory and follow the middle way.

May Allah be praised Who permitted us this facility and economy in our religious duties, for if He had not led us to it; we could never have found it by ourselves.

"Contentment is an inexhaustible treasure."

CHAPTER 4

ELEMENTS OF BELIEF IN THE RELIGION BROUGHT BY THE PROPHET MUHAMMAD (S.A.W.S.)

The first principle is to adjust what one believes, in consideration of the principles of Islam, so that the believer is able to apply his creed to his life. The foundation of Islam is the oneness and the unity of Allah. Nothing resembles Allah. He is neither matter nor form, neither an essence nor a quality: He is indescribable. Allah has neither beginning nor end. No location determines where He is, and He fills no space. He is neither born nor gives birth, He does not eat or drink: nothing is ever equal to Him. Time does not apply to Him, nor can He be related to the six directions. He is in none of these dimensions. He is not in need of anything, yet everything is in need of Him. Nothing created relates to His essence. He does what He wills and has no obligations. He is perfect and free of all incompleteness; His perfection cannot be improved. He is before the before and after the after, eternal. His attributes are permanent and eternal, yet they are not He. Neither are they other than He. These attributes are: Ever-Living, All-Knowing, All-Powerful, All-Hearing, All-Seeing, the One and Only Will, the only One who makes things become; and His is the Word without letters and without sound.

The Holy Qur'an is Allah's word. It is and will be forever with Him; it is not created. Although Allah is invisible in this life, the promise to the believers that they will see Him in the Hereafter is admissible to reason and proper by tradition. He will be seen without being in a place, without being in this or that direction, without being limited by distance nor needing light to be seen.

This universe of matter—from its tiniest atom and most minimal quality to its vast end, including all the actions of all those in it, both their good and their evil deeds—was created by the will and knowledge and power of the One and Unique Creator. Those whom Allah has created to inhabit the earth are His servants, yet they are given a will to choose what they shall do. In accordance with their actions, they are either rewarded or punished. The good deeds are those which they choose in obedience to Allah's wish, in harmony with His will and, above all, for the love of Him. A reward is not a payment but a gift, a sign of Allah's generosity. Punishment is not a necessity, but a manifestation of justice. Allah is not obliged either to reward or to punish His creation, which has no right to demand anything from Him.

The ability of a created being to act is within the very deed which it is meant to perform. One's capacity to do something is hidden in the cause and in the means for the accomplishment of that deed. The sign that an act meets with the pleasure of the Lord is the ease of its cause and its means, and the beneficence of its effect. No action is proposed to a created being by its Lord which is not within its power.

The one who is born is brought to life by Him. The one whose life is ended, abides with His appointed time of death. The time of death is fixed, and can neither be advanced nor delayed.

Lawful sustenance is that which is obtained by lawful means. Sustenance is destined. We cannot eat anything other than what is given to us. We cannot touch sustenance destined for someone else, nor can anyone else touch sustenance destined for us.

The pain suffered in the grave is a punishment for disbelievers and for believers who sinned in life. The blessings for believers who obeyed Allah and did good deeds are accorded by Allah's wish, and are known only to Him.

The angels questioning the dead in their graves; the raising of the dead on the Day of Judgment; the accounting for actions; the Book of Deeds appearing in either one's right hand or one's left; the crossing of the bridge, thinner than a hair and sharper than a sword, that passes over Hellfire; the intercession of the Messenger of Allah (s.a.w.s) and other lovers of Allah for sinners: all these are truths. Paradise and Hell are already in existence, and will always exist, until eternity, with their inhabitants.

The Ascension of the Prophet Muhammad (s.a.w.s), during which he was brought, bodily and in a conscious state, from the Sacred Mosque in Mecca to the Mosque of al-Aqsa in Jerusalem and from there to the heavens, up to wherever Allah took him, is true. The signs of the last day of the worlds given by the Messenger of Allah, including the appearance of the Antichrist, *Gog* and *Magog*, and the descent of the Prophet Jesus (s.a.w.s) from the heavens, as well as the rising of the sun from the West and other signs: these are all true.

Great sin is not enough to make a guilty person an infidel. It does not cancel our religion, nor abolish our worship and good deeds, nor condemn us to stay in Hellfire forever. The only person Allah does not forgive is the person who assigns partners to Him. He may forgive all other sinners if He so wills. Even if a person guilty of great sins does not repent, one may still hope for the forgiveness of Allah. Yet we remain always liable to be punished for even our lesser sins.

Allah responds to all prayers, and satisfies our true needs.

Faith and Islam are one. Islam is our confirmation and acceptance of that which Allah commanded the Prophet to bring and to teach. It means to act and to live in accordance with his teaching. Yet though one's actions may be at variance with the truth of one's faith, faith itself neither increases nor decreases. This is what is expressed when a believer says, "I am truly faithful." It is not appropriate to say, "I am faithful, if Allah so wills." When faith is only confirmed and admitted in that way, it has been treated as a created quality. Yet, when one considers that faith is the Lord's action of bringing His servant to the knowledge of Himself, it can no longer be thought of as created, but belongs to the eternal.

The faith of the one who imitates faith is true—but if he gives up looking for the proof and confirmation of the One in whom he professes faith, he is sinning.

There are great secrets and hidden wisdom in the reasons why certain people were chosen to be the messengers of Allah, in their teaching of the divine words sent through them, and in their miracles. The prophets were cleansed of all faults, great or small, and of any trace of disbelief, faithlessness, untruth, ambition for what was not destined for them, or violation of the rights of others. They manifested no character, word, or action that could hurt other people.

The first of the prophets was Adam (s.a.w.s) and the last and the best is Muhammad (s.a.w.s). The number of all the prophets whom Allah sent is not known with certainty. When they die, their mission and their prophethood do not end. The prophets are superior to angels.

The saints, who are brought close to their Lord, are made able to cross long distances in very short times; to produce sustenance and things needed instantly; to fly in the air; to walk on water; to speak the languages of animals, plants, and rocks; and to perform other wonders. These are facts. When prophets perform similar supernatural actions, the term "miracle" is applied. Yet no saint ever did or shall reach the spiritual level of a prophet, and none of them may claim that obligations and prohibitions established by Allah do not apply to them.

The best of all the saints was Abu Bakr the Truthful. Next after him was `Umar the Discriminating, then `Uthman, Master of the Two Lights, and `Ali the Preferred One, may Allah's pleasure be upon all of them. Indeed they became the leaders of Islam after the Prophet in the same order. After these are ranked the other Companions of the Messenger of Allah. We love and honor them, and none do we reproach with anything unbecoming. We witness that the ten Companions to whom the Messenger of Allah (s.a.w.s) gave the good news of their place in Paradise (Abu Bakr, `Umar, `Uthman, `Ali, Talhah, Zubayr, Sa`d, Sa`id, Abu `Ubaydah, Abdur-Rahman ibn `Awf); Fatimah, his daughter; Hasan and Husayn, his grandchildren; and others whom the Messenger of Allah (s.a.w.s) mentioned by name, are indeed in Paradise. The closest to Allah after the Companions of the Prophet were their followers in the next generation.

We believe it is a necessity for all Muslims to have a leader who is adult, free, and a Muslim. There are some who believe that, when all the Muslims are united, their leader must be from the tribe of Quraysh to which the Prophet belonged, and from the family of Hashimi. They do not insist that he should be totally sinless, nor known to be the best among the men of the time.

The *imam*, the leader of a community, cannot be overthrown, whether because of impiety or even because of tyranny, as long as he does not interfere with prayer.

It is permissible to perform congregational prayers under the leadership of someone who might be either good or bad. It is permissible to participate in such people's funeral rites.

It is acceptable, while taking ablution during battle or travel or in dire conditions, not to remove the shoes to wash the feet, but to wet the surface of one's shoes.

To drink date juice, if it is not an intoxicant, is not unlawful.

The souls of the dead do profit from the prayers of the living as well as from alms given for their souls.

There are special places possessed of a spiritual aura from which visitors profit. First among them are Mecca, Medina, and Jerusalem.

Possessing knowledge is superior to being intelligent.

Children of disbelievers who have not reached puberty do not necessarily go to Paradise because they are sinless, as some believe (among them Imam Nawawi).

There are protecting angels even for disbelievers.

Something which does not exist is not worthy of consideration.

Sorcery does exist. The maleficence of the evil eye does exist.

It is possible that an expounder of Islamic law may fall into error, although he considers proofs and precedents in his judgment. There is only one truth with Allah, but justice is rendered based upon existing conditions and situations.

These things are unlawful: to leave concrete proofs in favor of abstract considerations favored by people who like to claim they can see the inner meaning of things, thus negating religious precepts; to consider that which is unlawful as permissible; to give attention to the declarations of soothsayers; to be in doubt of Allah's mercy and forgiveness; to think of Allah as a vengeful, harsh punisher. Such attitudes are fit for disbelievers.

It is stated in the *Tatarkhaniyyah*:

Whoever says that any of the attributes of Allah Most High is created is a disbeliever. Whoever says that the Creator is only the origin and foundation of created things is a disbeliever as well as the one who believes that He creates actions which have no sense or reason.

If one believes and says that Allah has ordinary hands and feet, ears and lips, he is declaring that Allah resembles created beings and is therefore a disbeliever.

If someone says that Allah's knowledge is in the heavens, attributing a place to His knowledge, he is guilty of innovation, but is not a disbeliever—

especially if he is trying to make a point in the form of a story. But if he is claiming that Allah is in the heavens, attributing a place to Him, he may be suspected of being a disbeliever.

If someone says that nowhere is without Him, yet He is not anywhere, his intention may be to express that Allah's knowledge and power embrace all things, although no place can be attributed to Him. But if he means, instead, that the attributes All-Knowing and All-Powerful are to be assigned a place in the material world—then he is considered to be a disbeliever. It is better to say that Allah knows everything than to say that Allah's knowledge is everywhere.

To seek Allah above oneself or in front of oneself or in any direction whatsoever is disbelief.

To think that Allah might do something without any reason is to accuse Him of irrationality, and therefore is disbelief.

To say that Allah existed before anything else existed and that He will exist when all else disappears is a sin, because it insinuates that Paradise and Hell and other eternal existences will disappear. Some others believe that to deny the existence of eternal peace and bliss in Paradise and of eternal punishment in Hell is a sign of disbelief.

To deny the Last Judgment, or the Balance for the weighing of good deeds against sins, or the accounting for actions, or the book of one's accounting given either to one's right or to one's left hand, or the test of crossing the bridge over Hellfire, or Paradise and Hell, is a sign of disbelief. Someone who says that the scale for weighing sins and good deeds on the Day of Judgment is not an instrument, but a symbol of justice, is an innovator but not necessarily a blasphemer. So is someone who denies the existence of the punishment in the grave before the Day of Judgment.

Someone who claims that people guilty of the greater sins will stay in Hell for eternity is an innovator.

Someone who denies the intercession of those to whom Allah has given the right to intercede on the Day of Judgment is a disbeliever.

Someone who denies that the believers will see the Lord in Paradise as one sees the full moon is not a Muslim.

Someone who denies that all good and bad come from Allah, yet whether good or bad, that man himself is the creator of his deed, shows signs of disbelief.

Someone who believes that God invents new things, instead of believing in the preexistence of everything, is a disbeliever. So is someone who believes in reincarnation and the transmigration of souls; that the divine soul has entered the twelve *imam*s and each of those *imam*s is a deity; that a hidden *imam* will appear, and until he appears all religious orders and prohibitions are canceled; and that the angel Gabriel made an error by bringing God's revelations to the Prophet Muhammad instead of `Ali (r.a.). Such are outside of the community of Islam.

The blasphemous *Khariji* sect, a separatist sect, condemned the blessed Companions and friends of the Prophet—`Ali, `Uthman, Talhah, and Zubayr as well as the beloved wife of the Prophet, the blessed `A'ishah—in fact all of the community of Muslims, as disbelievers. Therefore, they themselves must be considered to be disbelievers. Their leader, Yazid ibn `Unaysah, instructed his followers to anticipate that someone would appear among the Persians to change the religion brought by the Prophet.

Those who belong to the heretic *Najjari* sect, whose leader was Husayn ibn Najjar, claim that the Holy Qur'an, whether written or read, is only created.

The *Jabriyyah* believe that no actions or behavior, thoughts or words, belong to any person, but all are forced upon one by God. This concept is held by some to be heretical and by others, not.

Contrary to this concept, a branch of the sect *Qadriyyah* claim that the human being is immaterial, eternally alive, all-powerful, creator of his own actions, and the proofs of his being alive depend neither upon his moving nor upon his being motionless: nothing that characterizes his physical being applies to him. This is a misguided philosophy that does not correspond to the principles of Islam and these people must be considered as disbelievers.

Among the separatist sect of *Mu`tazilah* are some who say that God cannot either be seen nor can see. Such a statement is blasphemous.

One of the leaders of the *Rafidi* sect, Muhammad ibn Nu`man, whose nickname was Tariq the Devil, claimed that God does not know about anything until after He has willed it and it exists. Such a statement is a sign that he had left Islam.

The same heresy is repeated by Jahm ibn Tafwan, leader of the *Mu`tazilah* sect. He also claimed that the human being has neither power nor responsibility.

The misguided people of *Qadriyyah* also refuse to apply the attribute of the All-Knowing to God, claiming that things only exist when they become. Thus there is nothing, there can be no knowledge, before existence. Consequently God Himself can only know about a thing after it exists.

The people who belong to the sect *Murji`iyyah* leave everything in the hands of God and claim that His compassion and forgiveness will include everybody, even those who deny Him. They declare that they leave both the life and the state of believers and disbelievers alike in God's hands, and that He will do whatever He wills with them. They say that both this world and the Hereafter belong to God, and as in this world God may make some of the faithful suffer while some of the faithless are blessed, the same situation will apply in the Hereafter. That is their notion of divine justice.

They say that their good deeds are accepted and praised and all their sins are forgiven, and they believe that there are no obligations for human beings, including the prayers, fasting, almsgiving, pilgrimage, and so forth, which are obligatory for Muslims. They do not deny that these are good deeds and that whoever does them is praiseworthy, but they also hold it is perfectly fine if one does not perform them. These beliefs are in direct opposition to God's prescriptions, and therefore lead people out of the religion of Islam.

Some of them say that while they do not associate with people who declare themselves faithful yet ignore the religion and sin, neither do they blame them. These are considered to be Muslims, but innovators.

Some among them say that only God knows the state of the faithful, and therefore we must leave them in His hands. We are not the ones who are going to punish them in Hell or forgive them and bring them into Paradise, nor do we have the right to justify or condemn them; yet we are not going to choose sinners as our guides in religion. These are the ones who are on the straight path.

Some who belong to the *Khariji* sect believe totally in the Holy Qur'an, yet some of their interpretations of God's words are erroneous. They firmly believe that ritual prayer, fasting, almsgiving, pilgrimage are the pillars of Islam and obligations for all the faithful. They believe in one God, His angels, the Holy Books, all the prophets, and the Day of Judgment. They also believe in the necessity of the indicated behavior and actions, and that whoever abandons them is led to disbelief. Yet they say that a person who abandons prayer is only sinning during the time of the abandoned prayer, and that a person who gets drunk or commits adultery is a disbeliever during the sinful action, but neither before nor after. These are misguided people who are guilty of innovation.

All the faithful should be informed about such people who have fallen into error and sin, avoid their presence, protect themselves from their words and actions, and oppose them wherever and whenever they can.

O seeker of the way to truth, increase your efforts to find the path under the conditions told and shown by the Messenger of Allah! Learn and strive toward heedfulness and understanding, without doubt, until you reach certainty. Then take refuge in God so that you do not slip, so that you do not lose your faith under the influence of the misguided and the uncertainty of the doubters.

There are many in our times who call themselves Sufis and claim that their *shaykh*s look upon God twice a day—while even the Prophet Moses (a.s.), who spoke to God, when he wished to see Him was told, "You certainly cannot see Me!" Other people may be fooled by this pretense, and wonder whether such mystics might not be above the level of prophets, since seeing God is the highest level to which a human being can aspire.

Of all God's creation, only the Prophet Muhammad, during his Ascension, saw Him. And according to Islamic tradition, the prophets certainly occupy a higher spiritual level than any saint, so that to consider any saint to be above any of the prophets is equal to infidelity. Yet I have heard some of these misguided Sufis say that with the exception of the Prophet Muhammad all other prophets have reached only to the sixth level of revelations and inspirations, while they themselves have passed beyond that! They also claim that although Abu Bakr, the blessed Companion of the Prophet, had reached the appropriate level to guide and teach the community of Muslims, they themselves exceed him in spiritual level. These people not only offend the souls of those closest to God, but offend the beloved Messenger of Allah, master of the past and the future and the mercy of God upon the universe.

RELEVANT PROPHETIC TRADITIONS
Ibn Mas`ud reported that the Prophet said:

> The best people of all times are those who are alive in my time. The next best are those who will come after them. After these will begin the period of untruth. Do not heed their words or their actions. (Bukhari, Muslim)

`A'ishah, the wife of the Prophet, reported:

> Someone asked the Messenger of Allah (s.a.w.s) about the worthiest among men. He answered, "The people who live in my time, and the generation that will come after them, and the generation that will come after them." (Muslim)

Abu Sa`id al-Khudri reports that the Messenger of Allah (s.a.w.s) said:

> Don't insult my Companions. Even if someone should donate as much gold as the mountain of Uhud, he will not receive praise from Allah equal to that received for half a handful donated by my Companion. (Bukhari, Muslim)

`Abdullah ibn Mughfal reported that the Messenger of Allah (s.a.w.s) said:

> Beware of the treatment of my Companions, and fear God. He who treats them with love, loves them because they love me. Who hates them, hates me; who hurts them, hurts me. Who hurts me, hurts God, and very soon God will catch him by the throat. (Tirmidhi)

Anas ibn Malik reported that the Prophet said:

Abu Bakr and `Umar are the masters of all the perfect men and the inhabitants of Paradise. They are above all people with the exception of the prophets. (Tirmidhi)

Abu Sa`id al-Khudri reported that the Messenger of Allah (s.a.w.s) said:

There is no other prophet who had two helpers from Heaven and two from this world. My two helpers from Heaven are Gabriel and Michael, and my two helpers among men are Abu Bakr and `Umar. (Bukhari)

Muhammad ibn Hanifah related:

I asked my father, "Who is the best among men after the Messenger of God?" He answered, "Abu Bakr." "And after him?" "`Umar." Then I was reticent to ask who after him, thinking that he would say `Uthman. Instead I said to my father: "For me, after them the best of men is you." And my father said: "No, I am just one Muslim among others." (Bukhari)

The blessed `A'ishah said that she heard the Messenger of Allah (s.a.w.s) say:

If Abu Bakr is among them, they have no need for another guide. (Tirmidhi)

She also said that `Umar said:

Abu Bakr is the best of us, and our master the Messenger of God loved him more than we do. (Tirmidhi)

Jabir related:

I heard `Umar address Abu Bakr, saying: "O best of men after the Messenger of Allah!" (Tirmidhi)

Whoever belittles the Companions of the Prophet, `Umar, `Uthman, and `Ali is cursed by God. But whoever insults Abu Bakr is a disbeliever, because God Himself mentioned Abu Bakr in His Qur'an:

When he [the Prophet] said to his companion, "Do not be sad." (*Tawbah*, 40)

CHAPTER 5

ON KNOWLEDGE

There are three categories of knowledge: knowledge about things we are obliged to do, knowledge about things we are forbidden to do, and knowledge about piety. When we do not know, God tells us:

If you do not know, ask the people who know. (*Nahl*, 43)

And the Messenger of Allah (s.a.w.s) said:

To seek knowledge is an obligation for all Muslims, men and women alike. (Anas ibn Malik)

It is an obligation for believers to know the right things to do in every condition and in all affairs that may concern us in our lives. For instance, one of the obligations of every Muslim is to perform the ritual prayer five times a day. Obviously it is also an obligation to know every aspect of the performance of this duty.

There are other necessary duties that are incumbent upon us. To know the methods of performing those duties in the way God expects is also incumbent upon us: how to fast, how to pay alms, how to perform the pilgrimage. But there is more to it than this. We need to know how to conduct business, how to deal with other people, how to lead our lives while avoiding unlawful actions; how to fear and love God, how to depend on Him, how to seek His approval, how to try to come close to Him. We need to know how to deal with the manifestations of our characters, such as miserliness or generosity, cowardice or courage, arrogance or humbleness, hard-heartedness or forgiveness.

Knowledge is obtained through information or experience.

It is an obligation to inform ourselves of what is right and what is wrong, what is permissible and what is forbidden, what is the tradition and the example of the Prophet. It is also an obligation to act upon our knowledge.

It is not sufficient only to act upon one's knowledge (though it is an obligation). There are also duties the observance of which will help others. Therefore we should also teach others, to induce others to do right and prevent them from doing wrong.

To know, and to act upon one's knowledge, is a personal obligation, called *fard `ayn*. To guide others toward truth is a social obligation, called *fard kifayah*. Obligations that must be fulfilled by society as a whole include the provision of education in canon law, in the interpretation of the Holy

Qur'an, in the knowledge of Prophetic traditions, in theology, in the fundamentals of Islam, in the science of Qur'anic recitation, and so forth. Mathematics is also included among these sciences, for many Muslim scientists believe that mathematics is a quarter of all knowledge.

To learn the Arabic language is also a part of our duty, for it is believed that Arabic is superior to other languages in many ways. God promises to reward those who learn it and teach it. It is the language in which God has addressed human beings, and the ones who know it will truly understand the literal meaning of the Holy Qur'an and the Traditions of the Prophet.

There is also knowledge that is disadvised or forbidden. For instance, although oratory may be necessary to subdue the claims of those who oppose the religion and to convince them of its truth, we are counseled not to become masters of this science or to learn more of it than is necessary to communicate the truth. Argument is disadvised in Islam.

Abu Nasr reported:

Hammad, the son of Imam Abu Hanifah, was an excellent orator and loved to debate. When his father forbade him, he said to Abu Hanifah (r.a.), "I have witnessed you yourself practicing oratory—why do you forbid me to do the same?"

The imam answered: "My dear son, when we expounded our knowledge in public, we were so afraid to slide into pride that we were as shy to move as if a bird were sitting on our head! You, these days, use oratory to praise your friends and to accuse their adversaries of blasphemy, thus leading them into arrogance and disbelief. You don't realize that when you accuse someone of blasphemy you are the first to blaspheme."

Abu Layth al-Hafiz said:

The name of the one who practices oratory is erased from the list of people of knowledge.

Abu Hanifah said:

With the exception of attempting to eliminate doubt, the use of oratory is not permitted. But it is an obligation to eliminate doubt as soon as it appears. If one sees a man on a shore throwing himself into the sea, it is an obligation to save him.

This declaration of Abu Hanifah indicates that oratory, used for its real purpose, is one of the knowledges to be acquired, by which one may help others. But it is not for everyone to practice. It is only for those who are pious, whose intelligence is able to discriminate the true from the false, and who are able to devote themselves to the salvation of others. In the hands of weak people, oratory may draw the practitioner, as well as those who listen to him, into false beliefs.

The knowledge of the stars is among the sciences we are advised not to study in depth. Some claim that to know the exact times of ritual prayer and the direction of the *qiblah* to which one turns during prayer is sufficient knowledge of astronomy. On the other hand, the blessed `Ali said, "The study of the stars and the heavenly bodies strengthens one's faith." Yet the blessed Ibn `Abbas said: "Anyone who derives any knowledge from the study of the stars has established a line of sorcery. The more knowledge you derive, the greater is the desire to apply it to sorcery."

The study of predicting events by the stars and planets is unlawful. It is like a contagious disease that spreads in one's being as well as around one. The deeper one goes into it, the more one becomes dependent upon it. It has no use, but it does a lot of harm. We cannot escape our destiny, even if we were to know it. Even if one could predict the times of the eclipses of the sun and the moon and even if one could foretell earthquakes and other disasters, what great benefit could result from it compared to the arrogance of being able to say, "We knew it"?

The knowledge that is forbidden and considered a sin is sorcery, soothsaying, and casting spells. Yet, as the poet says, "I learned about that which is wrong so that I do not do it." The one who does not know the wrong may fall into it.

The study of philosophy and logic as well as geometry and the natural sciences is acceptable, except for some aspects of them that are against the religion.

About the knowledge of debate: We are advised not to use floriated words in decorating lies so that they appear acceptable, nor to stubbornly persist in our opinion when our adversary has proved it to be wrong. We should be sincere and use discussion as a method of finding the truth, as well as a means of evaluating the character of our opponent. However, all techniques are permissible to defeat one's opponent's argument if his premise is unjust.

Today, in our times, it is best not to debate with anyone, as no one seems to have an ear to hear the truth.

That which is best in acquiring knowledge is to learn to judge the quality of one's actions. We need to know which of our actions correspond to God's ordinances, which follow the example of the Prophet, which do neither, but are undertaken with good will. We must know which are acceptable and which are undesirable. But this is to be judged neither by personal opinion nor by general consensus, but by proofs given by the Holy Qur'an and the Traditions.

One of the praiseworthy knowledges is the knowledge of medicine and hygiene. We should all know enough of it to care for ourselves. Some say that this is not an obligation. Others say that medical care is one of those sciences which must be present in society, and which become the duty of those who wish to help others.

It is believed that someone who stops eating despite having the means to feed himself—even with the intention of fasting—and dies of it, dies in sin. It is an obligation to feed oneself for the maintenance of life. Otherwise it is considered that we are tyrannizing ourselves.

To turn to medication to cure our ills, or to seek other medical intervention, is not obligatory. It is said that there are three ways of caring for oneself. The first is through diet, such as taking water for dehydration, or taking appropriate food for malnutrition. This is the most effective. The second is more conjectural, such as taking medication, counteracting heat with cold or cold with heat, bloodletting, and so forth. These kinds of treatments may make one feel better but do not necessarily cure the ill. The third is external surgery such as cauterization and lancing, the beneficial effect of which is doubtful at best. Charms and spells are also included in this category.

Not to seek a cure is not necessarily a sign of trusting in God and leaving everything in His hands. In fact, if the result of this kind of attitude is loss of life, it is unlawful. Only when the means are doubtful is it permissible to abandon seeking a cure for one's ills, giving the situation over to God's unmediated grace.

Ibn Mas`ud reported:

> The Prophet said, "In Mina all the nations of the world were shown to me. Among them I saw my people. They covered the plains and the mountains. Their numbers and their behavior pleased me immensely. I was asked if I was satisfied, and I said, 'Yes.' Another voice told me that 70,000 among them would enter Paradise without passing through the Day of Judgment."
>
> Then his Companions asked the Messenger of God: "Who are these 70,000 people?"
>
> He answered: "They are the people who, when they were sick, did not have themselves cauterized, neither sought charms and spells, nor did they think that their sickness was a sign of ill-omen. And they trusted in God, the curer of all ills."
>
> One of the Companions, `Ukashah, said, "O Messenger of Allah, pray that I be one of them."
>
> And he prayed and said: "O Lord, include `Ukashah among them."
>
> Then someone else asked him to be included among the blessed, and the Messenger of Allah (s.a.w.s) said: "`Ukashah is ahead of you." (Bukhari, Ibn Abbas)

To abandon medical intervention that has been proven to be a sure cure is wrong, but to abandon doubtful methods of curing is not necessarily wrong, and in some cases and for some people it is best. For someone who is ill to trust exclusively in God's grace is only right for those believers whose faith is complete. These truly believe that nothing is created by anything but God, that there is no cause of events other than He, and that the true health and the true cure can only be from Him. It does not matter whether such people of perfect faith seek medical help or not: their trust in God is complete. People whose faith is incomplete, who believe that good health depends on medical intervention and medicines, are not trusting in God in any case. Trust in God does not depend on the causes and effects of things, nor is the outcome important.

In another tradition, reported by Jabir:

> The Prophet was told that the family of `Amir ibn Hazm were making spells against scorpion bites, although people had heard that he forbade the use of charms and spells. The Prophet said: "No, in this case I do not see anything wrong in what they are doing. Let them use spells, if it serves for anything good for other Muslims." (from *Bustanu-l Arifin*)

It is possible that charms and spells are forbidden only to those who think that they are the only means of cure. Those who believe that both sickness and its cure are from God, and that medical intervention is a means in the hand of God, may also use charms and spells.

In a sense, any means is permissible to seek health. Some say that during the battle of Uhud, the Prophet rubbed rotten bones upon his wound. Some say he burned a piece of straw matting and put its ashes on his wound. He ordered someone else whose wrist vein was cut to have it cauterized. And he used to recite *Surah Falaq* and *Surah Nas* thrice into his palms, and rub his hands over his blessed body.

The science of medicine is not an obligation for everyone to acquire, but it is desirable and religiously laudable in Islam for some people to acquire it. Imam Ghazali agrees that it is one of the sciences some Muslims should maintain in order to help others.

All Muslims, after acquiring the knowledge which is an obligation for them, are free either to devote themselves to the practice of their religion and piety, or to acquire other sciences that are useful in helping other people. And the second choice is the better one.

QUR'ANIC VERSES ON THE IMPORTANCE OF KNOWLEDGE

The Holy Qur'an has many verses on the importance of knowledge:

> And God taught Adam (a.s.) the names, then He placed them before the angels and said: "Tell me the names of these, if you are right." They said,

"Glory to Thee, of knowledge we have none save what Thou hast taught us. In truth it is Thou who art perfect in wisdom and knowledge." God said: "O Adam, tell them their names." When he had told them, God said: "Did I not tell you that I know the secrets of Heaven and Earth, and I know what you reveal and what you conceal?" (*Baqarah*, 31-33)

He grants wisdom to whom He pleases, and he to whom wisdom is granted receives indeed a benefit overflowing. But none will grasp the message but people of understanding. (*Baqarah*, 269)

Those who are firmly grounded in knowledge say, "We believe in the Book; the whole of it is from our Lord." And none will grasp the message except people of understanding. (*Al-i `Imran*, 7)

There is no god but He: that is the testimony of God, His angels, and those endued with knowledge, standing firm on justice. There is no god but He, the Exalted in Power, the Wise. (*Al-i `Imran*, 18)

It is not (possible) that a man to whom is given the Book and Wisdom and the prophetic office, should say to people: "Be my worshipers rather than God's." On the contrary (he would say): "Be worshipers of Him Who is truly the Cherisher of all. For you have taught the Book and you have studied it earnestly." (*Al-i `Imran*, 79)

Be not in haste with the Qur'an before its revelation to you is completed, but say, "O my Lord! Increase me in knowledge." (*Ta Ha*, 114)

And such are the parables We set forth for humanity, but only those understand them who have knowledge. (*`Ankabut*, 43)

Those truly fear God among His servants, who have knowledge ... (*Fatir*, 27)

Say: "Are they equal, those who know and those who do not know?" It is those who are endued with understanding that receive admonition. (*Zumar*, 9)

God will raise up to (suitable) ranks those of you who have faith and who have been granted knowledge. And God is well acquainted with all you do. (*Mujadilah*, 11)

PROPHETIC TRADITIONS ON THE IMPORTANCE OF KNOWLEDGE
Kafur ibn Qays reported:

While Abu Darda', one of the most beloved companions of the Prophet, was in Damascus, a man came from Medina to see him. He asked the man what was the purpose of his coming to Damascus. The man said: "I wish to check a tradition that I heard you had reported from the Prophet."

"Is that all you came for? You have no other business here?"

The man said "No. I came to hear you confirm what you heard from the Prophet."

Then Abu Darda' said to the man: "Without any doubt, I heard the Messenger of Allah (s.a.w.s) say: 'Allah leads to Paradise the one who travels far seeking knowledge. The angels spread their wings under his feet for him to tread upon. All that is in heaven and on earth, even the creatures in the sea, beg God for the forgiveness of the sins of the one who seeks knowledge. The superiority of the one who knows over the faithful who spend their time in prayer is like the brilliance of the moon over the stars. There is no doubt that the wise holders of knowledge are the inheritors of the prophets, for the prophets did not leave gold and silver as their legacy, but left knowledge. Whoever received from this inheritance is certainly the richest.'" (Abu Dawud, Tirmidhi)

`Abdullah ibn `Umar said that he heard the Messenger of Allah (s.a.w.s) say:

The best of worship for the faithful is to know what is right and what is wrong, with the intention of applying it in their lives. And the best of piety is to avoid that which is doubtful. (Tabarani)

`Abdullah Ibn `Umar also reported that the Prophet said:

Even a little knowledge is better than a lot of worship. (Tabarani)

Ibn `Abbas reported that he heard the Prophet say:

If death comes upon a person while in the pursuit of knowledge, that person is received by his Lord. The spiritual level he attains is so high that the difference between him and the prophets is in the prophethood given to the prophet. (Tabarani)

Abu `Umamah reported that the Prophet said:

On the Day of Judgment the pious person is told to enter Paradise, but the holder of knowledge is commanded to stay, to intercede for humankind. (Isfahani)

`Abdullah Ibn `Umar reported that he heard the Prophet say:

A man of knowledge is seventy times better than a pious man, and each of the seventy levels is as wide as the distance covered by a fast horse in seventy years. (Isfahani)

Abu Hurayrah reported that the Prophet said:

There is no greater worship in the opinion of God than the knowledge of one's religion. A scholar is a warrior against evil, and his strength is a thousand times greater than that of the pious. Everything has a support that holds it. The support of this religion is the people of knowledge. (Bayhaqi)

Abu Hurayrah also reported:

An hour spent in the evening to study the fundamentals of my religion is better than praying the whole Night of Power. (Bayhaqi)

Abu `Umamah reported:

Somebody asked the Prophet about a very devout, pious man and about a man of knowledge. The Prophet said: "The superiority of the man of knowledge over the pious man is like my state as compared to the worst of you. Certainly God and His angels, and all the inhabitants of this world and the heavens—unto the very ant in its hole and the fishes in the sea—pray and ask forgiveness for the one who seeks knowledge to teach humanity to do what is right." (Tirmidhi)

`Uthman ibn `Affan reported that the Prophet said:

On the Day of Judgment, first the prophets, then the holders of knowledge, and then the martyrs will intercede for humankind. (Ibn Maja)

Mu`awiyyah reported that he heard the Prophet say:

O people, knowledge is only acquired by learning, and the knowledge of the fundamentals of your religion is acquired only by those who are intelligent. Whenever God wishes to bless someone, He gives that person intelligence. Only the people of knowledge truly fear and love God. (Tabarani)

Mu`adh reported that the Messenger of Allah (s.a.w.s) ordered the Muslims:

Learn! For seeking knowledge is worship, and to seek knowledge for God's sake is a sign that you love and fear Him. To exchange knowledge with others is to praise God. To inspire people to learn is to struggle in God's way. To teach is the best way of giving alms. To be generous in imparting knowledge brings one close to God. (Ibn `Abdil-Barr)

Abu Dharr reported that the Prophet told him:

O Abu Dharr, to learn one verse from God's Book is better for you than performing a hundred cycles of prayer. To learn a chapter in any of the sciences, even if you do not use it, is better for you than making a thousand cycles of prayer. (Ibn Maja)

Knowledge is the criterion of the right and the wrong, the lawful and the unlawful. It is the light that enlightens the path of the people destined for Paradise. It is the best friend of those who feel alone in the exile of this world. It is a beneficent colleague, a guide for those who feel lost, a sword in the hand of the warrior of God, an adornment that beautifies you to your friends and your enemies alike.

God raises the fortune of some people and makes them leaders: their legacy guides future generations. People follow their example and solve their problems using their opinions. Angels follow them wherever they are, caressing them with their wings. The wet and the dry, the warm and the cold, the fishes in the sea, the lambs and the tigers of this world pray for their sins, because knowledge is that which gives life to hearts and light to eyes.

The one who knows reaches the level of the service of God, which is the highest level to which anyone can aspire in this world or the Hereafter. To meditate is better than fasting. To teach is better than praying. Knowledge brings people together. The right and the wrong, the lawful and unlawful are known by it alone.

Knowledge precedes action. Action depends on knowledge. Those who are blessed are inspired by it. Those who disobey God are punished by the lack of it.

"To withhold knowledge from others is sinful."

CHAPTER 6

ON RIGHTEOUSNESS

Grammatically, *taqwa*, righteousness, is derived from the root verb *waqa*, which means to protect oneself from dangerous things. It has two meanings according to the religion. The general meaning of *taqwa* is the care one takes to distance and protect oneself from conditions that could bring harm in the Hereafter. A highly developed version of this pursuit is to avoid any thought, feeling, or action that might be construed as assigning partners to Allah. Its very highest point is to avoid everything that might distance one from the truth, and to undertake everything that might bring one close to the Lord. Allah Himself describes righteousness as fearing Him as He should be feared.

The particular, private meaning of righteousness is to fear and distance oneself from everything that deserves punishment, from all that is sinful, unlawful, and undesirable.

Some say that little errors in judgment, small sins, are not important: if one keeps oneself clean from greater sins, that effort causes the forgiveness of small errors, and one is not punishable for them. But little sins add up to greater sins—and an attempt to keep oneself safe only from the greater sins is no assurance, for some say that the number of "greater sins" is seven, some say it is one hundred, yet others say that it is seven hundred.

Tirmidhi related that the Messenger of Allah (s.a.w.s) said:

If a person does not abandon doing things while thinking there is no harm in them, he will never reach the level of righteousness. (Ibn Maja and Hakim)

Nu`man ibn Bashir said: I heard the Messenger of Allah (s.a.w.s) say:

What is lawful is clear, and what is unlawful is clear. There are other things in between that are doubtful. Many do not take them into consideration. Whoever avoids that which is doubtful truly has saved his faith and himself. Whoever is involved in doubtful things will sooner or later fall into sin. It is like a shepherd who grazes his sheep near a private garden: sooner or later the sheep will enter the garden.

Beware! All kings have a private garden. Allah's private garden holds the things He has declared unlawful. Be heedful! There is a piece of meat in your bodies that, if it is well, your whole being is well, and if it is sick, your whole being is sick. That is your heart. (Bukhari and Muslim)

Much of the religious meaning of words depends on their literal meaning. The literal meaning of *taqwa* is extreme care for one's protection:

therefore it must include taking care to protect oneself from small sins. Yet in modern times, it is very difficult to avoid doubtful situations. The principle is that obedience is due to the limit of ability. Thus, a person's strength and capacity, and the situation itself, will determine whether undesirable things, even prohibited things, are to be considered unlawful. Allah knows best.

There are more than 150 verses on the importance of righteousness and the fear of Allah in the Holy Qur'an. All cannot be included. The few quoted here should suffice. Allah says:

... and made you into nations and tribes, that ye may know each other [Not that ye may despise each other]. Verily the most honored of you in the sight of God is the most righteous of you ... (*Hujurat*, 13)

Recite to them the truth of the story of the two sons of Adam. Behold! They each presented a sacrifice [to God]: It was accepted from one, but not from the other. Said the latter: "Be sure I will slay you." "Surely," said the former, "God accepts the sacrifice of those who are righteous." (*Ma'idah*, 30)

But what plea have they that God should not punish them, when they keep out [people] from the Sacred Mosque and they are not its guardians? No men can be its guardians except the righteous; but most of them do not understand. (*Anfal*, 34)

... But God is the Protector of the righteous. (*Jathiyah*, 19)

... for God loves the righteous. (*Bara'at*, 4)

He knows you well when He brings you out of the earth, and when you are hidden in your mothers' wombs. Therefore, justify not yourselves: He knows best who are the righteous. (*Najm*, 32)

... and know that God is with the righteous. (*Baqarah*, 194)

... but the Hereafter is for righteousness. (*Ta Ha*, 32)

The end is [best] for the righteous. (*Qasas*, 83)

The Hereafter, in the sight of thy Lord, is for the righteous. (*Zukhruf*, 35)

... and verily, for the righteous, is a beautiful place of [final] return. (*Sad*, 49)

Be quick in the race for forgiveness from your Lord, and for a Garden whose width is the heavens and the earth, prepared for the righteous. (*Al-i `Imran*, 132)

Such is the Garden which we give as an inheritance to those of Our servants who are righteous. (*Maryam*, 63)

And those who feared their Lord will be led to the Garden in crowds until, behold, they arrive there. Its gates will be opened; and its keepers will say: "Peace be upon you! Well have you done! Enter you here, to dwell therein." (*Zumar*, 73)

But the home of the Hereafter is best for those who do right. Will you not then understand? (*Yusuf*, 109)

But verily the reward of the Hereafter is the best, for those who believe and are constant in righteousness. (*Yusuf*, 57)

To the righteous, the Garden will be brought near. (*Shu`ara'*, 90)

[Here is] a parable of the Garden which the righteous are promised: in it are rivers of water incorruptible; rivers of milk of which the taste never changes; rivers of wine, a joy to those who drink ... (*Muhammad*, 15)

The Beloved of Allah advises mankind on the necessity of righteousness and of the fear of Allah, the fear of losing His love, and care for His creation.

Abu Dharr al-Gifari (r.a.) reported that the Messenger of Allah (s.a.w.s) said:

Surely you are no better than the one whose skin is black or red. It is only the one who is more righteous who is better than others. (Ahmad ibn Hanbal)

Jabir ibn `Abdullah reported:

It was during the days of idolatry that the Prophet of Allah addressed us and said: "O people, your Lord is one Lord. Neither are the Arabs better than the rest of the world, nor is anyone else in the world better than the Arabs. Neither is the person with red skin better than the person with black, nor is the person with black skin better than the person with red. All of you have a common father. The best among people is the one who is most righteous. The best among you in the eyes of Allah is the one who fears and loves Him most. Let it be known. Have you heard what I said?"
His companions said: "Yes, Messenger of Allah."

And he said: "Let the ones who are present tell the ones who are absent." (Bayhaqi)

Abu Hurayrah reported that the Messenger of Allah (s.a.w.s) said:

On the Day of Judgment, Allah Most High will order the criers to say: "Surely I have created connections among you, and between you and Me, depending upon the love and fear that you feel for Me. But you have devised your own connections among yourselves based on your worldly concerns. I have chosen those among you who obey and submit to Me as the best among you, but you have not accepted them. Instead you have chosen as best among you so-and-so, son of so-and-so. Now, this day, I cut them off from My care. See what you can do among yourselves! I call only the righteous, wherever they are." (Bayhaqi)

Abu Dharr al-Gifari reported:

Day after day, for six days, the Messenger of Allah (s.a.w.s) said to me, "From now on, try to hear and understand what you are being told. Use your mind!" On the seventh day, he said: "I advise you this: Fear Allah in all the ways you are, whether evident or hidden. When you do something wrong, try to do right immediately after. If a stick in your hand falls to the ground, don't let anyone help you: bow down and pick it up yourself. Don't ask anything from anybody. Don't let anyone entrust you with anything." (Ahmad ibn Hanbal)

Abu Sa`id al-Khudri reported:

Someone asked the Prophet of Allah to give him advice. The Messenger of Allah said: "What is necessary for you is to fear your Lord, because all good comes from that feeling." (Qushayri)

Abu `Umamah reported that the Messenger of Allah (s.a.w.s) said:

Nobody has ever received greater profit from anything than a person receives from feeling the fear of Allah and His Ever-Presence. After that, the greatest benefit comes from a faithful, pure, and kindly wife who gives a man peace and pleasure when he looks at her; who obeys him; who is sincere and tells him the truth; and when he is absent, protects herself and what belongs to her husband. (Ibn Maja)

Ibn `Abbas reported:

The Prophet had either returned from a battle, or from seeing off his people going to battle, when he called his daughter, Fatimah, and said:

"Fatimah, strive to save yourself from the wrath of Allah! Even I may not be able to help you. Give this advice to all the members of our household and our family: tell them that they are not any better for belonging to the tribe of Hashim, nor are the Quraysh the best of my people. The best of my people are those who fear Allah most, and who take the most care to follow His precepts. Neither are the Helpers more privileged; the best of all of you are the righteous. You are like a handful of grain produced from one single seed. All of you came from one father and one mother. None is better than another, except the righteous." (Tabarani)

The sign of the righteous person, whose heart contains the fear and love of Allah, is being distant from what the Lord forbids and intent on what the Lord commands. If a person simply gives up doing wrong, but does not begin actively doing right, sooner or later that person will return to sinning. First will come sins involving the flesh, like drinking and debauching. Abandoning religious duties such as obligatory prayers and fasting may come later.

Abandoning worship could have been considered the greatest of sins. It is one of the mysteries of Allah that He has decreed otherwise. Therefore, in this book, the sins of the flesh will be dealt with first, and spiritual and religious delinquencies will be discussed afterwards.

What is harmful to one's material being is either particular to a single part of the body or common to all. Of the various members of the body, only eight parts usually act: the eyes, the ears, the tongue, the hands, the feet, the stomach, the sexual organs, and the heart. Anyone who takes the path to truth should keep these members from sinning. One should exercise a conscious and continuous control over them until doing right becomes a part of one's nature. This in itself would already include a person among the righteous.

Know that the education and purification of the heart are more important than concern for any other part of your physical being. The heart is like a king whose decision is law. The other parts of your body are like that king's subjects. The Prophet said:

Be heedful! There is a piece of meat in your bodies that when it is well, the rest of you is well, and when it is sick, the rest of you is sick. Know that it is the heart. (Bukhari, Muslim, from Nu`man ibn Bashir)

A heart is healthy when it is cleansed of wrong concerns and negative feelings by good morals and beneficent feelings. We will now try to describe what is meant by "character" and "morals"; what things constitute good and bad morals; the causes of each; and the ways to turn bad morals into good morals.

Our first care should be to study the ways of acquiring good habits and character, to keep them, and to improve and reinforce them. Good morals are such a discipline that they develop into good character, and good character in turn is responsible for good actions. Character can be changed: in fact, the aim and purpose of religion is exactly that. The ability to change differs from one person to another, depending on the strength of each person's wish and native ability, as well as upon the environment.

The forces that can change character are existent in everyone. The first is the ability to communicate. This ability depends upon the strength of one's understanding, and also upon one's equilibrium. Even if a person's capacity for understanding is only average, the door to wisdom is open. Wisdom is the ability to distinguish right from wrong.

The extreme development of understanding is a sharp intelligence, a quick-wittedness, which allows one to decipher hidden secrets such as destiny, or allegorical and ambiguous verses in the Qur'an. Excess of wit may push one to do things that are harmful to other people. Too much of this kind of intelligence leads to unreasonableness, lack of conscience—indeed to stupidity—which blinds the eye of the heart. It may leave a person in such a state that he can no longer tell what is good from what is bad.

The situation with intelligence is similar to the situation with anger. Anger is a necessary capacity. We require it in order to eliminate influences dangerous to our existence. The moderation of anger is called valor—a strength that enables a person to fight destructive forces. But excess of anger is fury, a madness that makes us forget both the reason for fighting and its results. And the deficiency of anger is cowardice, a state that renders us passive before a deadly danger.

Another great power in our being is lust. It is always in motion, seeking what the flesh desires. In equilibrium it is called chastity—the pursuit of our loves and desires in an exclusively lawful manner. Excess of lust is shamelessness, debauchery, which prods us toward whatever we fancy without any consideration either of the object itself, or of the physical or spiritual consequences to ourselves. And deficiency of lust leads to total loss of interest in all that is desirable, a state of complete lack of emotional involvement.

Wisdom, valor, and chastity are gained when consciousness manifests in communication among all the parts of ourselves, and between ourselves and others. Then we can draw our wit, our anger, and our lust under our control—we can, in fact, take them into our service. And stupidity, fury, cowardice, licentiousness are the result when anger, lust, and self-regard overcome our consciousness, reason, and conscience. The obverse of wisdom, valor, and chastity are vicious and perverse influences leading to vileness and disgrace. Most bad habits and character are caused by these and related excesses.

The cure of every ill depends on realizing that one is sick. When we recognize the harm of our condition, we can seek its cause and the ways to counteract it. Finding these, we can believe firmly in the beneficence of the measures necessary to counter our ills. And we will know the source of our cure.

Knowing our ills requires that we inspect ourselves, our actions, and our relations with others. It is helpful to listen to and accept the criticisms of real friends—even the accusations of our enemies—because, often enough, our friends merely excuse our faults, while our enemies see those faults magnified. The criticisms we make of others are a good means of seeing the same faults in ourselves. Each person is a mirror to other people, and those who realize this can see their own faults elsewhere, and take lessons from them.

Once you know your ills, you should not attribute them to a general and total failure. Learn to identify each separately and seek its causes, both outside and inside yourself. Then attempt to eliminate or change those causes.

All ill is cured by the action of its opposite. It is difficult, when one is used to a state, to face the uncertainty of a contrary state. It necessitates forming an intention and making a great deal of effort. The intention and the effort consist of self-evaluation, critiquing both our evident state and our hidden feelings and thoughts, and then taking action to oppose our habitual way of being. For instance, if you are a miser, act like a spendthrift. If you are a coward, be brave—but not so as to endanger yourself!

In all these attempts, be conscious. Calculate and reflect upon your actions and their effects, and be firm in your intentions and decisions. You must continue until your evil-commanding self, your ego, realizes that the effect of these efforts is a more natural, better, and easier life. Good health is easy to keep. All one has to do is be moderate.

To cure yourself of a bad feature of character is an obligation. It will save you from the disasters of this world as well as of the Hereafter.

Ma'munah related that the Messenger of Allah (s.a.w.s) said:

In Allah's estimation, there is no greater sin than bad character, because when someone has bad character, before he completes one sinful act, he begins another. (Isfahani)

The blessed `A'ishah (r.a.) reported that the Prophet said:

To attribute one's state or one's actions to bad luck or ill omen is a sign of bad character. (Tabarani)

The blessed `A'ishah also related that the Messenger of Allah (s.a.w.s) said:

One can repent for any sin but bad character—because with bad character, before a person can attempt to ask forgiveness for one sin, he commits a worse. (Tabarani, Isfahani)

Ibn `Abbas (r.a.) reported that the Prophet of Allah said:

Good character and morals transform errors as water melts ice, while bad character alters good deeds as vinegar cuts honey. (Tabarani, Bayhaqi)

Wisdom, valor, and chastity and innocence—in their pure state, without any false intentions—are the three guardians of an honorable condition. That condition is called justice. Whatever generates from justice is a manifestation of good character.

A person who has been blessed with good character, whether given naturally or acquired through effort, can preserve it only among other people of good character. Such a person should avoid the company of evil friends who indulge in fun and games, debauchery and drunkenness, and the exchange of gossip and meaningless debate, for this is the environment in which the ego feeds and strengthens and takes over.

What keeps the ego weak and obedient is applying learning and knowledge in good actions; being aware of one's state; meditating upon causes and effects; appreciating the gifts bestowed by good character; and listening to the advice of others engaged in the same pursuit. On such food, our ego will obey its Lord.

Allah Most High tells His beloved Prophet:

Indeed, you are of an exalted character. (*Qalam*, 4)

Anas ibn Malik reported that the Messenger of Allah (s.a.w.s) said:

A person reaches the best and most honored levels in the Hereafter as a result of good character, though to maintain good character is the easiest form of worship. And bad character condemns a person to the lowest depths of Hell. (Tabarani)

Abu Hurayrah reported that the Prophet said:

I have been sent for the perfection of character. (Imam Ahmad and Bayhaqi)

Anas ibn Malik reported that the Prophet said:

The one with good morals and character already owns the best of this world and the Hereafter. (Tabarani and Abu Dawud)

Abu Hurayrah reported that the Prophet said:

Allah does not beautify the appearance and the character of a person only so that, at the end, he will be thrown into Hell-fire. (Tabarani)

Abu Hurayrah related:

The Messenger of Allah addressed me, saying: "Abu Hurayrah, what you need most is the best of character."
   I asked him, "Please describe to me what good character is."
   He replied: "When someone abandons you, seek his company; when someone tyrannizes you, forgive him; when someone leaves you destitute, give him whatever you have." (Bayhaki)

O seeker on the path to truth, what you need most is to cleanse your heart of all that is evil and decorate it with beautiful behavior. The truth of Islam is no more than two things: to leave what is bad, and to advance what is best, in one's character.

In studying roots of bad character, we have identified principal features of maleficence. We have sought their causes, and will propose cures for them.

CHAPTER 7

ON THE DENIAL OF GOD

The worst and most destructive of all the features of bad character is faithlessness. Infidelity is the lack of faith shown by someone who is perfectly capable of believing in the existence of God, and yet will not. For a Muslim, faith is to believe that the Prophet Muhammad (s.a.w.s) is the Messenger of Allah and that what he has brought to humanity is the word of his Lord. We must confirm this in our hearts, say it with our tongues, and follow it in our lives. We are permitted to refrain from declaring our faith publicly if that would endanger our lives or the lives of others.

The faithful and the unfaithful are at opposite poles.

The denier of God is not the only nonbeliever. The person who doubts is also considered to be one. In the case of the doubter, to question the existence of God is equivalent to rejecting His presence.

There are three kinds of disbelief. One is the denial of the ignorant. This is the condition of the commonest sort of disbeliever. Such people don't listen to the words of Allah nor to those of His Messenger, close their eyes to the signs of the Creator, and refuse to accept proofs.

Ignorance is a grave sickness of the heart through which a person refuses to seek knowledge despite the ability to seek it. There are two kinds of ignorant people. The first kind are confused. They have lost their reason and their sense of discrimination and are reduced to a state worse than an animal's, because even a dumb animal has the instinct to differentiate what is good for it from what is bad for it.

The condition of not knowing what a human being is obliged to know is in itself unlawful, a sin according to Islam. (Ignoring that which it is not an obligation to know is not considered sinful.) The cure for this kind of ordinary ignorance is to show such people the troubles that their refusal to learn will cause them and the benefits they would receive if they knew, and then to teach them what they must know.

Occasionally some manifest proofs may appear contradictory. This is also one of the causes of ignorance. However the condition might better be called doubt, hesitation, awe. It causes some people to stop learning. The cure of the state is to teach such people the elements of reasoning and the methodical use of their intelligence until they are freed of their vacillation between the two proofs, each of which may be invalid by itself but become valid through contrast with the other.

(Sometimes it is difficult to eliminate a doubt when two Traditions of the Prophet seem to be contradictory, especially if one does not know when and under what circumstances the Prophet said or did the things in question. It is not a solution to prefer one Tradition over the other. In these cases it is acceptable to be doubtful in a positive way. Even the wisest among the interpreters, such as Abu Hanifah, have not been able to decide as to whether children of nonbelievers who have not reached puberty will be left in limbo between Heaven and Hell or will enter Paradise without being judged on the Day of Judgment; or the proper age for circumcision of male children; or the real meaning of the word *dahr*, generally taken to mean "time," in the 76th Surah of the Qur'an; and so forth.)

There is a worse kind of ignorance than avoidance of the difficult. It is a chronic sickness of the heart, an attitude of refusing reality. This is the case of the heedless person who lives in his imagination. It is a sickness hard to cure, because the one who is afflicted with it does not accept that he is ill, but thinks that his ignorance is itself a sign of wisdom and perfection. Therefore he neither wishes to change his state nor looks for a cure. These people can only be saved by a divine intervention that undeniably shows them the disaster of their state.

The cause of the state is an unjustifiable arrogance and the fear of losing an imaginary high position seeming to offer precedence over others. Such a person may even think that he is already a master over other people, and fear to lose his distinction. This was the situation of Pharaoh, who actually had material wealth and power, but claimed divinity. Allah Most High, mentioning the kings of ancient Egypt, says:

> These behaved insolently. They were arrogant people who said: "Are we going to believe two men [Moses and Aaron] who are only human and whose followers are our slaves?" (*Mu'minun*, 46-47)

Most of the people who deny God are found among the heedless, who do not know themselves and are either brought to high positions in this world or hope to attain them. They imagine that they should rule people. They either really have fortunes, power, and fame; or imagine themselves to have worldly power; or aim for it. They do not know that these are the causes of the sickness of their hearts, which become the slaves of this world.

Ka`b ibn Malik reported that the Prophet said:

> The destruction that worldly fortune and fame, or the ambition for them, inflicts upon one's faith, is worse than what a pack of wolves could do to a flock of sheep. (Tirmidhi)

Anas ibn Malik reported that the Messenger of Allah (s.a.w.s) said:

> To be pointed out as someone famous suffices as the worst disaster in this world and the Next, except for those whom Allah protects. (Bayhaqi)

Ibn `Abbas reported that the Messenger of Allah (s.a.w.s) said:

The praise of people renders one blind and deaf to truth. (Daylami)

To believe oneself to be exceptional, better than others, having a right over others—or to wish to be in that state—has three causes. The first is weakness of faith, which reduces us to being a slave of our egos and the desires of our flesh. That makes a person consider what is unlawful to be lawful.

The second is a more complicated condition. Sometimes a person is given some worldly privileges as well as some religious knowledge. That enables him to take what belongs to others, but also to spend some of it on useful deeds, such as the building of schools, hospitals, mosques, roads, and bridges. These people imagine that these deeds—which are actually a product of their tyranny—are their own religiously effective good actions. Their laying claim to them is nothing less than hypocrisy. On the other hand, if a person who holds worldly power is devout, with pure intentions, and convinces those under him to do good deeds, while not claiming to be the one who executed these deeds, his action is considered to be acceptable. Allah says that he employs some believers to be the guides of others. Yet good intentions do not make something unlawful, lawful.

The third cause is to believe that the high station one is given in this life is due to one's own qualities and perfection; to feel that one's possessions are a proof of one's greatness. Usually such people have stepped on many heads to reach that height, and have denied many their rights. While they seek the approval of the world, they lie and cheat and end up as arrogant, hypocritical tyrants. There are a few people who have received high positions honorably and without hurting others—in fact, while bringing those under them to higher worldly levels as well. Even for these, but certainly for the ones who have succeeded through their blind ambition, to be placed in a high position is dangerous. The cure for that danger is the realization that a high worldly state is not due to any kind of superiority, and that such a state is not permanent, nor are the awe and respect shown to the powerful permanent. The higher a person climbs, the greater the fall will be, and those who defer to the "successful" person today will not know him tomorrow, when all is lost.

A story is told that a king was invited for dinner by a shaykh who prepared a good meal. During the feast the shaykh ate voraciously, which shook the faith of the king in him, and the king left early. The shaykh, suffering from the sacrifice which he made by overeating, said: "May Allah be praised that this was sufficient to take you away from me!"

The surest way to rid oneself of the desire to be superior to others is to separate oneself from others—if not literally, then by freeing oneself from their opinions and considerations. The only time a place above others ceases to be dangerous is when one is neither attached to it nor ambitious for it.

Another cause leading to faithlessness is the fear of criticism and blame by others who are without faith themselves. Usually this is coupled with a desire to be praised and respected by everyone, without making any distinction about who they are.

The fear of criticism and the love of praise are very much like the sickness of feeling or hoping that one is superior to others. To rid oneself of the fear of criticism we should try to see the truth in it. This practice helps us to see ourselves and our faults, or to remind us of our faults.

Blame is rarely completely without truth. Therefore we should be thankful to those who are critical of us, even if their intentions are insulting—for they make us aware of flaws in our character or our actions of which we were unaware. Our critics are our allies against our enemy, which is our own ego. If you are absolutely sure that you do not deserve to be criticized, the criticism is still good for you—although disastrous for your critic! Therefore you should pity him and pray for his forgiveness, because he is guilty of slander. On the Day of Judgment, Allah will take his good deeds and give them to you, and take your sins and give them to him. But in any case, if you recognize the fault mentioned by him in yourself, you must do all that is possible to correct it.

The pain that comes from criticism is felt only by people whose whole life and care is for this world. For those who care for the Hereafter, criticism is a gift and a cause of salvation and peace.

People love justified praise because it makes us taste human perfection. If not totally, at least in some aspects of our character we are made to feel better than we are. The love we feel toward those who praise us captures their hearts and friendship in turn—and perhaps through them, captures the hearts and respect of still other people. Yet the effort to hold onto this love and consideration distorts our character. For in reality the praiser is our enemy, since he is the ally of our enemy—our ego.

If the approval of others relates to your attitude and actions in this world, simply remember that what they have praised in you is temporal, as are this life, this world, and their very approval, respect, and friendship for you. If their praise relates to your spiritual state, the medicine against the sickness is to increase your efforts to acquire knowledge and apply it in your spiritual life; and to hold on to sincerity.

The one who praises is perhaps in a worse state of faithlessness than the one who is praised.

Alas, most of the time, the causes and effects of ambition, praise and criticism, and the damage they produce, are totally ignored by the ones who are affected. All the explanation and advice we have given here cannot even be heard by many people, because the evil-commanding ego is their master.

Knowledge and living according to our knowledge lead to a state of awe and fear of Allah, which is a defense against all evil within and without ourselves. That state is better than the state of those who take refuge in their worship, caring only for the eternal life in the Hereafter, and living in security and peace. Allah says:

> Only the people of knowledge among Allah's servants are those who love and fear Allah. (*Fatir*, 28)

> Those who live with the fear and love of Allah in their hearts, and are generous, are the ones who race with each other to do good deeds. (*Mu'minun*, 60-61)

The third and last of the causes of the denial of God, in addi tion to faithlessness due to ignorance and faithlessness due to arrogance, is found in those exterior states that are considered by religious law to reduce one to infidelity.

Generally these include all words and actions that might indicate a rejection of Allah and His messengers—for example, considering invalid or unimportant God, the prophets, the holy books, angels, the Hereafter, the Day of Judgment, destiny, religious law, spiritual knowledge—which are the bases of faith. To allow the negation of these fundamentals that are to be respected and obeyed—even to excuse oneself for ignoring them—is infidelity in itself. Even to approve of others in this state is considered faithlessness.

To make a blasphemous declaration without being forced to it or uttering it by mistake—even if one did not know that it was blasphemy—is considered by many to be faithlessness. It is also widely held that any action produced by purposefully ignoring the religious law or believing in a principle that contradicts the religious law is a sign of faithlessness, even if one claims or truly believes that one is a Muslim in one's heart.

Often enough the causes of actions or statements that the religious law considers to be signs of faithlessness are negligible. They include, for example, words spent with an intention to show one's wit and literary abilities; an attempt to tell interesting and original stories; a desire to be popular and witty in a social situation; to take serious affairs lightly and to turn them into jokes; to spend vulgar and negative words in anger; and so forth. To tell stories that are immoral or against religious precepts, to be frivolous, to belittle religious principles, to behave loosely—these and other incidents, if they falsify or mock at sacred things, are considered to be signs of disbelief.

To protect yourself against these maleficent causes, you must first have faith—and then the fear of losing it. So realize that the loss of your faith, according to religious law, should not only produce an automatic divorce, make the food you prepare unlawful to other believers, and in many ways keep you isolated from good people, but if you die before being able to repent, you could be condemned to Hellfire for eternity! If you think of this, you will spend the effort to take your life seriously and control your tongue, even in moments of lightheartedness. Learn when to speak and when to keep quiet, consider the effects of your actions and words, and pray to your Lord to protect you from all that leads to faithlessness.

Abu Musa al-`Ashari reported:

> In one of his sermons the Prophet said, "O people, protect yourselves from attributing partners to Allah, because this unforgivable sin is as silent and hidden as an ant walking."
>
> Someone asked: "If it is as difficult to know as an ant moving, how are we to protect ourselves?"
>
> Our Master said: "Pray to Allah thus: *Allahumma inna na`udhu bika min an nushrika bika shay'an na`lamuhu wa nasta`firuka lima la na`lamuhu.* (O Lord, we take refuge in You from knowingly attributing partners to You, and we beg Your forgiveness for things we do not know.)" (Ahmad ibn Hanbal)

Hadrat Hudhayfah reported the same tradition, adding that the Messenger of Allah (s.a.w.s) asked his people to repeat that prayer three times every day.

Faith is a natural state uniting the created to the Creator: to realize it means salvation, and to lack awareness of it spells disaster. Not everyone is able to bring faith to consciousness. Only those who seek the signs of the Creator within and around themselves, who reflect upon the where and when and why and ultimate outcome of things, will become aware of it.

Only those have faith who reach conviction in the Existence that creates all while remaining uncreated, that sustains all, while requiring no sustenance. All came from Him and will return to Him. He is the One and Unique, unlike anything He has created; perfect, without lack; Who always was and always will be, though all else passes away. Those who have understood this then realize that all belongs to Him, all is from Him, yet is not He; and in the end there is nothing but He. He has created all things because of His love for them, expecting nothing in return. He has traced the lives of all persons and leads them to the straight path through sending prophets—human beings among human beings like themselves—to carry His divine messages. Faith is incomplete without believing in the truth of His words and His messengers and in the existence of another life, an eternal life after this temporal one, and that there is an accounting to be given on a Day of Judgment when it will be decided whether each person is to enjoy eternal bliss in Paradise, or to suffer eternal misery in Hell.

All the little samples of Hell and Paradise that we taste in this life are temporary, yet they impress and affect us enormously. From our own experience we should realize that the greatest benefit we may hope for from our faith and obedience to Allah is to be saved from eternal suffering in Hell, and to attain peace and joy forever in Paradise. May He who is All-Forgiving and All-Generous bless us with this end.

CHAPTER 8

ON SELF-INDULGENCE
AND BLIND IMITATION

There is a disease of the heart between faith and faithlessness, which shows itself when people get involved in trying to alter the precepts of the religion. The cause of this illness is total dependence on limited human logic and intelligence; total faith in one's own opinions; obedience to the desires of one's flesh and the ambitions of one's ego; or simply blindly following someone who is misled. The worst of these is slavery to the ego.

Our Lord says:

> Do not be misled by your egos, or you will be led away from the truth and into lies. (*hadith qudsi*)

He also says that your egos will lead you away from your Lord. And He promises:

> For such as had entertained the fear of standing before their Lord's judgment and had restrained the ego from its desires, the abode will be Paradise. (*Nazi`at*, 40-41)

And He warns us:

> Have not you known the ones who take their whims and desires as their god? (*Jathiya*, 23; *Furqan*, 43)

And:

> Who is more led astray than the ones who follow the fancies of their ego? (*Qasas*, 50)

And:

> Nay, the wrongdoers merely follow their own lusts, being devoid of knowledge. But who will guide those whom God leaves astray? For them there will be no helpers. (*Rum*, 29)

Anas ibn Malik reported that the Messenger of Allah (s.a.w.s) said:

> What destroys the human being is arrogance, following lusts and the desires of the ego, and miserliness. (Bazzaz)

The blessed `Ali ibn Abi Talib reported that the Prophet said:

What I fear for you most are two habits: to go along with the dictates of your egos, and to be ambitious for this world. (Ibn Abi Dunya)

Shaddad ibn `Aws related that the Messenger of Allah (s.a.w.s) said:

The sign of a person who is aware and intelligent is that he has his ego under control and devotes his life to the preparation for the Hereafter. The sign of the weak person is that he continues being a slave to his ego and hopes for his Lord's forgiveness. (Tirmidhi)

Our egos and the appetites of our physical being contain a tendency toward wrongdoing. They have the strength to impose their wishes in our lives—but to obey all their desires is surely the way to our downfall. Almost always they lead to forbidden things, harmful even to our material being and life in this world, in addition to being disastrous for the Hereafter. They push us to revolt against Allah's prescriptions and the path of salvation, leading us to regions of pain, confusion, disaster, and sin by pretending that these are desirable conditions and good for us. And those of us who remain slaves to their egos become lowly, immoral, tyrannical, selfish, stingy, hypocritical, lying, cursed beings, enemies of the public and of themselves.

It is necessary to fight an endless battle in this life in order to protect ourselves against this greatest of evil enemies. A continuous effort must be made to repel it, or at least to reduce our acquiescence to its demands. Perhaps the first attempt should be to change our habits, which usually already represent the established rule of our egos. That struggle is the true sign of the righteous. It is the only way to take hold of the force that leads us astray. We must fight to bring our egos under control, in order to save our souls and afford them their rightful ruling place in our lives.

O seeker of truth, if you wish your Lord to lead you on the straight path to truth, first you must eliminate the hindrance of your ego on that path. Then Allah will certainly act upon what He promises:

And those who strive in Our cause, We will certainly guide them in Our path, for verily Allah is with those who do right. (`Ankabut, 69)

In the struggle with the ego, we should be careful not to tyrannize ourselves. Among the desires of our flesh there are things permissible, even necessary. One should be able to gauge the strength and insistence of these desires: it is excess that makes them blameworthy. Indeed, it is not possible for human nature totally to deny what the flesh and the ego desire. The exaggeration of asceticism is forbidden in Islam. Even in our worship, moderation is advised.

The blessed `A'ishah, may Allah be pleased with her, reported that the Messenger of Allah (s.a.w.s) said:

O people, only do things that you are able to continue doing, for otherwise you will soon be discouraged and stop. The actions that Allah considers to be the best are the constant and continuous ones, even if they are small. (Bukhari)

The blessed `Ali ibn Abi Talib advised:

Give comfort and rest to your heart. For if you oppress your heart with heavy tasks, it will tire of them, and leave them and everything else.

Abu Darda' said:

At times I give rest and comfort to my ego. When I do this, it helps me on the path to truth.

Imam Ghazali advised:

When your wish and desire for prayer and worship diminishes, if you feel that some rest, sleep, amusement, or recreation would restore it, do it without delay. This rest is better than making one's prayers unwillingly.

To seek rest, comfort, and recreation, not for their own sake, but to give one strength and motivation to live a righteous life, is to abide by the rules of religion.

BLIND IMITATION

Often enough the ego fools us by presenting attractive examples and suggesting that we imitate them. Hidden under the make-up that makes them beautiful, these attractions are evil and hideous. Heedlessly one takes them as friends, partners in fun and games, drunkenness and debauch, or even as guides and leaders.

Following the example of a way of behavior or an appearance with unwarranted trust, without investigating and seeking proofs of its being desirable, is blind imitation. According to religious precepts, imitation is strongly discouraged—unless one has reached the decision to follow after closely examining the suggested exemplar (even if only in a summary manner). Allah orders us to look carefully at whatever exists on earth and in the heavens. Over and over again, in the Holy Qur'an, there are warnings against imitation. We are urged to investigate and carefully consider everything in existence before we follow its example.

By general concurrence and agreement, even religious practice, when it is merely an imitation, is considered a sin. There are a lot of people talking who only pretend to be wise, and a lot of books written that will lead one astray. Of course, long accepted and respected interpreters should be followed. But even in these cases, one should not blindly imitate the branch of Islamic teaching to which one belongs, but study and learn its origins and principles. Only by so doing will one will be following the principles of the Holy Book and the Tradition of the Prophet.

Even with the best of intentions, students remain in danger of creating distortions. If you are arrogant, and see and decide on things wholly according to your own mind and opinions, you will establish your own destructive innovations in the practice of religion. That is even worse than blindly following innovations instituted by others. Such danger is yet another example of the power of our egos to fool us into sin.

"The superiority of men of knowledge over others is like my superiority over one of you."

CHAPTER 9

ON SANCTIMONY AND HYPOCRISY

Yet another sickness of the heart and cause of faithlessness is sanctimony. Sanctimony in the ordinary sense means attempting to succeed in this world through one's devotion, worship, and prayers, while also making public these acts of devotion. Even simply telling someone about your religious practice without being asked, or without an intention of teaching or correcting religious concepts, is sanctimonious.

Sanctimony is a form of hypocrisy, which is the attempt to appear to be what one is not. Its opposite is sincerity, the foundation of true faith. Sincerity means to undertake good deeds and behavior in harmony with our actual faith and religion, out of concern for salvation and peace in the Hereafter and a pure wish to come close to our Lord. Such actions, devotions, worship, and prayers are kept hidden, away from the sight and hearing of others.

The reward for sincerity is the greatest gift of Allah in this world: the conviction that you are in the plain view of Allah while you are performing your worship.

If you are unable to see Him, certainly He sees you. (Muslim, Ibn `Umar)

Sometimes hypocrisy enters the heart simply as an ambition for worldly success. That is the beginning of the hypocrisy of the world-bound. But when the profit of the Hereafter is also included in one's wish, the situation becomes more complicated. Then a struggle arises as to which is more important, the benefits of this world or those of the Hereafter.

If all of our wish is to succeed in this world, we expect to obtain that success either from the Creator or from the created. The benefits we look for in this world are either control over other people, or wealth, or pleasure, or protection from the loss of the first three. Some people are confused, thinking that their worldly ambitions are a way to reach the benefits of the Hereafter. And indeed, if they wish for all the worldly goods with the intention of using them for Allah's sake, and if they depend upon Him alone to obtain them rather than upon human beings, their condition is not hypocrisy. To wish for worldly benefit through one's religion is lawful. The proof is the legality of praying for rain or of making special prayers to ask Allah to direct us to the right decisions in worldly matters, or praying to be relieved from pain, sickness, and trouble.

There are many signs of hypocrisy in our being. The first kind is in the appearance of our physical body. Examples of sanctimony, religious hypocrisy, are exhibiting thinness as a sign of spending one's days in fasting and one's nights in prayer; pretending that the paleness of one's face is due to fear and love of Allah; lowering the voice and eyes as an affectation of humility; feigning distraction as if one were preoccupied in meditation, and so forth. The physical signs of hypocrisy in the world-bound are different. They include being corpulent, red-cheeked, with a smiling self-confident face, a well-kept appearance, and so on.

Beautifying one's appearance and one's clothes may indeed be an indication of hypocrisy. To be carefully groomed, fashionably and strikingly dressed, in order to attract the notice of others, and to behave extravagantly in order to draw attention to oneself, are signs of hypocrisy in the world-bound. But in pretentious ascetics, hypocrisy shows in wrongly-sized, torn and patched clothes, unkempt long dirty hair, and worn-out shoes, all trumpeting abroad that this person has no time left after his religious duties to care for his appearance.

If you suggested to such a man that he wash and comb his hair and presented him with normal clothes, he would refuse them. He would worry that people would say that he cares about what people say! And he would resist looking like everyone else. Yet these hypocrites will not hesitate to change their appearance according to what they expect from the people among whom they find themselves. If perchance they have an occasion to rub shoulders with important and rich people, they dress in a way that is acceptable in such circles, for fear that their dirty and torn clothes would make potential patrons turn their backs. When they are together with the righteous, they feel it is more advantageous to appear ascetic.

The environment of a hypocrite is also arranged for show. The worldly hypocrite rides in expensive vehicles, lives in beautiful houses, serves his guests with elaborate table services. But when he is alone in his house, he wolfs down leftovers in his kitchen.

Both the worldly and the religious hypocrite like to sell themselves to the public by advertising the importance and honor of their ancestors and their ancestors' achievements—which, of course, have nothing to do with them.

The nature of hypocrisy in the religious zealot is the worse and more elaborate of the two. Such a man tries hard to give the impression that he has wisdom by speaking publicly without invitation, using incomprehensible, complicated words and sentences. He gives lengthy interpretations of verses of the Qur'an and Traditions of the Prophet in which the original meaning is lost or totally changed, while criticizing others for doing what he is doing: he charges other people with falsifying the Holy Scripture. Pretending that he has the whole Qur'an and thousands of Traditions in his memory, he engages in unwarranted debates with people of knowledge in an aggressive way, name-dropping about famous scholars, claiming them as his teachers or colleagues, talking about his personal experiences in long devotions and meditations. Even when he is silent, he moves his lips as if in interior prayer, showing exaggerated anger, or pain and tears, about the wrongdoings of others. He raises his voice as a sign of ecstasy during the recitation of congregational prayers. In these and many other ways he hopes to demonstrate his superiority over or difference from the rest of the believers.

The parallel signs of the worldly hypocrite are simpler. He tries to attract the attention of others by quoting philosophical or material explanations for certain phenomena of common interest. Better still, he pretends that these ideas are his own, by neglecting to mention the original authors. He recites poetry, unusual stories, humorous anecdotes, all in a very literary language and with appropriate gestures, in order to make people take notice of him.

It is to be suspected when, in congregational prayers, a particular person stands out from the crowd through a pose of utter humbleness, or through delaying his bows and prostrations as if rapt in complete awe while alone in his private prayers, he is very loose and in a hurry to get them over with.

The secular hypocrite publicizes his arrogance by lifting his chin, standing very erect, and walking slowly with a grave pace while turning his head slowly to the right and the left to see if he is observed.

When the religious hypocrite goes somewhere—usually public gatherings (to which he tries very hard to get invited) or Friday congregational prayers—he likes to have company. He is very careful to walk ahead of his companions so that it appears that they are following him, since he hopes that people will think he is a great spiritual leader with a lot of disciples.

The worldly hypocrite does the same thing, only he hopes that people will think him to be famous, powerful, and wealthy, with lots of clients depending on him and respecting him.

The kind of hypocrisy that counts on fame and power to attract people's love and respect has a specific object in mind. It exists either as an attempt to obtain personal benefit from the people whose hearts have been captured; or as a device to make the hypocrite's sins and wrongdoings (which, according to him, are right) appear commendable in the eyes of others as well.

To summarize, we can divide the manifestations of both secular and religious hypocrisy into four types.

A typical example of a hypocrite who hopes to attract the attention, approval, and respect of the public is the one who pretends to be already famous because of his wisdom and piety, the sign of which is the multitude of his followers and supporters. So he walks ahead of a crowd—fast, if they are walking fast, and slowly, if they are falling behind. He is so self-centered that he thinks that everyone is always looking at him. He is so totally concerned with the opinion of others that, even when he is walking alone, he will walk fast and then slow his pace so that people do not suspect this trick when he pretends to be at the head of his followers! Attitudes like this one magnify his hypocrisy many times.

If he ever finds a moment's relaxation from his terrible fear of attracting people's contempt, so that he jokes and laughs and loses his usual state of somberness, he catches himself, takes a deep breath, and excuses himself, saying that even the best of us have occasional moments of heedlessness. God, whose existence he rarely remembers, knows well that this man, when he is by himself, is the most unconscious and loosest of people. His fear and care are only for the opinion of other men.

This is the example of the first kind of hypocrite, who pretends to fast while he is not fasting—and if he is caught, pretends to be sick, or puts the fault on circumstances beyond his control. He may even cite his concern for his mother, whose excess of love and compassion for him is the cause of his lack of extra effort in worship! All of this, of course, is lies.

A possible cure for this and all other kinds of hypocrisy is to be wary of one's concern for the opinions of others. It is best to totally ignore people's opinions, unless your behavior is harmful to them. Indeed, your fasting or praying is between you and Allah and has nothing to do with human beings. If you seek other people's recognition of your piety, you are setting up partners to Allah—unless you want to set an example for them and you believe that they will follow you in your good deeds. But if your intention is to be a leader by being an example to others, you are the same as the secular hypocrite who wishes to become the commander of the army by showing false valor in battle, and gets himself killed.

The second kind of hypocrite is the one who wants to be superior to others by appearing to be truthful, dependable, and just. He shows off his fear of Allah and claims to do nothing but the lawful. Sometimes he even confesses to errors as a proof of his truthfulness, and in order to secure a reputation among ordinary people as a trustworthy person. His aim is to obtain a profitable position, such as the management of a trust or a judge-ship, by displaying himself as a truly respectable individual to whom one can safely entrust one's property, fortune, or dependents. Then he means to misuse these trusts, and is devious enough to avoid getting caught.

Or he shows himself forth as a mystic or preacher and by his manner and speech attracts women and young men whose attachment, trust, and love for him he misuses.

The third kind of hypocrite is the one who pretends to care for oth-ers. He appears compassionate and ready to help. He hurries with his ritual prayers and other worship in public, pretending that to be useful to people is more important. At the same time, he is careful to appear to be a strict believer. He collects from others by claiming to distribute to those in need—but he keeps a great deal for himself. Yet even with the little he gives away he attracts the gratitude and love of the poor and needy, from which he also profits.

The fourth kind of hypocrite, although privately very negligent about practicing his religion, in public makes an elaborate show of it. His advertised piety exists to enable him to reap worldly benefit from the people who believe in him. Yet he remains convinced that what he does is religiously lawful, because it resembles the attitude of those righteous men who become examples to others with their good deeds, and whose intention is to encourage others to follow the straight path. He in fact believes that Allah is going to reward him for his hypocrisy.

What is most pernicious is hidden hypocrisy—hidden even from the hypocrite himself. It is more difficult to detect than the sound of an ant's footsteps. That is why a sincere person must take great care to learn the signs of hidden hypocrisy.

Sometimes we find joy, satisfaction, and a little pride in people's approval and praise of things we have done with the true intention of helping others, leading them to the straight path, or serving as an example of selfless obedience to Allah. If we do these things without remembering that they are all undertaken for His sake and that He is the one who rewards us by hiding our faults and showing us only His beautiful side—then there is a danger of hypocrisy. To be happy and satisfied in yourself, thankful to Allah for making you act like a human being, and hopeful of His favors in the Hereafter, is not a sign of hypocrisy. The test is in our ability to look into ourselves in sincerity. Allah says:

O Muhammad, say: "All these are gifts due to Allah's infinite beneficence." Let them be happy only for this. (*Yunus*, 58)

It is permissible to feel a certain security and satisfaction in hiding one's piety, one's good deeds—even hiding from our left hand what our right hand gives—as a proof to ourselves that we seek only Allah's approval. However, hypocrisy may raise its ugly head and make us expect people around us to behave well toward us in consequence. We may expect people to offer us respect, to be fair when we buy something, to show us honor, kindness, thankfulness, as if we deserved those considerations for hiding our good deeds! If our efforts were untainted by hypocrisy, we would neither expect people's regard nor mind their ingratitude and disregard.

Unless you waste no thought or care on people's reactions when you behave according to the orders of Allah, unless there is no difference between your cat seeing you pray or your neighbor, the question of hypocrisy in your actions remains.

When we are confident of our truthfulness with ourselves, we may purposefully accept recognition from people in order to feel the sting of hidden hypocrisy. Allah sees and knows all; nothing is hidden from Him. The sincere believer should also be able to see in himself what Allah knows.

We should also suspect the existence of hypocrisy in our relations with our friends and acquaintances. Do we prefer one person over another because he is rich, famous, known and admired by others? Or do we care more about his righteousness, his knowledge and wisdom and good character—even if he is also rich and famous? If our preference is dependent on wealth and fame and the recognition of others, our care for that person is certainly hypocritical.

There are signs of hypocrisy particular to people who are put in the positions of teachers, preachers, mystical leaders, and the wise. One is a change of attitude and an affectation in speech when talking to important people. However if spiritual teachers appear to be especially polite, caring, and generous to the rich and famous with the intention of correcting their wrongdoings and leading them to repentance and to the straight path, thus hoping to lead others to salvation through their influence, their actions are correct and not hypocritical.

Another sign of hypocrisy among such people is the expression of envy and disapproval, and the belittling of others in their position. Yet envying someone for his piety, righteousness, and religious knowledge is perfectly acceptable.

Following are a few examples of religious edicts concerning hypocrisy.

For the sake of success in business or other worldly affairs, certain misrepresentations and exaggerations, if they are not intended as purposeful deceit or lies and are not clearly forbidden by the religion, are not considered to be unlawful. If such ruses are undertaken for a quick profit or a beneficial and pleasurable end, they are not considered to be good deeds. In politics, promises the realization of which are doubtful, or other propaganda, or an agenda put forward in order to gain power, are also acceptable.

On the other hand, all hypocrisy—showing off that which is not real—is unlawful, especially if one's intentions are dishonest. Such is the case of someone who doesn't do his ritual prayers privately, but appears in public communal prayers pretending to be devout. In the opinion of many scholars such an attitude is considered to be faithlessness, because the person guilty of it is making a mockery of his religion. Ibrahim ibn Yusuf said:

> If someone makes his prayers only to show off to others, he receives no spiritual benefit from them. On the contrary, he is sinning; and because he is showing contempt for Allah's orders, he is classed as a nonbeliever.

The famous theologian and jurist Abu Layth said:

These people are destined for the lowest levels of Hell, with the Pharaoh and others like him.

A person may make a public show of religion in order to protect people from talking against him and being guilty of the sin of gossip, or in order to learn how prayers are made, or to please his devout parents. Although such intentions are acceptable in themselves, they do not save such prayer from hypocrisy. In worship, the only valid intention is to act for Allah's sake. All other intentions are deceit.

In such misuses of the act of prayer, there is almost a belittling, even a ridiculing of religion. The purpose of the ritual prayer is not to obtain worldly benefits. Allah has made it an obligation upon believers for the achievement of our salvation in the Hereafter. At the same time, He has established it to organize and regularize our lives and worldly affairs. A person who uses the act of worship for other purposes than those Allah has ordained is daring to change the meaning of Allah's own intention. Allah says:

We give both worldly benefits and the benefits of the Hereafter to those who wish the Hereafter. And We give the benefits of this world to those who want them, but We give them no share of the benefits of the Hereafter. (*Shura*, 20)

According to the general consensus, if there is hypocrisy mixed into our devotions and undertakings in the pursuit of our religion, the results of our efforts are not void. Allah in His generosity only reduces His rewards. But if those acts have no religious motivation and are performed exclusively for worldly benefit, then Allah considers them null and void and they are, in fact, sinful.

Purity of intention in all one's acts in the practice of one's religion is an obligation. Ibn `Umar reported that the Messenger of Allah (s.a.w.s) said:

All actions depend on their intention and purpose. And all actions are rewarded in accordance with their intentions. (Bukhari)

Intention is a decision to act, together with the will to come closer to the Lord, seek His approval, and follow His orders. The will necessary to making an intention is not simply the abstract pronunciation of a wish, which could very well be influenced by one's ego and become hypocritical. The will to be close to the Lord is an expression of sincerity, devoid of any other purpose.

A sincere intention at the beginning of every act prevents other wishes and purposes from intervening during that act. In consequence, according to religious precepts, it is impossible to formulate a valid intention to offer tomorrow's morning prayer, or to fast during next year's Ramadan, or to fast for the whole month as a bloc. Such statements can only represent a hope, a wish that, if the Lord allows, one would prefer to perform those duties. Such hopes are not equivalent to the concrete intentions required by religion.

Religious practice allows of some exceptions in advancing or delaying our intentions. For instance, you may make the intention to pay the obligatory poor rate while you are gathering the funds for it, well before they are collected. You may make the intention to fast for a day on the night immediately before. If you are delayed from performing an act of worship, you may, at the time it is due, make the intention to perform it afterwards. If for some valid reason you cannot fast, you may intend the necessary expiatory charity later. And if you forget to formulate the ritual intention to offer prayer, you may do so at any time up until the first bowing.

CHAPTER 10

ON AMBITION

Ambition is a sickness of the heart whose principal symptom is a desperate desire for a very long life, without any thought of death. The person stricken with this sickness forgets any intention to improve his spiritual state, and gives no thought to the dangers that may befall him. These are four.

The first danger is to waste one's lifetime merely accumulating worldly goods. While doing so, one forgets about the existence of the Hereafter.

The second danger is to completely ignore death and the life after death. This hardens hearts and removes from them all compassion and concern for others.

The third danger is to delay the necessary. Even if such a person considers that what he is doing is wrong, even if it occurs to him that he has to repent, he puts it off until later, and is never able to accomplish it before the end comes.

The fourth danger is to abandon prayer and the practice of religion. Although well able to undertake these duties, the ambitious person is unable to see their importance.

The ambitious one thinks he will live forever. Thus even when he is old and sick, he increases his efforts to accumulate wealth, believing that his age and his sickness make it necessary for him, more than ever, to have money and what comforts it can buy. Many of these have enough means to last them and their families for ten lifetimes.

Even the ascetics of Islam say that it is permissible for someone to put aside enough money to support himself and his family for a year. They do not consider this to represent a lack of trust in Allah, because, according to tradition, the Prophet of Allah himself put aside means to support his family for a year. Therefore, according to religious law, to store sustenance for one's household for a year is accepted as a necessity and not a luxury. Some reduce this period to forty days or even just a month. But whoever plans for over a year is considered to be deficient in trust for Allah's generosity.

To hope for a long life with the object of preparing yourself to meet your Lord by doing good deeds, improving your character, and practicing your religion is not blameworthy. On the contrary, it is desirable.

Abu Bakr reported:

The Messenger of Allah was visited by someone who asked him: "Who is the best of men?"

He answered: "The one who has a long life and spends his time in good deeds."

"And who is the worst of men?"

"The one who has a long life and spends it selfishly." (Tirmidhi)

Jabir ibn `Abdullah reported that the Messenger of Allah (s.a.w.s) said:

Do not wish for death, because it cuts off life with a terrible shock. A long life is a passage of salvation and felicity with which Allah blesses some, leading them to truth. (Bayhaqi)

`Amr ibn `Anbasah reported that the Prophet of Allah said:

If someone's hair turns white in the practice of religion, the whiteness of that hair turns into a divine light on the Day of Judgment, illuminating his path. (Nasa'i)

`Ubayd Ibn Khalid reported:

The Prophet assigned two young men to be each other's companions in religion. One of them was martyred in a battle. A week later his companion died naturally. During the funeral prayers of the second young man, the Messenger of Allah (s.a.w.s) asked the congregation, "What have you wished for him in your prayers?"

Some in the congregation said, "We prayed to Allah that his sins be forgiven and that he be together with his martyred friend in Paradise."

The Prophet said: "During the week between their deaths, what deeds, what prayers did this man perform to bring him together with his martyred brother? The difference between the two is like the difference between the earth and the heavens." (Abu Dawud)

The cause of the maleficence of ambition is the love of the world and the worldly, forgetting that the end is near, and being fooled by one's youth and good health. Its cure is to overcome these causes. Remembering death will eliminate the love of the world. That recollection will make it clear that youth and health are no guarantee. In many places in the world, more children die than old people, and there are many sick people who live much longer than the healthy.

Anas ibn Malik reported that the Prophet of Allah said:

Remember death often: it will prevent you from sinning and help you to repent for your sins. (Ibn Abi Dunya)

Bara' reported:

The Prophet sat at the edge of a grave and shed tears until the earth in front of him became wet. He said, "O my brothers, prepare yourselves for a day like this when your time comes." (Ibn Maja)

`Amr reported that the Messenger of Allah (s.a.w.s) said:

The remembrance of death suffices you for counsel, and a sincere faith suffices you for riches. (Tabarani)

Abu Hurayrah reported that the Messenger of Allah (s.a.w.s) said:

Remember death, which will take away the pleasure of all you taste. You will find that you will be relieved in moments when you are troubled—and you will find out that if you do not remember it when you are happy in life, you will be troubled. (Ibn Hibban)

Ibn `Umar reported:

Ten of us came to visit the Prophet. One of the Helpers from Medina asked, "O Messenger of Allah, what person is the most intelligent and clear-sighted?"
He answered, "The one who remembers death most often, and prepares for it. People like that are really intelligent. They leave this world in honor and with the blessings of the Hereafter." (Ibn Abi Dunya)

Umm Mundhir reported:

One day close to sunset the Holy Prophet passed by a group of us and said, "O people, aren't you ashamed before Allah?"
We asked, "What is it that we would be ashamed of?"
And he answered, "You gather from this world that which you cannot finish eating. You are ambitious for things you can never have. You build things you do not need." (Bayhaqi)

Abu Nu`aym reported:

Abu Sa`id al-Khudri bought a very young servant named `Usamah ibn Zayd from Zayd ibn Thabit. He made an arrangement to pay him the price of a hundred *dinar*s after one month. When the Messenger of Allah (s.a.w.s) heard of this arrangement from Abu Sa`id, he said to the people around him, "Are you not amazed at the ambition of Abu Sa`id? At his expectation that `Usamah, whom he bought, will live a month, and that he himself will live a month to be able to pay his debt? As Allah is my witness, I myself feel death to be so close. At each blinking of my eyes I expect that Allah will take my soul and that I won't be able to close my eyes again. When I turn my eyes to one side, before I can look at some new thing, I think of death coming upon me. When I put a morsel in my mouth, I don't expect to swallow it before I die. O sons of Adam, if you have any sense, count yourselves among the dead! Certainly that is the sole certainty. Do you think you can prevent Allah from taking your life?" (Tabarani)

Hasan al-Basri reported:

The Messenger of Allah asked a group of his people, "Don't you all wish to enter Paradise?"
   They answered, "Yes, O Prophet of Allah!"
   "In that case, lessen your ambitions. Know that the end of your life is between two blinks of an eye, and have shame in front of Allah." (Ibn Abi Dunya)

Ambition is unlawful if its aim is to acquire and taste things that are forbidden, because just as unlawful causes make their effects unlawful, unlawful effects make their causes unlawful. To plan to do or to deal with things that are lawful is not unlawful.

To have lengthy hopes is not considered right even if you plan to increase your worship or good deeds, or to protect yourself from future dangers to yourself and your religion. In any kind of ambition there is doubt, for it is never sure. In the process of pursuing your distant goals you will experience tastes of the pleasures of success or resentment toward failures. These may produce harmful states. Ambition rests on a false belief in our ability to deal with things unknown, and to tamper with our destiny. It also involves tampering with the future of others.

Sa'd ibn Abi Waqqas reported:

Someone came to the Messenger of Allah (s.a.w.s) and asked for advice. He said, "Stop wanting and hoping for things that are in the possession of others. Stop being ambitious. Wanting what others have is certainly the worst of poverty. Make each of your prayers as if it will be your last prayer. Prevent yourself from doing things for which you will later be sorry." (Bayhaqi)

Even the wish, the desire to have or to taste something unlawful, is unlawful. To wish for something it is permissible to have, although obtaining it and having it may be dangerous, is not necessarily unlawful. But it is disadvised.

The worst of ambition is coveting what belongs to someone else. That is a form of degradation which includes not only ambition but envy, laziness—for you do not even try to be worth that thing yourself—and lack of faith in Allah's generosity, knowledge, and ability to satisfy your needs.

The opposite of maleficent ambition is to commit yourself into the care of your Lord, knowing that you do not know what is good for you, but Allah knows. It is to ask Him for, and trust Him to give you, exactly what you need and are worth. He is the one who knows what is beneficial for you, while you cannot be sure; and He is the only one who can prevent something bad for you from coming upon you. Your own experience with things you have desired, and were able to obtain or were prevented from obtaining, provides clear proof of this.

When we trust in Allah, His next blessing upon us is to become our guardian who protects us. In the Qur'an He advises that we say:

Allah is enough for me. He is the one who knows best for His servants. (*Mu'min*, 44)

CHAPTER 11

ON IDENTIFYING EVIL

B e aware that both hypocrisy and sincerity are apt to be influenced by the Devil. Therefore it is well to know the temptations, tricks, deceptions, and doubts suggested by the Devil, the necessity of fearing their influence, and the ways to avoid them.

First we have to be able to identify whether the influences that affect us are of evil or beneficent origin. This knowledge enables us to distinguish right from wrong. Influences may be either external or internal. It is more difficult to analyze interior influences because exterior influences are more obvious.

An idea comes into your head. You are in doubt: if you act upon that thought, will it be good for you or will it cause disasters? But these thoughts are the result of a certain need that Allah creates in our being. They lead us either to make an effort to satisfy some apparent lack in our lives or, on the contrary, to stop doing something that may be harmful. Such thoughts come without any recognizable intermediary. They are called inspirations. To fit them into the categories of "good" and "bad" without any doubt necessitates good will and sincere effort.

Inspirations can be identified as good if they correspond to the principles of faith. A beneficent result is reached when one recognizes them as a gift of God. Such an event is called "spiritual guidance" or "God's grace."

Allah says:

And those who strive hard for us, We shall certainly guide them in Our ways. And Allah is surely with those who do right. (`Ankabut, 69)

And those who follow guidance, Allah increases them in certitude, and puts in their hearts the fear of God. (*Muhammad*, 17)

We mentioned that these beneficial inspirations come into one's mind without an intermediary. In some cases, however, an inspiration is sent to someone by Allah Most High through an angel who interjects it into the upper right chamber of the heart of the faithful. That angel is called the Inspirer, and the invitation it places in the heart of a faithful person is called angelic inspiration. This kind of inspiration can only lead to good. Angelic inspirations may be identified through their being repetitive and their being followed by inspired advice as to how to act to reach the desired end.

Maleficent inner influences are usually triggered by an exterior, worldly entity affecting you through your senses. They are generally sensuous, lustful, exciting the desires of the flesh. This is called "the evil-commanding self." It can lead only to pain and trouble for oneself and others. These urges are constant. Desires that are forbidden press continuously until their hunger is satisfied. No manner of prayer, remembering Allah's admonitions, or resistance, can expel, weaken, or diminish them.

The worst kind of malignant temptation arises from the interior of one's being. It is injected by the Devil into the lower left chamber of your heart, and is called "imagination." This is an alternating temptation: if the Devil does not succeed in leading you to one mischief, he proposes a different one. The result is pain, stress, and confusion.

One sin leads to another. Yet sometimes imagination incites us to do a little good to prevent us from doing a greater good. Or it deceives us into "doing good" as an excuse for great harm.

The sign of good deeds that are precursors of great harm is that when we undertake them, we feel a great sense of elation and pride in what we have done. We become fearless. We are in a hurry in everything we do, we are sure, we do not think nor care where we are led. We cease to see the consequences of our actions.

Ibn Mas'ud related that the Messenger of Allah (s.a.w.s) said:

There are two points in the heart. One impresses a person with the touch of the angels—the confirmation of truth and the promise of good. The other tempts a person with the infection of your enemy, the Devil—the denial of truth, prevention from doing good, and the promise of evil. (Nasa'i and Tirmidhi)

It was reported by Anas ibn Malik that the Prophet also said:

Satan sticks his trunk into the human chest. If the son of Adam (a.s.) takes refuge in Allah, the Devil steps back. If the person forgets Allah, he sucks his heart out of his chest. (Ibn Abi Dunya)

The general opinion about how to save ourselves from a maleficent influence is first to take refuge in Allah's protection from the accursed Devil, as He orders us to do in the Holy Qur'an. The Devil is a pet created to persistently attack us: therefore we have to call upon its owner to prevent it from biting us. Like a vicious dog, it will chase you if you run. If you respond to it or even look at it, it will keep barking at you. But if you hold your position and ignore it, it may leave you alone.

If all this does not help, we must accept the influence as a trial from Allah to test our fortitude, our faith, and our ability to fight for the right cause. This test is similar to our Lord's intent when He sends upon us the tyranny of His enemies, while He has the power to annihilate them, so that we gain His approval and His blessings with the courage and patience we show in fighting against them. As He says in the Holy Qur'an:

> Do you think that you will enter Paradise, while there has not yet befallen you the like of what befell those who have passed away before you? Distress and affliction befell them and they were shaken violently so that the Messenger and those who believed with him said: "When will the help of Allah come?" Now surely the help of Allah is near. (*Baqarah*, 214)

The gates of salvation are only reached through struggle.

There are four tests by which we may distinguish whether an influence is good or ill. The first and the best is to compare our wish to do something with the rules indicated by the Holy Qur'an and the Traditions of the Prophet. The second is to ask the advice of those who know: theologians, spiritual guides, people of wisdom. The third is to compare the influences that affect us with the experiences of sincere, honest, devout people and then with the experiences of selfish, tyrannical, hypocritical ones. The fourth is a course of self-criticism to determine whether the influence is agreeable to our ego—pleasing to our lust, sensuality, self-satisfaction, and pride—or whether it will lead us to do something selfless, for the good of others, for Allah's sake. One or all of these four tests will tell us what is right and what is wrong.

If we know how the accursed Devil operates, it is possible to protect ourselves against his temptations. Generally speaking, there are seven ways the Devil leads people astray.

1. The main goal of the Devil is to prevent us from obeying our Lord. He wants to steal our faith. He will attempt to prevent us from praying, fasting, paying the poor-rate, from performing the Pilgrimage, from doing good deeds. He presents the ego with attractive alternatives: wealth, fame, fun, ambition, attachment to the world and the worldly. But the heedful, wise, and faithful person can respond: "I am here in this world for a moment and I will be in the Hereafter for eternity. I can only care for this world for the short time I will spend here, but I must work for the sake of the Hereafter where I will stay forever."

2. If the evil influence cannot prevent us from doing what Allah has ordered us to do, it tries to delay the good actions we intend. It tempts us to do what is pleasurable to our egos first. What Allah asks us to do, it prefers we do later. In this case, the devout, under the protection of their Lord, can respond: "My life is not in my hands. I do not know when the end will come. If I leave what I was ordered to do today until tomorrow, tomorrow may never come. Every moment of my life is for a purpose. Now is the time to do what is to be done now. And now is the only time."

3. When the Devil cannot prevent us from following Allah's ordinances in our lives, nor force us to delay our duties, he pushes us to hurry. He says: "Do it quickly, so that you will have time for other things." The wise can resist by saying: "Less done, but completely, is better than much which is incomplete."

4. Then the Devil incites us to show off our deeds. If the faithful are protected by their Lord from hypocrisy, they can say: "People can neither help me nor harm me except by the will of Allah. Neither their praise nor their curse touches me. My Lord is All-Seeing and He is sufficient for me."

5. The most dangerous of evil temptations induces us to be proud. The Devil whispers in our ear: "How wise and heedful you are, while the whole of humankind is asleep!" If we are guided by our Lord, we can respond: "All praise and thanks are due to my Lord if I am heedful. His is the guidance, His is the success. All I have is His gift. If it were not so, all the good that comes through me would not reduce the swamp of my sins by a single drop."

6. Then the Devil says: "Indeed you are sincere and not a hypocrite, so you do not have to do any good deed for others to praise. Strive inwardly! Let none see you pray or how good you are. Live your spiritual life in seclusion; leave the world to the worldly. Your Lord will know." Thus the Devil tries to pull the devout into hidden hypocrisy. If they follow this bad advice, in their seclusion they will feel that they are protecting themselves from the rest of the world, who are worse than they are. The faithful who are well guided will say: "I was born into this world and am no better than any other person in it. We are all the servants of our Lord. Some He uses to benefit others, some He uses to tyrannize others. He knows what I do and He knows what is in my heart. I cannot hide anything from Him. If He wills, He exposes what I am; if He wills, He hides who I am even from myself. He is the Master, I am the slave."

7. Then the Devil says: "If all is His doing, then you do not have to intend to do anything. If all is His will, then you do not need your will. It is decided in your mother's womb if you are doomed or you are saved; nothing you will do will change your destiny." The wise will know that we do not know our destiny. But we do know that we are created to praise our Lord, to know our Lord, and to serve our Lord. Whatever our destiny is, our good deeds will profit us. If we are created fortunate by birth, we still need to do good deeds and to protect ourselves from evil. If we are created to do ill, we need to do even more good as repentance to compensate for our misfortune. How could the Lord punish a person for obedience? If one is destined to be thrown into Hell, it is better to enter the fire as an obedient servant. Allah promises that if a person comes to Him with faith in his heart and a lifetime full of good deeds, the fire will be forbidden to him. And He promises:

And those who keep their duty to their Lord are conveyed to the Garden in companies until they come to it and its doors are opened and the keepers of it say to them: "Peace be unto you! You led pure lives, so enter it to abide." And they say: "Praise be to Allah Who has made good to us His promise..." (*Zumar*, 73-74)

There is no doubt that Allah is the cause of all causes. Yet it seems to be His way to make everything that exists in this world and in the Hereafter to appear as the result of another existence. What we are able to observe is that the rain causes plants to grow, a child is born from sexual contact between a man and a woman, warm weather in summer ripens fruits, and Paradise is the reward for good deeds. He offers the Garden to humanity, saying: "You inherit Paradise as a reward for what you have done," and "Are the ones who do right the same as the sinners?" And the accursed Devil whispers in our ears, "If Allah is the cause of all things, then who can change that which is destined to happen? What if your efforts are against that which Allah has predestined for you? Is it not a great sin? If He wills you to do good, it will happen regardless of your will. If anything you want to happen does not meet His will, it will not happen. There is no need to judge, for all good and bad is from Him ..."

The wise can respond to this sacrilegious insinuation. "Indeed, the Lord is the Creator of all beings, as well as of their actions and what happens to them. Yet He has given the human being a will with which his heart and his mind dictate him to choose the right or the wrong. Neither the person nor the will created themselves: they are created. They do not exist independently, by themselves. Therefore a human being is neither able, nor does he need, to create anything with his will, by himself. Allah has made the human will conditional upon His overpowering greater will. Although surely whatever will happen to a person has been decided by the divine will and knowledge and is written in the Divine Tablet, we do not know what that destiny is until it happens. Nor does Allah's decision mean that a person's destiny is going to happen against his own will and is somehow forced upon him."

If someone somehow knew what was going to happen to you and wrote it down on a piece of paper, could it be said that he was forcing you to do those things, even though you do not know what is written on that paper? Whatever you do, even if it leads you to the destined end, is done by your own decision and is not enforced upon you.

Some believe that whatever happens to us is neither done to us by others, nor enforced upon us by an irresistible power; rather everything depends on our own will. This is an evil wishful thinking and has no truth in it.

The truth is that we are free to choose our actions, but our choices are compelled, forced upon us. That is what is called "interposed enforcement."

One may ask, What is the difference between having a power insufficient to change the result and having no power at all? But the choice of a desired result itself is dependent on another choice, and on a whole sequence of affairs of which we have no knowledge or control. Our will is created and necessitates the enforcement of a preexistent greater will. Allah's will is that preexisting self-created greater will. It is in no need of anything.

Our plans and efforts are surely subject to our fate. But there is an interdependence between our will and our fate. And in our fate there is a sequence of results, each depending upon another. If you make a choice and your intended result is canceled by another opposing choice, that opposing choice must have preexisted. But if the choice corresponds to your destiny, there cannot be a preexisting opposition to it. The right choice appears to be natural, obvious, dictated by your conscience.

According to the theologians, to choose without preference is acceptable, even if what one has chosen is not possible. If a preferred result is not a part of your intention, then whatever happens is acceptable and right. But is this result a product of the person who acts without preference, or is it imposed on him? Whether the result of what he wills and acts upon is from him or brought upon him, there is a joint liability between his will and his fate. And this is as it should be.

Once, God willing, this introduction about the temptations of the Devil and our ability to resist them is understood, we may start an investigation into hypocrisy versus sincerity.

DISTINGUISHING HYPOCRISY AND SINCERITY

Suppose an individual is in the company of very devout people who fast the day and spend the night praying. Although it is not his habit to do what they do, he may bring himself to fast and pray with them. Is he a hypocrite? He himself may doubt it. That doubt, before he has seriously evaluated his intention, is certainly wrong.

In the course of self-examination, he may reflect that in his customary life he was heedless of the practices and attitudes of the people among whom he now has come. He may observe that the comforts of the world—and the work and concern and ambition to secure those comforts—do not exist with these people. He may admire how free, at peace, content, and happy they are. When he truly wishes to be like them, to do what they do, he will join them. Certainly such a decision is not hypocritical. On the contrary, it is a right step toward salvation and felicity.

On the other hand, if he wishes to join these pious folk to gain their approval, praise, and favor; or if he fears their criticism of his negligence in worship and devotion; then he is indeed a hypocrite. This is especially so if he lies to himself, thinking that if he did not do in the past what he is doing now, it was due to circumstances beyond his control. This attitude is a sin, for the hypocrite is preferring the approval of the created to the orders of the Creator. Even if the result of such hypocrisy is a manifestation of apparent signs of devotion, it is better that one stay with what little worship one was already in the habit of performing.

Even in the case of a laudable intention, such as the intention to repent, there can be doubt as to whether a person is sincere or hypocritical. There are some people who publicly appear to be humble, their heads bowed, often audibly saying, "Lord forgive me …" Are they indeed God-fearing, heedful people, constantly remembering their faults, feeling shame and regret? Or are they seeking the confidence of others through their apparent honesty? Only the ones who know their hearts will know the truth.

There are also those people who openly publicize their devotion, piety, and good deeds. It is permissible, even laudable to do this if one is worthy to be an example and a leader, because then the public knowledge of one's acts will induce other people to undertake them.

Ibn `Umar reported that the Messenger of Allah (s.a.w.s) said:

> A good deed hidden from the view of others is better than one performed in public. But a good action undertaken by a well-known person whom others will follow is still better. (Bayhaqi)

Even for such leaders there is the risk of hypocrisy, for the Devil's tricks are often devious and hard to detect. If we have the slightest doubt of our sincerity in leading others to follow our example to do good, we should prefer privacy, for there is no risk in it. Public participation in communal prayers, pilgrimage, and other gatherings of the faithful which Allah has made obligatory are excluded from these concerns.

Some persons are in the habit of relating their religious and spiritual experiences to others. This is not different from the case of someone who publicizes his good deeds to teach or to encourage people. But even if the intention of such a person is hypocritical, in that he is trying to attract the admiration and respect of other people, still it does not detract from the reward he has already received from Allah—if the experiences are true. Yet if his intention is to draw benefit from the disclosure of his experiences, he may be sinning when he tells them.

There is the person who is lax in private religious practices but shows fervor when among the pious. And then there is the contrary case: a devout person who falls among people who are not religious. If such a person were to abandon his practices, not because he feared the people's reproach or ridicule, but because he thought that it might be hypocritical to continue, he would be making a wrong decision. Indeed, to do what he had always done would be proof of his sincerity, while that fear of hypocrisy would be to his credit. Even if he merely pretended to adopt their heedless behavior and change his usual pious ways, delaying or abandoning his prayers in consideration of his secular companions, he would be truly a hypocrite. Even worse, he would also be guilty of abasing companions who might very well admire his devotion.

In these situations strange ideas come into one's mind. You might think that you are protecting people from the sin of gossip, since they might talk about you behind your back on account of your different behavior. This again is an unjust accusation of one's companions. In addition, according to our religion one may only abandon things that are merely permissible—not those which are obligatory or even those which are desirable—in order to save other people from sinning. If we go so far as to neglect our religious obligations or the practices of the Prophet, for whatever reason, justifying ourselves without regret or reproach, it can only mean that we consider Allah's ordinances to be negligible, even shameful in certain circumstances. If he reflected on the consequences, a person of sound mind would certainly see that these considerations are no more than the Devil's worst contrivances.

There are some circumstances that involve our conscience and leave us in doubt as to the sincerity or hypocrisy of our acts. Suppose a friend asks to borrow money from you. Although you have the means to give him what he wants, you feel selfish and do not wish to lend him the money. On the other hand, you feel ashamed to refuse. If he had only sent somebody else to ask for the loan, you would certainly have refused! Then again, what would people say? You might even be at fault, since there is a tradition of our religion stating that while there is one divine reward for giving alms, there are eight divine rewards for lending money! Anyway if you pay him what he wants, he will owe you a favor. And others will praise you as a beneficent and generous person.

Any and all of these thoughts and motivations are signs of hypocrisy. The only sincere decision is this: if you have it, give your friend what he wants simply to satisfy his need and to please him.

There are times when sincerity, qualms of conscience, and hypocrisy force themselves upon us all together. On these occasions we must be careful of the balance of influences. If sincerity dominates, the situation is acceptable.

Suppose you are attempting to repent: you wish to stop sinning. Often enough this commendable aspiration becomes very complex. Do you wish to stop doing wrong for Allah's sake, because of the fear and love of your Lord? The sign of this is the care you give to your actions in private, since you fear the All-Seeing, All-Knowing Allah even when you are secluded from the sight of others. Or are you ashamed and wary of the criticism of other people? Or are you taking thought for your children, dependents, and friends, who might imitate your wrongdoing, so that you are trying to protect them as well as yourself by behaving in accordance with the morals of your religion? Are you afraid that you may be belittled, rejected, even punished by society? Or do you think that by behaving in a model manner in public, you save people from the sin of gossip and slander?

If you are sincere in your consideration for others, you should mind neither their praise nor their blame. Yet it is right and natural that we are hurt by other people's criticism. Often there is truth in it, and we should feel pain at the sight of what is wrong with ourselves. That pain may lead us to try to correct the wrong: therefore it is lawful. It is only our denial and resentment of criticism that is not good.

We are not blind to what is happening around us. And, alas, one sees some Muslims offering their formal prayers even to excess, though meanwhile they continue to sin. Although impressions like these are critical of other people, if they serve as lessons to us and help us to stop sinning ourselves, then they are a good influence.

Abu Hurayrah reported that the Messenger of Allah (s.a.w.s) said:

All of my people are likely to be forgiven by Allah except those who do not hide their sins, who proudly exhibit them. Those are the people who tear Allah's veil, under which He hides their faults. I fear that on the Day of Judgment, Allah will tear their veils and put them to shame. (Bukhari, Muslim)

To hide our sins from others is the better course, even if the reason is hypocritical. Shame is a commendable feeling usually dictated by conscience. A common example is our general behavior in public. Suppose, while walking in the streets, somebody rushes, bumps into people, is inconsiderate and impertinent to others. Suddenly he encounters an important person whom he knows. He becomes dignified and civil; his behavior becomes exemplary! In both cases he is acting hypocritically—but he may have become ashamed of his behavior when he met the person he knew.

Shame sincerely felt because of our wrongdoings, even when brought on by fear of other people, is a good deed. But if we feel ashamed of performing pious, laudable actions dictated by our religion because we are in the company of the irreligious, that shame is blameworthy. Someone whose faith is strong feels a shame before Allah far more intense than what he might feel in the presence of the most powerful of men.

We have mentioned events and actions that are induced by a mixture of influences, motivations partly sincere and partly hypocritical. The perfection of sincerity is in becoming invisible in the eyes of others. At a lesser level, perfect sincerity dictates that the opinions of others should not matter, because all of us are helpless. All that matters is to follow Allah's prescriptions, and all reward and punishment are solely from Him. Yet people with these motivations are indeed very few.

ON WAYS OF CURING HYPOCRISY

The ability to cure hypocrisy depends on our being able to detect its symptoms, realizing the troubles and pain it causes, and knowing how it is generated. Only then can we see the benefits of sincerity, wish for it, and seek its sources.

The causes of hypocrisy are three: the wish to be known, respected, honored by people, with the intention of profiting from such a situation; envy of the good fortune of others, and a desire to have the same for oneself; fear of being criticized and blamed for one's actual state.

About the troubles that hypocrisy causes, Allah warns:

... so whoever hopes to meet (the approval) of his Lord, he should do his deeds for His sake and join no one in the service of his Lord. (*Kahf,* 110)

Ibn Mas`ud reported that the Messenger of Allah (s.a.w.s) said:

If someone prays properly in public and is lax when alone, that person belittles his Lord. It is nothing less than a great insult to Allah Most High. (Ya'li)

Mahmud ibn Labid related:

The Messenger of Allah said, "What I fear most for you is that you commit, in a hidden way, the unforgivable sin of attributing partners to Allah."

The blessed Companions asked, "How could that be done, O Messenger of Allah?"

And he answered, "By acting hypocritically! When the hypocrite faces Divine Justice, Allah will tell him, 'Now go and seek help from the ones upon whom you depended, see if they will be able to save you.'" (Ahmad ibn Hanbal)

Ibn Abi Dunya reported that the Prophet said:

On the Day of Judgment, the hypocrite will hear himself addressed, "O you thankless, depraved sinner, you broke your trust, you lied even to yourself, you spent your life in vain. All you have done is lost, nothing is left in your favor." (Jabala)

And Dahhaq related that the Messenger of Allah (s.a.w.s) said:

Allah Most High tells us, "I am the best of your companions. If someone undertakes something that is not for My sake—even if it is for My sake and someone else's—that person is attributing partners to Allah. And that action is considered as performed wholly for the sake of whatever was set up as a partner to Allah." (Bazzaz)

Therefore let us undertake to do all that we do for the sake of Allah alone. Then each of our actions will be for the benefit of all. Since the right action as accepted by our Lord is the one intended only for His approval, if you think: "I am doing this for Allah's sake and for the benefit of this person whom I pity or for the benefit of someone who has shown me mercy"— your deed will not be for the sake of your Lord at all. It will be for another human being. If you say, "I do this for you, for Allah's sake," you are doing it for me. Your claiming it to be for Allah's sake will be hypocritical.

There are many more verses in the Qur'an, and innumerable Traditions of the Prophet, on the subject of hypocrisy. But this much should suffice for someone who is faithful and intelligent. An intelligent believer finds the right path with little effort.

The real meaning of hypocrisy is to distort devotion, which is given to us as a means to come close to the One who is sacred and powerful, by using it for other purposes. There are other devices through which one may seek people's favor, but to pretend godliness and piety in order to gain people's attention, love, and confidence is blasphemy and an insult to God. Indeed, if people knew his intentions, the hypocrite would receive the opposite of what he seeks: distrust instead of confidence, hate instead of love. People may not see through a hypocrite, but nothing is hidden from Allah. He certainly knows. And His wrath far surpasses the worst punishment we may receive from human hands.

The least harm a hypocrite should expect is that his actions will be unlawful in the eyes of God. His willful falsification, his presenting something as real while it is not, will turn against him. Although there are degrees of hypocrisy, and divine punishment is in accordance with the gravity of the offense, the hypocrite can expect that all his fraudulent efforts will be in vain. Not only will he gain no favors, but in the eye of God he will stand condemned.

If we are reminded of the benefits of sincerity, we may be able to prevent ourselves from falling under the influence of the evil-commanding ego that leads us to hypocrisy.

The main sources of sincerity are faith, love, and hope. Its nourishment is wisdom, intelligence, and knowledge. These causes become active when all our actions, behavior, thoughts, and feelings are dependent on our faith in God, and the love, joy, and security it brings.

The faithful and the sincere are praised by Allah:

... they are enjoined naught but to serve Allah, being sincere to Him in obedience, upright, and to keep up prayer and pay the poor-rate, and that is the right religion ... Those who have faith and do good, they are the best of creatures. Their reward is with their Lord: gardens of prosperity wherein flow rivers, abiding therein forever. Allah is well pleased with them, and they are well pleased with Him, that is for whoever loves and fears his Lord. (*Bayyinah*, 5-8)

Anas ibn Malik related that the Messenger of Allah (s.a.w.s) said:

Whoever leaves this world believing in one God, alone, without any partners or anything like Him, and who has worshiped Him sincerely and paid his due share of the poor-rate, goes to a Lord who is pleased with him. (Ibn Hibban and Hakim)

Mu`adh ibn Jabal related:

When the Messenger of Allah (s.a.w.s) sent me to Yemen as his emissary, I asked him for advice. He said, "Be sincere toward Allah in your faith. Even if your achievements are few, if they are sincere, that is sufficient for you." (from *Hakim Mustadrak*)

Ibn Thawban reported that the Prophet said:

Good news for those who are sincere! They are the lamps enlightening the path to truth. They uncover the darkness of all who cause mischief. (Bayhaqi)

Abu Darda' related that the Messenger of Allah (s.a.w.s) said:

This world is damned, and it is given to the man of the world. What is in it, having lost its purity and sanctity, is also damned, and is given to the worldly. The only exception is that which is done sincerely for God's sake. (Tabarani)

Abu Dharr al-Gifari reported that the Prophet said:

If someone's heart is sincere in faith, if he protects his soul against spiritual ills, if he is assured and at peace in himself, if his character is honest and upright, if his ears hear the truth and his eyes see reality—then that person is saved from all fears and has realized every hope. (Bayhaqi and Imam Ahmad)

Your ears are a path to your heart; your eyes are its windows. The person whose heart understands what enters it and keeps it safe has found salvation. The sincere person is safe, secure, and at peace in this world and the Hereafter. His actions find divine reward. Allah is pleased with him, and he is pleased with his Lord.

The hypocrite can be cured and find his felicity by pulling the roots of hypocrisy out of his heart. Those roots are the love of the world, the immediate desire and lust for the tastes of this life, and the preference for this life over the Hereafter.

This world is turbid. Its inhabitants have no power. Helpless, they can neither harm nor save anyone. The eyes in people's heads, without the insight of faith, are blind to reality. And the life in this world is temporal. It shrivels, decays, and passes away very fast, while the life in the Hereafter is forever, clear and eternal.

O you who have received the great gift of intelligence from your Lord, use it! Use it to test your deeds and your praise of your Lord. Your Lord knows what you do: it is enough achievement that you know what you are doing. No one else has to know. Is not the One who created you and everything else sufficient for you?

When you evaluate your actions, do not forget to remember the benefits of sincerity and the damage done by hypocrisy in your life. The best decision is to stop exhibiting your good deeds: only this will close the gates of hypocrisy altogether. Yet there are certain circumstances when your actions should be shown in order to encourage others to follow your example.

Even when your intentions are the best, you will be obliged to defend your heart against the evil temptations of your ego. Hypocrisy enters the heart through three gates: the hope that your deeds will be recognized by the public; the wish to be praised and given honor and high position as a reward for your actions; the acceptance and enjoyment of this popularity and the rewards it offers.

We must reject all these temptations. We should consider that in reality, to be publicly singled out—even by people's praise for a devout, pious, honest, and generous person—is sufficient to lead us into the worst troubles of this world and the Hereafter. We must believe that the one who praises us is our enemy, because he is the ally of our ego, our worst enemy. And we must know that succumbing to these temptations will eventually attract Allah's wrath and punishment upon us.

If you resist in this way, your resistance will let you see the ugliness behind the false facade of momentary attraction. Then you will be able to refuse.

The decision to refuse the temptations of hypocrisy is made by the mind. The mind obeys whichever is the stronger; attraction toward, or aversion from, a stimulus.

There are three sure ways to strengthen your resistance to hypocrisy. You can know its causes and effects. You can consider undesirable even the most seemingly attractive results of a hypocritical action or attitude. Best of all, you can make sincerity your purpose in life.

Suppose that, with the purpose of sincerity in your heart, you start performing your prayers. You still may not be aware of the infusion of hypocrisy in your concentration. It whispers to you, urging ambition in your devotions, fear of failure, need of acceptance. Then your heart becomes flooded with hypocrisy. There is no space left to remember the magnificent causes and effects of the lost sincerity. You will experience no aversion to hypocrisy, for both aversion and attraction only occur when we are aware and know the consequences of our actions.

On other occasions, we may realize the insidious penetration into our heart but be unable to oppose it because the taste of the hypocritical state is pleasing to the ego, which is stronger than our will. Many a wise person of knowledge is not safe from this. Such people teach, but their actions do not correspond to their words. The more knowledge they pour out, the deeper they sink into their hypocrisy. They know perfectly well what they are doing, and its consequences. Because they know what they are doing, divine punishment on them will be greater.

No one can escape totally from the insidious infiltration of hypocrisy into his or her being. It is hoped that Allah will forgive the person who fights it even though afflicted with it, if that person does not willfully choose it, want it, enjoy it, or profit from it. The ability to stop the imagination and to be displeased with praise and attention is not in human nature. But intelligence to see the evils of hypocrisy, and the will not to choose it and to fight against it, are within human ability. These can help us at least not to put hypocrisy into action and to attract Allah's compassion.

Aversion to hypocrisy and the ability to resist it only become possible through faith in Allah and abiding with one's religion. Whoever wills to be sincere in actions and in state can protect themselves from the effects of hidden hypocrisy only through the fear of Allah. This is not only a fear of the punishment and wrath of Allah; it is also a fear of losing the love of one's Lord and of His rejection.

This care toward and fear of one's Lord has to exist during and even after every action. Its place is not at the beginning. At the beginning we need an intention containing a firm faith in our sincerity that we hope for nothing other than Allah's approval and pleasure in our forthcoming action. The meaning of a good intention is to start an action with sincerity, purpose, and resolution. Doubt, confusion, and neglect cannot be part of a well-made intention.

A sincere person begins each action with a clear certainty. In the course of the action, the certainty may wear off, and forgetfulness and heedlessness may affect the work.

The fear of Allah is felt by people who are afraid of the consequences of their egotism and hypocrisy.

Theologians are in dispute as to whether fear or hope has more value. Some of them claim that hope best overcomes fear. Others say that fear should supersede hope. So is it lawful when a sincere person with a clear intention of starting to work for Allah's sake, then comes to doubt if his sincerity was true? According to the accepted rule in Islam, "Certainty of sincerity in intention, when doubted by the person in the process of the action, is not annulled by that subsequent doubt." Yet it is commendable to fear and to be anxious that our sincere intentions might be adulterated during the process of our actions, and to pray and supplicate Allah to turn our wrong into right.

The majority of the legalists say that fear should supersede hope.

> Someone asked Saint Rabi`ah al-`Adawiyyah, "What do you count on in your hope to receive Allah's favors?"
> She answered, "On my doubt of the value of any of my actions undertaken for His sake."

Whether fear of Allah or hope of His compassion is more to be counted upon depends on the person and the circumstances. For people just starting to understand the value of religion, fear of Allah is best. For people who, while aware of the traces of egotism, pride, and self-satisfaction in themselves, are lazy and think that some outside circumstance will provide them with what they want, fear of Allah is best.

For the faithful who have studied and know right from wrong, and who are sincere in their attempts to do right, fear and hope of Allah are best. Allah knows best.

"The one who does not wish for others that which he wishes for himself, is not a true believer."

CHAPTER 12

ON ARROGANCE AND HUMILITY

Arrogance is a state in which we are convinced that we have the right to be above others. Justifiable self-regard, without comparing ourselves to others and feeling superior, is not the same thing. That is, at worst, vanity. Arrogance is unlawful in Islam. It is considered to be a disgraceful state.

The opposite of arrogance is to look at ourselves with the intention of truly knowing ourselves. Self-examination is a virtue, and one that is expected of a Muslim. Whether our self-regard is justifiable or not, whether truly in our hearts we believe that we are superior to others or not, if our conceit is exteriorized, manifested, communicated to others by mind or deed, it is a sin. The worst version of this sin occurs when no justification exists for the feeling of superiority we cherish. Allah Most High, one of whose attributes is the Proud One, is the only one with a right to that name.

The only occasion when the attitude of pride is not a sin is when it is manifested against an aggressive, arrogant person or against a tyrannical enemy, when we are waging battle in defense of our religion or country. In fact, to show pride toward an arrogant person is considered to be a good deed.

Jabir related that the Prophet said:

> The only state of pride Allah permits is the one shown in battle or while performing a generous act. (Abu Dawud)

The meaning of pride while helping a person in need is belittling our own generosity while pretending that we could have done much better.

Modesty, to appear less than we are, is commendable. Yet, the exaggeration of humbleness to the extent of appearing abject is a sin. Mu`adh ibn Jabal reported that the Messenger of Allah (s.a.w.s) said:

> Showing excess attachment and appearing abject, reducing oneself to the state of a beggar, does not suit the character of a believer. The only exception is the humbleness of a student toward a teacher, seeking to receive knowledge. (Ibn Adiy)

Only knowledge is worth begging for, and worth humbling ourselves to receive.

To illustrate the right and wrong way to manifest humility, imagine a totally coarse, ignorant person entering into the company of the wise. If these wise people show excessive respect to the newcomer, stand up to greet him, offer him the best place, see him to the door when he is leaving, that is definitely wrong. On the other hand, if they show him kindness so as not to make him feel unwelcome, listen to and answer his questions at the level of his understanding (even if the questions are beneath them), and especially never think of themselves as better than he, doing all they can to make him feel he is their equal, then indeed their behavior is proper.

Another example of unlawful humility in Islam is to beg while we have shelter and food, even if only enough for one day. To give someone a small gift with the hope of receiving a greater benefit is equivalent to begging.

Allah Most High says:

Do no favor seeking gain. (*Mudaththir*, 6).

To go to feasts without being invited is humiliating and a kind of begging. `Abdullah ibn `Umar reported that the Messenger of Allah (s.a.w.s) said:

If a person refuses an invitation, he is revolting against Allah and His Messenger. If someone goes to a feast or a wedding without being invited, he has entered that house as a thief and left as a plunderer. (Abu Dawud)

To seek out, visit, and frequent dignitaries, people in power, high government officials, judges, generals, or influential rich people, with the hope of obtaining benefit from these relationships, is forbidden humility according to our religion, unless these people possess the means of our receiving what is rightfully ours and we are in real need of it. When in the company of such people, to remain standing, to bow, to show excessive respect in action and speech, are demeaning, and the wrong kind of humility as well.

To work hard—even far beneath our qualifications—to support our families, to help with the menial chores of our houses, shopping, cooking, cleaning are commendable signs of true humility. To be ordinary in appearance, to wear inexpensive and worn clothes, to befriend the poor and disadvantaged, to eat simple food and not throw away leftovers, not to seek reputation-building, self-glorifying jobs, not to consider it beneath you to be a shepherd, a gardener, a porter, a carpenter, or a mason—these are signs of true humility. These kinds of manifestations of humility are worthy of great divine rewards, for they resemble the behavior of prophets and saints. But many people do not know it and think of a life like this as reprehensible. They are the arrogant ones who do not know themselves.

Arrogance becomes more dangerous when it is manifested and directed. Some people are arrogant toward human beings. They are not any better than the accursed Devil who refused to obey Allah when He asked all the angels to prostrate to Adam (a.s.). The Devil thought that he was created of fire while Adam was created of earth, and that fire was superior to earth. He did not know himself and he did not know Adam. Therefore he was punished and rejected from Allah's mercy until the end of time.

Some are arrogant toward Allah, like the Pharaoh who said, "I am your Lord, the Supreme." Or like Nimrod, who said to the Prophet Abraham (a.s.), "Your God may be the Lord of the Heavens. I am the lord of this world," and dared to challenge Allah to fight him. Allah drowned the Pharaoh and his armies while they were chasing the Prophet Moses (a.s.) and the children of Israel. Nimrod was killed by a mosquito that devoured his brain.

Some are arrogant toward the Prophet of Allah, like Abu Jahl, who said, "Is this who God chose as His Messenger? Couldn't He have revealed the Qur'an to a celebrated man of Mecca or Medina?"

Allah seals the eyes and ears and hearts of the arrogant so that they cannot know the truth. He declares in the Holy Qur'an:

I shall turn away from My revelations those who are unjustly proud in the Earth. Even if they see every sign, they will not believe in it. And if they see the right path to salvation, they will not take it. If they see the wrong path to error and sin, they will take it. This is because they reject Our messages and are heedless of them. (*A'raf*, 146)

Abu Hurayrah said that the Messenger of Allah *(s.a.w.s)* reported from Allah Himself:

Grandeur is My shirt, majesty is My lower garment. Whoever compares himself to Me is arrogant. I throw him to the Fire and do not regret it. (Abu Dawud)

Ibn Mas`ud related:

The Prophet said, "Whoever has an atom of pride in his heart will not enter Paradise."
Then one of his Companions asked, "What do you say about someone who likes to dress in fine clothes?"
He answered, "Allah is beautiful and likes that which is beautiful. Arrogance is to deny reality and to consider others beneath oneself." (Muslim and Tirmidhi)

Thawban reported that the Messenger of Allah (s.a.w.s) said:

A believer who dies free of debt, treachery, and arrogance enters Paradise. (Tirmidhi)

Anas ibn Malik reported that the Prophet said:

In Hell the proud will be locked in coffins of fire and kept there forever.
(Bayhaqi)

`Abdullah ibn Salam was seen in the marketplace with a heavy load of wood
on his back. Someone said to him, "What makes you do this? Allah has
freed you from doing such chores."

Ibn Salam answered, "I wished to rid myself of all signs of pride with
this, as I heard the Messenger of Allah (s.a.w.s) say, 'The one who has
pride in his heart, even as little as a mustard seed, will not enter Paradise.'"
(Tabarani)

Abu Hurayrah reported that the Messenger of Allah (s.a.w.s) said:

There are three kinds of people Allah Most High will not address nor will
He forgive on the Last Day. They are adulterers, rulers who lie, and poor
people who are arrogant. (Muslim)

During his caliphate, `Umar ibn al-Khattab (r.a.) was marching upon
Damascus with his army. Abu `Ubaydah ibn Jarrah was with him. They
came upon a little lake. Hadrat `Umar descended from his camel, took off
his shoes, tied them together, and hung them on his shoulder. He took
the halter of his camel and together they entered the water. Seeing this
happening in front of the army, Abu `Ubaydah said, "O commander of the
faithful, how can you be so humble in front of all your men?"

Hadrat `Umar answered, "Woe, Abu `Ubaydah, if anyone else other than
yourself thinks this way! Thoughts like this will cause the downfall of the
Muslims. Don't you see? We were indeed a very lowly people. Allah raised
us to honor and greatness through Islam. If we forget who we are and
wish other than Islam, which elevated us, the One who raised us surely will
debase us."

Ibn Tirmidhi reported that the grandfather of `Amr ibn Shu`ayb heard
the Messenger of Allah (s.a.w.s) say:

On the Day of Judgment, the haughty will be raised as small as ants but
in their own countenance. They will be guided by huge hordes of horrors
to a dungeon called Bulis. There they will be fed with poisonous human
excretions like dirty blood and pus.

Muhammad ibn Zayyad reported that when Abu Hurayrah was appointed the governor of Medina, he used to walk into the marketplace with a
load of wood on his back and shout, "Open the way, let the governor pass!"
and others would cry, "Open the way, let the people see their leader pass!"
(Muslim)

Imam Tirmidhi related that Jubayr complained that people thought he was proud. He said, "I ride a donkey, I wear the coarse wool clothes of the poor, I milk my goats myself. I heard the Messenger of Allah (s.a.w.s) say that whoever acts thus is not proud."

Seven qualities are said to be causes of pride: education and knowledge; religious piety; the fame and nobility of one's family and ancestors; physical attractiveness or physical strength; wealth; achievement; and the number of one's admirers and followers. In reality, none of these qualities necessarily produces arrogance. On the contrary, they are positive values for which every person strives. The real cause of arrogance is stupidity, and the inability to comprehend what is offered as knowledge. Yet there is no other medicine but knowledge for curing this stupidity.

A superior education and acquired learning are the first and most dangerous cause of pride. This case is most difficult to cure because its cause is also its medicine. To acquire knowledge is an obligation for every Muslim. Therefore to refuse to learn so as not to be proud of one's knowledge is not a solution for this problem. The solution is in educating ourselves that the superiority of knowledge depends solely on the sincerity of the intention to act upon it. To learn how to apply our knowledge in everyday life and to teach it to others for Allah's sake alone, without any wish to receive compensation or recognition from people, is a whole spiritual and social education in itself. Anyone who has achieved this state will not feel superior to the lowest and most ignorant person in existence.

Ibn 'Umar reported that he heard the Messenger of Allah (s.a.w.s) say:

Whoever seeks knowledge in order to have recourse to something other than Allah, or for the pleasure of anyone except his Lord, might as well prepare himself for punishment in Hell. (Tirmidhi)

Abu Hurayrah related that the Prophet said:

Whoever studies his religion in order to secure his livelihood and to benefit materially, or in order to seek fame, is bound to distort religious knowledge. He will interpret it for his personal purposes, removing all that is holy in knowledge. Such a holder of knowledge will not have even a whiff of the perfumes of Paradise on the Day of Judgment. (Abu Dawud)

Ibn 'Abbas reported that he heard the Messenger of Allah (s.a.w.s) say:

There are two kinds of men of knowledge among my people. One spends all that Allah has taught him freely, offering it to anyone who wants it without accepting anything in return. All the birds in the skies, all the fish in the seas, all the creatures on land pray to Allah for his forgiveness. The other man of knowledge who has received his knowledge from Allah does not share it with any other creature. He keeps it to himself or sells it for the lowly benefits of this world. He thinks his price is high. He does not realize that he is exchanging the finest for the coarse. On the Day of Judgment, this sort of man will be made to wear a collar of fire attached to a chain. A demon of Hell will pull him around and show him to others, shouting, "This is the creature who was stingy with the greatest gift of Allah. Knowledge was given to him, and he sold the most valuable thing in existence for the lowest price: the comforts of temporal life." (Tabarani)

`Usamah Ibn Zayd reported that he heard the Messenger of Allah (s.a.w.s) say:

On the Day of Judgment, a man of knowledge will be thrown into Hellfire. They will tie his intestines to a pole and he will turn round and round like a donkey working in a mill. Other inhabitants of Hell, curious about the punishment, will ask him what terrible sin he committed. He will answer, "I used to teach people to do good but I did not do it myself. I used to teach them not to do wrong, but I did it." (Bukhari, Muslim)

In another tradition reported by `Usamah, the Prophet said:

On the night of my ascension to the Heavens, I saw some people whose tongues were torn from their mouths with red-hot pincers. I asked the angel Gabriel who they were. He answered, "They are those of your people who taught others to do that which they did not do themselves." (Muslim)

Anas ibn Malik reported that the Messenger of Allah (s.a.w.s) said:

The demons of Hell will begin by torturing the men of knowledge who have the whole Qur'an in their memory. When these complain, asking if they were worse than the people who denied Allah, that they should be punished before them, they will be asked, "Are the ones who know and the ones who do not know the same?" (Tabarani and Abu Nuaym)

Anas ibn Malik also reported:

The Prophet said that the holders of knowledge are the inheritors of the prophets. They should be fully trusted by the people as long as they do not become tools in the hands of worldly rulers and are not trapped by the false attractions of this life. But if they are submerged in the world and seek the company of rulers, they become traitors to the station bequeathed to them by the prophets. (Hakim)

Mu`adh ibn Jabal reported:

While we were circumambulating the Ka`bah, I asked the Messenger of Allah, "Who is the worst among men?"

The Prophet said, "O Lord, forgive me! O Mu`adh, why do you ask about bad things? Ask about that which is good. But the answer is that the worst among men are the men of knowledge who behave badly." (Bazzaz)

Abu Hurayrah reported that he heard the Messenger of Allah (s.a.w.s) say:

The ones who suffer the most punishment in Hell are the learned whose teaching did not do anyone any good. (Tahrani, Bayhaqi)

Mansur ibn Za`dan reported that he was told:

The sinners in Hell will complain of the stench coming from some new arrivals to Hell, and they will tell them, "Woe to you! What terrible things you must have done that you add to our misery by the terrible stench you emanate!"

And they will say, "We were men of knowledge, but we did not improve ourselves with it." (Bayhaqi)

Abu Hurayrah and Abu Darda' reported that they heard the Messenger of Allah (s.a.w.s) say:

A wise man is not wise until he acts upon what he knows. (Bayhaqi, Ibn Hibban)

Anas ibn Malik reported that the Prophet said:

There will come a time when many among the devout will be ignorant, and many among the people of knowledge will be sinners. (Hakim)

Abu Sa`id reported that the Prophet said:

Whoever hides from the people something he knows about Islam, the knowing of which would profit the Muslims, will find a bit in his mouth made out of fire on the Day of Judgment. (Ibn Maja)

`Umar ibn al-Khattab reported that the Messenger of Allah (s.a.w.s) said:

As long as people voyage upon oceans and ride over land freely and safely by the permission of Allah, Islam will be victorious. Then will come a time when people will recite the Qur'an and say, "There is no one who understands Allah's words better than we do; there is no one superior to us in knowledge of anything." Those are people from among my people, just like you. Those people! You will know those people. They are the fuel of Hell. (Bazzaz, Tabarani)

Ibn 'Umar reported that he heard the Prophet say:

Whoever claims to be wise is surely ignorant. (Tabarani and Mujahid)

It is indeed rare to find a possessor of knowledge who is also a possessor of conscience, who guards himself against these evils. A wise man is he who sees his shortcomings and is not proud; for whom the more he knows, the more he realizes how little he knows.

Of course, to stop pride, one first has to admit that arrogance in any form whatsoever is a sin, and that only Allah the Proud One is worthy of that attribute.

It is said that only the ones who know can fear Allah. By the same token, only the ones who fear Allah can know. These are free of the sin of keeping their knowledge to themselves, selling it for personal benefit, being proud of it, or becoming guilty of any of the other forms of evil that superior knowledge may induce. These rare servants of Allah are the true inheritors of the wisdom of the prophets who were without exception fearful of their Lord and humble, in spite of being the best and most knowledgeable of all human beings.

That which befits the true servant of Allah is not to have (or at least not to express!) any feeling of superiority toward anyone.

Such a person, when he encounters an ignorant sinner, thinks, "He sins because he does not know, yet I sin in spite of my knowledge. Therefore, he is certainly better than I." When he encounters knowledgeable people, he considers them more devout than himself, for who may judge the quality and quantity of wisdom? When he meets an older person, he considers the elder more devout than himself, for he certainly has had more time to pray. When he sees a younger person, he reflects that he himself has had more time to sin than the youth. When he encounters someone of his own age and status, he considers that while he knows nothing of the life of the other, he knows very well how he has conducted his own life, and something known is more justifiably open to criticism than something unknown. Even when he meets someone who is without faith and openly denies God, he thinks: "How secure is my own faith? How do I know that I will end my days as a believer? And how do I know that this poor man will not be honored by Islam before he leaves this world?" Let him even look upon a dog or a pig, and he will lament that these creatures have not revolted against their Maker, so that there is no judgment nor punishment for them, yet he himself, created as the best of creation, has revolted against his Lord and is deserving of punishment.

These are the good servants of Allah who see themselves clearly and are making their accounting before they are obliged to make it. Engaged in repentance, they have no occasion to criticize others or show pride.

One may object that Allah Most High has ordered us to oppose the faithless and the sinners, so how are we to see ourselves as beneath them? Indeed, we are urged to help such people to mend their ways; and if they cannot be helped, to fight them to prevent their harming others. However, we cannot do this for our own benefit, but only for Allah's sake. We cannot undertake that struggle while thinking that we are the saved and they are the damned. You should know that Allah is aware of the wrongdoings you are hiding from others while you are busy reprimanding them for sins that show. You must consider that in the end you may be worse than the ones you oppose, and fear for yourself, rather than fearing the effects of the acts of the people you blame.

When you are led into a situation in which you are obliged to reprimand a sinner, you should behave like a nurse charged by a great lord to educate his children. That nurse, when necessary, may reprimand and punish the children of the lord, but will never feel superior to them, for he knows that those children are dearer to their father than he is himself. Only Allah knows who is dearest to Him. The best way is to think that everyone else is better in the Lord's opinion than one is oneself.

The second cause of arrogance is a feeling of superiority in one's spiritual and religious state. Someone who has chosen the lifestyle of an ascetic, who has devoted his life to praying, fasting, and meditating, withdrawing from the world, runs the greatest danger of this sin. The real cause of it is very much the same as the cause of pride in one's knowledge. Just as in that case, the lack of knowledge and wisdom is responsible. A pious person should know that our spiritual state as Muslims does not depend on prayer, fasting, meditation, or seclusion from the world. We are given numerous actions in life that bring spiritual rewards, and warn off many others that we are forbidden to pursue. And in whatever we do, we are taught that our intentions, sincerity, and love and fear of Allah are of the greatest importance for our salvation.

Allah Most High indicates that salvation is only possible through the love and fear of Allah, and that the truth of our love and fear of Allah is known only to Him. He says:

Do not feel superior and claim that you are pure. Allah is the one who truly knows those who forbid themselves from doing wrong for the love of Allah. (*Najm*, 32)

The third cause of sinful arrogance is to be proud of one's ancestors and their merits, nobility, and distinction. Is this reasonable, if those attributes are not also one's own? How can we hope that the virtues possessed by somebody else will benefit ourselves? A poet has written:

If you are proud of your forefathers:
You are indeed telling the truth.
Woe to them! How their souls must suffer
That they have fathered such a bad son!
What safety did Cain find in Adam's nobility?
Was Kanan saved from the Flood by being the son of Noah?

Abu Hurayrah reported that the Prophet said:

The one who does not act for himself cannot be saved by his parents.
(Muslim)

The fourth reason that some people are arrogant is their physical beauty. This pride most often afflicts women. Why do they not know that exterior beauty is but temporal and passes very quickly? Allah has created only animals to be attracted to exterior beauty. Allah and the wise look at the beauty of the heart in human beings. The fact is that our beginning is a blood-clot in our mother's womb, and our end is a foul-smelling, decaying corpse thrown into a grave. How attractive can that body be? Its belly is filled with excrement, its bladder with urine. Mucus comes from its nose, spittle from its mouth, blood from its veins, pus from under its skin, its armpits stink. Thinking on all this and more will reduce vanity. In any case, eventually our tight skin will sag and our shiny hair turn into a donkey's tail, and make us feel humble.

The fifth reason for some to be proud is their strength. Physical power, like beauty, is short-lived. Even more temporal and fragile than good looks, strength melts away with a few days of fever or sickness. One need not wait for old age: an accident, a broken bone, takes it away for good. And when you think of it, elephants, bulls, even donkeys are more powerful than men. How can one be proud of a quality in which animals are superior to human beings?

The sixth cause of pride is wealth and fame, and the seventh is numerous followers, students, employees, and dependents. These two reasons are the most unseemly causes of arrogance because they depend on conditions entirely outside of ourselves. These conditions, though so difficult to obtain, can very easily be lost. The sickness of these causes of pride is common to all people, faithful and faithless, honest and dishonest alike. When we find ourselves in these conditions, we feel like kings. When we lose them, we feel ourselves the lowest of the low. How can someone be proud of possessing a thing that pleases a thief when he succeeds in his misdeed?

There are other influences from outside ourselves that may induce arrogance. Hatred and vengeance, which are great sins in themselves, will give birth to yet another great evil: pride. When we are angry at someone above us, especially, our ego will immediately raise us to a level above the superior adversary. We imagine ourselves more righteous, more intelligent, more powerful, closer to Allah. Even if the adversary is right, he is wrong. If he is powerful, that is temporary, he is a soldier of Satan. If he is devout, his devotion is hypocritical. If our enemy wins, then vengeance sets in. The injustice has to be righted! The arrogance of the imagined victim is very long-lasting.

Then there is envy; again a great sin in itself. It forces us into denial of Allah's will, questioning His justice. Why should somebody who is inferior to us be blessed with more sustenance and a better life? Woe to the arrogant who think that they know the value of the envier and the envied, and what each deserves, better than God!

Hypocrisy, to think of ourselves and to behave as other than we truly are, is likewise tied to pride. An arrogant person is truly the worst of hypocrites, for he certainly thinks and behaves as if he is worth more than his actual value. But the person whose arrogance derives from prior hypocrisy has two faces. In public, he sells himself as better than the people who are better than he. But in the presence of a person with whom he is in competition, he pretends to be respectful and humble. Excessive attention to the judgments of others while expecting their good opinion reveals that even simple acts like dressing better in public, living above one's means, putting on airs in company, are signs of the arrogance of the hypocrite.

The only cure for arrogance induced by hatred, envy, or hypocrisy—all greater sins—is to remember in our combat against these that further evils will attach to us if we fail to stop them.

It is best to mention some of the common signs of arrogance so that we do not feel safe from the evil of pride. Suspect the presence of arrogance:

- If you need to be recognized by people and are pleased when they show you signs of respect, such as standing up when you enter a room, saluting you on the street, or paying you compliments. In fact, arrogance should be feared if you do not feel embarrassed and uncomfortable when these things happen.
- If you feel important and pleased when surrounded by admiring companions who insist on walking one step behind you. Abu `Umamah reported:

The Messenger of Allah was walking from his house to the graveyard of

Jannat al-Baqi, and many of his blessed companions were following behind him. He turned and asked them to walk in front of him. When he was asked the reason, he said, "When I heard the shuffling of feet behind me, I feared that pride might enter my heart." (Imam Ahmad, Ibn Maja)

- If you refuse to visit someone, making the excuse that it would serve no purpose.
- If you refuse to sit next to someone whom you consider inferior.
- If you refuse to enter the company of the sick and the lowly.
- If you refuse to do any housework in your home.
- If you refuse to carry heavy loads in public.
- If you refuse to wear cheap or worn clothing.
  Abu `Umamah related that the Prophet said:

To wear old and worn clothing is a sign of the faithful. (Abu Dawud)

- If, while enjoying the invitations of the rich and important, you refuse to accept the invitations of the poor.
- If you are embarrassed to shop for cheap things in inferior markets.
- If you put yourself forward, ahead of other people, on occasions of introduction to important personages.
- If you put yourself forward, in discussions and debates, against what happens to be right, and hope to be convincing nonetheless.

These are just a few samples of behaviors that, if engaged in privately, are signs of arrogance, and if manifested publicly, are signs of both arrogance and hypocrisy.

Love of oneself is a very maleficent character; especially when people are proud of their achievements; worse still if they are enamored of their imagined religious or spiritual state. Such may forget that the honor bestowed on them because of their achievements, as well as those achievements themselves, belong to Allah Most High alone. People forget this because they are unaware and heedless that every person is created by the Creator, and that each person's actions are his destiny decided by Allah. The realization that all is done by His will, and that everything belongs to Him, will cure us of this ill. Then we will be thankful for everything that happens to us or through us, and be obedient to the will of our Lord.

To save ourselves from egoism, it should suffice to see its results in ourselves and others. The egoist thinks of his state as a blessing. He thinks that he knows everything and that he controls his life, and even the lives of others. He is heedless of the suffering he causes for himself and others. He thinks that he is physically, socially, and spiritually on the top of the world. Yet he has no thought for an occasion when he might fall from the heights to which he has climbed, nor does he recognize any other power other than the one he imagines he possesses. He takes himself as his own God—and he will be devastated when Allah acts upon what He says:

Woe to the one whose evil deed is made fair-seeming to him, so that he considers it good. (*Fatr*, 8)

Anas ibn Malik reported that the Prophet said:

Three things are devastating: to believe in the good of avarice, to cater to one's lust, and to be an egoist. (Bayhaqi)

The same source reported that the Prophet said to his Companions:

Even if you have never committed a sin, I would be afraid for you of the greatest sin: pride in one's spiritual state and self-regard.

To know some of the vast benefits of humbleness encourages us to fight the evil of arrogance. Humbleness is the profession of prophets and saints, of the truly wise and pious servants of Allah. It is this character praised by Allah that brings one to the highest spiritual levels.

To be humble, we have to know ourselves: where we come from, where we are going in this life. We must be aware of the facts and exclude the inventions of our ego and imagination. The ego is not only resistant to accepting religious norms but also defies reason and awareness of facts. It prefers imagination and exaggeration. It loves heights and loves itself. It likes to see itself up above everything and everybody. It is blind and deaf to reality. To know ourselves, we have to stop doting on ourselves and become objective. We must look at ourselves with neutral eyes, the eyes of the norms of revealed law. Surely every believer will be able to locate generosity between avarice and wastefulness; honest work between ambition and laziness; courage between brazenness and cowardice; hope between doubt and rigidity. The median is the center of perfect balance. That is what one has to discover in oneself. But because our ego is apt to push us upwards, it is best to consider ourselves as lesser than we have found ourselves to be. That is what humbleness is.

The safest state of being is to consider oneself lower than everybody else. That was the way of the generation of Muslims after the Prophet.

Imam Shibli said:

Abasing myself stopped the aggression of my enemies.

Abu Sulayman al-Darani (q.s.) said:

If the whole world tried, they could not have reduced my self-regard to a lower level.

Can you sincerely bring yourself to admit that you are even worse than the accursed Devil? If not, then think! The Devil and those like him are where they are because Allah chased them out of His mercy, while He has blessed us with faith, the ability to obey, and His Beloved as our guide. These and all the good we possess are His gifts. If we do right, it is from Him, not any doing of ourselves. When we behave like Satan, it is our own doing and we have no excuse for having tyrannized ourselves. Yet we do not blame ourselves: either we ignore or we forget our faults. We do not even know our faults, yet we count our every little deed as if it were a great achievement. The unknown is always infinitely greater than the known. May Allah protect us, but our unknown wrongs, unadmitted by us, may by their weight pull us to the depths. There we may end up sharing the punishment of those who were chased from the mercy of Allah. When one reasons this way, indeed one should feel humble.

Ibn `Abbas reported that the Prophet said:

Surely Allah Most High ordered us to be humble. I tell you that none among you shall belittle any other, nor are you permitted to insult them. (Abu Dawud)

Rakb al-Misri reported that the Messenger of Allah (s.a.w.s) said:

I bring good tidings to the one who is humble while mindful of the honor of being created a human being; also to the one who has given up his self-regard, yet does not beg for favors; to the generous one who spends freely for Allah's sake from what he possesses; to the one who seeks the company of the wise and knowledgeable; to the one who is compassionate to those in need. I bring good tidings to the one who gains his livelihood lawfully with his own hands; to the one who cleanses his heart; to the one whose inner beauty shines in his face; to the one who holds back his anger; to the one who does not say what is not to be said; and to the knower who acts upon his knowledge. (Tabarani)

Abu Sa`id reported that the Prophet said:

Whoever humbles himself for Allah's sake, Allah raises to the highest levels. Whoever is arrogant against Allah, Allah reduces to the lowest of the low. (Ibn Hibban)

Abu Hurayrah reported that the Messenger of Allah (s.a.w.s) said:

When someone is humble toward fellow Muslims, Allah raises that person's state. When someone tries to belittle fellow Muslims and claims to be better than they, Allah lowers that person far below the others. (Tabarani)

Sometimes some people will abase themselves in front of the powerful out of fear, or in front of the rich because they want to get something from them, or in front of people in general in order to receive their sympathy or pity, or simply to be accepted by them. All these and similar shows of hypocritical humbleness are fraudulent and wrong.

CHAPTER 13

ON ENVY

A ccording to the knowers of Islam, envy is defined as the wish that a person whom one dislikes should not receive a good that Allah has bestowed upon him, although his having this gift does not in any way harm anyone in this world or the Hereafter. Or else it is to wish that he might lose what he has already received. To agree with someone who feels this way is also considered to be envy.

If envy comes upon you unintentionally and is undesired, so that you feel ashamed of it, scholars of morals rule that it is excusable.

Envy becomes one of the greater sins when one is guilty of intention, premeditation, and desire to harm some innocent person, hoping he might lose what is due to him and trying to influence events so that he does. Some authorities say that envy is a sin only if one acts upon one's envy. Abu Hurayrah reported that the Prophet said:

> My Lord in His mercy does not consider sinful the maleficent thoughts of my people as long as they do not declare them or act upon them. (Bukhari and Muslim)

An unintended urge or thought that comes upon us can be controlled and left unexpressed, for

> On no soul does Allah place a burden greater than it can bear. (*Baqarah*, 286)

Once such things are not acted upon, they cannot be considered sinful. And such divine mercy is not a privilege of Muslims alone, but applies to all creatures, who are all the people of that Prophet who was sent as Allah's mercy upon the whole world.

Ibn Abi Dunya reported that the Prophet said, "There are three dangers from which nobody is able to save himself: doubt, ill luck, and envy."

We may suggest a solution to these three problems: When you are in doubt or consider something to be bad luck or are envious, you should simply not act upon these impressions, not even contemplate them or talk about them. Then, if Allah wills, they will not pose a danger.

Someone asked the saint Hasan al-Basri his opinion on envy. He said, "It is a painful and distressing feeling, yet if you don't act upon it, it will not harm you."

One might ask how is it that denying Allah or inventing deviations in religion, even if not expressed, are considered to be great sins, while other ugly characteristics such as envy, arrogance, and hypocrisy, if unexpressed or without effect on other people, may be excused. Are they not all subjective, hidden in one's heart, and perhaps unintentional? It must be realized that faithlessness, disregard for religious law, and inventing one's own law, are beliefs that affect one's whole being, becoming an identity and determining all of one's actions. Envy, arrogance, and hypocrisy are only part of a person's character. They are isolated traits. Although they are considered sinful in themselves, when by the effort of the envier, envy is kept out of action, it is like an idea that has not taken form. Therefore, it does not exist, and is not blameworthy.

Unfortunately, if these ugly faults exist in us, they very seldom stay hidden unless we have made it our life's goal to cleanse our hearts from evil influences and to beautify them with characteristics meeting with Allah's pleasure.

A hypocrite pretends to be an obedient servant of Allah and does the right thing in public. On these occasions he may even appear to be inwardly praying or being meditative. Although those acts in themselves are commendable, as capitulations to insincerity they become sinful. However a person afflicted by envy, when he prevents himself from manifesting his feelings, acts in opposition to what envy demands. Therefore one who is smitten by this ugly state but does not act upon it is forgiven.

(Arrogance, selfishness, is usually not a temporary state but a constant characteristic, like being a disbeliever or inventing one's own religion. Therefore it is particularly evil. Allah knows best.)

There is also a kind of envy in which one wishes for oneself what some other person has. Such an envier does not wish the other person to lose the thing; he only wants it for himself as well. If the object of this desire is a worldly benefit, it is a permissible ambition. If it is directed toward someone else's religious and spiritual superiority, so that one wishes and tries to be like him, this kind of envy is even commendable.

Another state related to envy is resentment felt toward someone who has many benefits, yet does not use what he has either for the enhancement of his spiritual state or for the advancement of his religious community. On the contrary, his wealth, power, or intelligence is used to sin and to create discord among the believers. In such circumstances, to wish that what such a person possesses should be taken away, and even to act upon the wish, may be considered as a pious act of jealousy.

Abu Hurayrah reported that the Messenger of Allah (s.a.w.s) said:

> Surely Allah is jealous for His good servants. So should the faithful be for each other. Allah's jealousy for the faithful is against the temptations of evil. (Bukhari)

This commendable jealousy is a protective attitude toward someone dear, aimed at preventing any wrong from coming upon him. Allah is jealous of human beings to protect them from setting up partners to Him, giving themselves false gods. And the worst sign in human beings, which separates us from our Lord, is the thought that we are free—free to do whatever we wish without considering whether it is right or wrong. The faithful should be jealous for their own selves and for their families and others entrusted to them against misbehavior, revolt against Allah, or acts or tendencies that will lead to either. We should be jealous of anyone who might be instrumental in leading us and our dependants toward evil. That is one of the most important necessities of our religion.

Abu Hurayrah reported:

Sa`d ibn `Ubadah came to the Messenger of Allah (s.a.w.s) and asked, "O Messenger of Allah, if I catch a man who is committing adultery with my wife, should I leave him alone unless there were four witnesses to the act?"

The Prophet said, "Yes."

Sa'd said, "I hope this is not your personal judgment. By Allah, if I hadn't heard this order from you, I would finish off such a man with my sword, four witnesses or not!"

Then the Prophet said to those present: "Listen to me well. If Sa`d thinks he is jealous, I am more jealous than he, and Allah is the most jealous of all." (Muslim)

This quality of protectiveness must not be confused with the ordinary jealousy between men and women, or between friends and competitors.

Hadrat `A'ishah recounted:

One night the Prophet left my room and I became jealous, thinking that he was going to one of his other wives, and followed him. When the Messenger of Allah (s.a.w.s) saw me, he said, "What is happening to you, `A'ishah? Are you jealous?"

I answered, "Indeed, it is normal for a woman like me to feel jealous over someone like you."

Then the Prophet said, "I see that you have come with your own devil."

And I said, "Does everyone have a private devil?"

He said, "Indeed, they do."

I asked, "Do you also?"

And the Prophet said, "Yes, but by the help of Allah, I was able to make my devil into a Muslim and submit to Allah Most High." (Muslim)

The cure of envy is through its opposite: the antidote is wishing people well. To wish well for people is a kind of beneficence to which our religion orders us. That is especially so when we see that the abundant blessings poured upon someone are bringing spiritual as well as material benefits to that person and to the people around him. Then we should not only wish that his good fortune lasts and increases, but try to help see that it does.

Tamim al-Dari reported:

The Prophet said, "The practice of religion is to wish others well."

Someone asked, "Specifically whom should we wish well?"

He answered, "Allah; His words in the Qur'an; the leaders of the people; and all Muslims." (Muslim)

A part of helping people to obtain the good things we wish for them is to advise them. Hudhayfah (r.a.) reported that the Messenger of Allah (s.a.w.s) said:

Whoever does not spend effort to give good advice for the well-being of other Muslims is not one of us. Whoever does not remember Allah, His Messenger, the leaders of Muslims, and all the believers, think well of them and wish well for them morning and night, is not truly one of us. (Tabarani)

Envy, in addition to being maleficent in itself, becomes an instrument to bring upon the envier at least eight other major evils:

The first is that envy may erase the rewards we hope to receive from our devotions, good deeds, and obedience to Allah. Abu Hurayrah related that the Messenger of Allah (s.a.w.s) said:

Beware of envy, because it burns to ashes all of one's good deeds. (Abu Dawud)

Although according to religious law a sin does not cancel a good deed, in the end greater sins overwhelm a person's good deeds and may drive one to faithlessness in this world and overturn the balance of fate when good deeds are weighed against sins on the Day of Judgment.

Zubayr ibn `Awwam reported that the Prophet said:

You have inherited some of the bad habits of those before Islam: envy and hostility among yourselves. Both shave parts of you all. I am not talking about shaving your hair. These bad behaviors shave off your faith. I vow upon the One who holds Muhammad's soul in His hand that unless your faith is perfect, you will not be able to enter Paradise. And as long as you do not love each other for Allah's sake, your faith is not perfect. Shall I teach you something that will help you love each other? Greet each other saying "Allah's peace and compassion and blessings be upon you." (Tirmidhi)

The second evil that envy may cause is revolt against our Maker, because the envier gossips, lies, curses, fights against the one he envies unjustly, although his victim does not deserve it. This is tyranny, which Allah detests. Damrata ibn Sa'lebe reported that the Messenger of Allah (s.a.w.s) said:

> People are considered to be doing good for each other as long as they are not envious of each other. (Tabarani)

The third evil that envy may bring upon us is the anger of the Prophet and the loss of the opportunity of his intercession on the Day of Judgment. `Abdullah ibn Busr reported:

> The Messenger of Allah said, "The envier who envies, the two-faced hypocrite, and the sorcerer who tells of the future do not belong to me, nor I to them." Then he recited the verse from the Qur'an:
> Those who tyrannize a believing man or woman by accusing them of a sin they have not committed are liars, and will bear a heavy load of sin. (*Ahzab*, 58) (Tabarani)

The fourth danger of envy is that it may transport one to the gates of Hell. Both Ibn `Umar and Anas ibn Malik reported:

> The Messenger of Allah said, "There are six kinds of people who because of their six faults will be sent to Hell even before being judged on the Day of Judgment." Someone asked who they were. The Messenger of Allah answered, "Tyrannical rulers because of their injustice; bigots because of their idolatry; celebrated people because of their arrogance; dishonest businessmen because of their cheating and lying; the people of backward places because of their ignorance; and the people who know better because of their envy." (Daylami)

The fifth maleficence of envy is its effect on the person envied. If not checked, it may cause disasters for its object. That is why Allah orders people to take refuge in Him from the attack of the envier, just as He asks us to take refuge in Him from the temptations of the accursed Devil. Mu`adh ibn Jabal reported that the Messenger of Allah (s.a.w.s) said:

> When you receive in abundance from your Lord that which you needed, keep it a secret. For anyone who is thus blessed will suffer the envy of others. (Tabarani)

The sixth pain that envy brings is the totally unnecessary trouble, hardship, and suffering that envy causes to the envier himself. A saintly man among the Muslims of the second generation after the Prophet, Ibn Sammak, has said:

I have never seen a tyrant who appears to be a victim like the envier. He is constantly troubled and in pain, his mind has abandoned him, and he is continuously punished by none other than himself.

The seventh ill that envy brings is blindness of the heart, which becomes unable to see reality. Sufyan al-Thawri said:

If you can avoid being envious of others, you will be quick to understand all and everything.

And finally, envy is a barrier that prevents us from ever reaching our wish or our goal, whatever it is. For when envy affects us, we are not able to see the real causes and effects of things when they happen, nor do we receive the sympathy and help of anybody in obtaining what we hope to achieve. It is said that a person who is afflicted with envy will never be a leader of men.

There are two encouragements to help us resist envy. One is intellectual and the other is practical. Intellectually, we have to be convinced that the evils envy causes in our daily life and our spiritual life, both in this world and the Hereafter, must be blamed on ourselves alone. The one we envy is totally innocent and our envy is not ever going to cause him any harm. On the contrary, it may do him good here, and certainly will enhance his spiritual life in the Hereafter. On the religious level, we must realize that our envy is a sign that we neither accept nor believe in God's will and justice: it indicates that we are critical of God, even angry at Him. This is close to denial and a great sin. Meanwhile the one whom we envy will not lose Allah's blessings: perchance they may even increase, and certainly he is not sinning. In the Hereafter, as an innocent victim of tyranny, he will benefit. Each word, each action the envier spends against his victim is a spiritual gift to him that will be deducted from the envier's good deeds and given to the envied one on the Day of Judgment. And in this life, certainly, public opinion will be against the tyrant and his condemnation will be a victory for the victim.

Practically, we may resist the feeling of envy coming upon us by an effort to turn things around. If you have an urge to talk against the one who attracts your envy, you should praise him instead. If you feel superior to him, you should behave humbly toward him. If your envy demands that you work against the one you envy, you should force yourself to be kind and generous toward him. Instead of cursing him and hoping he will lose the thing you envy, you should pray to Allah to increase His blessings upon him.

These attempts may not be sufficient to prevent us from envy if we have this bad character well rooted in us. To uproot envy from our being for once and all, we have to analyze the causes of this bad habit and eliminate them. There are six principal origins of envy in human beings: egotism, arrogance, fear, ambition, bad intentions, and vengefulness.

1. Egotism is the conviction that nobody has any right to preference over oneself. An egotist cannot bear the thought that somebody might claim to be superior to him because of attaining more wealth or knowledge or higher position or esteem or any other qualities that are better than what he himself possesses. When other people also agree to the superiority of his adversary, he may well wish him dead. If an egotist detaches himself by not comparing himself to people who are better off than he and not wishing them to be reduced to a level below him, but remains content with his state, comparing himself to others who are not as fortunate as himself so that he becomes thankful, then he has found his cure for envy.

2. Arrogance is less an acquisition than it is an aspect of a person's character. Usually an arrogant person's pride is not justified by any quality he possesses. That is why when others truly possess the qualities the arrogant one imagines are his, he wishes their loss, since he fears his rivals may ascend to a state superior to his own. The cure for this is in trying to know oneself, as well as in recognizing admirable qualities in others and respecting them. If you are not able to admit any inferiority because of the rooted evil of your arrogance, then imitating humility may help to save you from the disastrous effects of your condition, and one day your imitation may become real.

3. Fear is usually created by a real or imaginary adversary to whom we might lose whatever we have. We may be afraid to lose our life, our well-being, our possessions, our position, our honor, our love, our neighbors' esteem. Then we become envious of anything that may come into the hands of our adversary, since we fear it will strengthen him against us. This is perhaps the commonest cause of envy. We find this competitiveness not only among the highest officials of the government and highly placed people of business, and among religious scholars and respectable people of knowledge, but in every home between husband and wife or among children jealous for attention or between men and women competing for someone's love.

4. Envy caused by ambition is related to envy caused by the fear of losing what we have. The difference is that while the latter is defensive, the first urges us to attack. The ambitious person feels secure in what he has, but wants something that is in somebody else's hand. He wants to be on top with nobody above him, and he wants to be recognized as such. Because of this, nobody is safe from him. If he learns that somebody at the other end of the world is above himself, he will feel competitive and become envious of him. The ambitious one is usually envious of other people in the field in which he feels he excels, whether that is in possessions, in a profession, in strength, or in looks. But sometimes he may be jealous of qualities and

possessions of other people that have made them renowned even when he has no wish to excel in their fields. For the strongest motivation driving an ambitious person to be envious has little to do with real competition, not even with reality. All he wants is to be praised.

5. Some people have bad intentions and thoughts almost indiscriminately against everybody. They wish no one to have anything good. They are not arrogant or ambitious, they are not even jealous of other people's good fortune and covetous for themselves. They are simply negative. They suffer when they hear praise of somebody they don't even know; they suffer at news that something good has happened. When they hear about a disaster that has befallen a stranger, they are happy and wish that other people might suffer the same misfortune. It is as if any good received by anybody has somehow been taken away from them. If anyone loses anything, it is as if they gain it themselves. The people for whom they wish the worst are not necessarily their enemies. They may not even know them. This sickness is the worst kind of envy, practically impossible to cure unless such a person fully realizes his sickness, wishes to be cured, and is ready to go through a long period of education at the hands of an enlightened teacher.

6. Envy caused by vengefulness is graver than any of the other causes, because vengeance is a disaster capable of destroying lives. There are three aspects of vengeance to be considered. The first is that we must know what vengeance really is: a destructive feeling of hatred toward some person or group of people, or even toward an idea or a concept, that urges us not only to feel justified but even obliged to destroy our adversary.

According to religious teaching, this feeling (unless produced by genuine injustice) may be unlawful even if it is not exteriorized or acted upon. Also, someone may become incensed by a just action taken against him to prevent him from doing wrong, or to force him to do right. If he reacts vengefully, he is certainly sinning.

If we are wronged, we should try to right the wrong. If we are incapable of exacting our rights, then instead of being vengeful we should leave matters in the hands of God and wait for justice on the Day of Judgment. Allah Most High says:

Whoever forgives and makes reconciliation, his reward is due from Allah. (*Shura*, 40)

and

Let forgiveness be a part of your nature, guide people to do good, and do not associate with the ignorant. (*A'raf*, 199)

Abu Hurayrah reported that the Messenger of Allah (s.a.w.s) said:

Allah gives His promise and honor to the one who forgives and the one who behaves humbly for the sake of Allah; and generosity never decreases anyone's riches. (Tirmidhi)

If we forgive someone who has done us wrong when we are unable to obtain his just punishment, that is commendable. But if we forgive the one who has done us wrong while we could easily have him punished, it is highly praiseworthy.

In some exceptional circumstances, it is better to pursue your right than to forgive. These are the cases where forgiving the injustice would encourage the wrongdoer and cause him to tyrannize others, whereas fighting for your right might stop him. However in such cases we must be very careful not to try to obtain more than what was taken from us. The punishment must be equal to the wrong done and never in excess, because in that case, the victim would be tyrannizing the tyrant.

The second aspect of vengeance is that there are many evils that a vengeful person both causes and suffers himself. Among them are envy, taking pleasure in other people's misfortunes, belittling, lying, gossiping, giving people's secrets away, mocking people, tyrannizing, hiding the truth, and preventing justice. All these darken the heart, hurt others, and cause a person to sin.

Wasila ibn Eskaa reported that the Prophet said:

Do not rejoice at the misery of your brother. For if you do, Allah will give him well-being, and try you with calamities. (Tirmidhi)

To rejoice at misfortunes that befall your adversary, especially to believe them a response to your prayers asking for his punishment, is certainly worthy of blame. If someone you dislike is made to suffer, you should consider that it may be a test of how you will react, and fear Allah's retribution. Instead of feeling avenged, you should feel sad and pray that the misfortune be lifted from your enemy. Only when the punishment of your enemy will surely prevent him from tyrannizing others, and may be a lesson to other tyrants, does a feeling of satisfaction at his difficulties become other than condemnable.

Even between friends, when one is unjust to the other and causes him harm, the victim stops talking to his fellow and cuts all relations. Abu Hurayrah related that the Prophet said:

It is not lawful for a believer to be angry at another believer for more than three days. When they meet, they should salute each other. If both do, they will share Allah's pleasure. If one does not respond, he will be sinning. (Abu Dawud)

In another version of the same tradition, it is said:

Whoever is angry and hostile toward a believer for over three days is at risk of Hellfire.

This reconciliation dictated by the Prophet only relates to animosity between believers pertaining to worldly affairs. If the matter pertains to moral or religious affairs, and if an immoral and irreligious person is guilty of persecuting a decent person, it is permissible, in fact advisable, for him to seek justice and to keep away from the guilty party.

According to our religion, whether a person unjustly maltreated by another belittles his adversary, acts arrogantly, lies or gossips about him, gives away unsavory secrets of his opponent, makes ugly jokes about him, causes him pain in any way, injures his relationship with his family and friends, prevents him from performing his obligations to others, or prevents him from receiving mercy and forgiveness, he himself is sinning. Such are the sins that vengefulness brings upon us.

Ibn `Abbas related that the Prophet said:

If a person is without three bad characteristics, Allah may forgive his other sins. They are setting up partners to Allah, engaging in sorcery, and indulging in vengefulness and hatred against Muslims. (Tabarani)

In another tradition, Jabir ibn `Abdullah related that the Messenger of Allah (s.a.w.s) said:

On every Monday and Thursday the angels report the states of all humanity. All who have realized, admitted, and repented their sins are forgiven, except for the vengeful, who cannot repent because of their vengeance. (Tabarani)

In yet another tradition from the same source related by Mu`adh ibn Jabal, the Messenger of Allah (s.a.w.s) said:

On the night of the 15th of the month of *Sha`ban*, Allah Most High looks upon all His creation with love and compassion and forgives their sins, except for the ones who take other gods besides Him and the ones who seek vengeance. (Tabarani)

The third aspect of vengeance is that one of its principal causes is anger.

CHAPTER 14

ON ANGER

A furious person who does not have the strength to take revenge swallows his anger. Then his inner being becomes inflamed with vengefulness, destroying him.

Wrath is a passion produced by the agitation of the blood in the heart at an encounter with danger. It is also a release of anger, which comforts a person after being unjustly hurt. In some cases it is a necessary feeling, as the world and sacred things may be protected by it.

Courage is a characteristic praised by people, religion, and justice alike. Yet both its lack and its extreme are blameworthy. The lack of courage is called cowardice. That is a sickness of the heart that renders one paralyzed, unable to act to help either oneself or others. The coward becomes a rag under everyone's feet, attracting tyranny and injustice from certain people, and thereby causing them to sin.

Our Lord says in a Divine tradition:

In defense of your rights, let the enemy find both patience and valor in you. Neither let your sense of gentleness and compassion prevent you from executing Allah's orders against those who have broken the Divine Laws.

Hadrat `Ali reported that the Prophet said:

The best of my people are those whose strength of religion is like steel. (Bayhaqi, Tabarani)

To rid yourself of your fears, you should face what you fear and gradually force yourself to fight it. And you should remind yourself that while fear surely will lead you to defeat, in courage there is hope of victory, no matter how strong the enemy is, if you persevere.

On the other hand, an excess of anger becomes a sickness of the heart called fury. It causes great damage and injury to the one who is furious, perhaps more so than to his adversary. Worse, it is a contagious sickness, infecting in full force whoever is around. Fury renders a person totally mindless and unaware of the consequences of his ravings and violence.

The opposite of fury is forbearance or gentleness. This quality enables one to be patient, considerate, and calm instead of flying into passion when encountering an unpleasant and aggressive situation. As the effect of anger is violence and destruction, so the effect of forbearance is compassion and peace of mind. If we were able to remember that during the very few seconds before the flame of fury envelops us, we might be able to save ourselves.

There are four medicines to cure anger. We can use our intelligence to realize the consequences of our violence. We can take certain actions to prevent anger's flaring up. We can foresee and prevent the occasions that may create anger. And we can learn forbearance.

Emotions are much swifter than reasoning. But if you are intelligent and experienced enough to be firm with yourself even for a short while before the explosion of anger, you may be able to stop its occurrence. That is only possible when the reason for anger is slight and not devastating. If you know and have the time to consider the following four losses suffered through expressing anger, and the seven following benefits you may reap by suppressing your fury, the recollection may save you.

Intelligence demands we consider the consequences of our actions that are against our interests. The worst result of fury is a loss of all control. This in turn can make us do or say something so awful that it corrupts and subverts our faith. It can even lead a person to lose faith and become an infidel.

Bahz ibn Hakim related that his grandfather heard the Prophet say:

Anger subverts religious feeling as bitter substances spoil honey. (Bayhaqi, Tabarani)

You should also consider that in that rabid condition you are liable to inflict great unjust pain upon your adversary—especially if you are more powerful than your enemy. You should realize that Allah is All-Powerful, and on the Day of Judgment may inflict upon you a punishment whose extent cannot be imagined.

If you attack your enemy in anger, you should expect retaliation from him, and it may perhaps be much harsher than the punishment you have inflicted yourself. Furthermore, you will never know when it may come. The anxiety will poison your days for a long time, unless reconciliation is reached.

If you were to see yourself in a state of fury, if you looked in a mirror, you would see that your face changes from that of a human being to that of a wild animal. And it is not only the expression on our faces, but the whole of our rational human nature that turns into the worst of animal nature.

Even if we are unable totally to prevent the negative feeling, if we simply manage to stop expressing our anger, we may save ourselves from the disasters mentioned above.

You may find it helpful to remind yourself of the seven benefits you can reap by swallowing your anger.

1. Allah Most High says that He has prepared His Paradise for those who are able to swallow their anger and forgive the ones who did them wrong.

2. If someone has the strength to obliterate his enemy but restrains himself, Allah promises he may choose his own rewards on the Day of Judgment. Sahl ibn Sa`d heard the Messenger of Allah (s.a.w.s) say:

> He who has the strength, the opportunity, and favorable conditions for success in expressing anger by violence, yet restrains himself, will be shown to the resurrected crowds on the Day of Judgment as an honored servant of Allah and asked to choose his own rewards. (Abu Dawud, Tirmidhi)

3. Anas ibn Malik reported that the Prophet said:

> Allah Most High abandons the punishment due to anyone who can abandon his own anger. (Tabarani)

4. Ibn `Umar reported that the Prophet said:

> There is nothing a servant of Allah may swallow that is considered as praiseworthy as the swallowing of anger. (Ibn Maja)

5. Allah protects from misfortunes and afflictions whoever protects himself from the violation of anger.

6. Allah's compassion reaches whoever escapes from the battlefield of the manifestation of his anger.

7. Allah loves the one who can put out the fire of fury in his heart. Ibn `Abbas reported that the Messenger of Allah (s.a.w.s) said:

> Whoever possesses these three qualities will receive the compassion of Allah and is made worthy of His love: to be thankful for all that the Lord gives; to forgive instead of punishing when one is wronged; to be able to restrain oneself from expressing one's anger and hurting people. (Hakim)

Over and above these seven benefits that we may hope to receive by suppressing our anger, there is a much greater reward if we are able to forgive the cause of our anger. Impatient and weak as we are, if we can manage to forgive, how should Allah the All-Powerful and Most Merciful not forgive our sins in return? Indeed He says in a Divine tradition:

> Forgive and forget! Don't you want Allah to forgive your wrongdoings?

The anger that bursts out so quickly after the initial emotional reaction to an irritation can be subdued by four measures to be taken immediately:

The first is to make a ritual ablution with cold water. `Atiyyah reported that the Messenger of Allah (s.a.w.s) said:

> Anger comes from Satan and Satan is created from fire. Fire can only be put out by water. So whenever one of you is stricken by anger, make an ablution. (Abu Dawud)

The second remedy is to sit if you are standing, and to lie down if you are sitting. Abu Dharr al-Gifari reported that the Prophet said:

> If you become angry sit down; if it does not pass, lie down. (Abu Dawud)

The third remedy is to take refuge in Allah. Sulayman ibn Sured related:

> Once, in the presence of the Prophet, two people cursed each other. Their faces became bright red from anger. The Messenger of Allah said, "I know a phrase that, if you would have said it, the anger you feel would have totally left you. Say *A`udhu bi-Llahi min ash-shaytan ar-rajim* ('I take refuge in Allah from the accursed Devil')." (Bukhari, Muslim)

To achieve total freedom from the maleficent effects of anger, we must study the causes and effects of negativity and try to avoid them. As we have already learned, the worst causes of anger are arrogance, selfishness, and excessive ambition. If someone afflicted with one of these moral ills feels slighted in the smallest thing he imagines to be his due, he erupts with fury. Yet if the same sort of short exchange should happen to somebody else, it would have no negative effect whatsoever. The difficult cures for arrogance, selfishness, and ambition have already been mentioned.

Then there are a number of exterior causes, each not too grave by itself, which may create anger in some people. They include bad jokes, criticism, opposition, lies, gossip, duplicity, harsh discussions and debates, stubbornness, cursing, hitting, destroying property, stealing, inequity, and so forth. All this may be summarized as tyrannical behavior, which invariably produces a negative reaction in the majority of people. Certainly one should never participate in such behavior. And unless you have patience and strength of will, compassion and ability to forgive, you should escape from places where tyrannical people are present.

There are some people who consider anger to be a sign of manliness, valor, zeal and ardor, self-respect and a sense of honor—thus something commendable. This is stupidity, and one sign of a diseased mind. Indeed stupid or sick people are liable to get angry more quickly and more often than intelligent and healthy people. They may even be proud of it.

Alas! There are some scholars and teachers who preach the truth of religion in a harsh manner, blaming their listeners with sins they may not have committed, threatening them with the wrath of God. They become causes of anger. A house of worship is no place for anger. Those who provoke it there are none other than hypocrites and pompous, arrogant, and selfish creatures. For even if what they say is true, by the tone of their speech, the words become their own instead of God's. Then instead of preventing people from sinning, they cause them to sin by inciting them to fury.

Anyone who advises people to do right ought first to know certainly what the right is. That certainty is in the Words of Allah—in the Holy Qur'an and in the words and actions of the Messenger of Allah, which were not his own but came from Allah Most High.

Next he must make sure that the people whom he is addressing can understand what he says. He also has to be so convincing that they will agree with what he says. And the advice must be such that people are able to act upon it once it is given. If any one of these conditions is missing, it is best not to say anything at all. Obviously kind and sweet and encouraging words are the primary means of obtaining a useable result.

Finally, if the one who preaches does not do what he advises others to do, his words will have no positive effect whatsoever.

As for people who are listening to advice, they ought to consider the good intentions and fervor of the speaker, even if what he says is offered in an aggressive way. They should consider the truth of the words, not the tone in which they are presented. If the words are critical of the behavior of the audience, even if that criticism is unjustified, it is best to remember the principle that those who criticize us are our friends, since they are the enemy of our enemy, our evil-commanding ego, while the ones who praise us are our enemies, since they are the friends of our enemy, our ego.

How often a stone thrown at something else accidentally falls on our heads and enrages us against the one who cast it! Such unintended events hurt us or the ones we love or our property and create angry retaliation, and retaliation to our retaliation, sucking yet others who are totally innocent into the conflict. All this results in wars. In order to avoid the accidental causation of anger, people must be heedful of what they are doing, especially when undertaking actions that may be dangerous. And if perchance our actions cause unexpected harm to someone, we should immediately ask for forgiveness and try to compensate the harm done. In such circumstances, the one who has suffered from harm should realize that the negative act was accidental and show patience and acceptance and excuse the person who caused the accident.

Yet another cause of anger is excessive desires and demands from the life of this world. Often, when we wish for a thing that is not our due, if we consider our actual state rather than identifying with the state of those who have what we want, we can reconcile ourselves to what we already possess. But the poor want what the rich have. And when they ask for it and are refused, both the poor and the rich are angry. The one who wants what is not his due is guilty of arrogance, while the one who won't part with what he holds is guilty of avarice.

When a person is promised something and the one who made the promise breaks his word, again anger may arise on both sides. Abu Sa`id al-Khudri reported that the Prophet said:

> On the Day of Judgment there will be a big sign pointing behind all those who have promised something and broken their word. (Muslim)

If we make a promise that is conditional, therefore breakable, we should warn the other party about the condition. Otherwise, even when the excusing situation arises, breaking our word will be unlawful for keeping one's word is a religious duty.

Promising something while knowing perfectly well that the promise cannot be kept is treachery, which is a great sin. Its opposite, trustworthiness, is one of the great religious accomplishments. Anas ibn Malik reported that the Prophet said:

> A person who is not trustworthy does not have faith. The religion of the one who does not keep his word is not true religion. (Tabarani)

Treachery and trustworthiness do not merely apply to the loss or security of material things. They go much deeper than that. Abu Hurayrah reported that the Messenger of Allah (s.a.w.s) said:

> Whoever is consulted must be trustworthy. An ignorant person who gives erroneous opinions on religious legal matters suffers the punishment for the sins he has created. And whoever gives bad advice to his Muslim brother certainly has been unfaithful to him. (Abu Dawud)

Allah Most High declares through His Prophet:

> Why promise something that you will not do or that you are unable to do? A false promise draws Allah's wrath on the liar.

Abu Hurayrah reported that the Messenger of Allah (s.a.w.s) said:

> Three signs indicate a hypocrite: He lies when he talks, he breaks his promises, and he is a traitor to what is entrusted to him. (Muslim)

In another tradition, Ibn `Amr ibn al-`As reported that the Messenger of Allah (s.a.w.s) said:

> Whoever is afflicted with four bad characteristics is certainly a hypocrite, and whoever has even one of them is liable to insincerity until he gets rid of it. They are to betray a trust; to lie; to dishonor one's own promise; to try to distort the truth of a matter in one's own favor. (Muslim)

To promise something while knowing that you will not fulfill the pledge is a purposeful lie and religiously unlawful. But a promise made with an honest intention that cannot be fulfilled because of circumstances beyond your control is permissible according to our religion. According to Abu Nu'man the Messenger of Allah (s.a.w.s) said:

> If you promise and cannot keep your promise, it is not a sin. (Abu Dawud)

According to Imam Ahmad and his followers, to keep one's promise is an obligation and to break it is a sin in every case. Since there are Qur'anic verses on the subject that lead in several directions, one may be in doubt about this matter. We should avoid doing things that involve doubt concerning the religious law.

Anger may arise from association with melancholy and irrational people, with children having tantrums, with raving madmen, with ill-trained animals. Indeed it is unreasonable to react in such situations, since the conditions that produce our anger are not the fault of those we blame, but facts of life and a natural part of affairs. Worse still is becoming angry at lifeless things—things falling, breaking, burning, disappearing; or a stone that causes us to trip. These objects have no will of their own and have no intention to cause trouble to anyone. When, after an outburst, we realize this, we may get angry with ourselves—but this also is unreasonable and disapproved by the religion.

On the other hand, to be annoyed at yourself because you have been lax in worship or you realize that you have sinned is correct, so long as it is not excessive. When your anger leads you to decide to redeem yourself by good actions and extra prayers, it is commendable.

The worst kind of anger among all we have enumerated is to become angry at Allah and His Messenger. This usually happens in reaction to some other person who cites Qur'anic verses or Traditions of the Prophet to substantiate his criticism of us. Our anger at him may develop into anger against our Sustainer and our Prophet. We take refuge in Allah from such an eventuality. That is why our Prophet said:

Anger corrupts one's faith and one's religion.

To become upset when you observe people sinning or hurting each other is right—as long as you do not overreact. For this is a feeling inspired by faith and attachment to the teachings of one's religion, as well as by compassion for fellow human beings. But to accuse such people of infidelity, hypocrisy, dishonesty, adultery, and so forth, insulting them or attempting to punish them, is a sin. Trying to advise them gently and reasonably, if possible—that is the good deed. Many people are sensitive to other people's behavior and think of themselves as reformers. Unfortunately, they are often too harsh in their criticism. They do more harm than good, and this is something to be aware of.

CHAPTER 15

ON FORBEARANCE

Forbearance is a kind of behavior superior to the suppression of anger. When an adverse situation seems to violate our well-being, it creates a nervous upheaval. Great effort is required for us not to manifest this upheaval in anger, and it takes time for us to calm down. Forbearance is a condition that prevents such upheaval altogether: it keeps the nervous system in balance at all times. People who possess forbearance have patience and gentleness of character. These are signs of faith and wisdom, which enable such people to use their minds to govern their emotions.

The gentle in character hope for God's love in response to their forbearance. Such response is promised by the Messenger of Allah, as we see in the following prophetic traditions.

Hadrat `A'ishah, the beloved wife of the Prophet (r.a.) reported that the Messenger of Allah (s.a.w.s) said:

> Allah's approval and love are due to whoever is gentle and resists anger. (Isfahani)

Hadrat Fatimah, the beloved daughter of the Prophet (r.a.) reported from her father:

> God certainly loves the one who is well-behaved, well-bred, well-mannered, honest, and gentle, who does not expect anything from anyone and is not envious of others. He certainly does not love those who use foul language and are constantly asking and expecting favors from others. (Tabarani)

The ones who are gentle also hope for the love of the Prophet, since they are imitating him in his behavior. Ibn `Uyaynah related that one of the private prayers of the Messenger of Allah (s.a.w.s) was:

> My Lord, enrich me in wisdom, beautify me with gentleness, honor me with piety, and be good to me in preserving my health so that I may serve others. (Ibn Abi Dunya)

The gentle person realizes that his ability to control negative emotions creates a favorable condition for acquiring knowledge and wisdom, as (according to Abu Hurayrah) the Messenger of God said:

> When you wish to acquire knowledge, pray that you be given a calm dignity and a gentle manner, whether you are learning or teaching. Be

softhearted and put on your best behavior. Don't be one of those pretentious scholars who are arrogant and overstep the bounds of decency. That
will be a sign that your stupidity has vanquished your noble forbearance.
(Ibn Sina)

The one with forbearance is promised spiritual advancement by the
Prophet of Allah who said (according to `Ubadah ibn Samit):

Shall I tell you how Allah Most High will raise the spiritual status of people
and communities? That will be His blessing upon you if you deal gently
with the one who has offended you, if you forgive the one who has tyrannized you, if you are generous with the one who deprived you, if you
befriend the one who has abandoned you. (Tabarani, Bazzar)

There are many benefits for the compassionate, soft-hearted, mellow-
mannered faithful, and the fiery punishment of Hell will never touch them.
It is reported by Ibn Mas`ud that the Prophet asked his Companions:

Shall I tell you who is safe from Hellfire? The one who is humble, who
cares for all of God's creatures, and who serves them with gentleness and
dignity. (Tabarani)

The noble wife of the Prophet, Hadrat `A'ishah, reported that the
Messenger of Allah (s.a.w.s) said:

To be compassionate and gentle is one of God's blessings. To be coarse
and stupid is one of God's curses. (Tabarani)

Jarir reported that the Prophet said:

The one who is deprived of compassion and gentle manners is deprived
of all good. (Abu Dawud)

Forbearance beautifies its owner and attracts God's love to him. Hadrat
`A'ishah related that the Messenger of Allah (s.a.w.s) said:

Wherever there is gentleness, there is beauty. Wherever gentleness has
disappeared there is shame. (Muslim)

Forbearance is not a characteristic easy to assume. It becomes permanent through long efforts in enduring controversy, injustice, tyranny, and
all other conditions that weigh heavily upon one's ego, and through cur-
tailing anger and the desire to retaliate. Many a pious man has declared
that he achieved forbearance by purposefully seeking the company of
obnoxious men and suffering their impudence, anger, and violence, practicing patience with them.

Abu Darda' reports that the Prophet said:

Knowledge is acquired by learning. Forbearance is acquired by suffering the impudence of others without reacting. Whoever makes an effort to obtain that which is good, God gives him good. Whoever is able to stand controversy is saved from suffering. (Tabarani)

Every aspect of good character, such as generosity, humbleness, and valor, is obtained by long practice in fighting corresponding faults, such as stinginess, arrogance, and fear. The worst handicap to acquiring forbearance is harboring doubts about the goodness in other people, especially the other faithful, and imagining bad things about them. This suspicion of one's associates leads to the terribly sinful state of doubting the goodness in God.

Allah Most High says,

O you who believe, avoid suspicion, for surely suspicion in some cases is a sin. Do not look for each other's faults and slander each other. Would you like to eat the flesh of your dead brother? (*Hujurat*, 12)

And according to Abu Hurayrah, the Messenger of Allah (s.a.w.s) said:

Beware of suspicion, for suspicion is a lie. Do not seek to know each other's secrets. Do not vent your feelings in reproaches or envy the lives of others; do not slander anyone for what they are or for how they act. When you give and take among yourselves, be fair: neither more nor less than is due. Do not cheat each other. When one of you leaves a woman, another should not propose to her until the first has actually departed. O God's creatures, be like brothers! A Muslim is the brother of all other Muslims. A brother does not tyrannize his brothers, nor leave them helpless when they are tyrannized.

Then he pointed to his heart and said thrice,

This is where the fear of God should be—in your hearts. If you dare to hurt your Muslim brother, that is sufficient to earn you God's curse. It is forbidden by God to harm the property, the honor, or the physical being of another Muslim. God does not look only upon your actions, but sees also your thoughts and the intentions of your hearts. (Muslim)

Forbearance does not mean permissiveness. It is permissible, in fact it is incumbent upon a Muslim to act for the sake and in the name of God against people who are flagrantly and undoubtedly sinning, revolting against God, committing indecencies, hurting others—in order to make them stop. For God says:

Why should you be divided into two parties about the hypocrites? God has upset them for their evil deeds. Would you guide those whom God has thrown out of the way? For those whom God has thrown out of the way, never shall you find the way. (*Nisa', 88*)

Suspicion is very wrong as a basis for action. Sufyan al-Thawri says that there are two kinds of suspicion. One is a sin: that is when you pass judgment against someone based upon your suspicion. The other is not a sin: that is when you suspect someone of having done something wrong, but refrain from judging or condemning him. This point of view is the right one.

The opposite of suspicion is to think well of everybody. Even if there are signs to make you doubt the innocence of someone, it is still best to think of that person as innocent. To think badly and continue to be suspicious of someone who has been proven innocent is a sin. Thus it is best for you to have good will toward one and all. Above all, you should think well of your Lord.

Abu Hurayrah reported that the Messenger of Allah (s.a.w.s) said that God says:

I am as My servant thinks of Me. If he thinks well of Me, I am good to him. If he thinks ill of Me, I am bad to him. (Bukhari)

According to Ibn Mas`ud, the Prophet said:

I swear upon the one and only God who created all and everything that He only offers you what you hope for from Him. All good is in His power. (Tabarani)

And Abu Hurayrah reported that he also said:

To think well of God is one of the best forms of worship. (Abu Dawud)

Jabir ibn `Abdullah added, "When your life in this world ends, hope for God's mercy at your last breath."

Abu Hurayrah reported that the Messenger of Allah (s.a.w.s) said:

On the Day of Judgment, God will condemn a sinner to Hellfire. When he is brought to the edge of the fire, he will look back and say, "O my Lord, I always thought well of You!"

Then God will pull him back from the fire and say, "I am as My creature thinks of Me." (Bayhaqi)

Another affliction that keeps us from developing the good characteristic of forbearance is to believe in bad omens and bad luck. This conception can even drive people to consulting fortunetellers, soothsayers, and oracles in order to thwart imagined bad signs. This is a sin in our religion, which is based on intelligence. There are many prophetic traditions on this subject. One is reported by Ibn Mas`ud, who reported that the Prophet said:

> Considering something or somebody to be ill-omened and a bringer of bad luck is a form of the unforgivable sin of attributing partners to God. Whoever does this is not one of us. If people are affected by such a sick feeling in their hearts, they should summon up their faith in God, who does only that which is best for His creatures. Let them count upon God and submit to Him. (Abu Dawud)

Abu Hurayrah reported that the Prophet said:

> There is no such thing as bad luck, nor do one person's troubles pass to another person like a contagious sickness. There is no one who can bring you bad luck. (Bukhari)

In another tradition reported by Ibn `Umar, the Messenger of God said:

> There is no such thing as bad luck or a bad omen. If you have a shy and nervous horse that throws you off, or a mean wife who makes you miserable, or too small a house surrounded by bad neighbors, you may attribute it to bad luck, but it is your own doing and your own fault. (Bukhari, Muslim)

The opposite of believing that others can bring you bad luck is to believe that somebody or something can bring you good luck. You may feel elated by being in the presence of a saintly person and believe that the contact will bring you good fortune. You may be surprised on a sacred religious holiday by meeting someone you love whom you have missed, and consider that a good omen. A deep saying or the counsel of a wise person may touch you and seem to change your life. Positive incidents like these are to be accepted as good.

According to Anas ibn Malik, the Prophet said:

> There is no such thing as bad luck, but I like good omens.
> The Companions said: "What kind of good omens, O Messenger of God?"
> And he said, "The best are good words." (Abu Dawud)

He also liked to hear well-wishers say, "Guide us well," "Lead us to success," and such words when he was about to start on a voyage.

To believe in such omens enforces our positive wishes and strengthens our will to do good. There must not be any belief that such incidents have some influence over God's will or over one's destiny! They should only increase our hopes to receive good news, which can only come from God.

`Urwa ibn Amir related:

When some people were talking about luck in the Prophet's hearing, he told them, "Think positively. No bad luck can prevent a Muslim from what is required of him or what he has to do. If some among you encounter difficulty, pray to your Lord that He bring you success or eliminate the obstacle. He is the only one who can grant success and remove the difficulties in your lives. People have no power unless God gives it to them." (Abu Dawud)

Some people confuse the Prophet's acceptance of good omens in Islam with such practices as opening the pages of the Holy Qur'an with eyes closed and putting one's fingers on a verse, hoping to receive an answer to one's problems. This is not permissible, as it resembles the practice of the pre-Islamic pagan Arabs, who drew straws to decide what to do. It is an insult to the Holy Book to use it as a fortuneteller, seeking news in it from the unknown.

Another hindrance to forbearance, in fact a sign that a person has no capacity for forbearance, is avarice.

"Wealth is not from abundance of possessions. Wealth
is but from wealth of spirit."

CHAPTER 16

RELATING TO THE GOODS OF THIS WORLD:
AVARICE, WASTEFULNESS, GENEROSITY, DETACHMENT

Avarice is a sign of lack of faith in God, who provides the sustenance of His creatures. A stingy person both suffers himself and causes suffering in his dependents by skimping with what he possesses because he imagines that someday he may not have his present means. Thus from a fear of imaginary hard times for which he has no forbearance, he causes immediate pain. He lacks the faith necessary to accept that what he has in his hand is not his. He believes that his future is guaranteed only by his own efforts. He also lacks the humanity and the intelligence to realize that what has been given to him is to be delivered to his and others' needs.

Allah says:

And let not those who are niggardly in spending that which God has granted them out of His grace, think that it is good for them. Nay, it is evil for them. They shall have a collar of their niggardliness on their necks on the resurrection day. God's is the heritage of the heavens and the earth. And God is aware of what you do. (Al-i 'Imran, 179)

The reverse of avarice is to be a spendthrift, to waste away all one's substance unnecessarily, for pointless things. This behavior is unacceptable both for humanitarian reasons and according to Islam. Yet generosity is a laudable characteristic in a Muslim. It means spending from one's means for the near of kin and the orphan and the needy and the wayfarer, for God's sake, not for glory or praise: the generous person does not look for thankfulness from the recipient of help. Large-heartedness is even superior to generosity, and signifies three traits: to give away to the needy things one needs for oneself; to feel the needs of others and to satisfy them even before they are aware of those needs themselves; and to hide from those whom one aids, and everyone else, one's involvement in providing help. God Most High says:

They prefer them before themselves, though poverty may afflict them. These it is that are the successful. (Hashr, 9)

If you practice economy because you wish to live simply and humbly, even if your economy extends to your family and dependents, it is a good thing. But if economy becomes excessive, causing harm to your health and

hygiene or to the well-being of your family, friends, and society at large, it is unlawful according to Islam. Such a person is as bad as a spendthrift. A balance has to be found between excessive expenditure and being remiss.
God Most High says:

And make not your hand to be shackled to your neck, nor stretch it forth to the utmost of its stretching forth, lest you sit down blamed and stripped off. (*Bani Isra'il*, 29)

And:

They who, when they spend, are neither extravagant nor parsimonious, and the just mean is ever between these. (*Furqan*, 67)

Ibn `Umar reported that the Messenger of Allah (s.a.w.s) said:

If one of you feels that you need something for yourself and you sacrifice your need in favor of satisfying the need of someone else, some of your lesser sins will be forgiven. (Ibn Hibban)

Hadrat `A'ishah, the blessed wife of the Prophet, reported:

I have not seen the Messenger of Allah (s.a.w.s) satiated three days one after the other. None of us in his household had enough food, while we certainly had the means. But he preferred others over himself, and let them eat. (Bayhaqi)

Ibn `Umar reported that the Prophet said:

Eat what a generous person offers you, for it brings you health and restores you, while the food offered by a miser makes you sick. (*Dar-i Kutni*)

Hadrat `A'ishah told us that the Prophet said:

The ones who are loved by God are created generous and with good morals. (Abu Shaykh)

Abu Hurayrah reported that the Messenger of Allah (s.a.w.s) said:

Generosity is a tree whose roots are in Paradise. The generous person is held at one of its branches and he stays there until he is pulled into Paradise. Avarice is a tree whose roots are in Hell. The miser is tied to one of its branches and will not be saved until he is pulled into Hellfire. (*Dar-i Kutni*)

Abu Hurayrah reported from the Messenger of God:

The generous person is close to God, heaven, and humanity, and far away from Hell, while the miser is kept far from God, heaven, and humanity, and is in Hell. In God's opinion, an ordinary person lacking in devotion who is generous is closer to Him than a wise and pious person who is niggardly. (Tirmidhi)

Ibn `Abbas reported that the Prophet said:

Generosity is one of God's greatest characteristics. (Abu Shaykh)

Abu Hurayrah reported:

The Messenger of God said to his Companions, "I give you good news: the one who is generous is in Paradise. This is in accordance with God's act, and I am a guarantor and a witness for it. And beware, the one who is miserly is in Hell. This, too, is in accordance with God's act, and I am a guarantor for this also."

The Companions asked, "Who are the generous and who are the miserly?"

And he answered, "The generous are those who know that others have rights over whatever fortune God has bestowed upon them, and He gives it to them. The miser is the one who keeps what belongs to God, and is stingy not only toward man but toward God. But beware also: generosity does not mean to gain money unlawfully and throw it away on the unworthy. (Isfahani)

Another saying of the Prophet as reported by Abu Sa`id al-Khudri:

There are two characteristics that will never belong to a faithful person: they are immorality and stinginess. (Tirmidhi)

It is reported by Abu Bakr that the Prophet said:

A creator of social calamity, a cheater, a miser, and a person who helps the needy only reluctantly, expecting thanks and recognition, will not enter Paradise. (Tirmidhi)

Abu Hurayrah related:

The worst traits found in human nature are an insatiable avarice and a heart-wrenching cowardice. (Abu Dawud)

`Abdullah ibn `Umar reported that the Prophet said:

The glory of my people at our beginning depended on their sincerity and righteousness, their piety and asceticism. Their downfall at the end will be caused by their love of the world, their avarice, and their doing the wrong thing. (Tabarani)

Excessive attachment to this life and this world is not good, for that is what causes avarice and other wrong states and actions. God says,

Your wealth and your children are only a trial. The great reward is with God alone. (*Tagabun,* 15)

Work for the world to the extent of the time you will spend in it, and work for the Hereafter to the extent of the eternity you will spend in it. `Abdur-Rahman ibn `Awf related that the Prophet said:

The accursed Devil says that the wealthy will not be safe from him because of three things. First, he will make them live in fear of losing what they have. Second, he will push them to gather wealth without regard for other people's rights. Finally, he will make them love what they own so that they cannot part with it. (Tabarani)

Abu Hurayrah reported the Prophet having said:

Cursed are the ones who are the slaves of silver and gold, cursed are the ones who take this world as their god. (Tirmidhi)

Ka`b reported that the Prophet said:

All people pass a test in their life. The test of my people is what they do with the goods of this world. (Tirmidhi)

What causes attachment to the goods of this world? Rightfully and naturally people love their children and family and feel the obligation to support and nourish them and make their future secure. But in our excessive attempt to gather wealth to achieve this duty, we forget that the One who created us and our families and our children also created our support and nourishment. We fail to take a lesson from children who inherit great fortunes and squander them, becoming destitute. We do not observe the children of the poor who are better off and much happier than the children of the rich. It is especially common that when a person gathers wealth by stepping on people and causing harm to others and by being a slave to the world, his children spend their inheritance on luxury and sin. Wealth leads them astray rather than to salvation, peace, and contentment.

God addresses the world in a divine tradition reported by His Prophet:

O world, be a friend to My servant who remembers Me while looking at you, and be an enemy to the one who forgets Me while being involved in you. To those who serve Me in their lifetimes, be a servant yourself. To those who serve you, be a vicious master.

Then there are those who gather the goods of this world for no other reason than to pile wealth in their safes and count it as it increases. In reality, the gold is not in their safes, but stuffed in their hearts, so that there is no space left for any other love. This is one of the worst sicknesses of the heart and very difficult to cure, especially if one is afflicted with it at an older age. The best cure is the remembrance of death, for the one who is afflicted with avarice is sick because he has forgotten death. Perchance through remembering it, the benefits due to generosity may dawn on him, and that thought will permit him to spend money on good deeds. If he is able to continue long enough, perhaps giving will become a habit and cure him of the worst of sicknesses.

There are also people who wish to enjoy their lives in this world to the full, without any regard to right or wrong, good or evil. They lust for fun. Fun costs money. They spend for their fun today, but need to make and keep a lot of money for tomorrow—which for them will never end. For them is God's warning:

Know that the life of this world is but play and amusement, pomp and mutual boasting in the multiplication of your wealth and children. It is as rain causing the vegetation to grow, pleasing the heedless farmer, but then all withers away, turning yellow, and becomes chaff. And in the Hereafter is a severe chastisement. (*Hadid*, 20)

Abu Hurayrah reported that the Prophet said:

This world is damned, and all that there is in it is damned, except the things that remind you of God and of which God approves, and the ones who learn from these, and the ones who teach them. (Tirmidhi)

And he said (reported by Sahl ibn Sa`d al-Sa`idi):

If this world had the value of a single wing of a mosquito in the opinion of God, He would not have given a drop of water to the ones who do not believe in Him. (Tirmidhi)

Ibn `Umar reported that the Messenger of Allah (s.a.w.s) said:

What a man receives from this world only decreases his value in the opinion of God, even if he is good and pious, unless he spends it according to God's will and for His sake. (Ibn Abi Dunya)

Abu Musa al-Ash`ari related that the Messenger of God (s.a.w.s.) said:

The one who loves this world loses the Hereafter; the one who is concerned with the Hereafter loses interest in this world. I hope you will choose the lasting over the passing. (Imam Ahmad, Bazzar, Ibn Hibban, Hakim)

And Anas ibn Malik related the Prophet having said:

Have you ever seen anyone who could walk in water and keep his feet dry? The one who treads in the swamp of this world is also like this. He is covered with the mud of sin and cannot keep himself clean. (Bayhaqi)

Hadrat `A'ishah related from the Prophet who said:

This world is a home for those who feel homeless because they have forgotten where they came from. This world is wealth for fools who have forgotten they possess the treasures of their Lord. The fool passes his life gathering the goods of this world, which will never be his, but will stay with the world. (Imam Ahmad)

Hasan al-Basri reported that Messenger of God (s.a.w.s.) said:

Attachment to this world is the foundation of all the errors in life. (Bayhaqi, Ibn Abi Dunya)

Musa ibn Yassar reported that the Prophet said:

In all God's creation, there is nothing He loves less than this world. He has not looked at it once since He created it. (Bayhaqi)

Hadrat `Ali reports the Prophet having said:

What you do right in this world will gain you no more than long interrogations on the Day of Judgment. And what you do wrong will gain you entrance to Hell. (Bayhaqi, Ibn Abi Dunya)

Ibn Mas`ud reported from the Prophet:

Gather, in this world, no more than you need and no more than you can carry, for on the Day of Judgment, you will be forced to carry all that you owned in this life. (Tabarani)

Ibn Bashir reported from the Prophet:

The sign of God's contempt for a person is that He makes him spend what goods He has bestowed upon him on building monumental homes for himself. (Tabarani)

It is obvious that the life of this world is a harsh test, full of temptations. Damned and detested by God, this world prevents us from remembering our Lord. It causes us to fail in our duties as a human being. Inviting humanity to sin, it leads us to destitution in the eternal life of the Hereafter while offering very little in return.

The worst trick of this world is that it consumes the very short lifetime allotted to human beings, forcing its slaves to kill themselves by working for it, or by drowning themselves in drugs, alcohol, and gambling in the name of fun and games. Worse still, in doing so it pushes people to hurt and violate other persons and other creatures of God—animals, plants, earth, water, and air alike. And the ambitions of this world's slaves have no end until they destroy themselves and those around them—unless they come to see the true purpose of this world and this life.

One can pass the test of this life and save oneself from the calamities of this world by learning to oppose the false attractions it offers.

Anas ibn Malik related the following traditions from the Messenger of God:

If someone has a strong hope for the Hereafter and makes an effort to prepare for it, God will show him the beauty of it and take the love of this world out of his heart. All his scattered efforts to achieve success in this world will be united in the single thought of preparing for the Hereafter, and he will be satisfied. While if someone's only hope and wish is for this world, his efforts are all in vain. God places a third eye in between his two eyes, an eye of insatiable ambition, and he is never content. God scatters his attention and his efforts to many objects of desire, and does not offer him any divine gifts, but grants him only what he can get himself. Possessing only that, he feels very poor. (Tirmidhi)

Don't you hear the herald calling? O believers, let the ones who wish take the world: it is not for you. Every breath, every step, every turn you take in this world precipitates your death. Take as little as possible from it, just enough to survive. (Bazzar)

A man grows old, but two things stay young in him—the wish to live forever and the wish to own the world. (Bukhari, Muslim)

If people had enough gold to fill two deep valleys, they would wish to have a third. Nothing will fill such people's stomachs but the earth in their graves. (Bukhari, Muslim)

To oppose this blind ambition for the world, one should learn to be satisfied with little, with nothing more than one truly needs.

Abu Hurayrah reported that the Prophet said:

Oppose the desires of the world by pious asceticism. This will bring comfort both to your body and to your heart and mind. (Tabarani)

Dahhak reported that a man asked the Messenger of God what was meant by asceticism. He said:

An ascetic is one who thinks about death, who recalls that one day this body he pampers will return to earth. He does not count upon tomorrow, nor wish for the pleasures and joys of this world today. He is one who does not count himself among the living, but counts himself among the dead, and prefers that which is everlasting to that which has an end. (Ibn Abi Dunya)

Hadrat `Umar related from the Messenger of God:

To be rich is not to own the goods of this world, but to "realize" the treasures God has placed in you. (Bukhari, Muslim)

And `Amr ibn al-`As related that the Prophet said:

A believer has found salvation only when he has just what he needs, and is satisfied and pleased with the share that God has bestowed on him. (Muslim)

Abu Hurayrah reported that the Prophet prayed:

Our Lord, give me and my people no more than we need. (Muslim)

Abu Darda' reported that in the home of the Messenger of God they never sieved the flour to separate the fine from the coarse, but baked bread with rough flour; and that the Messenger of God had only one robe to wear. (Tabarani)

Hadrat `A'ishah, the blessed wife of the Prophet, related that in the household of the Prophet there was never even a slice of barley bread left for the next day. (Tabarani)

Abu Talhah said that the people of the household complained to the Messenger of God of their hunger, and showed him the stones they had tied around their bellies to suppress it. And he showed them that he also kept a stone pressed against his stomach. (Tirmidhi)

Hadrat `A'ishah reported that a month could pass without a cooking fire burning at their home: they suppressed their hunger by eating a few dates and drinking water. Wheat bread was rare, and rarely were they satiated eating rough barley bread. (Bukhari, Muslim)

Abu Darda' reported the Prophet having said:

There is a very narrow passage in front of us: none but the light in weight will be able to pass through it! (Bazzaz)

Anas ibn Malik saw Hadrat `Umar from the back. The future caliph had three large patches on his shirt, sewn one on top of the other between his two shoulders. (Tabarani)

`Umar ibn Husayn reported that the Prophet said:

God loves the poor person who has a large family and very little to support them but keeps working hard, is upright, doesn't ask help from others, and maintains his self respect. (Ibn Maja)

And he said:

The poor will enter Paradise 500 years ahead of the rich. (Tirmidhi)

Abu Sa`id al-Khudri reported that the Messenger of God said to one of his companions whom he loved best:

O Bilal, die as a poor man, do not die as a rich man. (Tabarani)

Abu Dharr al-Gifari reported that the Messenger of God said:

The attitude of a believer toward the goods of this world is not to consider them all wrong, so that when you earn or are given them, you throw them away in disdain. Everything that comes to you is from God's infinite treasury and passes through human hands for your own and others' needs. But do not count on what you have and try to keep it: rather depend on God's grace. And do not despair because of little good fortune and many trials in life. Trust that there is great benefit deriving from these in this world and in the Hereafter. Need brings you closer to God than having more than you need. (Tirmidhi)

CHAPTER 17

ON MONEY: HOW TO USE IT AND NOT WASTE IT

All the warnings about the temptations and dangers of the goods of this world should not make us forget that money, wealth, and property are also God's gifts. A fertile field is given to us to till and plant and water. Thus we grow an orchard whose fruits we will gather, not only in this world, but also in the Hereafter.

Money is necessary both to lead our lives here and to prepare for the Hereafter. Our physical existence—a strong healthy body, which needs to be fed, clothed, protected, educated, and cared for—is the carriage of our souls. It is the tool of our virtues and good deeds, our worship and devotions. Only money will secure the energy, health, and security for it. And how are we to protect ourselves against our enemies, help our family, our friends, and the needy, pay our dues and debts, go to the Pilgrimage, educate ourselves, help build schools and hospitals, roads and bridges, secure our community and country and save ourselves from being dependent on others, without money?

But one must work, and work lawfully. God does not give other than what we work for. To work hard and earn money by lawful means and to spend it on good deeds is considered by God to be more worthy than spending time and effort upon making extra prayers and empty acts of devotion, hoping for personal salvation. God esteems that the best of people who are bound for Paradise are those who are good to others.

Abu Qabsha al-Ansari reported that the Prophet said:

God gives a man knowledge and money. And if he is thankful, and loves and fears God, and feels that his family and others have rights over what he has, so that he shares his knowledge and his wealth with them—he is purchasing the palaces he will receive in Paradise. (Tirmidhi)

The Prophet said to `Amr ibn al-`As that for an upright and righteous person, lawfully gained wealth is an excellent gift of God. The Messenger of God prayed for Anas ibn Malik, "O Lord, increase the wealth of Anas and the number of his children, and make his wealth bountiful and sacred for him." And when Ka`b wanted to donate all his money to the community of Muslims, the Prophet said, "No, keep some of your wealth, for it is a favor to you from your Lord."

As God says:

... and God found you in want, so He enriched you ... so the favor of your Lord, proclaim. (*Duha*, 8, 11)

Sufyan al-Thawri said, "Today, wealth is your sword against your enemies."

Sa`id ibn Musib said, "There is no good in someone who does not work
hard to make money, because such behavior is proof that a person does not
recognize his responsibilities to the world, whose debt he can only repay
with money. Neither does he realize that he can only defend himself and
his dependents and their honor with money. He neither cares for the ones
who will remain after he is gone, nor for his own Hereafter."

Ibn Jawzi said, "When your intentions are right, to gather and keep
wealth is better than to abandon it."

And again it must not be forgotten that a coin has two sides. Money has
a good and a bad side: the good aspect of it is to be praised, while the bad
aspect of it is to be condemned. The danger of material wealth is that it
may render the wealthy arrogant and cause them to forget God, death, and
the Hereafter. Then they rebel against Him, neglect religion and responsibility, and become world-bound, immoral, selfish, and mean.

It is very difficult to realize that our possessions are not our own, but a
gift of God lent to us to be spent on our needs and the needs of others.
Yet to believe that our wealth is purely the result of our own efforts and
belongs to us to keep, rather than treating it as a trust from God, is a sin. It
signifies either that one does not believe in God, or else that one belittles
God's generosity as the Sustainer of His creation, and is unthankful.

God says:

If you are grateful, I will give you more, and if you are ungrateful, My
chastisement is truly severe. (*Ibrahim*, 7)

The ungrateful sooner or later will lose what they were given. One of the
usual ways that wealth is lost is through waste.

Prodigality is as much a sin as avarice. To squander wealth, to throw away
God's gifts, is an insult to God and an act of violence toward humanity.
More is said and written against miserliness than against waste only because
human nature is more inclined to hold on to things than to throw them
away. Miserliness expresses fear, insecurity about the future, and doubt of
God's generosity. It keeps the miser in want and misery. But the prodigal
is as arrogant as Pharaoh, who took himself to be God and built himself
pyramids as high as mountains. When such a person squanders his wealth,
it generally benefits no one. On the contrary, his wastefulness leads himself
and others to degradation in this world and in the Hereafter.

God forbids throwing away your wealth, saying:

And give not over your wealth, which God has made a means of support
for you, to the weak of mind. (*Nisa'*, 5)

And:

> O children of Adam, wear your best clothes when you present yourselves
> to God at prayer in the mosques. Eat and drink, but waste not by excess,
> for God does not like the spendthrift. And share your wealth; give their
> due to the near of kin and the ones in need and the wayfarer, and squan-
> der not wastefully. Surely squanderers are the Devil's brethren, and the
> Devil is ever ungrateful to his Lord. (*Bani Isra`il*, 26-27)

The Prophet said:

> On the Day of Judgment the children of Adam will not pass the test until
> they have answered four questions: How did they spend their time? What
> did they receive for their efforts and actions in their lifetime? How did
> they spend whatever wealth they received? And how did they spend their
> health and strength? (Tirmidhi)

It is useful to understand that receiving or paying interest on borrowed
money is unlawful in Islam because of the sinfulness of prodigality. Interest
causes waste—certainly when it is paid, but also when it is received. For
anything given and taken, when it has changed in kind and quantity or in
value between the time it was given and the time it is taken, is considered
depreciated and therefore wasted.

The definition of squandering is to throw money into a place from which
you cannot retrieve it or receive any benefit from it. If you cast it into the
sea, burn it, or tear it to pieces, if you gamble, drink, and debauch with
it, or if you lend it improperly, it is all the same. Such behavior resembles
permitting ripe fruit to rot on the tree, letting wheat go unharvested in the
field, not repairing a roof when it leaks, leaving flocks to wander unpro-
tected, and not taking care of yourself and your dependents. These are
similarly wasteful and wrong.

To avoid waste, one must take care even of the details. We must preserve
our property, including stored food and clothes, books and papers, from
vermin, humidity, heat and cold, or any other potential harm. Not finishing the food on one's plate, throwing away leftovers, or leaving crumbs of
bread on the table are subtle offenses of prodigality.

It is wasteful to eat too much; to eat when not hungry; to keep eating
to satiation; and to eat something merely because it appears. To eat more
than you need is permissible if you intend to fast the next day, or in order
not to embarrass a hungry guest who is overeating at your table.

Hadrat `A'ishah reported that when the Messenger of God saw her eat
two meals a day, he reproached her, saying:

O `A'ishah, have you not anything to do except satisfy your stomach? To eat twice a day is wasteful, and God does not like those who waste his gifts. (Bayhaqi)

Anas ibn Malik reported that the Prophet said:

To eat everything that whets your appetite is considered excess in the use of God's allotted sustenance. (Ibn Maja, Bayhaqi, Ibn Abi Dunya)

To be bored with what remains of one kind of food and to cook another dish, to be choosy, to leave the staple foods and favor appetizing ones, are all considered wasteful, yet not prohibited, because Allah Most High says:

O you who believe, make not unlawful the good things that God has made lawful for you. But commit no excess, for God likes not those given to excess. (*Ma'idah*, 87)

And:

Say: Who has forbidden the beautiful gifts of God, which He has produced for His servants, and the things clean and pure that He has provided for sustenance? These are for the faithful in the life of this world, and there is better for them on the Day of Judgment. Thus do We make Our messages clear to those who understand. (*`Araf*, 32)

The Prophet asked his companion Jabir, who left traces of food on his plate, to eat them all, and even lick his fingers. He said that one does not know in which drop of one's sustenance God's grace resides. He said that the Devil stands next to the one who eats, and whatever is left on one's plate is food for the Devil.

The Prophet himself certainly cleaned his plate at every meal. Any bit of bread or grain that fell upon the ground was gathered and scattered for birds and ants to eat. Any leftover food unfit for human consumption should be fed to animals.

The Messenger of God said, "God cares for those who care for His creatures. So care for the creatures on the face of this earth: those in Heaven will care for you." He also said, "There is divine reward for whoever quenches the thirst of a thirsty creature."

To use too much water while washing, or too much oil in your lamps, too much wood or coal to cook or warm yourselves, are considered wasteful actions.

When you sell something, to charge less than its real value, and when you buy something, to pay more than its true worth, even if you were cheated into doing so, are considered points against you. So also is living in a large house and paying excessive rent. There is no harm if one purposely pays more than a thing is worth in order secretly to help the one who is selling it, because that person is in need.

Even to be wrapped in a shroud more ample than needed, or to use more water than is necessary in washing the dead, or to waste water while taking one's ritual ablution, is considered prodigality.

Ibn `Umar reported:

> One day the Prophet saw Sa'd ibn Abi Waqqas taking ablution and said to him, "O Sa'd, how wasteful you are!" Sa'd asked if water could be wasted in taking one's ritual ablution. The Prophet answered, "Yes, even if you are using the running water of a river." (Ahmad ibn Hanbal)

It must be understood that prodigality is sinful, not just because it wastes substance, but because this bad habit signifies a deeper depravity, such as ingratitude, carelessness, self-centeredness, arrogance, even faithlessness. Someone who is free of these transgressions and has good intentions, who eats well, dresses well, resides in large houses and lives well, careful not to spend his wealth on things God has forbidden, is not doing wrong. So long as he is not living as he does in order to show off, so long as he does not presume that he is better than others, so long as he shares his good fortune and is thankful, he is doing right. As the Messenger of God said, according to Ibn `Abbas:

> Eat as well as you like and dress as well as you wish as long as arrogance and prodigality do not lead you to transgression. (Bukhari)

On the other hand, spending in excess for God's sake and in His way is the best of deeds. Mujahid said:

> If someone had a pile of gold as high as the mountain of Abu Qubays and spent all of it in God's way, it would not be excessive. But if you spend a coin or a handful of corn against God's will you are guilty of the sin of prodigality.

Someone said to Hatim at-Ta`i, "There is no good in wastefulness," and he responded, "There is no wastefulness in doing good."

Yet one also has to be careful of extravagance even in charity. God says:

> And God is the one who provides in your gardens fruits of various sorts and olives and pomegranates, like and unlike. Eat of its fruits and pay the dues of it that are proper on the day the harvest is gathered. But be not excessive, for God does not like those who are wasteful. (*An`am*, 142)

Many knowledgeable interpreters of the Qur'an like Razi, Qadi, and Zamakhshari agree that to "pay the dues of it that are proper" means the obligatory poor rate that every Muslim has to pay—one-fortieth of his fortune—as well as the voluntary alms and expenditures for good deeds. Then "be not excessive" would refer to spending for good deeds beyond that. According to some respected sources, "be not excessive, for God does not like those who are wasteful" was revealed on a day when Thabit ibn Qays distributed all his wealth to the poor, leaving nothing for his family. `Abdurazzaq reported from Ibn Jurayj that it was Mu`adh ibn Jabal who gave all of his date harvest to the poor, forgetting his own family's needs, prior to the revelation of the above verse. Jabir ibn `Abdullah and Ibn Mas`ud give another account. According to them, the verse was revealed when a child came to the Messenger of God and said that his mother wanted such and such an item from the Prophet, but the Prophet did not have it. "In that case," the child said, "she will want the robe you are wearing!" The Messenger of God took off his robe and gave it to the child. Since he was then not sufficiently dressed to proceed to the mosque, people's attention was attracted, and God revealed the above verse.

Abu Hurayrah reported that the Messenger of God said:

When you help people or give alms, it is better to give more than is needed. But first see to the needs of your extended family, for whose well-being you are responsible. Indeed the hand that gives is better than the hand that takes. Start your good deeds with satisfying the needs of those whom you are obligated to support. (Bukhari)

Abu Hurayrah also reported:

Someone came to the Prophet and said, "I have a coin to spare." The Prophet said, "Keep it for yourself." The man said, "But I have another." He said, "Then spend it on your children." When he said he had another coin to spare, the Prophet said, "Spend it on your household." The man said he had yet another, and the Prophet said, "Give it to the ones who serve you." When the man said that he had yet another coin, the Prophet told him, "I leave it to you to do whatever you wish with it." (Baghawi)

Bukhari says that if someone is not well-to-do and has a family not properly taken care of, or is in debt, it is better for him first to pay his debt and then to spend on his family's needs rather than trying to help others. For God throws back in such a person's face what he spends in the name of charity, since a debtor has no right to spend other people's money on his own magnanimity. Abu Layth as-Samarqandi, in his book called *Advice to the Heedless*, reported that Ibrahim Adham said that someone who is in debt does not have the right to butter his bread. Muslim scholars such as Ibn

Hajar al-Asqalani and Ibn Battal are in agreement that it is unlawful for a debtor to give alms until he pays off all his debt.

Tabari and other scholars agree that it is permissible to give away everything you own in charity if you are sound in body and mind, do not owe anything in money or kind to anyone, have no dependents, and are sure that you can support the burden of being penniless. If even one of these conditions is lacking, it is better to keep some wealth for yourself. But scholars who base themselves on the opinion of Hadrat `Umar state that God does not accept this kind of excess as a good deed.

Now that we have discussed different aspects of prodigality and examined its various iniquities, it is best to learn how to avoid wastefulness once and for all.

If you are afflicted with this sickness, having read and believed in the troubles and difficulties caused by squandering God's gifts (as we have attempted to prove by verses of the Holy Qur'an and Traditions of the Prophet) will certainly encourage you to do something about it. But if you find yourself incapable of not being a spendthrift, then find someone close and dependable and place him legally in charge of your affairs

It is usually one of the following six causes that prevents a wasteful person from becoming normal.

1. Arrogance, displayed in thinking that one can do whatever one wishes with one's wealth, since it has been gained by one's own efforts. This attitude signals lack of faith in God the Sustainer.

2. The hypocrisy of pretentiousness, which pushes one to spend more than one can afford in order to win the admiration of others.

3. The hypocrisy of dissimulation, which urges one to cover up incompetence and laziness by spending more money than one can actually make.

4. Attachment to the life of this world, which inclines one to living according to self-defined high standards in the name of the "good life."

5. Ignorance, which keeps one from distinguishing waste from liberality (and indeed, in some cases it is difficult to distinguish one from the other.)

6. Simplemindedness.

Simplemindedness is often inborn. Such abnormality frequently manifests itself by irresponsibility and sometimes in exaggerated actions, including excessive spending. It is God's order not to let such persons have control over money and property, but to assign them a dependable person who is legally responsible for the protection of their wealth. God says:

And make not over your property which God has made a means of support for you to the weak of mind, but maintain them out of it, feed them and clothe them, and counsel them well. (*Nisa'*, 5)

But the "weak in mind" include heirs to fortunes who mindlessly squander their inheritance because they have not themselves spent any effort in making the money, or are under the influence of bad friends who take advantage of them. God also forbids every believer from befriending bad people.

Sometimes perfectly normal people fall under the baleful influence of high positions they have attained. Ruthless politicians, administrators, even religious figures become spendthrifts, thinking that they will thus measure up to the praise and respect of the people around them. They squander the wealth of nations, organizations, and sectors for which they are supposed to be responsible.

Recklessness and immoderation caused by mental illness can only be prevented by assigning such people a custodian who will protect their wealth from being squandered.

Spoiled heirs of rich fathers may be helped by convincing or preventing them from associating with bad friends and frequenting places which lead them astray.

People who do not know the difference between extravagance and liberality can be taught what is right and what is wrong.

People who take pleasure in showing off can be reminded of the punishment that awaits hypocrites in the Hereafter.

If someone is ready to sacrifice all for the earthly good life, it would be useful to remind him that he is sacrificing eternal bliss for a moment of fun and games in this ephemeral world.

And the loser who is trying to hide his laziness and failure behind a screen of excessive expense ought to realize that God says:

... man can have nothing but what he strives for. (*Najm*, 39).

It was reported by Anas ibn Malik and Hadrat `A'ishah that the Messenger of God said:

I take refuge in God from the curse of laziness. (Muslim, Bukhari)

The lazy one should seek the company of hard-working honest people and an environment that encourages work.

The arrogant one who denies the gifts of God will only learn when God takes back what He has given and leaves him destitute and bankrupt and alone by himself.

May God grant that we realize the gravity of wasting His blessings upon humanity. And for those who are afflicted with this sickness, may God grant them the wisdom, determination, and strength to fight against one of the worst of human characteristics. Our Lord is the best of helpers: He renders easy that which mortals find difficult.

CHAPTER 18

ON CARELESS HASTE

Haste is an urge; an emotional impulse, into which it is difficult to intervene with intellect, as emotions are quicker than reason. It pushes a person hurriedly in the direction of a thing wished for, without much reflection or examination as to whether the thing itself is really desirable or right, or whether one's hurried action is the right action. It is a bad habit, for it fools people into thinking that the work done is complete, although (since one has not given the necessary attention to its integral parts and details) it will eventually fall apart.

Haste seems harmless, even desirable to some people. Yet in addition to causing waste of valuable time, effort, and means, it is the root of many disastrous human failings. God warns us:

Man is a creature of haste. Soon enough will I show you My signs; then you will not ask Me to hasten them. (*Anbiya'*, 37)

When the angel Gabriel was dictating God's revelation to the Prophet, he used to recite while the verse was not yet complete. God said even to him:

And make not haste with the Qur'an before its revelation is made complete to you, and say: "My Lord, increase me in knowledge." (*Ta Ha*, 114)

One may counter haste by serious reflection upon whether the desired goal is worthwhile and right. If it is, the time taken in planning one's actions logically and knowledgeably, taking into consideration all the possibilities of failure and the measures available to counter them, will be of great help in attaining that goal. So will giving ample time to the completing of details, the parts which will make the whole. The Prophet said:

A good state of being and action, right intentions, and seriousness and prudence in the use of God's gifts is one twenty-fourth of the character of a prophet. (Tirmidhi, Ibn Sarjis)

Haste has strange after-effects. Even if you are intending to do a good deed, if you hurry, you will probably fail. At best, the work will be incomplete when you had hoped it would be finished. This state of affairs causes resentment, doubt, and hopelessness. It can discourage and dispirit even the person who approaches a task with the best of good will. The excessive exertions made while in a hurry will cause physical and mental fatigue, and lethargy will set in. Then not only will the work attempted fail, but discouragement will prevent one from doing further work. Rashness in one's actions may even make one forget one's initial good intentions, and alter the sincerity of the work.

If he has not thought of the consequences of his hurried actions and they cause harm instead of good, a hasty person who does not have the patience to bear the weight of such a failure will crumble under it, and curse himself. God foresees this and says,

> And man curses, which is a prayer for evil, while he ought to pray for good, for man is given to hasty deeds. (*Bani Isra`il*, 11)

Some hasty people even hurry their daily ritual prayers. Shortening and hurrying their recitations, and rushing through their bowing and prostration, they may miss the prayers in the proper positions or make mistakes, thus causing their observance to be unacceptable to God and failing in their religious duties. Precipitateness in one's actions, spoken declarations, and thoughts and emotional reactions often cause breaches in the good behavior and character befitting the faithful.

Even if he realizes that his rushing about is a flaw, a hasty person may find excuses for it. He may tell himself that lengthy precautions and considerations that delay action are the mark of a lazy person who wastes time; the most valuable gift of God. That is indeed true in spiritual matters concerning the Hereafter, but not with regard to worldly affairs. God says:

> They believe in God and the Last Day, they enjoin what is right and forbid what is wrong, and they hasten to good works: they are the ones who are in the ranks of the righteous. (*Al-i `Imran*, 114)

And:

> Be quick in the race for repentance, asking forgiveness from your Lord, and the Paradise, whose width is that of the heavens and of the earth, prepared for the righteous. (*Al-i `Imran*, 159)

In one of his sermons, the Messenger of God said:

> O man, repent, and ask your Lord's forgiveness before you leave this world. Before the world occupies all your time, hurry to do deeds to save yourself. Remember your Lord often, so that you honor the solemn oath your soul made when it was created. Help others openly and secretly, for God helps those who help others. If you do these things, what you have missed in your obligations will be compensated. (Ibn Maja, Jabir)

And he said:

> What are you waiting for? Are you waiting to be rich, which will only make you rebel against God, or to become so poor that you will forget your worship? Are you waiting until you get older, when you won't have the strength, or to become sick, which will weaken your spirit? Are you counting on the coming of the notorious antichrist, *Dajjal*, to push you to move? Or are you going to wait until the last day of the worlds? (Tirmidhi, Abu Hurayrah)

He also said:

> Value five things before they are finished and gone. Value your life before death comes, your good health before sickness comes, your youth before old age comes, your spare time before worldly affairs leave you none, and your wealth before it is lost. (Ibn Abi Dunya, Ibn `Abbas)

Thus make haste in seeking salvation, in obeying your Lord, and in preparing for the Hereafter. But wait and be careful and take your precautions in worldly affairs—for your haste may lay waste your efforts to gain your eternal life in the Hereafter.

Another maleficent effect of haste is that it causes harshness, coarseness, and hard-heartedness. In one's hurry, one neglects considering other people. The Prophet said:

> The one who does not show concern and compassion for other people will not receive care and compassion. (Bukhari and Muslim, Abu Hurayrah)

The Prophet considered a hard-hearted person, who shows no care for other people's suffering on account of his actions, to be as bad as a murderous bandit.

> God tears away compassion only from the hard hearts of rebellious, tyrannical brigands in God's kingdom. (Tirmidhi, Abu Hurayrah)

God Himself warns His Prophet:

> Thus it is by God's mercy that you are gentle to them. If you had been rough, hard-hearted, they would have certainly broken away from around you. So forgive them their faults and ask for God's forgiveness for them, and consult them in matters. But when you have determined what to do, put your trust in God. Surely, God loves those who trust in Him. (*Al-i `Imran*, 158)

Hurrying one's decisions and actions makes for negligence, not only in regard to what happens to others, but also in regard to what happens to oneself. One may lose all sense of shame about one's mode of behavior— and shamelessness is an abominable thing, detested by God. Shamelessness is either an attitude of total unconsciousness, or else an arrogance whereby a person thinks that all he does is right, no matter what harm it causes. Even when the harm done is proven to such a person, he is likely to smile.

The first rule of noble shame is to be ashamed before your Lord about things you do that God considers to be detestable and sinful. Then shame appears concerning lesser misbehaviors, such as lack of consideration for others' feelings, rights, or well-being; carelessness about your own appearance, speech, and behavior; impoliteness, selfishness, aggressiveness, and so on. One should have shame in the presence of people with whom one interacts without forgetting to have shame in front of one's Lord.

Shamelessness is a sign of arrogance, weakness of spirit, and lack of religious seriousness and conscience. It is a sure sign of hypocrisy, especially if one manifests shame before other people but not before God and His Prophet. Who but a hypocrite would show himself to others as sorry for the thing he has done wrong, but not repent to God who has created and sustained him, given him a mind to understand, and taught him how to live? Woe to the one who is hurrying through this life careless of God and man, and woe to the shameless hypocrite who shows regret to men for his lawlessness, seeking their pardon and approval, while forgetting the witness of God.

> The Prophet commanded his Companions, "Always have shame in front of God." They said, "O Prophet, praise be to God! Indeed, we are ashamed in front of our Lord." And he said, "No, not like this. To really have shame, you must guard the head on your shoulders, and the mind and thoughts in it. You must guard its seven openings: your eyes, your ears, your nostrils, and your mouth. You must guard your body and what it contains: your heart, your stomach, and what is between your legs. You must guard what your hands hold and where your feet go. And remember death: that all but your soul will return to earth. Thus those who choose the eternal life in Heaven must keep under control their attachments to the attractions of this world and have shame in front of their Lord." (Tirmidhi, Ibn `Abbas)

And he said:

> Shame is a clear sign of faith, and the faithful are in Paradise. Shamelessness is a sign of suffering and cruelty, and the cruel are in hell. (Tirmidhi, Abu Hurayrah)

Shame, which indicates having a conscience, is a great gift of God. It is a means of security against doing wrong, and a means of repentance and regret when one does wrong involuntarily. God loves the repentant. The Messenger of God said:

Misbehavior unbefitting a believer dishonors a man and renders him ugly, while conscience and good behavior render one beautiful and likable by men and God. (Tirmidhi, Anas ibn Malik)

As mentioned previously, haste causes people to fail. Failure causes disappointment and discontentment with our lot. Then we complain. We forget that all the good things that happen to us come from God, while all the bad things are our own doing. And when we complain about our lot, we are complaining about God: we should fear God's punishment. God says:

O My servants who believe, fear your Lord. Good is the reward for those who do good in this world. Spacious is God's earth! Those who patiently persevere will surely receive a reward without measure. (*Zumar*, 10)

Patience is the antidote to the poison of haste and the failure and despair it causes. It is a quality praised by God and man. It brings people close to God. It is a key to success, both in overcoming the problems of this world and in opening the door to Paradise. The Messenger of God said:

God shows compassion and forgives the sins of those who show patience, do not complain, and hide their troubles from others when a misfortune befalls themselves or their property. (Tabarani, Ibn `Abbas)

Faith has two halves. One half of it is thankfulness, and the other half is patience. The highest form of patience is shown at the moment when misfortune strikes. (Daylami, Anas ibn Malik)

Try and show patience at the very moment the misfortune strikes, as this is the best. Patience is the essence of devotion and the foundation of saving oneself from sin. (Bukhari and Muslim, Anas ibn Malik)

Failure through haste leads to disappointment, not only with oneself but also with others. While a person may have received a great deal of help in his endeavor, he is apt to attribute his failure to conditions such as social rules and regulations, other persons, and even God, all of which appear to the ungrateful to have opposed his attempt. With this terrible ingratitude for all the help he has received past and present; he begins to hate and fear everyone. This is a very dangerous situation. It is a clear case of unthankfulness toward man and God, for the one who is unthankful toward other people cannot be thankful toward God. The Prophet said:

> The one who is unthankful for whatever little he gets will not become thankful when he is given a lot. Whoever is unthankful toward others who help him will not be thankful to God. Thankfulness is to realize that all you receive is given; to value what you receive; to express your gratefulness to the one who gave. This creates love and unity among people, and unity is mercy. To be unthankful creates division among people and disunity causes pain. (Ahmad ibn Hanbal, Nu`man ibn Bashir)

> The one who is thankful when he eats receives the same blessing from God as the one who shows patience and fasts for God's pleasure. (Tirmidhi, Abu Hurayrah)

God warns against ingratitude:

> God sets forth a parable: a city enjoying security and quiet, abundantly supplied with sustenance from every quarter; yet it is ungrateful for the favors of God. So God made it taste of hunger and terror from every side because of what they wrought. (*Nahl*, 112)

While ingratitude causes troubles and attracts God's wrath, thankfulness is a way to abundance in sustenance and God's grace. God says:

> ... and when your Lord made it known: If you are grateful, I will give you more, and if you are ungrateful, My chastisement is truly severe. (*Ibrahim*, 7)

And:

> Why should God chastise you if you believe in Him and you are thankful? And God knows, and even multiplies His rewards. (*Nisa'*, 147)

Haste is difficult to control because our emotions take hold of us much faster than our intellect can intervene. The worst of all emotional upheavals is anger. Usually a person suffers this violent feeling when he cannot have what he wants, when what he thought was right turns out wrong, or when he feels that his rights are being violated and he calls this injustice and reacts. Selfishness makes him blind to the fact that what he wants may belong to someone else; that what he thought of as right may be in direct opposition to law, order, and the customs of society; that what he felt as a violation of his rights may be a restraint put upon him to save him from disaster. Above all, he forgets that what happens to him is a part of his destiny, designed by God. When one reacts violently against men and God, and totally loses one's reason and mind, then a human being turns into a wild animal. That is why anger is a curse, and one of the greater sins.

In a divine tradition revealed to the Prophet, God says:

Those who do not show patience toward troubles and pains predestined for them and revolt against the fate that I set right for them may as well search for another Sustainer than I. (Tabarani, Abu Hind al-Dari)

And the Prophet said:

If you wish to know what God thinks of you, look at your own hearts and see how you feel about Him. He is the way you think of Him. If you resent Him, He will resent you. (Hakim, Jabir ibn `Abdullah)

An angry person can try to change his character through moral exercise, through purposefully showing acceptance and consent toward whatever happens. And it is necessary to educate oneself by studying multiple sides of an affair in order to become convinced that one is not always right, and that things appearing to be wrong at first sight may not turn out to be so in the long run. Above all, one should remember that "everything good, and everything that appears to be bad, comes from God." And God is Good and Merciful.

Let it not be forgotten that neither troubles, real or imaginary, nor sins committed, are destined in themselves. They are a potential in everyone's fate, which some arrogant people draw upon themselves as tall trees draw lightning.

Anger directed against a specific person or establishment is usually caused by disappointment. Disappointment occurs when someone depends on someone else for something and the one upon whom one depended does not deliver. People forget that a dependent has no claim to raise against the one upon whom he depends: the provider is neither obliged to deliver, nor is his ability to deliver guaranteed, nor has he obliged the dependent to depend on him. On the other hand, God has obliged us all to depend on Himself; His Treasures and Power are infinite, and adequate to satisfy our needs. All of us should depend on God alone.

God is the Source of all, but He uses people and things as means. Therefore, depending on God does not mean not to look for help from His creation. Neither does it mean that one should not work toward the good and take precautions against the bad. But having done what a person is capable of doing, we should entrust our efforts into the hands of God, who will give whatever result He esteems to be right, for whatever comes from God is good and right. God says,

But in God put your trust, if you have faith. (*Ma'idah*, 23)

Is not God enough for His servant? (*Zumar*, 36)

Surely, those whom you depend on besides God control no sustenance for you. So seek sustenance from God and serve Him and be grateful to Him. To Him you will be brought back. (*'Ankabut*, 17)

... and He provides for him from sources he never could imagine. And if anyone puts his trust in God, sufficient is God for him, for God will surely accomplish His purpose. Verily for all things God has appointed a due proportion. (*Talaq*, 3)

And the Messenger of God said:

Those who depend on magic and charms or cures such as cauterizing to regain their health are far from having trust in God's healing powers. (Tabarani, Mughirah ibn Shu'ba)

And `Umar ibn al-Khattab reported that he said:

If you truly believed and trusted God, He would feed you as He feeds the birds. The birds that are hungry in the morning are all fed by the evening: only God knows how. (Tirmidhi)

If a person who trusts God has today's sustenance, he does not worry about tomorrow's. Abu Darda' reports that the Messenger of God said:

As your appointed time of death follows you all through your life, so does your God-allotted sustenance. (Ibn Hibban)

One day, the Messenger of God saw a date half-buried in sand. He pulled it out and offered it to Ibn `Umar, who was with him, and said:

If you had not come upon it, this date would have found you wherever you were. (Bayhaqi, Ibn `Umar)

Anas ibn Malik reported that someone asked whether he shouldn't just leave his camel untied, entrusting it to God. The Messenger of God said:

No, first take all precautions. Tie your camel, then depend on God to keep it safe. (Tirmidhi, Anas ibn Malik)

Thus trust in God does not require leaving everything to Him without doing anything yourself. Conversely, working to obtain what you need or asking for other people's help does not mean that you do not trust in God. Indeed, to have a hand in fulfilling your own needs is the best endeavor available to recommend you to God's favor.

But in his hurry to accomplish something, a hasty person will not hesitate to cooperate with, befriend, even offer support to, a depraved, faithless sinner. This is most unbecoming to a believer and extremely dangerous, even if these people occupy the highest positions and are very powerful. God warns us:

> And incline not to those who do wrong, lest the fire touch you. And you have no help beside God; otherwise you will not be helped. (*Hud*, 113)

And the Prophet said:

> Do not show respect and call a deceitful hypocrite "master," even if you mistakenly think of him as one. You will anger your Lord by taking an enemy of God as your master, and will suffer His wrath. (Tirmidhi, Buraydah)

Thus shy away from, or oppose, those who rebel against God, and fight those who attempt to pervert God's rules and prescriptions with their words and actions—for that is the worst of tyranny to the believers. Fight them with your actions. If you cannot, then fight them with your words. And if you cannot even speak against them, fearing for your life and the welfare of your family and friends, then at least deplore them in your heart.

People who work for and sympathize with tyrants who oppose God and the godly do not like decent people. Pious and righteous believers and spiritual teachers are their particular enemies. Since the faithful love for God's sake and strive for justice, and hate for God's sake and oppose tyranny, they should oppose people who take themselves to be gods. God tells to His Messenger:

> Say: If you do love God, follow me, then God will love you, and forgive you your sins; God is oft-forgiving, most merciful. (*Al`Imran*, 31)

And the Messenger of God said:

> The best a man can do is to love for God's sake and hate for God's sake. (Abu Dawud, from Abu Dharr)

> Tyrants, who are guilty of the unforgivable sin of ascribing partners to God, are hidden like a black ant walking on a black stone in the middle of the night. (Hakim, Hadrat `A'ishah)

One who does not love for God's sake and hate for God's sake does not feel the truth of faith in his heart. Only when one loves for God and hates for God is one loved by one's Lord. (Ibn Hanbal and Tabarani, `Amr ibn Jamuh)

One of the signs of faith is to love God's creation, not because one benefits from the beloved, but because one loves for God's sake. (Tabarani, `Abdullah ibn Mas`ud)

Someone asked the Prophet what he thought of a man who loves pious people who do good deeds, but is neither as good as they nor able to do good as they do. He answered: "A person is united with the people he loves." (Bukhari and Muslim, Ibn Mas`ud)

All these failures in human behavior—hurrying through this life, which is our only chance to prove ourselves worthy of God's love; squandering His most valuable gift, our allotted time—come about through heedlessness, being asleep. Because of heedlessness we become daring, fearless, dreaming that we are invincible knights while at best, we are powerless tools in the hands of God.

The cure for all ills is consciousness: to wake up from the sleep of heedlessness. What is needed is fear, fear of God—not so much the fear of His punishment, but the fear of losing His love and care.

Religion is the awe of God. It is the conviction that you, and all and everything, are His. Everything that happens to you and to the universe is in His hands. You have no power except that which comes from Him. You have no say except as He directs you and orders you. And all He is and does and gives, and everything He directs you to do, is good. Thus the fear of God is this awe of His greatness and power in contrast to human nothingness. It should lead humanity to heedfulness of what is happening to us, and of what we are expected to do. And it should make us realize how we have failed and thus draw us to repentance, to working with patience, to enduring the tests, to gratitude for the rewards we receive, and to an awareness of our unworthiness in the face of all God's gifts.

All this in turn brings people closer to God. It will bring you certainty instead of dreaming and enable you to see the real reality. The saintly Dhunun al-Misri said:

Certainly seeing reality reduces ambition and haste. It increases fear of God and piety in one's heart, and asceticism in one's needs and actions.

Heedfulness—seeing the truth about yourself, your world, and your life, seeing God's hand in everything—will raise you to the level of being God's servant. Divine servanthood is the highest spiritual level to which any human being can aspire, because it is the level of the Prophet of God. To be a servant of God is total freedom: it is freedom from being a slave to the world. This freedom in turn frees one's will from being a slave to customs and habits, and permits it to seek with sincerity the Truth, the universal conscience. Finding that, you will be freed from all fault and rewarded with salvation and peace in this world and with spiritual bliss in the Hereafter. God says:

> Among His servants, only those who are possessed of knowledge fear God. Surely God is mighty, forgiving. (*Fath*, 28)

And:

> Their reward is with their Lord: gardens of perpetuity wherein flow rivers, abiding therein forever. God is well pleased with them, and they are well pleased with God. That is for the one who fears his Lord. (*Bayyinah*, 8)

God says in a divine tradition revealed to His Prophet:

> Upon My Might and My Glory, I will not allow two fears and two certainties in My servants at the same time. If My servant fears Me during his life in the world, I will give him certainty and security on the Day of Judgment. If he is fearless of Me, sure and secure in the world, let him fear My wrath on the Day of Judgment. (Ibn Hibban, from Abu Hurayrah)

Someone asked the Messenger of God what he should do to save himself from Hellfire. The Prophet answered:

> Cry! Eyes that shed tears with the fear of God are eternally safe from Hellfire. (Isfahani, Zayd ibn Erkam)

The following words of the Prophet, and of the virtuous saints who know better than we, describe their fear of God. The Prophet said:

> I am able to see what you cannot see and hear what you cannot hear. The heavens are moaning and groaning. There is not an empty space there as big as your palm where there is not an angel crying in prostration in fear of God. God is my witness, if you knew what I know, you would laugh little and cry much. You would not be able to enjoy your wives in bed. You would wander out into the desert lamenting, begging for God's mercy. Oh I wish I were a fallen tree, instead of a man. (Tirmidhi, Abu Dharr)

The saintly Fudayl said:

> I do not envy either the most perfect man or a prophet sent by God or

his angels closest to Him, because they too will be present on the Day of Judgment. I envy the one who is not born.

`Ata' ibn `Abdrabbih, a pious ascetic from the generation after the Prophet, said:

If there were a fire and I was told that I would not be reborn on the Day of Judgment if I threw myself into it, I fear my heart would stop from joy before I could throw myself into it.

The famous Sufi saint Sari al-Saqati of Baghdad said:

How many times a day I look to the tip of my nose, crossing my eyes, to see if God has turned my face black because of the faults and sins I have committed.

He also said:

How I wish they would bury me somewhere other than Baghdad. I fear that the earth will reject my corpse and spit me out of my grave and embarrass my friends.

O my readers, my brothers in faith, woe to us whose shoulders are heavy with sin! Hear how the pure ones, the beloved ones of God, feared Him, though there was no reason for them to fear. What makes us so secure? It is because we are asleep, unaware of our reality. Wake up from the deadly sleep of heedlessness. Love the ones who loved God and whom God loved. Try to follow them. Perchance God will count us among them, as His Prophet promised:

A person is together with the one he loves in this world and in the Hereafter. (Bukhari, Anas ibn Malik)

O You who run to help the desperate who cry for help, O You who forgive all but the one who takes himself to be god, O Most Merciful of all who are merciful: We are guilty of ingratitude for all that You have given us, and we confess. Forgive us for the sake of Your chosen Prophet, Your most beloved creation, whom You have sent as a mercy upon the worlds, Hadrat Muhammad Mustafa (s.a.w.s)—may Your blessings be upon him, and upon all the prophets You have sent before him, and upon Your angels closest to You. You love them and they love You. You are pleased with them and they are pleased with You. Accord us their intercession and forgive us for their sake: cleanse our hearts and our acts and hide our faults. You are the Veiler of sins, You are the All-Forgiving, You are the All-Merciful, O Generous, All-Compassionate God. *Amin.*

CHAPTER 19

ON HOPELESSNESS

Hopelessness is a curse: a source of much mischief that eventually may lead to loss of faith. It starts with doubting God's beneficence and ends in believing that He does not exist. When someone loses faith in God, there are no bounds to his mindless and heedless actions and behavior. When one does not fear God, it seems that misbehavior has no consequences. One loses track of all obligations, duties, consideration of others, ethics and morals.

When a person has lost hope of God's beneficence, his only concern is himself. He has lost his faith in God, so his ego becomes his god. He does not believe in the Hereafter or the Day of Judgment, so the worldly life is his only domain and his only chance is to make the best of everything in it. As he does not believe either in divine justice or in divine punishment, he has no scruples about committing criminal acts as long as he is not apprehended by human justice—which he tries to sway in his favor if he can.

God is ever forgiving and compassionate. Hopelessness is a madness that makes a person vulnerable to falling into the betrayal of faith. Caught in time, like any sickness, it can be cured. It suffices to remember God's compassion, manifest in all the good things with which one is blessed, and how similar troubles in the past faded away and were replaced by better conditions. Remember that the solution to problems does not depend entirely on our own precautions. Often these do not work, and sometimes, miraculously, they do so unexpectedly.

The Prophet said:

> When you see someone who is better off than you are, look at someone who is less well off. Doing this will keep you from belittling the blessings God has given to you. (Abu Hurayrah)

Just this kind of reasoning suffices to turn hopelessness into hope, attracts God's mercy and generosity upon the despondent one, and strengthens his faith.

God says:

> O my servants who have transgressed against themselves, despair not of the mercy of God; surely God forgives sins altogether, for God is Forgiving, Most Merciful. (*Zumar*, 53)

The Prophet said:

On the Day of Judgment God will come out with such mercy and forgiveness for sinners that none could have expected or imagined it; even the accursed Devil will hope to be forgiven. (Ibn Abi Dunya, Ibn Mas`ud)

And he said:

When God created the creation, He inscribed upon His throne, "My mercy far surpasses My wrath." (Bukhari, Abu Hurayrah)

Our Creator divided His mercy into one hundred parts. He kept 99 portions, and sent one upon this world to be divided among His creation from the beginning of time until the end. That is what makes the wild beast pull in its sharp claws so that it does not hurt the cub; that is what makes people show care and compassion for each other. God kept the other 99 portions of mercy to be spent on the faithful on the Day of Judgment. (Bukhari and Muslim, Abu Hurayrah)

Abu Ayyub al-Ansari, when he was on his deathbed, said that he had hidden up until then something he had heard the Prophet say, fearing that it might be misunderstood, and he recited the following prophetic tradition:

If humankind had not sinned, God would have taken them away and replaced them with sinners so that He could forgive them. (Muslim)

Hopelessness primarily affects those who are attached to this world. They love the worldly life, so if any pleasure they lust for is denied to them, they are devastated. In fact, for most of humanity, the source of all unhappiness is disillusionment concerning worldly ambitions. When people attain what they had hoped for, instead of thanking God, they are thankful to the world. Disappointment may lead to hopelessness, which God dislikes, instead of patience, which God loves, but contentment too may lead to arrogance and rebelling against God, instead of gratitude toward God. Both the good fortune and the trials of life may lead people to sin.

Know that people do not know what is ultimately good for them, but God does. And nothing happens in this world, or in our lives, except with the will of God. If we have faith, whether that which comes from God seems good or bad to us, it should make no difference. Such acceptance is the sign of a true Muslim, who submits to the Lord. God says,

... so that you may not despair over matters that pass you by, nor exult over favors bestowed upon you. For God does not like vainglorious boasters. (*Hadid*, 23)

Although he is vain, the hopeless one who counts only upon himself and upon the world is full of fear. He is not afraid of God, but he is afraid of the world and the trials of the world. He is afraid of sickness, of poverty, and of any harm that might come from another person. Such fear is deeper and more devastating than the fear of someone who is naturally a coward. A cowardly person is not violent, for he does not have the courage to fight. But a hopeless person who is afraid is dangerous. Because he has no hope, he does not think of the risks when he fights. Scratching and scrambling, he tries to gather the goods of this world, and then he lives in terror of losing them. By contrast, the righteous who count on God, when they are poor, remember that poverty is the state of prophets and saints. The hopeless eat their fill when their neighbors are hungry, fearing for their own health and well-being. The faithful hope for God's promised reward of a hundred times the care they give to the ones in need. A hopeless person is afraid of everyone, because he thinks everyone is like himself. A faithful person thinks well of everyone, and considers the other faithful as his brothers.

> The Prophet visited Hadrat Bilal, who was sick, and was brought a plate full of dates to eat. He said, "What extravagance is this, Bilal?" When Bilal said that he had saved them to offer to him, he said, "Do not gather and keep anything. Are you doubting that God, the owner of all, will sustain you? Anything you save will be fuel for Hellfire." (Tabarani, Abu Hurayrah)

O you who love and fear God and have unshakable hope in His beneficence, do not fear poverty! To fear poverty is an insult to God because it means distrust in His generosity. If poverty comes upon you in spite of all your precautions, accept your destiny, and find consolation in having been brought to the way of the prophets, the saints, and the pious ascetics.

Your personal devil, your ego, will tell you that being poor and ill-fed will make you and your family sick, and may even kill you. If not, it will at least prevent you from working, which may finally force you to beg and lose your dignity. Use your mind: being poor does not make you sick. In fact, an affluent way of life is often the cause of sickness. Poverty never prevented anyone from working. On the contrary, it encourages people to try harder to better their condition. Rather it is arrogance, hypocrisy, and laziness— bad qualities mostly produced by power, fame, and riches—that are the causes of not wanting to work. Begging and needing the help of others is a good deed, as it enables the charitable to perform a good deed. Besides, if to be sick is in your destiny, it will happen whether you are rich or poor. If your sickness prevents you from fasting and praying, God accepts that, and in your incapacity will continue giving you the benefit of your customary worship. If you show patience with the pain and suffering of your sickness, God will load you with His pleasure, forgiving your sins. The blessed companions of the Prophet, when they received the announcement of the benefits due on the Day of Judgment to those who are patient in sickness, wished their sufferings were like those of the Prophet Job, whom God praised to His angels.

For those who lack patience with suffering, the Prophet taught the recitation of the following prayer, mornings and evenings:

O Lord, I beg from You good health in this world and safety in the Hereafter.

O Lord, I beg for Your mercy and beneficence in the affairs of my life and my religion; in what I own; for myself and my household. Make us feel secure from the things we fear, and hide our faults.

O Lord, I take refuge in You from evil coming from before me and behind me, from my left and right; and from above. Protect me from what may come from below to destroy me. (Abu Dawud, Ibn `Umar)

Above all, do not fear human beings. People who fear God will not harm other people. A believer is a person from whose tongue and hand others are safe. Keep your distance from those who rebel against God, but do not fear them, for if they attack you, God considers them to be attacking Him. He is the best and most powerful of helpers, and He is sufficient for you.

The one who has lost hope in God is capable of taking advantage of other people, for he has also lost his conscience. He is deceitful, treacherous, swindling, double-dealing, lying. The Prophet said:

The one who cheats is not one of us. (Muslim, Ibn `Umar)

One day, in the marketplace, the Prophet passed by a bag of wheat. He liked the look of it and wanted to buy some. But when he dug his hand into the bag, he felt that under its surface, the wheat was wet. He asked the merchant how he could sell such wet wheat. The man replied that it had been rained on. The Prophet asked him, "But how can you hide it, by putting dry wheat on top of it and fooling people?"

It is an obligation for the righteous, when they sell or even give something away, to inform the recipient if the thing changing hands has any deficiency. It is also not permissible to praise something changing hands above its true value, with the intention of selling it above its actual worth. In such a case, the buyer has the right to return the merchandise. On the other hand, one has a right to sell something well above the price one originally paid, if the market permits, as long as one does not have the intention of cheating.

Cheating does not apply only to commerce. Deception is wrong in other human relationships, whether in the characterization of a future bride or groom prior to marriage, or in the self-description of someone seeking employment, or in the terms of a job being offered, or in the conditions of any kind of deal between two parties.

Deception injures people through a pernicious influence that they cannot foresee. It is wholly wrong when undertaken for personal benefit, for the person cheated does not deserve such treatment. But in self-defense against a tyrant or in war, deception is acceptable. It is said, "War is won only by deception."

A believer must put himself in the place of the person with whom he is dealing in all human relations, including conflict. The Prophet said:

I swear upon my Lord in Whose hand is my soul, that if any one of you does not wish for his fellow Muslim that which he wishes for himself, he is not truly a believer. (Abu Hurayrah)

Intrigue and mischief-making are other dirty tools in the hands of the hopeless from which they think they can reap some benefit. Instead, in the creation of disorder, sedition, and rebellion among people they consider to be their enemies, the hopeless themselves also drown. God says:

Mischief-making among people is worse than committing murder. (*Baqarah*, 191)

It doesn't matter who is responsible for inciting people to revolt against authority, law, and order, setting people against each other, creating anarchy: that person is a sinner. Even an authority who speaks to the public in a way they may not understand, so that they misinterpret his words, has committed a sin. Even a spiritual teacher or a religious scholar who speaks over the heads of the congregation, or who tries to enforce upon them long-forgotten customs or ways of worship, well above their endurance, or who forbids them things that might be slightly undesirable according to religious law, but which people are used to doing and cannot do without, is guilty of mischief-making. Carelessness of the tongue is the cause of much bitterness among human beings. The Prophet said:

Talk to people only in a way that they will understand.

O believer, watch your tongue! It can produce the sweetest or the bitterest reaction. Have a care for the one who listens to what you say. Do not say anything unless you are sure that the one who hears it will understand it as you meant it, that he will agree with it, and that he is able to apply what you say to his life. If one of these conditions is missing, you had best not say anything. Otherwise, even if you have the best of intentions, you may lead people astray. And for each wrongdoing you have provoked in others, you will be doubly punished by God.

Silence is better than useless speech. But speak loudly and clearly against tyranny, and against those who act against God and your faith. For no matter how humble your place in society, if you are aware of a wrong being done, to be silent is equally wrong. The Prophet said:

> The one who does not speak out against tyranny and injustice is nothing but a dumb devil.

He also said:

> Do not fear to tell the truth, even if the result is bitter. (Abu Dharr)

God mentions such believers as

> ... people whom He loves and who love Him: humble toward believers, mighty against disbelievers, fighting in the way of God and never afraid of the reproaches of such as find fault. (*Ma'idah*, 54)

Although the reward goes to the courageous who speak out against what is ungodly, the Prophet permits silence for persons who may with certainty expect a disaster to fall upon them and those around them if they speak the truth. God is Ever-Forgiving.

While fearing, cheating, and fighting with other people, the one who has lost hope in God has no one to depend on except men. Therefore he desperately seeks their company and their help. When he is without them he feels isolated and desolate because he cannot exercise his arrogance, egoism, and selfishness. His greatest joy is being the center of attention. Such persons become attached to and dependent upon others. They are over-demanding, thinking the help they receive is their right, and soon they are rejected. Abu Bakr al-Shibli said, "To depend on men is a sure sign of bankruptcy."

What is proper for the righteous is to limit their relations with others. We serve as instruments in God's hands. Thus we should care for other people and help them, since "the hand that gives is better than the hand that takes." But neither depend on people nor spend too much time with them. People often congregate not to pray or remember God, but rather to forget. In such gatherings of careless acts, senseless talk, laughter without mirth or joy, noise instead of peace, men lead each other to heedlessness. God says:

> Keep up prayer, enjoin good and forbid evil, and bear patiently that which befalls you. Indeed this is an affair of great purpose and determination. Turn not your face away from people in contempt, nor go about in the land exultingly. Surely God does not like any self-conceited boaster.

Pursue the right course in your going about, and lower your voice. Surely the most hateful of voices is the braying of an ass. (*Luqman*, 17-19)

If you are ever forced to be together with people of this character, do not ever attempt to discuss any serious matter, especially spiritual and religious subjects. What you will encounter is an obstinate adversary in debate. Such a person will never accept the truth, but will try to win the debate with a jumble of words that are clearly insincere, hypocritical, subjective, untrue, and delivered in a very loud and ostentatious way. You will never be able to change such people's minds, but they may be able to disturb your peace. Having lost hope in God, they are not only rebelling against God and truth: their life is a rebellion against law and order, morals and decency, and especially against anything or anybody they loathe seeing as an authority above them. Their banners in this war with the world are ambition, arrogance, greed, envy, lust, and revenge. The swords they use in their fight are denial of the rights of others, lack of compassion and love, selfishness, ignorance, stupidity, perverting the truth, hypocrisy, and shamelessness. Sinning is a way of life for them. Even major acts of sin such as destruction, violence, rape, and murder can be justified in their minds. As they have no conscience, even the slightest sense of repentance does not occur to them. If only they could repent! In spite of all they have done, God might forgive them. But repentance is a sign of hope in God's compassion and forgiveness, and they are the way they are because they have lost that hope.

Here is a summary list of the awful states that those who have lost their hope in God may suffer. Such a person will be angry; distrustful, faithless, and untrustworthy; hypocritical, arrogant; and ungrateful; hating and hateful; tyrannical, violent, and destructive; ambitious, greedy, and lustful; critical, yet hating criticism; loving to be praised while feeling inferior; hostile, vengeful, cowardly, noisy, cheating, lying, lazy, hasty, ignorant and stupid, hard-hearted, shameless, immoral, excessively worldly, and never regretting what he has done.

Yet God says:

Surely God loves those who repent and loves those who cleanse themselves of their faults. (*Baqarah*, 222)

And:

And repent to God all, O believers, so that you will have the deliverance from your sins that you hope for. (*Nur*, 31)

And:

O you who believe, turn to God with sincere repentance. It may be your Lord will remove from you your evil and cause you to enter gardens wherein flow rivers, on the day in which God will not abase His Prophet and those who believe in him. (*Tahrim*, 8)

And the Messenger of God said:

The one who repents for his sins is like the one who has not sinned. (Bayhaqi, Ibn `Abbas)

But he also warns,

The one who asks God for forgiveness of his sins yet continues sinning is mocking his Lord. (Bayhaqi, Ibn `Abbas)

(Hamid al-Tawil asked Anas ibn Malik, "Is it true that you have heard the Prophet say 'Just to regret what one has done wrong is the same as repenting?'" and Anas said "Yes.")
The Messenger of God also said:

When God knows that His servant regrets what he has done, even if he does not declare it, He forgives him even before he repents. (Hakim, Hadrat `A'ishah)

And:

Even if you have sinned so much that your piled-up sins would reach the sky ... God will accept your repentance. (Ibn Maja, Abu Hurayrah)

May God have mercy upon the one who has lost his hopes, and upon all of us. And may we all hope for the intercession of His Prophet, whom God has sent as His mercy upon the Universe. *Amin.*

"Obeying one's parents is like obeying God."

CHAPTER 20

THE USE OF THE TONGUE

ON SPEAKING IN GENERAL

On the Day of Judgment our own organs—our tongue, our eyes, our ears, our hands, and the rest of our physical being—will be witnesses against us. Above all, watch your tongue, for speech is the unique gift that God has bestowed only upon the human being. The welfare of the rest of you depends on your tongue. The Messenger of God, when asked about the best thing a person can do to gain God's approval, said:

Watch your tongue. (Abu Shaykh and Bayhaqi, Abu Juhayfah)

And he said:

Every morning when a person wakes up the whole body begs the tongue, "Fear God for our sake, for our salvation depends upon you! If you are true, we will be truthful. If you are false, we are doomed." (Tirmidhi, Abu Sa`id al-Khudri)

And:

No one is truly a servant of God until he is able to watch his tongue. (Tabarani, Anas ibn Malik)

And:

No one is truly faithful unless truth enters his heart, and truth does not penetrate the heart unless the tongue is truthful. (Ahmad ibn Hanbal, Anas ibn Malik)

And:

Learn to lock up your tongues in the prison of your mouths. (Tabarani, Anas ibn Malik)

And God says about us:

Not a word he utters but there is by him a watcher at hand. (*Kaaf*, 18)

Sufyan ibn `Abdullah related:

I asked the Messenger of God : "O Prophet, tell me an act that will save me from Hellfire."

He answered, "Believe that God is your Lord and be true to Him."

Then I asked: "What should I fear most in life?" The Prophet pointed to his tongue and said: "Your tongue." (Tirmidhi)

Aslam related:

One day `Umar went to visit Abu Bakr and when he entered his room, he saw Abu Bakr pulling at his tongue violently. He protested, "Stop, Abu Bakr, may God forgive you, what are you doing?"

And he answered, "It is this that always gets me into trouble!" (Tabarani)

The Messenger of God said:

If you can promise me that you will be able to control your tongue in your mouth and what is between your two legs, I can promise that God will take you to His Paradise. (Bukhari, Sahl ibn Sa`d)

The tongue is loose: it is hard to keep it straight. The best way to keep it from going astray is to close it inside the mouth and keep quiet. It has no control in itself: it babbles and makes noises unless it becomes a tool of the mind. To teach the tongue to speak only when necessary is a great exercise and demands a great effort. It is best to consider the following rule: Speak only when you know that what you say is in accordance with truth mentioned in the Qur'an or the Traditions of the Prophet, or with what the wise close to God or true scholars have said. Then make sure that those who listen to you understand what you say, and also that they will agree with you. Furthermore, make sure that people are able to put into action what they have heard from you. If any of these conditions is missing, it is best to stay silent.

The Prophet said:

Whoever among you believes in God and the Day of Judgment, either speak of things from which people will benefit, or keep silent. (Tirmidhi, Abu Hurayrah)

And he said:

Do not speak in a manner displeasing to your Lord. Empty talk hardens people's hearts, and people with hard hearts drift away from God. (Tirmidhi, Ibn `Umar)

Someone asked the Messenger of God for advice on how to live as a believer should. He answered:

To respect God as you should is the source of all good deeds. Be prepared to fight for God's sake: to fight against one's ego is the greatest of struggles. Remember God always, read God's prescriptions in the Holy Book, because that will shed light upon your life in this world and secure God's remembrance of you in the heavens. And watch your tongue even when you speak beneficently. If you do these things, you will resist the temptations of the accursed Devil. (Tabarani, Abu Sa`id)

And he said:

Most of the mischief that people suffer is from their tongue. (Tabarani, Abu Wa`il)

Amr ibn Dinar related:

One day a man came to visit the Prophet and spoke for a very long time. Finally the Prophet asked the man: "Tell me how many barriers there are between the tongue and the outside of the mouth." The man answered, "Two sets of teeth and two lips." Then the Prophet said: "How is it that none of those are able to make you stop talking?" (Ibn Abi Dunya)

And he warned us, saying:

A man utters a word, seeing no harm in it, but this very word makes him fall into Hellfire from seventy years' distance up in the heavens. (Tirmidhi, Abu Hurayrah)

And:

A good man comes so close to Paradise that the distance between him and eternal salvation is no more than the length of a spear. Then he utters a thoughtless word that throws him back the distance from here to Yemen. (Abi Dunya, Amat bint Hakim)

And:

If you talk a lot, you will surely slip. (Abu Nu`aym, Ibn `Umar)

And:

Those who hold their tongues are as blessed as those who keep some of their fortune to spend in charity. (Bazzar)

And he said:

The one who keeps silence is saved. (Tirmidhi, `Abdullah ibn `Umar)

Yet it must be understood that to keep silent when something essential and true must be said is also wrong. The point is that one must think before saying a word, passing it through the sieve of what is permissible or forbidden according to religion, conscience, and necessity. Then say what you must say clearly and briefly. If you keep quiet, it should not be because you are afraid of the adverse consequences of what must be said. One should keep quiet so as not to say things of no consequence, unnecessary and useless, or words that are sacrilegious, leading people astray, creating negativity or doubt.

SACRILEGE

The worst word the tongue might utter is the denial of God and His prophets. If that sacrilege is declared willfully and publicly, one loses one's religion. All the divine rewards promised for good deeds are lost, and such a person is considered by the religious community to be as dead, a sinner bound for Hell. The marriage of such a man is automatically annulled. If he dies before repenting, no religious funeral will be performed for him.

If those who have so spoken repent, publicly renouncing their sacrilegious declarations or abandonment of faith, their marriages may be reinstituted. If the penitent is a woman, her husband is obliged to take her back with a renewal of the marriage ceremony. If the penitent is a man, his wife need not take him back unless she so wishes, in which case they will have to be married again.

In any case, penitents who have the means must perform a Pilgrimage, even if they had already fulfilled that duty in the past. They need not repeat the other obligatory religious practices, such as daily prayers and fasting that were completed before the utterance of the sinful words. However any worship they might have performed during the period when their religion was invalidated must be repeated.

This grave infidelity occurs only in cases when one means inwardly, and confesses outwardly, that one denies the existence of God and rejects the religion of Islam. There are lesser cases when one may utter a sacrilegious word in jest or error. This is less reprehensible. It still necessitates sincere repentance, but it is not punishable as is intentional infidelity.

LYING

Another detestable utterance of the tongue is lying. Telling untruths is certainly one of the gravest of sins if it is done on purpose, when one knows perfectly well that the thing is untrue and intends to cause harm by saying it.

God orders us to avoid lying with all our strength, and threatens us, saying:

... and for them is a painful chastisement because they lie. (*Baqarah*, 10)

To lie is unnatural, because it is untrue. The Prophet said:

Humanity is created with a multitude of dispositions, and lying and disloyalty are not among them. (Imam Ahmad, Abu `Umamah)

And he said:

Someone who lies, makes fun of others, or is a hypocrite, hiding who he really is—even if such a person finds justification for his acts, he is not truly faithful. (Abu Ya`la, `Umar ibn al-Khattab)

And:

Lying is a black smear on your character that will never wash away. You will pay for slander, hypocrisy, and lying with the tortures of the grave. (Ibn Hibban, Abu Barza)

And:

When you lie, the angels around you run away from the stench to a distance of ten miles. (Tirmidhi, Ibn `Umar)

The blessed wife of the Prophet reported that the only people he disliked were the liars. When the Prophet knew that someone had lied, that person's love left his heart until the liar repented to him.

It was reported by his beloved friend Hadrat Abu Bakr as-Siddiq that the Prophet said:

Lying is the opposite of faith in God. The two cannot be together. And the worst of lies is slander. (Bayhaqi)

And the Prophet said:

There is no atonement for five wrongdoings: to assign partners to the One and Only God; to kill; to slander someone; to run away from the enemy in a just struggle; to swear to the truth of something one knows to be a lie in order to take what does not belong to you. (Imam Ahmad, Abu Hurayrah)

The Prophet said:

Whoever misappropriates someone's property through lying and cheating has lost his chance to enter Paradise and certainly deserves Hell. (Muslim)

And:

False witness is as punishable as the unforgivable sin of assigning partners to God. (Huzaymah ibn Fatiq)

Abu Bakr related:

I heard the Prophet say, "Shall I tell you which are the greatest among all the great sins? They are assigning partners to God, revolting against one's parents and abandoning them, and lying in bearing witness." When he said this, he kept repeating "Do not lie, do not lie ..." (Bukhari, Muslim)

The worst of lying and slander is to slander God and His Messenger. God says:

And who does more wrong than the one who invents a lie against God or rejects the truth when it reaches him? Is there not a place in Hell for those who reject faith? (`Ankabut, 68)

And the Messenger of God said:

When someone slanders me and lies about me it is not like lying against any other truth. Whoever purposefully lies against me had better prepare his place in Hell. (Bukhari, Mughirah ibn Shu`bah)

When a man, pretending to be a scholar of Islamic law and customs, promulgates wrong information on legal matters, he is distorting God's prescriptions either purposefully or in error. In either case his rulings are considered to be lying and slandering God, who warns such people:

But say not, of any false thing that your tongues may put forth, "This is lawful and this is forbidden," so that you forge a lie against God. Surely those who ascribe false things to God will never prosper. (*Nahl*, 116)

And:

And who does more wrong than the one who invents a lie against God or rejects the truth when it reaches him? Is there not a place in Hell for those who reject faith? (`Ankabut, 68)

And the Prophet of God said:

> If those who have authority over others give false rulings in legal matters, the divine punishment due to the ones who did wrong in consequence falls on them manyfold. (Ibn Abi Dunya, Abu Hurayrah)

It is equally wrong to attribute words arbitrarily to the Messenger of God. The science of authenticity of the Traditions of the Prophet is a trustworthy historical method depending on proofs of the times and places and relationships in the chain of people who reported the traditions, ensuring that they truly talked to each other. Anyone who attributes words and actions to the Prophet without being sure of their authenticity is committing a grave sin.

The Messenger of God said:

> Fear in your hearts the punishment of God when you repeat my words unless you are absolutely sure that I said those words. (Tirmidhi, Ibn `Abbas)

Repentance absolves sins. The repentance for lying and slander is undertaken in three steps. First you must make a firm decision not to repeat the wrong in the future. Then you must confess to and ask pardon from the person you have slandered or lied about. Finally you must confess to the people to whom you spoke falsely about the person you slandered.

God, whose mercy far surpasses His wrath, may forgive sins committed against Him. But He will not forgive sins committed against human beings until the person who was wronged forgives the person who committed the wrong.

Someone who claims that people other than his own parents are his parents is considered to be guilty of one of the worst lies.

The Messenger of God, who was an orphan and was cared for by his grandfather and his uncle in his youth, said:

> Whoever denies his father and claims another as such has lost his chance of entering Paradise. (Bukhari, Sa`d ibn Abi Waqqas)

And:

> The one who claims as his father someone other than his real father is guilty of a denial not much different from denying God as his Lord. The one who claims something as his when it really belongs to someone else is not a faithful person and had better prepare for his place in Hell. And if someone calls someone else an infidel while that person is faithful, the accusation will turn back on him and make him an infidel himself. (Bukhari, Abu Dharr)

Lesser forms of lying include promising something you know you will not be able to deliver; offering made-up dreams for interpretation; listening critically to the talk of people you dislike with the intention of repeating it, hoping to create contempt for them; repeating in public things you have heard said in private; and making fun of people.

The Prophet said:

If somebody listens to the talk of some people who do not want him to listen, molten lead will be poured into his ears on the Day of Resurrection. (Bukhari, Ibn `Abbas)

And:

It is enough evil for you that you repeat everything you have heard. (Muslim, Abu Hurayrah)

It is permitted to say something you know to be untrue in the following three situations. The Messenger of God said:

Lying is made lawful under three conditions: In marriage, when a husband compliments his wife with the intention of pleasing her. In war, for the best strategy in battle is misinformation. In cases of conflict and animosity between two believers, when someone may report to each that the other is saying good things about him, even if it is not true, in order to bring them together again as friends. (Tirmidhi, Asma ibn Yazid)

In another tradition the Prophet added:

A woman may lie to her husband to have harmony at home. If there is no other way, it is permissible to lie to save oneself from the hand of a tyrant and to receive justice. (Abu Dawud, Umm Kulthum)

Other acceptable untruths are:

- telling fables and fairy tales to children for the purpose of amusement or education,
- speaking ambiguously so as not to divulge one's own or other people's secrets when questioned about them,
- expressing one's inability to give something when asked by saying, "maybe, if I can, one day soon," and so forth, as a delaying tactic so as not to break people's hearts,
- exaggeration to make a point, such as, "I invited you a hundred times," "I told you a thousand times," "Thank you many, many times," and so forth.

These and other harmless untruths intended to comfort and help others are not considered to be lies.

While lying is considered one of the worst aspects of character and is blameworthy, truthfulness and sincerity are qualities appreciated by humanity and loved and rewarded by God. To be truthful, one has to know the objective truth, overcome the temptations of claiming one's own subjective truth as the truth, and have the strength, determination, and courage to tell and expose the truth, which is not welcomed by the society in which we live. Truth and justice are interrelated. Both are among the 99 Beautiful Names, the attributes of Almighty God, and should be an integral part of the character of every faithful person who wishes to be close to the Lord.

The Messenger of God said:

> Do not ever doubt that truthfulness always eventually will lead you to success and good, and that doing good will lead you to salvation and Paradise. If you live your life being truthful, God will count you among His sincere servants, while lying surely will lead you to failure and wrong. Wrong will pull you into Hellfire, and lies will be rejected by God. (Bukhari, Ibn Mas`ud)

Abu Jawza' asked the grandson of the Prophet, Hasan ibn `Ali, what he had retained as the most important among the words of his grandfather. He answered:

> Leave the things that are doubtful and don't ever act on them. Act upon things you know without doubt to be just and true. Truth makes the heart submissive to God and brings peace and calm in and around yourself, while doubt and untruth bring forth disturbance and pain for you and those around you. (Tirmidhi, Hasan ibn `Ali)

The Prophet said to his followers:

> Promise me that you will always follow six principles, and I will give you the good news of Paradise and guarantee that you will be admitted to it.
>
> Tell only the truth when you speak. Keep your promises. Protect well that which is entrusted to you. Be honest, and fight to save your honor. Shy away from that which is unlawful. Do not touch what belongs to others. (Ahmad ibn Hanbal, `Ubadah ibn Samit)

GOSSIP AND SLANDER

Beware: calumny, gossip, and criticism are the most harmful aspects of lying. They are reprehensible before God and the causes of mischief and violence among men. God says:

... Nor speak ill of each other behind their backs. Would any of you like to eat the flesh of his dead brother? (*Hujurat*, 12)

And the Prophet said:

On the Day of Judgment someone's book of deeds will be given into his hands and he will not see there any of the good deeds he did, in good faith, for God's sake. He will ask the Lord, "Why aren't my good deeds recorded in here?" and the Lord will answer, "They have been given to the ones you hurt and insulted by talking against them." (Ibn Hibban, Abu `Umamah)

And:

Gossip and slander make the good deeds of a two-faced person fall away like the leaves in autumn. (Isfahani, `Uthman ibn `Affan)

And:

The Prophet said that during his ascension he saw some people who were eating rotten human corpses. He asked his companion, the archangel Gabriel, "Who are these people who are punished thus?" Gabriel answered, "Those are the ones who slandered and gossiped during their lifetime ..." (Imam Ahmad, Ibn `Abbas)

And he said:

Those who backbite their fellow human beings in this life will be made to eat their corpses in the Hereafter: they will wail and scream in horror. (Tabarani, Abu Hurayrah)

Once when the Messenger of God was preaching to his followers, a man abruptly got up and left. Later his blessed Companions complained to the Prophet, commenting on how badly the man had behaved. The Prophet said:

Now you are guilty of backbiting your brother in faith. How does his flesh taste in your mouths? (Abu Ya`la, Abu Hurayrah)

The blessed wife of the Messenger of God, Hadrat `A'ishah, said:

One day I saw a tall woman leaving the presence of the Prophet and said to him, "How very tall that woman is!" The Prophet said, "Spit out what is in your mouth." And I spat out a rotten piece of flesh. (Ibn Abi Dunya)

Another time Hadrat `A'ishah criticized Hadrat Safiyyah bint Hayy ibn Akhtab, daughter of one of the beloved Companions of the Prophet, commenting on how short she was. The Messenger of God said:

O `A'ishah, you have said such a word that if it fell into the ocean it would pollute it! (Abu Dawud, Hadrat `A'ishah)

And the Prophet told:

During my ascension I saw in Hell some people with sharp nails made of copper tearing at their faces and I asked my companion, the Angel Gabriel, who they were. He said, "They are the people who dishonored human beings by backbiting during their lives." (Abu Dawud, Anas ibn Malik)

One day the Prophet asked his Companions; "Do you know what gossip really is?" They said, "God and His Prophet know best." And he said, "When you even think something about your brother in faith that he wouldn't like to hear, you are backbiting." One of the Companions then asked, "Even if it is true?" and he said, "Yes. If it is true, you are guilty of gossip. If it is not true, you are guilty of the greater sin of slander." (Muslim, Abu Hurayrah)

To criticize a believer concerning the state of his practice of the religion, even if he is guilty of acts contrary to the tenets of the religion, is also wrong, especially when such criticism is undertaken in public, harshly, in anger, with cursing and shouting. If correction is undertaken privately and gently, by speaking only to the person involved while none other can hear, it is not criticism but advice.

According to the scholars of the Hanafi school, if someone speaks critically about a particular society's or a whole town's practice of religion in general, and the majority in that town or society know the few who are guilty of the offense in question, the person who criticized is absolved of gossip, as he does not know the particular persons who are committing the wrong. It is considered that such a person is condemning the act, not the ones responsible for the act.

The same principle applies in the case of individuals. If you condemn an act, but do not direct blame upon the one who performs the act, your criticism is not considered to be slander. And it is not slander when a member of the governing classes, for the benefit of society in general, points out certain people guilty of creating disorder and mischief by their talk and actions—if the statement is absolutely truthful.

If a person or persons are guilty of openly creating dissension, violence, and harm to others, it is not wrong to criticize them openly.

In cases when you do not know the name of a person but need to identify him, to describe him by saying that he is blind, or lame, or fat, or old, and so forth, is permissible and not considered insulting.

The Messenger of God said:

Are you reticent to warn others of the dangers some criminals may cause? Tell everyone to protect themselves from such people. (Ibn Abi Dunya, Baz ibn Hakim)

And:

To tell others about the shameful acts of someone who shamelessly exposes his mischief in public is not slander. (Abu Shaykh, Anas ibn Malik)

One may classify gossip by its gravity into three categories.

The first and worst is to slander people unjustly and to claim that calumny is not a sin but a service. It is a clear case of infidelity, since the one who is guilty of it claims the unlawful to be lawful and commendable.

The Messenger of God said one day, "Slander is a worse sin than adultery." People asked why, and he answered, "Because if an adulterer repents and asks God's forgiveness, God in His compassion may forgive him. But the slanderer will not be forgiven by God until the person whom he slandered forgives him." (Ibn Abi Dunya, Jabir ibn Abdullah)

The second kind of gossip is to talk against someone in public with the intention that he hear about it. God may forgive this gossip if the slanderer is able to receive pardon from the one he slandered.

The third is to criticize someone while hiding his identity: this also is blameworthy. We may be forgiven it if we beg God not only to forgive us, but also to forgive the one we criticized for his wrongdoings.

The Prophet said:

You can only absolve yourself from the wrong you have committed by talking against someone, by praying to God to forgive you and him both. (Umm Abi Dunya, Anas ibn Malik)

Some scholars do not find this atonement sufficient. They claim that the one who talked against someone else must put his repentance into action by serving the one whom he condemned in whatever way he can. They base their claim upon the following words of the Prophet:

Someone may criticize his brother in faith, then regret what he has done. If he does not affirm his repentance in action by helping his brother in any way he can, he will find the wrong for which he criticized the other will come upon himself, either in this life or in the Hereafter. (Abu Shaykh, Anas ibn Malik)

And:

Whoever helps his brother in faith without his knowing, God will help him in this life and in the Hereafter. (Ibn Abi Dunya, Jabir ibn `Abdullah)

And:

Whoever protects the name and honor of his brother in faith in this world, will have an angel sent by God to protect him on the Day of Judgment. (Ibn Abi Dunya, Anas ibn Malik)

And:

If someone helps to eliminate a stain from the name and honor of his brother in faith, God will prevent Hellfire from reaching him in the Hereafter. (Abu Shaykh, Abu Darda')

Another sinful act of the tongue is to divulge the secrets of people one has spied upon. It is even wrong to tell people their own secrets if it will embarrass them. People who expose secrets are called informers. Some of them make a profession of it and cause great suffering to society, as well as to individuals. Telling other people's secrets is certainly a criminal act, equal to bearing false witness. There is only one excusable case: if a person is unaware that a dishonest informer has exposed his secret, one may advise him of that. In that case it is a kind deed.

God tells us:

O you who believe, avoid most suspicion, for surely suspicion in some cases is sin; and spy not, nor let some of you backbite others. Does one of you like to eat the flesh of his dead brother? You would abhor it! (*Hujurat*, 12)

Heed not the type of despicable man ready with oaths, who slanders others, going about with calumnies, hindering all good, transgressing beyond bounds; he is deep in sin, violent and cruel; with all that, base-born. (*Qalam*, 10-13)

Woe to every slanderer, defamer ... (*Humaza*, 1)

The Prophet said:

The person who divulges the secrets of two people to each other cannot be permitted to enter Paradise. (Bukhari, Hudhayfah)

Informers will be brought back to life as monkeys on the Day of Judgment. (Mu`adh ibn Jabal)

To swear at people and to inform on them are two fires that destroy truth and this fire and truth cannot cohabit together in a believer's conscience. (Jami` as-Saghir)

The informer is base-born either from a false marriage or by birth; he has a totally false character. (Hakim, Abu Musa al-Ash`ari)

The ones who make fun of you, talk behind your back, or tell people your secrets, and see nothing wrong in their mischief, will be brought to life as dogs on the Day of Judgment. (Abu Shaykh, `Ala ibn Harith)

To make fun of people and ridicule them, whether to their faces or without their knowledge, is wrong, even if the intention is not to belittle them but only to make people laugh. God says:

O you who believe, let not some women among you laugh at others; it may be that the latter are better than the former. Neither find fault with your own people, nor call one another names. Evil is a bad name after faith: and whoso turns not, these it is that are the iniquitous. (*Hujurat*, 11)

The Prophet recounted:

One of those who make fun of people reaches the gate of Paradise: the door cracks open and a voice tells him: "Get ready to come in!" As he approaches, the gate shuts in his face. Again and again the same thing happens, until he gives up. (Ibn Abi Dunya, al-Hasan)

CURSING

To curse people, even to curse at animals and things, is very dangerous. The damnation one wishes upon others sooner or later turns and hits whoever summoned it. Cursing is wishing another person great harm—to be damned, to be chased away from the mercy of God. No one has the right to wish that upon a believer, especially since there is no reason for it. Perhaps it is justifiable to curse a proven enemy of God. Yet even in that case, the person must be dead without having repented, as with Abu Jahl. How many such cases does one encounter in life? Yet many who call themselves believers curse their wives and husbands, parents and children, even their pets who do not obey them, or the stone upon which they tripped, and the wind that blew off their hats! The Prophet forbade people to damn even the flea that bit them, or the hurricane that wrecked their homes.

On the other hand, in various traditions it is mentioned that the Prophet condemned and cursed people who curse their parents; who are guilty of usury; who hide criminals from justice; who grab others' land; the rich who do not pay the obligatory tithe; thieves who steal the shrouds off dead peoples' backs; married couples who tyrannize each other; those who receive bribes as well as those who pay them; people who drink intoxicating drinks or who make, sell, serve, or force others to drink alcohol; people who do not respond when they hear the call to prayer; and men who lead prayers for a community of heretics. Yet he also advised Muslims not to curse or damn anyone or anything, as God himself asks human beings to abstain from damning even the Devil himself. The Prophet said:

For a believer to curse a believer is as bad as killing him. (Bukhari, Daqqaq)

It is not within the character of a believer to curse, to damn, to speak or act improperly. (Tirmidhi, Ibn Mas'ud)

Do not doubt that those who have damned others in this life, no matter how perfect they otherwise may be, will be forbidden from interceding for anyone else on the Day of Judgment. (Muslim, Abu Darda')

When a believer curses someone, that malediction escapes to heaven. The heavens close their gates to it, so it descends back toward the earth, but the earth closes its gates to it, too. It runs hither and thither to escape and cannot find a way. Then it falls upon the person who is cursed. If he is innocent, the affliction cannot touch him. So finally the curse returns back to the one who invoked it, and destroys him. (Abu Dawud, Abu Darda')

If a Muslim calls another Muslim an infidel, that word strikes either the one or the other. If indeed it was true it hits the one at whom it was aimed, but if not it returns back to the one who uttered it, and hits him. (Bukhari, Ibn 'Umar)

For a Muslim to curse a Muslim is an immoral vice. For a Muslim to fight a Muslim is infidelity, casting him out of God's mercy and grace. (Bukhari, Ibn Mas'ud)

When two believers fight and abuse each other verbally, the one who swore first is guilty. But when the fight continues and the one who was initially attacked responds with curses, they are both guilty. (Muslim, Abu Hurayrah)

What is becoming to a Muslim, if attacked verbally, is to show patience and not respond. And if in addition he is generous enough to forgive the one who assaulted him, that will not only gain him God's pleasure but will cause God to forgive the one who attacked him.

To swear at animals and at inanimate objects is not only a sign of negativity and stupidity, but an attack on God's dumb creation, which cannot defend itself. Furthermore, animals, vegetation, and air, water, lightning, floods—all these act only with the will of God, and are totally submissive to Him, unlike human beings. The Prophet reprimanded a man who cursed a rooster. He said, "Do not curse the rooster, for it crows by the will of God to wake you up for your morning prayer."

To tell people their faults to their faces, even if your description is correct, is forbidden by God, who said, "Do not blame each other with your faults, as you will shame each other."

And the Messenger of God said:

Someone who accuses his brother in faith of faults will be guilty of the same faults before he leaves this world. (Tirmidhi, Mu`adh ibn Jabal)

Indeed, if you blame someone for a fault, you are certainly guilty of the same fault. If you didn't possess it, you wouldn't be able even to identify it. And if you wish to have totally faultless people as friends, you will be without friends.

OBSCENITY

Yet another obnoxious habit of the twisted tongue is to use bad words. Even in one's ordinary conversation; obscene words such as those which refer to private parts and bodily functions, when used out of context to insult or to ridicule or to make fun, are strictly forbidden in the morality of Islam. Even if these words must be used out of necessity, one must be discreet. The Prophet said:

Paradise closes its gates to the one who uses obscene words in his speech. (Ibn Abi Dunya, `Abdullah ibn `Umar)

WAILING OVER THE DEAD

Loud lamentation, wailing and screaming for the dead or for other misfortunes, is considered to be bad behavior and blameworthy in Islam. Yet if it arises as a natural manifestation of a broken heart, because of misfortune or having lost a beloved person, it cannot be helped. Elaborate mourning for the dead is not accepted in Islam, but that is certainly not because Islam encourages hard-heartedness. It does encourage patience, faith in God, and forbearance. Both good and what seems to us to be bad come from God, and for a true believer they should both be equally good and acceptable. The Messenger of God said:

> If someone screams and wails, lamenting a misfortune, and resenting and blaming God's will, he will be brought back to life on Judgment Day covered with hot tar. (Muslim, Abu Malik ibn `Ashari)

> There are two meannesses of character in some people that God considers to be denial and contempt for God's favors: they are lamenting and wailing over the dead, and swearing and cursing peoples' family and ancestors. (Muslim, Abu Hurayrah)

ARGUMENTATIVENESS

Discussion, argument, and debate are discouraged in Islam. Someone who knows the truth tells it, and those who do not know listen to it. When the subject is religious rules and precepts and canon law, these are clearly established and may be acquired by study. Yet there may be valid questions, depending on cases, situations, meaning, and intentions. Then it is permissible to ask, but not to rebut or contradict that which was claimed as right.

To insult a man of knowledge by saying, "What you say is right, but your intention is wrong," is considered ill-mannered at least and sacrilegious at most, because one is not able to know peoples' interiors: only God knows them. The proper attitude is to accept a truth when you hear it.

If you doubt the truth of something, and the subject is worldly, you should keep silent. But if an intentional lie is told about religious matters, you have the right to object if you are sure of the truth of the matter, as proven by the Qur'an and the traditions. In that case, your intention should not be anything other than to protect the listeners, as well as the one who uttered the words, from false information. On the other hand, to protect yourself from arrogance it is best to keep quiet. As the Prophet said:

> The one who realizes that he is wrong in his opinions, and does not get into an argument, has won a place at the edges of Paradise. The one who knows he is right and does not argue has won a place at the center of Paradise. And the one who shows the beauty of his character and manners in an atmosphere of controversy by staying quiet has won a place at the highest point of Paradise. (Tirmidhi, Abu `Umamah)

> Truly the first things my Lord forbade us to do were to worship idols, to take intoxicants, and to argue with each other. (Ibn Abi Dunya, Umm Salamah)

A believer will not be able to perfect his faith unless he forsakes arguing and debating matters with others. (Ibn Abi Dunya, Abu Hurayrah)

A Muslim is not permitted to argue with a fellow Muslim, to make fun of him, or to make him a promise that he cannot keep. (Tirmidhi, Ibn `Abbas)

To dispute about the principles, creed, and opinions of other valid sects in Islam, claiming one's own as better than the others, is very dangerous. The Prophet said:

No one has gone astray after having found the truth except those arrogant ones who claim their path as being better than others', whether they may be right or wrong. (Tirmidhi, Abu `Umamah)

Then he recited God's words from the chapter "Gold Adornments" in the Qur'an:

And they say: "Are our gods better, or is He?" They set it forth to you only by way of disputation. Nay they are a contentious people. (*Zukhruf*, 58)

Spite and antagonism, insisting on one's point of view whether right or wrong, using false witnesses, false proofs, and insulting words—hour after hour, day after day—to tire the adversary who may be right, is the worst form of arguing and is considered as a sin. The Prophet said:

The least liked among human beings are the spiteful. (Bukhari, Hadrat `A'ishah)

It suffices you for sin to be always contentious. (Tirmidhi, Ibn `Abbas)

Whoever argues without supporting his argument with knowledge is being punished by God in the process until he gives up his argument and confesses to being wrong. (Ibn Abi Dunya, Abu Hurayrah)

SINGING AND STORYTELLING

Music, singing, and tales are very strong instruments, influencing the emotions. The emotions are the principal human quality upon which religion is based. Intellect is supreme and superior to the emotions in the proper ordering of the human being, as it is the unique gift of God given to humanity, to which God speaks. The emotions are quicker and their effect is stronger, making it possible for them to distort intelligent decisions. Therefore in many religious opinions music is looked upon with suspicion.

Music, songs, poems, and tales that heighten carnal desires, attachment to the pleasures of this world, animal instincts, rage and violence, and make people forget God and their moral responsibilities to humanity are obviously wrong. Indulging in these is yet another guilty act of the irresponsible tongue. God condemns it, saying:

> But there are among men those who purchase idle tales, without knowledge or meaning, which mislead people from the path of God and throw ridicule on the path of God. For such there will be a humiliating penalty. (*Luqman*, 6)

And the Messenger of God said:

> God sends two devils upon the singer who rages in a loud voice, and they kick his chest hard while he is singing. (Ibn Abi Dunya, Ibn `Umamah)

Many scholars agree that such worldly music is objectionable and undesirable. Yet on special occasions such as public festivities, marriage celebrations, and so forth, to amuse and add joy at the gathering, appropriate and clean music has been made permissible.

Some scholars also object to the religious music of the Sufis, the mystic sects who use chants and drums during their ceremonies of remembrance of God. They object to spiritual music even more than to secular music, as this music and chanting is undertaken in the name of religion. Yet the chanting of the verses of the Qur'an with a beautiful voice and manner is commendable. Because such tones extend the meaning of God's words and bring religious fervor, excitement, and rapture, moving people with an intense emotion of the love of God, God and His Prophet recommend it. Allah's Messenger said:

> When you read the Qur'an, chant God's words beautifully. (`Abdurrazzaq, Al-Bara)

> Beautify the Qur'an with your chanting. (Abu Dawud, Nasa'i)

> God Almighty does not pay greater attention than when He hears His words in the Qur'an beautifully chanted. (Bukhari, Abu Hurayrah)

> The one who does not give attention to beautiful chanting when he recites the Qur'an is not following our path. (Bukhari, Abu Hurayrah)

On the other hand, chanting the Qur'anic verses and other religious chants should not distract from, but enhance, the words of God and the praises of God. If one's attention is monopolized by the beauty of the music to the detriment of listening to the content of the chant, then it is obviously wrong.

The following words of the Prophet and the theologians of Islam explain it. The Prophet said:

> Chant the Qur'an according to the Arab musical modes. Do not chant it the way Christians and Jews sing in their temples. In future times after me, there will come men who will recite the Qur'an reverberating in the manner of Christians singing in their churches. They will raise their voices in waves but the meaning of God's words will not come out from their throats, because their hearts will be filled with sedition, mischief, and arrogance. (Tirmidhi, Hudhayfah)

This confirms God's words:

> It is a Qur'an in Arabic, without any crookedness therein, in order that you may guard against evil. (*Zumar*, 28)

Imam Zayla`i said:

> When one chants the Qur'an cutting God's words in half or repeating them over and over again, causing confusion for the sake of the tune, it is sinful both for the singer and the listener.

But it is stated in the *Tatarkhaniyyah*:

> If the time and the trill or quaver in chanting the Qur'an do not take away a listener's attention from the content, and neither distort nor lose the meaning of God's words, but on the contrary enhance the attention of the believer and make him listen carefully so that he understands the divine message and is emotionally affected by it, then they are commendable. That is how Qur'an should be recited by the *imam* during communal prayers in mosques. But if chanting causes the meaning to be lost, the prayer is not accepted and should be redone.

Turpishti confirms this and says,

> Religious chanting [is good] when music does not cause distortion of the message, but on the contrary enhances the meaning by creating an emotional receptivity in the listener, who in rapture feels joy or sadness in his heart, gets tears in his eyes, and feels the love of God.

Thus as long as music does not lead people to worldliness, lust, and rage, as in the case of some secular music, and as long as it does not distort or annihilate the divine message, but on the contrary decorates and beautifies the message, and increases the love of God in the hearts of the faithful, it is good. If putting religious teaching and divine words into music either dilutes, distorts, or hides the good they are intended to have, that music is sinful for the one who sings it and for the one who listens to it.

DIVULGING SECRETS

Another mischief that the twisted tongue brings upon people is betrayal. Human beings live in society. When you hear something shameful about somebody, you are obliged to keep it a secret unless it is definitely against the law. Even if the matter is an infraction of the religious law, you are bound to keep it secret if it does not concern you. If it concerns and touches you, you are free to divulge what you heard; yet it is still better to keep silent, even in grave cases such as adultery or drunkenness. If what you heard is a violation against somebody's rights, seriously hurts another member of the community, or is legally punishable, then it is your right to divulge what you know, especially if the party who has unjustly suffered from this aggression asks you to be a witness. But if the wrong done did not cause any harm to anybody nor is punishable under the constraints of the law, it is best to keep one's silence.

The Prophet said:

When someone speaks to someone else in a gathering and then leaves, his words are a trust for those who heard them to protect. (Abu Dawud, Jabir ibn `Abdullah)

People who attend any gathering are under obligation to keep private whatever was said and done during the gathering, unless the shedding of blood, the commission of adultery, or the theft of property was discussed or undertaken therein. (Abu Dawud, Jabir ibn `Abdullah)

When two people speak together in a meeting, what they say to each other is a trust to be kept by all, even if what they heard does not please them. (Hakim, Ibn Mas`ud)

On the Day of Judgment, among the most shamed will be husbands and wives who heard each other's secrets and divulged them to others. (Muslim, Abu Sa`id al-Khudri)

One of the bad habits of the tongue of which most people are guilty is idle talk. Almost everybody babbles about real and unreal experiences, hoping to amuse other people. Instead they make fools of themselves and sin against God, involuntarily divulging their own and other people's shameful behavior by the slips of their tongues.

The Prophet said:

On the Day of Judgment the ones who have committed the most errors are going to be the people who indulged in the most vain talk during their lifetimes. (Tabarani, Ibn Mas`ud)

ASKING FROM PEOPLE

Perhaps the most important time for us to watch our tongues is when we wish to ask for something from others. This does not apply only to asking for money or material things, but also to asking for service, advice, opinions, and intercession.

Only when someone is totally incapacitated, destitute, and helpless, or gravely sick or weak, unable to help himself and his dependents to the extent that he lacks enough nourishment for a single day, is a person permitted to ask another for sustenance. To beg for help when there is no such need is unlawful according to our faith. Woe to the one who begs in order to add to what he already possesses.

Hadrat `Ali reported:

The Prophet said, "The one who asks people for things while he really is not in need is asking for fire to be added to the Hellfire in which he will burn." And when he was asked what describes destitution, he said, "If someone does not have food even for a single day." (Tabarani, Hadrat `Ali)

Hadrat Abu Bakr, Abu Dharr, and Thawban reported that the Prophet said:

If you drop your whip when you are riding, do not ask someone walking next to you to pick it up for you. (Tirmidhi)

And they indeed did not ask.

The most obnoxious manner in which some beggars ask for help is by mentioning God's name, such as "For God's sake! May God reward you and be pleased with you!" and so forth. This is sacrilegious.

The Prophet said :

The one who begs from human beings by mentioning God's name is accursed and damned. (Tabarani, Abu Musa al-Ash`ari)

It is appropriate to ask in God's name only when you beg Him for your forgiveness, for His Paradise, and for what He knows you need in this world.

The Prophet warned the ones who beg for favors from people while they are not really in need, saying:

Begging from people is such a stain on a person's face that it will not leave while a shred of flesh is left on his skull, until he meets his Lord. (Bukhari, ibn `Umar)

Each time anyone begs people for favors he is tearing his face with sharp nails. (Abu Dawud, Samurah ibn Jundub)

Shamelessly begging for things that one already has or is capable of working for and gaining oneself is sinful for anyone who has sufficient strength and health. (Tirmidhi, Hubshi ibn Junadat)

Women who ask their husbands for divorce although they have fulfilled a man's obligations in marriage and have not done anything prohibited by religious law, and furthermore demand the dower previously agreed to be paid to a wife at divorce, are considered to be blameworthy.

The Messenger of God said:

The woman who asks to divorce her husband while there is no violence nor has he violated his duties according to Islam, will have no scent of the perfumes of Paradise, for she has reduced herself to the level of a hypocrite. (Tirmidhi, Thawban)

It is permitted for you to ask when:

- an official institution owes you something that is your right,
- your employees, workers, or servants owe you work they are paid to do,
- your wife or husband is neglecting what is proper for the harmony and well-being of the family and the home,
- your children or students are not studying and learning, or respecting their elders,
- you lack a roof over your head and food enough for one day, so that others should be helping you without being asked.

And then there are the foolish, curious people who ask indiscriminately about their future, about destiny, about divine secrets concerning God's names, attributes, actions, and essence, inquiring whether these things were created or are eternal, and so forth, when these are not essential for them to know. The Prophet said about them:

People will keep asking each other about divine secrets and the essence of God, and how and when and who created this and that, up to the point of asking: Who created God? When someone feels such curiosity, it is best to say sincerely, "I believe in God and His Prophets" and take refuge in God and leave His secrets alone. (Bukhari, Abu Hurayrah)

The same message as related by Abu Dawud has the following words added to it:

When people ask you about divine secrets, tell them that God needs nothing, while everything is in need of Him. None created Him, He was not born, and none resembles Him nor is equal to Him. And tell them to take refuge in Him from the accursed Devil.

The Prophet forbade his Companions to ask such questions. In fact he discouraged them from asking too many questions on any subject, and likened such behavior to spending one's money on buying unnecessary things.

Questions like this are difficult to answer and difficult to understand when answered. Therefore they are apt to lead both the one who asks them and the one who answers them into error and sin.

That does not mean that someone with a sincere question, wishing to learn something pertaining to religious or spiritual matters that concern him directly, should not inquire of someone who knows the answers. In fact to reflect on such questions and answers as an intellectual exercise or to strengthen one's general knowledge is also permissible.

UNCONSCIOUS SPEECH
Especially in spiritual conversations, but also in everything one says, one should watch carefully to use the appropriate words to avoid all misunderstanding.

People prior to Islam used to use the Arabic word *karam* for grapes. The word literally means "generous." Since people who drank grape wine, which was not forbidden before Islam, supposedly became more generous in their stupor, the Arabs used the word for grapes. The Prophet forbade this, saying:

Do not call grapes "the generous." "Generous" is the proper word for a munificent Muslim. Call grapes, grapes. (Muslim, Abu Hurayrah)

He also said:

If you hear someone say that so-and-so will perish from the face of the world, know that he himself soon will perish, because he has uttered those words. (Muslim, Abu Hurayrah)

Because such people condemn others, thinking themselves superior, they are guilty of arrogance in their speech. The Prophet also forbade his Companions:

Do not say "God and so-and-so wish such a thing to be done." Say: "God wishes, and because God wishes, so-and-so advises this to be done." (Abu Dawud, Hudhayfah)

Someone came to the Messenger of God to ask about various matters concerning himself. During the conversation, he said, "You and God asked us to do it," in order to justify something he did. The Prophet objected by saying, "Are you considering me equal to God? Say: God so wished, and I obliged." (Ibn Maja, Ibn `Abbas)

He also said:

Do not talk about people who are under your care as "my servant," "my loyal wife," "my dependents," for they are neither your servants nor your dependents. We are all God's servants and depend only on Him. Call them your helpers, your companions, your sons and daughters. And no one who works for someone else should call him "my Lord," for we all have one Lord, God Almighty. (Muslim, Abu Hurayrah)

Neither is it proper to pray to God saying "for the sake of Your Prophet." Rather say, "for the sake of Your love for Your Prophet." For the prophets are also God's creations, and none of the created have any rights over the Creator.

It is also undesirable for the children to call their parents by their names, and for wives and husbands to call each other by their names.

The Prophet advised:

Do not say: "I feel awful," rather say: "I do not feel very well." Do not say: "I am ruined," rather say: "I am having some difficulties." (Bukhari, Sahl ibn Hanif)

Because words are alive, if you verbally attach bad conditions to yourself or others, they may come to be. In fact, the Prophet changed the names of people and places that were negative into names with positive meanings. He said:

The worst of names are Harb [war], and Murrah [bitter]; and the name

that is most disliked by God is Malik al-Amlak [the owner of all owned].
(Bukhari, Abu Hurayrah)

He advised people to give their children beautiful names, hoping they
would grow to be worthy of their names. He changed the name of `Asiyah
(the one who revolts) bint `Umar to Jamilah (the beautiful one); the name
of Hazn (the hard one) ibn Sa`d to `Aziz (beloved); and the names of the
people who were named `Atalah (wrench), Ghurab (crow), Harb (war),
Hakim (judge), Shihab (flame), and Shaytan (Satan) to Salim (safe one).
He also changed the name of a place called `Uffurat, meaning difficulties,
to Khudrat, meaning greenery.

We have to reflect about the meaning of words that we use not only to
be clear in our expression of our thoughts, but also to make sure that they
do not carry negative connotations. Especially in choosing proper names
for our children, names of our shops, workplaces and products, we have to
use words that express beneficence and beauty.

DUPLICITY

In behavior, showing ourselves as other than what we are is hypocrisy. In
language, speaking other than what we really think and feel is duplicity.
They are both the opposite of sincerity, which is one of the most praised
and worthy characteristics of a Muslim.

Ibn `Umar said:

These days we don't seem to worry when we talk to the faces of important
people differently than when we talk about them elsewhere. At the time
of the Prophet, we used to consider this as hateful duplicity. (Tabarani,
Ibn `Umar)

One day, the Messenger of Allah (s.a.w.s) said to Ka`b ibn Ujra', "May God
protect you from living under stupid rulers."

Ka`b asked, "Who would be the stupid rulers?"

The Prophet answered, "There will be rulers after me who will not
follow my path, neither will they be enlightened with what I said or did.
Neither they nor the ones under them, imitating them, claiming their
lies as truths and helping them in their tyranny are of us, and I am not
of them. On the Day of Judgment, they won't be able to drink from my
hand. Whoever opposes them and calls their lies 'lies', and does not participate in their tyranny is one of us and I am one with him. He will drink
from my hands on the Day of Judgment and I will intercede for him. O
Ka`b, mankind wakes in the morning as one of two kinds: He is either the
fortunate one who has tried to buy his share of punishment from God
and got rid of it and is free, or the fallen one who has sold himself to the

world and became its slave. The ones who seek the favor of rulers and powerful men are amongst the second kind." (Ahmad ibn Hanbal, Jabir ibn `Abdullah)

Duplicity is a dishonesty expressed in flattery, praise and approval of a wrong committed by someone from whom one hopes to receive rewards or from whom one is afraid. Usually, these are people who are lacking in faith and do not follow the precepts of religion. On the other hand, in some dire, dangerous situations, it is permissible to say what one does not mean to save oneself from the hand a tyrant.

`A'ishah, blessed wife of the Prophet, reported:

A dreadful man came into the presence of the Messenger of God. When he saw the man from afar, he said, "Woe, what a terrible brother of a terrible tribe, what an awful son of awful people!" But when the man came inside, he smiled at him and paid him compliments. Afterwards I asked, "O Messenger of God, why did you smile and speak kindly to this awful man?"

He answered, "When did you ever hear me talk in vain? Surely God approves of whoever protects himself and his people from the tyranny of a tyrant by putting distance between them by peaceful means. There are some terrible people. In order to save themselves from them, people have to use duplicity and praise them." (Bukhari)

But the hypocrite who talks, falsely praising one to his face and cursing him to others, with either selfish intentions or to breed hostility between people are double-tongued. The Prophet said:

The people who are two-faced during their lives will be raised in the Hereafter with two tongues of fire in their mouths. (Bukhari, Ammar ibn Yasir)

The ones who will be considered the lowest of the low on the Day of Judgment are the two-faced who say one thing to one person and another to someone else. (Bukhari, Abu Hurayrah)

Some people extend their duplicity to dangerous proportions, which may cause whole communities and nations to suffer. These are the people who intercede, support and talk in favor of inept, incapable, unsuited or simply bad people to gain high positions in government and religious circles such as governors, ministers, judges, religious prelates etc. They do this not because they are misinformed in good faith, but to gain profit and status themselves or for those close to them. Or indeed they are misguided by others who have the same motives or are afraid or ashamed of such people of bad intentions while they should fear and be ashamed of God for their actions. The Prophet said:

> Whoever opts for those who oppose God's precepts and those who follow them, opposes God. (Abu Dawud, Ibn `Umar)

God says:

> Whoever recommends and helps an evil cause shares in its burden, and God has power over all things. (*Nisa'*, 85)

God also says in the same verse:

> Whoever recommends and helps a good cause becomes a partner in it. (*Nisa'*, 85)

Thus, contrary to supporting an evil cause, to support a good cause is rewarded by God. Abu Musa reported that a poor man came to the Messenger of God, who was sitting with his Companions. When he saw him, he turned to his Companions and said:

> Help the one in need, and help him by asking for help for him. God will reward you for both your efforts. (Bukhari, Abu Musa)

And he said:

> I encourage you to ask for my help for your friends. I wish to do good but I hide it till someone asks me to do good for his brother. God expresses His will by the tongue of His prophets. (Abu Dawud, Mu`awiya)

Another harm that man's tongue brings upon others as well as oneself is to influence people and even force people if one is in a position of authority to do bad and sinful acts and prevent them from doing good deeds. This is an attribute of a hypocrite who has achieved a high position appearing as a good man. Strengthened by authority, he then cheats and tyrannizes people and orders his followers to do the same. Those who support and obey such people are as blameworthy as the one who propagates hate and tyranny, and are hated by God. And the ones who oppose them and generate good actions amongst people are loved by God. God says:

> Let there arise out of you a band of people inviting to all that is good, enjoining what is right and forbidding what is wrong; they are the ones who attain felicity. (*Al-i `Imran*, 104)

Someone asked the Messenger of God, "Who are the best of people?" He answered, "They are the ones who influence people to do most good, prevent them from doing wrong, whose hearts are full of compassion and who fear God." He added, "If one of you encounters bad being done, try changing it by the force of your hands. If you do not have the strength for that, then try to change it by your tongue. If you are unable to change it by your words, then feel the pain of the wronged in your hearts and pray for God's help. The last effort is a sign of the minimal faith in your hearts." (Muslim, Abu Sa`id)

These words of the Prophet are a proof that every believer is obliged to try to prevent wrong from being done and encourage good to be done. According to Imam Abu Hanifah and many Muslim scholars, to undo harm by their own hands is an obligation for people of authority and strength such as the ruling classes, to try to correct the wrong by one's words is an obligation upon scholars and wise men and to lament and to wish the tyranny to be gone falls on the ordinary humble people.

Anas ibn Malik asked the Prophet, "Should the one who himself is unable to do good deeds ask others to do them, and should the one who is not blameless ask others not to sin?"
The Prophet said, "Yes, indeed, even if you are unable to do all God asks us to do, ask others to do them. Even if you are guilty of doing some things God forbade us to do, ask others not to do them." (Tabarani, Anas ibn Malik)

Someone asked the Messenger of God, "Is a whole community blameworthy for the wrong being done even if there are many good people amongst them?" He said, "Yes."
The man asked, "Why?"
He answered, "Because they have been heedless and permissive toward what was being done and have done nothing to prevent it." (Tabarani, Ibn `Abbas)

On the other hand, he also said:

The leaders of a community are not rendered responsible and blamed by God for the wrong done by the ordinary members of the community if they do not have the capability to stop them from sinning. (Imam Ahmad, `Adi ibn Umar)

The Prophet took very seriously the responsibility of the faithful to convince others not to do wrong and to lead them to do good. He said:

All the good deeds you do, including risking your life for God's sake, are like a drop compared to the pleasure of God, as vast as an ocean, offered to the ones who prevent people from doing wrong and lead them to do good. (Yahya ibn `Utarid)

The scholars agree that doing good deeds are occasional, to risk one's life fighting for God's sake is a final act, while a life devoted to leading people to obey God and prevent them from doing harm is continuous and all-encompassing. That is why it is a superior deed in the opinion of God. And the people who are persecuted and die on this path are considered more worthy among the martyrs.

The Messenger of God said, "As long as you do not belittle its truth when you say 'there is no God but God,' you receive God's help and blessings upon you." The people asked, "How can one belittle the truth of *La ilaha illa'llah?*" He answered, "When you see around you people who are sinning and revolting against God and you do nothing to stop it." (Tabarani, Anas ibn Malik)

And he said:

The greatest of all the martyrs who give their lives for God's sake is Hamza, and then those who dare to oppose tyrannical rulers and are killed by them. (Hakim, Jabir ibn `Abdullah)

The worthiest of just wars is to tell the truth to a tyrannical ruler. (Abu Dawud, Abu Sa`id al-Khudri)

All of the prophets God sent before me had their blessed companions and followers who emulated them and obeyed them. And after them came people who claimed that they followed them, but said things that their prophets never said and did things that their prophets never did and distorted their religion. Whoever fights them with the strength of their arms are the true faithful ones. Whoever speaks against them are also good faithful people. Whoever only feels a grudge against them has the least of faith, and the ones who do not care have faith smaller than a mustard seed. (Muslim, `Abdullah Ibn Mas`ud)

INSTRUCTION
It is an obligation upon the faithful for those who know to teach those who do not know. It is incumbent upon us to prevent the ones who have fallen into error from sinning. But in doing so, harsh words are not convincing. On the contrary, harshness may push those who are astray to react and fall

deeper in sin. It behooves all Muslims to be kind to each other, to smile and greet each other, to use gentle words when they speak to each other.

Miqdad ibn Shurayh reported from his grandfather that he asked the Messenger of God what he should do in this life to get him to Paradise in the Hereafter. The Prophet said:

> Feed the hungry, greet your brothers in faith kindly, and speak kindly and gently to them. (Tabarani, Miqdad ibn Shurayh)

And:

> The Messenger of Allah said, "There are palaces in Paradise: from outside them you can see inside, and from inside them you can see everything outside, all around."
> Someone asked, "Who will inhabit them?"
> He said, "The ones who sweeten their tongues and talk kindly and beautifully, feed the hungry, and spend the nights praying while everyone else is sleeping." (Tabarani, `Abdullah ibn `Umar)

And he said:

> When you salute someone in need, smiling, with an open face, God counts it as if you have paid him a handsome alms. (Ibn Abi Dunya, Abu Dharr)

And he warned:

> If you see only the faults and errors of people and tell them harshly to their faces, even if your intentions are to free them of their faults, you may easily lead them deeper into mischief and sedition. (Abu Dawud, Mu`awiya)

And:

> O lowly one who claims to be a Muslim with his tongue, but whose heart is shut to faith! O one who seeks the faults of people in order to expose them! Whoever shames his brother in faith and exposes his faults risks God's showing forth his own secret faults. Even if he hides in his house, he will be exposed—disgraced and scorned by the whole world. (Abu Dawud, Abu Barza)

A believer should learn to hold his tongue, especially in front of people of knowledge. In the opinion of God:

> Are those who know and those who do not know the same? (*Zumar*, 9)

Indeed not! Therefore one should learn the code of behavior for a student to show toward his teacher, the attitude of a person who knows less in front of a person who knows more.

Zendosti writes in his book called *The Summary* that the ignorant before the knowledgeable, students before teachers, should remain attentive and silent. They should never start to talk unless they are asked, never contradict what has been said, and be brief when permitted to speak. When the teacher shows signs of fatigue or displeasure, they should never ask questions, but remove themselves. They should respect the times, and the limits of the times, when they are permitted into the teacher's presence, knock gently on his door, and wait for his answer. When the teacher is away, one should never sit where he sat, and one should never walk in front of him.

These and other manifestations of respect and care for the wise and the scholars are fitting behavior for believers. Surely you will benefit most from a teacher if you love him, seek his approval and pleasure, fear his anger, and obey him completely in any order not contrary to God's rules.

In most books on morals it is written that even to remind one's teacher of a religious duty, such as the time of prayer, is considered bad behavior.

When one hears the call to prayer, respect is due as to a teacher. From the tongue of the caller to prayer, God, the ultimate teacher, is speaking. To speak over the call is disrespectful. The exceptions are to say quietly *la hawla wa la quwwata illa bi-Llah* ("There is no power or strength save in God"), *ma sha'Allahu kana wa ma lam yasha' lam yakun* ("What God wills, happens, and what He does not will, shall not happen") at appropriate places, and during the morning prayer call to whisper *sadaqta wa bil-haqqi nataqta* ("You have spoken sincerely and uttered the truth") when *as-salatu khayrun min an-nawm* ("Prayer is better than sleep") is chanted by the caller. To utter those phrases is to follow the practice of the Prophet.

During the call to prayer, one does not verbally salute and greet people, nor respond verbally to salutation. Even making *dhikr*, repeating God's names, or reading the Qur'an, is held to be disrespectful during that time.

Obviously, in the course of one's formal worship, to utter words other than the required recitation of Qur'anic verses and other prayers invalidates that act of worship. It is also wrong to offer greetings to someone who is praying or reading the Qur'an. But if someone does so anyway, it poses a problem of behavior, as Muslims are supposed to respond to salutations of peace. According to Abu Hanifah, the worshiper who is greeted should not answer the one who greets him, but he may salute him silently from his heart. According to Imam Muhammad, one simply ignores the salutation. According to Abu Yusuf, one responds to the salutation after the prayer or the reading is concluded.

Another misbehavior is to speak during the sermon in Friday congregational prayers. Even words one might utter while reading the Qur'an, offering prayers, or engaging in other devotional acts are included in this code of silence. The Prophet says:

> Even the person who says "Keep quiet!" to a friend who is speaking while the sermon is delivered in mosques on Fridays, has uttered words wrongly. (Bukhari, Abu Hurayrah)

And:

> A person who cannot keep quiet and attentive while the sermon is delivered on Fridays is like a donkey carrying books on his back. As for the one who asks him to be quiet, his congregational prayer is imperfectly done. (Imam Ahmad, Ibn `Abbas)

If the preacher, in delivering the sermon, recites the verse *ya ayyuhalladhina amanu sallu alayh* ("O you who are faithful, send blessings upon him"), although it is proper to utter a blessing for the Prophet, that should be done inwardly, from the heart. Some scholars even say it is best to keep quiet altogether and give one's attention to the sermon. This is the case because listening to the sermon is obligatory, while reciting the blessing is a voluntary devotion. Therefore, following the practice of the Prophet, one can delay it until after the sermon is over.

Some scholars advise people who hear someone greeting them while they are listening to the sermon to salute them in their hearts, since response is a religious duty. Others prefer that you ignore that greeting, since it is neither right to speak during the sermon nor permissible to be distracted from it by anything.

Another fine point of this code of silence for the devout is that one should not pronounce a single word regarding worldly concerns between the dawn and the morning prayer, but devote this short time at the beginning of the day to meditation, remembrance of God, and reading the Qur'an.

It is also discourteous to speak while someone is chanting the Holy Qur'an. God says:

> When the Qur'an is read, listen to it with attention and hold your peace, that you may receive mercy. (*A'raf*, 20)

Although it is believed that this verse was revealed to admonish people who were talking during a congregational prayer, it is generally applied to all cases and places where the Qur'an is read publicly. The exception is when someone starts chanting the Qur'an unexpectedly at a place of work, or in a social gathering. Then the listeners are absolved of wrongdoing if they continue to speak, but the one who began chanting the Qur'an is to be blamed.

It is also considered wrong for people to salute each other while they are listening to the Qur'an. Saluting the speaker or the listeners in a religious gathering is also discouraged, for the same reasons that silence during the Friday sermon is required. Likewise one should hold one's peace in mosques while the congregation is gathering for prayer. The Prophet said:

> There will come a time when there will be Muslim nations who will discuss their worldly affairs in mosques. God does not need them to enter His holy houses. (Ibn Hibban, Ibn Mas`ud)

And:

> If someone raises his voice in a mosque and announces things, for instance if he seeks people's help in finding something he has lost, respond to him briefly, "May God not return to you that which you have lost!" For mosques are not built for such purposes. (Muslim, Abu Hurayrah)

But indeed one should keep one's tongue from praying or wishing for harm to fall on another person. The Prophet said:

> A Muslim is he from whose tongue and hand other Muslims are safe. (Tirmidhi, Abu Hurayrah)

The worst of curses is to pray that one's brother in faith die without faith. Some scholars say that whoever offers such a curse is a heretic. Others say that wishing anyone's damnation in the Hereafter is a major sin at the very least. Nor is it permissible to pray for the welfare of a tyrant or a denier of religion, wishing such people success in this world and the Hereafter, unless one prays for their conversion to truth and justice, and the transformation of their tyranny into beneficence.

TAKING OATHS

To take an oath swearing that something is true, while knowing well it is a lie, is the worst curse that your own tongue can bring upon you. The Messenger of God said:

> The worst sins are to assign partners to God, to disown one's parents, to kill, and to swear that something is true while it is a lie. (Bukhari, `Abdullah ibn `Umar)

And:

> To swear to the truth of something while knowing well it is a lie is an oath

against God, which has no atonement. (Hakim, ibn Mas`ud)

And:

The Messenger of God said, "If someone succeeds in taking something that does not belong to him away from another believer, by swearing it is his, God closes the doors of Paradise for him and makes it lawful for Hell to take him."

Someone asked: "Does that apply even if the thing he took is of no value?"

He said, "Yes, even if it is a little piece of a branch of the toothbrush tree." (Muslim, Abu `Umamah)

To swear in the name of something other than God is sacrilege, especially if one is taking an oath about something that is not true and trying to save oneself from mentioning the name of God while lying. But even if what you are taking the oath about is true, if you say, "I swear on the honor of my nation" or "on the name of my forefathers," and so forth, that oath is unacceptable. The Prophet said:

To take an oath in the name of God about something untrue is a lesser sin than taking an oath in the name of anything else, even if your oath is true. (Tabarani, Abdullah ibn Mas`ud)

And:

If one of you takes an oath in the name of another community than Islam, he is not a Muslim and belongs to that nation in whose name he has sworn. (Bukhari, Thabit ibn Dahhaq)

And:

God forbids us to swear in the name of our forefathers. If you have to take an oath, swear in God's name or not at all. (Bukhari, Abu Hurayrah)

When the Messenger of God heard someone swearing in the name of his forefathers, he said:

Do not swear in the name of your fathers. The one who takes an oath in the name of his Lord had better tell the truth, and the one who hears such an oath had better believe it. The one who is not satisfied with the truth of an oath taken in the name of God will not be protected by God's mercy. (Ibn Maja, Buraydah)

Ibn `Umar said that he heard the Prophet say:

The one who swears in any other than God's name has fallen into error, and is not taking an oath, but cursing. (Tirmidhi)

God says:

And make not God's name an excuse in your oaths against doing good, or acting rightly, or making peace between people, for God is one who hears and knows all things. (*Baqarah*, 224)

Islam also strongly advises against using God's name too often in one's oaths to confirm what one knows to be true. God says:

Heed not the type of despicable man ready with oaths ... (*Qalam*, 10)

Although it is permissible to swear to the truth of something important, as was practiced at the time of the Prophet by his Companions, later the saintly and devout among the Muslims shied away from swearing in God's name, because of their fear and love of God and respect for His ordinances. The Prophet said:

All that taking an oath in God's name brings upon one is either regret or sin. (Umm Hibban, Ibn `Umar)

A man falsely accused Hadrat Jubayr of owing him ten thousand *dirhams*. As he could not find any evidence or witnesses to prove his claim, he publicly asked Jubayr to swear that he did not owe him this fortune. And Jubayr, feeling shy before his Lord, refused to take an oath in God's name. He preferred to pay the liar a fortune that he did not owe.

In a similar case, another pious Muslim, Esh'as ibn Qays, paid seventy thousand *dirhams* that he did not owe in order to avoid swearing by God's name.

NAME-CALLING

Another offense of the tongue is name-calling—to give people bad titles or nicknames in order to belittle or insult them. This is an attempt to change somebody's identity for the worse in the eyes of other people, and can be very harmful. God says:

Nor call each other by offensive nicknames, giving names connoting wickedness to someone who is a believer. Those who do not desist are indeed doing wrong. (*Hujurat*, 11)

But there is no harm in giving a pleasant nickname to one or both of two people who have the same name with the intent of differentiating them.

SELF-PROMOTION
Many use their tongues to sell themselves, to make others believe that they are the right people for high positions in society or government. This is a form of begging for something that one neither needs nor deserves: therefore it is very wrong. People who do this are accumulating insurmountable trouble and pain for themselves and others. The Prophet said to Abdur-Rahman ibn Samura:

O Abdur-Rahman, do not sell yourself, seeking to be a chief or to hold a high position to rule over others. If such a position is offered to you without your asking for it, both men and God will be your helpers. But if it is given to you because you asked for it, you will be left by yourself to deal with it. (Bukhari)

The most difficult of high positions is that of a judge. To be truly just is a quality of God Most High, while to fail in justice is one of the worst crimes against God. The Prophet said:

Whoever becomes a judge has had his throat cut without a knife. (Abu Dawud and Tirmidhi, Abu Hurayrah)

And:

The one who is ambitious to become a judge, selling himself to obtain powerful supporters, if he succeeds, will be left by himself to fail. But if someone, chosen by all, is forced to take on this duty as a sacrifice, God will send as his companion a just angel, who will inspire him with divine justice at all times. (Abu Dawud, Anas ibn Malik)

The blessed wife of the Prophet, Hadrat `A'ishah, reported that he said:

Even the judge who strove to be just will have a moment on the Day of Judgment when he will wish that he had not even judged which of two people owned a single date. (Imam Ahmad)

One day, the Messenger of God said:

If those of you who want to be rulers over people wish to know what it means to be a ruler, I will tell you. You have three things to gain: one is universal blame; the second is regret for your acts and your wish to rule; the third is God's punishment on the Day of Judgment—with the exception of those who rule in justice. (Tabarani, `Awf ibn Malik)

He also said:

I do not doubt that many among you wish to rule over people, but know that you will regret it on the Day of Judgment. How fine is a mother who suckles a child, how terrible is the one who does not feed her child! (Bukhari, Abu Hurayrah)

And he said:

There will be no one who has commanded even ten people who will not be brought to justice in shackles on the Day of Judgment. Only the justice with which they ruled can undo their shackles. (Imam Ahmad, Abu Hurayrah)

The responsibility to command and to dispense justice among people has to be assumed by somebody, but it is arduous and difficult. To present oneself for that responsibility is foolish, to say the least. It is better to refuse it, even if it is offered. But unless there is someone else who is better qualified, a believer who is esteemed to be competent by others is obliged to accept this task.

All the scholars of Islamic law agree that the community should be reluctant to appoint someone who is ambitious to be director of a religious trust. People should choose someone who is known to be honest and competent and is hesitant to accept the responsibility. That is because the responsibility for the spending of religious funds is no less serious than carrying out the duties of a judge.

The responsibility of becoming a trustee, an executor for an orphan or a mentally incompetent adult, is an equally dangerous position. The Prophet said to his companion Abu Dharr:

O Abu Dharr, I see a weakness in you. I care about you and wish for you what I wish for myself. So even if there are only two people, do not be the chief of them, and do not ever accept to take charge of the property of an orphan. (Muslim, Abu Dharr)

The scholar Kaadihan says: "One should be reticent to accept the responsibility of becoming a trustee for anyone. It is like standing at the edge of a precipice." And Abu Yusuf related that the Prophet said, "To want to be a trustee for the first time is at best a mistake. If someone seeks it a second time, he must be inclined to deceit. If he wishes it a third time, he must be a thief." He also said that even a trustee as trustworthy as Caliph `Umar ibn Khattab would not be able to save himself from paying a heavy indemnity at the end of his career. Imam Shafi`i said, "Only a fool or a thief is anxious to become a trustee."

So stay away from these five positions: to be the trustee of an incompetent person; to rule over others; to act as an agent or attorney for someone; to be the custodian of another's property; and to dispense justice.

WISHING FOR DEATH

When a man is distressed and lacks faith, courage, and patience, his mind loses control over his tongue, and his tongue utters blasphemies. One of these blasphemies is to curse oneself and say, "I wish I were dead." Wishing to die before God brings death upon you is a revolt against Him and a sin. God says:

And man prays for evil as he ought to pray for good: and man is ever hasty. (*Bani Isra`il*, 11)

The Prophet said:

I forbid you to wish for death when a catastrophe befalls you. If you are totally desperate, pray not for death, but ask God to make you live as long as He esteems it is good for you and to take you to Himself when it is best for you. (Bukhari, Anas ibn Malik)

And:

Do never ask your Lord to take your life before God esteems to end it. Realize that when you die, your possibility of doing good deeds ends. You need all the good you do for the Hereafter. The whole life of a faithful person should be spent in doing good. (Bukhari, Abu Hurayrah)

And he said:

Do not ever wish for death: fear the time when your affairs will decide your salvation in the Hereafter. Wish for a long life. When God accords a long life to a believer, it is a sign that He has chosen him as a blessed person whom He will prevent from doing wrong and will lead to truth. (Ahmad ibn Hanbal, Jabir ibn `Abdullah)

`Ulaym al-Kindi reported that he and Abu Anbes al-Ghifari watched from the roof of their house as people carried away the bodies of those who had died from plague. Al-Ghifari, with terrible sadness and sincerity, said three times, "O damned plague, take me away, too!"

`Ulaym asked him, "How can you say that? Didn't you hear our Prophet forbid us to wish for death? He warned us that our book of deeds is closed by death, and that there is then no returning back to do things to please the Lord and save us on the Day of Judgment!"

Al-Ghifari responded, "And have you not heard him also say, 'When the following six catastrophes fall upon humanity, then hurry to end your lives: when the most foolish among them becomes their ruler; when whole armies of police tyrannize people; when judges sell justice for money and their own benefit; when crime and bloodshed become a daily occurrence;

when men lack care, and disown their families and friends; when God's holy books become rhymes chanted like songs to the accompaniment of music, and such singers, who have no knowledge of divine words, become the leaders of prayers in mosques.'" (Ibn `Abdil-Barr)

STUBBORN CONDEMNATION

Another regrettable utterance of the tongue is its rejection of people's excuses when they apologize for something wrong they have done. This is as bad as searching out their faults. The Messenger of God said:

The one who refuses to accept the excuse and apology of his fellow Muslim is like a dishonest tax collector, and is just as blameworthy. (Ibn Maja, Jud`an)

The Prophet said:

If you wish your wives to be modest, be ashamed of your own impudence. Be kind to your children if you wish them to be loving. Accept the apology of your fellow Muslim if you wish to drink from the fountain of *Kawthar* when you are thirsty on the Day of Judgment. (Tabarani, Hadrat `A'ishah)

This obligation to accept the apology of the faithful is dependent on our belief that the apologizer sincerely regrets what has been done. If we know the person is only pretending to be sorry, it is not an obligation—but it is still recommended for a compassionate believer.

SELF-INTERESTED INTERPRETATION OF SCRIPTURE

Another grave fault of the tongue is to interpret God's words in the Holy Qur'an so as to accord with one's own opinion. The Prophet said:

The one who interprets God's words in His Holy Book according to his own ideas, even if his interpretation is correct, is doing wrong. (Abu Dawud, Jundab ibn `Abdullah)

And he warned:

Whoever utters a word that is not based on a vast knowledge about the Holy Qur'an had better prepare himself for Hellfire. (Tirmidhi, Ibn `Abbas)

He also added a warning to take care in relating his traditions, saying:

Take care in relating my words and actions. Speak only if you are sure. Whoever attributes to me words that I have not said had better prepare himself for his place in Hell. Whoever assigns his own opinion to God's words in the Qur'an should also be ready to enter Hellfire. (Imam Ahmad and Tirmidhi)

It is obvious that the Prophet did not forbid all interpretation of the Qur'an. Otherwise thousands of volumes of interpretations would not have come to our day. This warning is for opportunists who interpret Qur'anic verses in order to justify their dubious actions, and ignoramuses who expound upon the Qur'an in order to gain a reputation as wise men. These warnings cannot mean that no interpretation except that undertaken at the time of the Prophet is allowed. Only a few such insights have reached our time. If there were no room for any other effort to understand God's instructions, then religious precedents applying to our own times would be impossible to discover.

The general consensus of the scholars is that there is no such interdiction, unless it perhaps applies to the allegorical verses, for which God Himself forbade people to establish a fixed meaning.

He it is who has sent down to you the Book: in it are verses basic or fundamental, of established meaning: they are the foundation of the Book. Others are allegorical. But those in whose hearts is perversity pursue the part thereof that is allegorical, seeking discord and seeking to determine its original meaning, but no one knows its original meaning except God. (*Al-i `Imran*, 7)

The Holy Qur'an has been revealed to humanity as a perfect proof of God's prescriptions. Because of its divine perfection, interpretation for human understanding is necessary. But only the faithful who are well versed in the Arabic language and the recorded occasions of the revelation of each verse, and who possess a share of worldly knowledge of the subjects mentioned in God's words, have the right to interpret the Holy Qur'an. Even if you are a scholar of Islamic theology, if you are not fully knowledgeable in Qur'anic Arabic and the context of the Qur'anic verses, you should not attempt to interpret the text beyond the ancient traditional variant readings of the Word of God as handed down by pupils of the Companions of the Prophet. Ignorant interpretations are no more than stories: they are not true commentary.

Someone may know Arabic well but not be aware of the tenets and fundamental articles of faith, nor the general agreement of Islamic jurists. That person will be unable to understand the sense of verses that appear to abrogate earlier passages in the Qur'an. Thus the interdiction also applies to those who think they can comment on the Holy Qur'an according to their own understanding and opinion simply because they know Arabic.

Opinions based on immense knowledge of all aspects of the religion and the language may vary, as may the spiritual inspirations of saintly people, such as the *imam*s of various Islamic creeds. A good example is the interpretation of the verse:

... if you have touched women ... (*Ma'idah*, 6)

Imam Shafi`i holds that if a man touches the bare skin of a woman with his palm, as in shaking hands, both will lose their ritual ablution. According to the interpretation of Imam Abu Hanifah, however, the same verse is interpreted as implying sexual intercourse, which necessitates a washing of the whole body before coming to prayer. Other forms of contact, according to him, do not necessarily break one's ablution.

INSOLENCE

When someone is speaking knowledgeably on any subject of interest, especially on religious matters, interrupting is considered bad behavior. It is especially rude to interrupt a public speaker. Even silent salutations are out of order, because they distract the speaker and attract attention to yourself. It doesn't matter whether a person is reciting or interpreting the Qur'an, transmitting Traditions of the Prophet, preaching, praying, or simply talking to people on a specific subject. If you interject a totally different or mundane matter, even by whispering to one of the listeners, it is a sign of bad manners, frivolousness, affectation, or simply arrogance.

What is proper for a speaker is to be organized, dignified, and orderly in speech and to keep the delivery strictly on the subject, without diverting to other matters. What befits an audience is to listen attentively in silence, even restraining random glances. To leave the presence of a speaker without a dire reason is insulting.

The same reproof is due to dependents who disrespect, oppose, reject, and disobey the rightful orders of the ones upon whom they depend. This applies to children's behavior toward their parents, students' toward their teachers, employees' toward their employers, husband and wife toward each other; the public's toward its government, and so forth. Traditionally, it is written that in a case of disagreement between two people, if one of them receives a judgment in his favor and his opponent contests the decision even in words, he should be reprimanded by society.

If you are offered a gift, it is reprehensible and insulting to ask whether it is ritually clean or if it has been obtained lawfully. Likewise, if you are invited to dine, it is shameful to question your host about whether the food contains anything forbidden by religion. And if you pray in someone's house and there is no dirt visible, it is unacceptable to be suspicious of the cleanliness of the place. This kind of attitude is a sure sign of failure of trust, hypocrisy, or arrogance, nosiness or ignorance, and is clearly a form of tyranny toward people of your own faith.

O seeker of truth! What is proper for you is to trust your fellow believer. The exterior is an expression of the interior. The owner is the banner of what he owns. If a person is clean, that which he possesses and offers is clean. To distrust this is to be lacking in faith.

It is true that God forbids the believers from helping others in wrongdoing, approving of wrongdoing, or even ignoring and permitting wrongdoing. He says:

> ... help one another in righteousness, but do not help one another in sin and rancor ... (*Ma'idah*, 2)

Thus the one who supports a sinner in sinning is a sinner himself. In cases of major sinful acts—such as being an accomplice to a murderer or a thief or supporting a tyrant—this is obvious. But even involuntarily to be a part of a group that generates anarchy and poverty, which are conducive to murder and robbery and injustice, is equally to be condemned.

The principle holds even to the fine point of a woman's rights as a wife. For instance a wife may not visit any man (outside her own family within the degrees of relationship that make marriage impossible) without her husband's approval. There are some traditions attributed to the Prophet, not certain to be authentic, that forbid women even to go to the public baths. Other jurists find this interdiction false. Some scholars interpret the verse in the Holy Qur'an where God addresses the household of the Prophet:

> And stay in your houses and display not your beauty like the displaying of the days of ignorance, (*Ahzab*, 33)

as a rule for all Muslim women, although this injunction was given in particular to the wives of the Prophet. And indeed Muslim women should not make themselves specially attractive when they leave their homes.

Yet a wife of the Prophet was not like any other woman. The Mothers of the Believers were in contact with a large number of people; men and women, who would come to them to learn the treasures of wisdom they received from the Prophet. An allusion to this is contained in the verse preceding the one quoted, where God says to them:

> O wives of the Prophet, you are not like other women. If you would keep

your duty, be not soft in speech, lest he in whose heart is a disease yearn: and speak a word of goodness. (*Ahzab*, 32)

Thus they were not forbidden to speak to men. But as a safeguard against possible inclination of the ego to evil thoughts, women are told not to indulge in soft and flirtatious conversation with the opposite sex. The same applies to men, who are told not to engage in superfluous conversation with young women unless it is necessary to talk to them about a serious matter. Some say a man should not even salute young women nor respond to their salutations unless they know each other as family. This clearly indicates that the intentions of the parties are dishonorable, as the Prophet said that the adultery of the tongue is in flirtatious conversation with the opposite sex.

It is also considered wrong for two people to whisper in each other's ears while a third person is present, because invariably it irritates the third person and creates suspicion. The Messenger of God said:

When you are three, let not two whisper in each other's ears in front of the third, because he will be insulted and hurt. Neither should a wife describe another woman to her husband as if he was seeing her undressed. (Bukhari, from Ibn Mas`ud)

Now that we have summarized what is forbidden or disadvised by our religion with regard to the troubles our tongues may bring upon us, we will further discuss the problems our tongues may cause us socially in our everyday life.

JOKING

To joke and to make fun of people and of things people do is a common behavior toward which we should show extreme caution. The Messenger of God certainly had a sense of humor. Abu Hurayrah said:

I often saw the Prophet stick out his tongue at his grandchild, Hasan ibn `Ali, whom he loved. The child would respond by running to him and hugging him. (Abu Ya`la)

He also reported:

The Companions said to the Prophet, "You are joking with us!"
He replied, "But I only tell the truth." Tirmidhi, Abu Hurayrah)

And Anas ibn Malik, the Prophet's adopted son, said that the Messenger of God summoned him one day with, "O owner of two ears!" suggesting that he heard and understood everything. It was a joke and a compliment.

Thus joking is permissible when what is attributed is pleasant and complimentary; true but at the same time loving, lighthearted, and humorous. Joking is wrong when it is insulting, untrue, harsh, mean, and mischievous.

`Abdullah ibn Saib reported that his grandfather heard the Prophet say to someone who took someone else's walking stick as a joke:

> As far as the harm done is concerned, it makes no difference whether you took it as a joke or stole it. (Tirmidhi)

And `Abdur-Rahman ibn Abi Layla reported that during a night journey with the Prophet, one of the Companions fell asleep riding his camel. Someone else took the reins from his hands and let the camel walk loose, as a joke. The poor man woke up in fear. The Prophet said:

> A Muslim who causes fear in another Muslim, even as a joke, is sinning. (Abu Dawud)

Indeed, exaggeration in humor and making fun, when practiced by many and too often, causes a society to lose its dignity and seriousness and creates hostility among people. Even if it only causes riotous laughter, too much laughing deadens the heart—especially when it is at the expense of someone else.

Abu Hurayrah reported:

> One day the Prophet said to his Companions: "Who among you is prepared to accept, act upon, and teach to others five instructions I shall give?" Without hearing the instructions, I volunteered. Then the Prophet said, "First, do not do that which is unlawful: among all the people, you will be the one who worships God best. Second, be content with what God has allotted you in your daily life: among all the people, you will be the richest. Third, be kind to your neighbor: you will perfect your faith. Fourth, want for others what you want for yourself: you will truly be a Muslim. And fifth, do not laugh too much, for laughter wounds the heart." (Tirmidhi)

And Abu Hurayrah also reported:

> A man utters a single word to make people laugh, and that single word makes him fall in the approval of his Lord as far as from here to the heavens. The fall one takes when one's tongue slips is much worse than the fall one takes when one's foot slips. (Bayhaqi)

PRAISE

Often when one makes fun of someone or of something, it is out of ridicule and criticism; and therefore unkind and harmful. Yet the opposite action—praising people—in some cases can be equally wrong. There are six conditions under which praises and compliments can be harmful.

1. To praise oneself is considered by man and God alike as a sign of arrogance. God says:

Do not try to absolve yourselves, for God knows best who is the one who is obedient to Him and who does right. (*hadith qudsi*)

The same disapproval applies to people who praise their own parents, progeny, dependents, students, or achievements. Their purpose is to praise themselves indirectly. Yet when something is worthy and laudable, its owner or maker certainly deserves equal praise. Someone asked a wise man, "What is undesirable and ugly even if in reality it is good and beautiful?" And the wise man said, "The good man who praises himself."

Yet there are conditions that make self-approbation permissible. One may speak well of oneself in self-defense, when wrongly accused or tyrannized, or to convince an authority to release property that is rightfully one's own. If someone has deep knowledge, perfect morals and behavior, and good deeds, that person may speak of them so that others might learn. Perhaps people will envy those qualities and try to emulate them. The Prophet said:

I am the leader of all the children of Adam, but I am not proud. All the prophets will gather under my banner on the Day of Judgment, and I will be the first to enter Paradise, but I am not proud. I will be the first who will intercede for sinners and my intercession will be accepted, but I am not proud. (Ibn Maja, Abu Sa`id)

2. It is wrong to praise people by attributing to them unverifiable deeds or moral and spiritual virtues (such as sincerity, faithfulness, honor, piety, chastity, and so forth) of which no one can have sure knowledge, since they are inner qualities. In such matters one can only rightly say, "It seems to me that so-and-so is this-and-that ..."

3. The worst praise is that offered to people known to be impious and sinful in an effort to absolve them. The Messenger of God said:

By praising a sinner one invites God's wrath upon oneself. (Ibn Abi Dunya, Anas ibn Malik)

4. If you are aware that your praise of someone will lead him to think himself better than other people so that he becomes arrogant, you will

have helped another human being commit the major sin of pride.

> Someone praised someone else to the Prophet. He said to him, "You are cutting your friend's throat." He repeated this sadly three times. Then he turned to the others present and said, "If anyone wishes to speak favorably about someone, say, 'It seems to me so-and-so is such and such ...' Only God knows the truth. I would not dare to praise anyone while He knows better." (Bukhari, Abu Bakra)

And he said:

> When you encounter someone who is loudly praising somebody else, throw dust in his face. (Muslim, Miqdad ibn Aswad)

5. To praise a sinful person or a sinful act so that they become desirable to honest people and lead them astray is the way of the Devil. Any elaborately and attractively embellished description that sets fire to people's lustful fancy may lead to disasters, including the innocent description by a wife to a husband of another woman's beauty. Finally, to praise rulers and people in authority in order to gain personal favors for oneself, to obtain things to which one has no right, or to get support for tyrannizing or punishing people is no less than criminal.

BLAME

Criticism may be a positive action: it may prevent the repetition of a wrong, or encourage a wrongdoer to repent. Yet even in this commendable form, criticism is an accusation, and it may not be taken kindly by the one who is criticized. Furthermore, it implies that the criticizing tongue is above the admonished ear, and thus may involve the critic in arrogance. Furthermore, much criticism is subjective. For instance, a food that is not liked by one person may be perfectly tasty for somebody else.

Abu Hurayrah reported:

> The Prophet never criticized any food that was offered to him. When he was hungry he ate, and when he was not hungry, he did not eat. (Muslim)

Expressing disapproval of things such as food, clothing, houses, or places—let alone people or situations—is a form of arrogance and therefore to be avoided.

POETRY AND RHETORIC
To use poetry or poetic language to make one's criticism, praise, ridicule, or persuasion to immorality more effective makes these errors of the tongue even worse. That is the reason God and our religion find poetry suspect: it may subtly encourage people to sin.
God says:

And the poets, only those astray follow them. (*Shu`ara'*, 224)

And the Prophet said:

A man is better off with a body filled with pus than with a heart filled with poetry. (Tirmidhi, Abu Hurayrah)

Poetry praising God and His prophets, describing the beauty and harmony of His creation, guiding people to the love of God and to the worthiness of good deeds, reminding them of the Hereafter and the Day of Judgment, or addressing other such topics is obviously commended by the religion.
If beautiful and colorful language is used to enhance emotional response without creating a hindrance to understanding the good advice given in preaching and teaching, it is permissible. But using rhyme and rhythm or displays of eloquence in political oratory or even everyday, ordinary talk is undesirable when it hides the truth and destroys clarity. The Messenger of God said:

God's wrath is upon those who twist their tongues in an effort to be eloquent, in order to fool people. (Amr ibn al-`As)

And he repeated thrice:

Beware! The ones who run up against causes with twisted tongues and incomprehensible words are lost to good. (Muslim, Ibn Mas`ud)

PRATTLE
The Messenger of God said:

The one among you who is furthest away from me and most odious to me is the one who jabbers at length about affairs without minding whether what he says is true or false, right or wrong. (Tirmidhi, Jabir ibn `Abdullah)

Good behavior prevents the faithful from engaging in useless and meaningless talk. Most people's talk is about superficial experiences they wish to share with others: food they ate, things they thought, places and people they saw. Even if such words are harmless—purely descriptive, not containing any criticism or negative comment—they represent a loss of valuable time and effort for oneself as well as for others. And one can rarely avoid untruth, exaggeration, gossip, hypocrisy, and pride from infiltrating into such conversations.

On the other hand, it is possible to use light conversation purposefully and with consideration to eliminate someone's pain, making him forget his troubles. We should risk our dignity by chattering about irrelevant things if we have helped someone who feels beholden and embarrassed, or if we have done a genuine good deed, or to amuse children who are distressed. On these and similar occasions, it is appropriate even to make fun about serious matters, for to keep silent and appear solemn may be construed as arrogance.

IGNORANT ASSERTIONS
The worst speech is to talk about things one knows nothing about.

> During a funeral at the time of the Prophet, the person who was performing the eulogy said, "O you who have left this world, I give you the good news that Paradise awaits you!"
> The Messenger of God told him, "And who has given you this news? You talk of things you do not know." (Tirmidhi, Ibn `Umar)

> The mother of a martyr in the battle of Uhud found that her son had tied a flat stone to his belly to suppress his hunger. She wiped the sand from his face and said, "Oh my son, Paradise is your abode!"
> The Prophet told her: "Let us not say things we do not know. Let us hope he was one of those faithful ones who do not chatter about matters that are useless both in this world and the Hereafter, and that he talked against things that hurt others, but did not touch himself." (Ibn Abi Dunya, Anas ibn Malik)

Peace and ease in the Hereafter are for those who will not have to pass through the Day of Judgment. That Day itself is a dire punishment, and the one who talks senselessly and unnecessarily will certainly be asked about every word he said, and will have to pay.

The Messenger of God said:

> The person who is likely to sin by saying the wrong things is the person who talks too much. (Abu Shaykh, Abu Hurayrah)

And:

The beauty of Islam shows in the face of one who keeps silent about things he does not know and that do not concern him. (Tirmidhi, Ibn `Umar)

What becomes the faithful is to talk briefly but clearly and precisely about things that have to be said, things that one is sure are true. But elaboration and repetition and lengthy explanations may be necessary when one is addressing people whose understanding is weak and when the subject is important enough that it has to be communicated under any circumstances.

ORDINARY SPEECH

In human social relationships there are certain interactions for the common good that must be handled with great care. Our religion has precepts for dealing with them: these must be followed. We refer to everyday activities such as buying and selling, forming partnerships and companies, settling conflicts, entering into marriage or divorce, forming trusts, making donations for good deeds, making settlements, assigning inheritances, and so forth. For each there are proper methods indicated in religious law. Any procedure contrary to these customs is considered wrong and sacrilegious.

Someone asked Imam Muhammad ibn Hasan why he had not written a book on piety. He answered, "But I did! I wrote a book on human relations in commerce and social affairs."

Piety is real only as it is exercised in people's decency and kindness toward each other. Fear of God is manifest when people do not hurt or cheat others. Details of this behavior are available in religious law and Islamic teaching. Everyone should refer to these before undertaking an action involving other people and society at large. It is a religious duty.

There are certain people authorized to disseminate knowledge whose words, actions, and behavior influence others. They are the scholars, the wise, the religious leaders, teachers, and preachers. Such people must be especially careful to study and learn from authentic sources. They should apply what they teach in their own lives, for they themselves must be examples of what they teach. Otherwise their preaching will be hypocritical and their influence on others will be either nonexistent or negative—and they will be responsible for the effects they produce. The divine punishment for misleading teaching is many times greater than for ordinary sins, for bad teachers also receive punishment for the sins of the people whom they have influenced.

The same care must be given to our private worship—our daily prayers, supplications, recitation of the Holy Qur'an and of the Beautiful Names of God. There are clear indications about the exact pronunciation of the Arabic words and the proper styles of reading the Qur'an aloud. It is also forbidden to pray publicly or to invoke the Names of God in places where people usually commit sin, or during commercial or business dealings, in order to assert one's own righteousness. Nor is it permitted to accept payment for praying or reading the Holy Qur'an for someone's benefit. We have elsewhere written three essays on this subject: *ad-Durr al-yatim* ("The Rare Pearl"), *Inkaz al-Khaliqin* ("Deliverance of the Created)", and *Ikaz an-Na'imin* ("Awakening of the Sleepers").

SILENCE

Thus far we have summarized the mischiefs and disasters this tongue in our mouths can bring upon us. But when it decides to keep still, silence also has its risks. If it refuses to testify to the unity of God and the prophethood of Muhammad (s.a.w.s), to pray, to recite the Qur'an, to enjoin the right, to prevent the wrong, to salute the faithful, to advise, to comfort, to save, or to express compassion and love, its silence is sinful.

The Messenger of God said:

> When you come into the company of others, salute them with God's peace and blessings, and stay with them if there is a place for you. When you leave, salute them again. The first greeting is not better than the last. (Tirmidhi, Abu Hurayrah)

The adopted son of the Prophet, Anas ibn Malik, used to greet lovingly every child he encountered. He said, "That is what the Prophet used to do." (Bukhari and Muslim)

The Prophet also said:

> The most miserable and most incompetent of men are those who cannot even pray. And the stingiest of men are those who do not greet others when they see them. (Tabarani, Abu Hurayrah)

And he said:

> A Muslim has six rights over other Muslims. When they see each other they should greet each other. When one invites another, if he has no valid excuse, he should accept the invitation. When one asks for advice from another, he should give his best advice. When one is sick, the other should visit him. When one sneezes and says "Praise God," the other should respond, "May God have mercy on you." When one dies, the other should accompany his funeral procession. (Muslim, Abu Hurayrah)

Sneezing has a special importance in Islam. It is believed that with a sneeze, the heart misses a beat. It is as if one is dead for a moment and is then brought back to life. That is why the one who sneezes ritually says, "Praise God," while other Muslims respond with "May God have mercy on you," as is said about the dead. The Prophet said:

God likes the ones who sneeze and dislikes the ones who yawn. When you hear someone sneeze and praise God, ask God's mercy upon him. Yawning is induced by Satan. When he makes you yawn while you are praying, don't open your mouths: swallow your yawning. If you open your mouths, the Devil will be pleased and laugh. (Bukhari, Abu Hurayrah)

When the Messenger of God sneezed he always covered his face either with a handkerchief or his hand, and sneezed with as much restraint as possible. He said:

When you hear someone sneeze, if he says, "Praise God," say, "May God have mercy on you" each time he sneezes. But if he sneezes more than three times, do not: he must have a cold." (Abu Dawud, Abu Hurayrah)

Do not enter someone else's house without announcing yourself with salutations, wishing the peace and blessings of God on those who live there, and asking their permission. This is recommended by God Himself, who says:

O you who believe! Enter not houses other than your own until you have asked permission and saluted those in them. That is best for you, in order that you may heed what is seemly. (*Nur*, 27)

The Prophet was in a house and someone from the tribe of Bani Amir came to visit him. When the man came to the door, he shouted, "May I come in?"
The Prophet, hearing this, asked his servant, "Please go and teach our visitor how to ask to enter a house. Tell him that first he should offer greetings, saying 'God's peace be upon you,' and then ask if he may enter." The visitor heard him and obliged, and was permitted to enter. (Abu Dawud, Rib'iy ibn Hirash)

The Prophet advised:

Knock at the door three times at most. If they open, enter. If not, leave. (Muslim, Musa al-Ash`ari)

Someone asked him if he should ask permission to enter even his mother's presence, and he answered, "Yes." (Tabarani, 'Ata` ibn Yasar)

The Prophet also said:

> If someone sends you a messenger inviting you to his house and you fol-
> low the messenger to the house, you do not have to ask permission to
> enter. (Abu Dawud, Abu Hurayrah)

Among the misdeeds of silence are:

- not to advise the right or forbid the wrong when you are sure your
  words will be effective and will bring harm neither to you nor to the
  people you are addressing,
- not to intercede for the wrongly accused and tyrannized,
- to stop talking to your parents and your family,
- to refuse to be a witness,
- not to say "Glory to God" or "God be exalted and blessed" when
  you hear the name of God mentioned, which indicates disrespect
  for the Lord,
- not to recite a prayer for the Prophet's soul when you hear his
  name, which is also disrespectful.

It is wrong not to ask others' help when one is totally destitute. And it is
wrong, when people know of such a case but cannot be of sufficient help
themselves, if they do not seek out further assistance. It is an obligation
upon every believer to support poor people to the extent that they have
enough sustenance to be able to function and to do their obligatory worship.

There are many more such cases when one might choose to be silent but
God and His Messenger have ordered us to become involved. In such cases
silence is sinful or blameworthy. In our times it is indeed difficult to avoid
them. But if we can only retain what has been written here, try to follow
the instructions, and reduce our connection with people who revolt against
them, we might have a chance to save at least ourselves.

SUMMARY
For the sake of making things easier to remember, let us summarize, enu-
merating the essential words that should not be uttered according to the
order of God:

- sacrilege,
- despair of God's beneficence,
- hypocritical talk,
- lying,

- gossip, accusation, criticism,
- impertinent, damning, cursing words about people, things, and situations,
- contradicting and opposing truth,
- divulging secrets,
- ridiculing and embarrassing people,
- asking for special favors,
- asking unnecessary questions,
- duplicity,
- inciting people to do wrong,
- excusing and interceding for the wrongs people do,
- preventing people from doing good deeds,
- coarse and impolite speech,
- shaming people,
- threatening divorce,
- wailing for the dead and advertising their good deeds,
- insolence toward one's superiors, teachers, and elders,
- conversing during the chanting of the call to prayer or, in mosques, during recitation of the Qur'an, preaching, and worship,
- praying for the success of a tyrant,
- praying for the punishment of a good person,
- taking a vow for something untrue,
- swearing in any other name except that of God,
- giving rude nicknames to people,
- putting oneself forward to become a high official, governor, judge, trustee, and the like,
- cursing oneself,
- wishing for death,
- refusing to accept the apology of a fellow Muslim,
- frightening a believer,
- interrupting someone's talk,
- contesting one's teacher's words,
- doubting whether some food or gift is religiously lawful or not,
- making fun of people,
- praising someone for personal benefit,
- reciting poems and singing songs of obnoxious content,
- lengthening one's talk and unnecessarily adorning it with oratory,
- whispering in people's ears in the presence of others,
- greeting the disbelievers with the greeting of believers,
- claiming permissibility for matters God has forbidden,
- leading people to revolt and disbelief,
- addressing young strangers with evil intentions.

This is not an exhaustive list. There are other words that can lead people astray and damage social harmony. To stay silent and uninvolved when others are guilty of such wrong statements and actions is also wrong.

We hope it is clear to the reader that the tongue is as important an organ as the mind that thinks and the heart that feels, because it is the tongue that expresses thoughts and feelings, making them evident and alive. It is said that the perfection of a human being depends on two little pieces of flesh: the heart and the tongue. The right interaction of these two organs in us can lead us to the love, hope, and fear of God.

O seeker of Truth, watch your tongue! Guard it especially from two failures: lying and gossip. The two greatest enemies of the heart are hypocrisy and pride. And as a heart safe from hypocrisy and pride is safe from all the other ills that might afflict it, so a tongue that cannot tell a lie and will not talk against people and things is protected from the other ills that might infect it.

Many verses in the Qur'an and many Traditions of the Prophet condemn lying and gossip. The venerable `Umar ibn `Abdul-`Aziz, `Umayyad caliph and grandson of the beloved companion of the Prophet `Umar ibn al-Khattab, said: "Since the day I learned to dress myself, I have not once lied." And Abu Layth al-Faqih relates that the good wife of a pious man bought some cotton yarn, but did not like it when she got home. She said to her husband, "These yarn merchants are crooks, they cheated me." The pious husband divorced her for these words. When people asked him why he divorced his good wife, he answered, "I fear God, and do not wish to be embarrassed on the Day of Judgment when all the yarn merchants will be chasing after my wife to receive what they are due."

"To report all one hears suffices as a great sin."

CHAPTER 21

ON LISTENING

To listen to all the harmful talk mentioned in the previous chapter is inviting trouble, unless there is a necessity to oppose it or to take precautions against a danger it may provoke in daily life. Your ears are the way to your mind and your heart. They must be protected. The Prophet said:

> Beware! In every man's destiny there are tests of adultery. There is no running away from it. It will catch up with you. (Bukhari, Abu Hurayrah)

The adultery of the eyes is to look at things that invite you to sin. The adultery of the ears is to listen to words and sounds that will poison your heart and mind. The adultery of the tongue is to speak vain words. The adultery of the hands is to take what does not belong to you and to hurt others. The adultery of the feet is to walk into disasters.

The ego loves adultery and directs the senses toward it. And the appetites of the flesh confirm or negate the adulterous desires of the ego, so watch them carefully.

God has created sounds in nature to remind people of Him. The wind whispers and howls; the rain patters, thunder roars, birds sing. But the best of music is silence, which comforts the heart and quiets the mind.

Words are given only to humanity. The human tongue can be the sweetest of all sweets and the bitterest of all poisons. It is the human tongue that the ear must most beware of. So do not listen to those who are disliked by God and man alike. Do not listen to lies and sacrilege and talk that tries to make the wrong right and the right wrong. Do not listen to meaningless noise and rhythm that makes your flesh crawl and turns you into an animal, yet which some people call music and amusing songs.

Many scholars have written against such noise. Imam Kaadihan, basing himself on prophetic traditions, said, "To listen to loud musical instruments is sinful. To go to places where such noise invites people to sin is to do what religion forbids. To take pleasure in it is sacrilege."

He also mentions that if one hears such noise accidentally, there is no harm. Yet according to some reports, the Messenger of God plugged his ears on occasions when he heard such riotous noise.

People who participate in this activity take pleasure in what they call excitement. "Excitement" abolishes all thought, consideration, decency, chastity, and humanity in people and turns them into animals. Certain people with an overexcitable nature shout and scream during funerals, sermons, and recitation of the Qur'an, and think of this as spiritual ecstasy.

Usually it happens when there is chanting and music on such occasions, which is strictly forbidden. So is the so-called ecstasy that amounts to loss of one's mind and control, and is the cause of unlawful acts in human behavior. The Messenger of God said:

Even in battle, but certainly during funerals, sermons, and prayers in mosques, it is unlawful to shout and scream. (from *Ikhtiyar*)

It is also recommended not to listen to the public recitation of the Qur'an when it is wrongly recited or wrongly interpreted. Either ask the reciter to stop, or better still, leave.
God says:

When you hear men engaged in vain discourse about Our signs, turn away from them unless they turn to a different theme. If Satan ever makes you forget, then after recollection, do not sit in the company of those who do wrong. (*An`am*, 68)

To listen to vague personal experiences of people that do not correspond to religious teachings, such as inspirations and dreams, is also harmful. The Prophet said:

Whoever tells a dream he has not dreamt will be asked to tie together two kernels of wheat without a string. Whoever listens to the talk of men hated by God and men alike will have hot lead poured into his ears on the Day of Judgment. And whoever makes images of men will be asked to give them life. They will all be punished. (Bukhari, Ibn `Abbas)

In addition to the things it is recommended we not listen to, there are also things we are required to listen to. It is wrong not to listen to the advice of people of knowledge. It is wrong for children to ignore their parents, for students to ignore their teachers, for the one who does not know to ignore the one who knows. When the people don't listen to their rulers, the soldiers to their officers, the workers to their employers, inferiors to their superiors, they will remain ignorant, at a disadvantage, even in danger.

On the other hand, those who issue advice, recommendations, and orders should also listen to the questions, ideas, comments, excuses, and complaints of the people under them. A judge who does not heed the words of the accused, a religious counselor who does not respond to the question of someone who asks for advice, a husband who does not listen to his wife, a rich man who does not care about the pleading of the poor are certainly guilty of playing deaf to words they are obliged to hear.

CHAPTER 22

ON LOOKING

God says to His Messenger:

> Say to the faithful that they should lower their gaze and guard their modesty; that will make for greater purity for them; and God is well-acquainted with all that they do. (*Nur*, 30)

Thus God orders us to turn our eyes away from evil. All that God has created is beautiful and useful for the one who can truly see, but woe to the blind who see their own evil in things! A pure man with an objective eye who knows that what he is looking at is a creation of God will not see any evil in the creation. But those whose eyes are blinded by their egos and the evil desires of their flesh cannot see the beauty of reality. Ugliness is in the eye, not outside it. It is the eye that sins: sinfulness is not in what is seen. What a dirty eye sees is its own imagination. That is why God says:

> And pursue not that of which you have no knowledge; for every act of hearing, seeing, or feeling in the heart will be inquired into on the Day of Reckoning. (*Bani Isra'il*, 36)

Those who are ignorant and blind to the truth are led by their egos, their personal devils, to distort the beauty, harmony, and purity of reality into the chaos of their imagination, where everything unlawful, ugly, and sinful becomes permissible. And God says in a divine tradition:

> To see things one should not see is one of the poisonous arrows of the Devil. Whoever hides from this due to his love and fear of Me, I will give him such faith that his heart will be totally filled. (Tabarani, `Abdullah ibn Mas`ud)

And the Prophet said:

> On the Day of Judgment, all eyes will shed bitter tears of blood except the eyes that did not see what it is forbidden to see, which shed even a small teardrop in shame and fear of God during their lifetime, and were not shut in sleep on the way to Truth. (Isfahani, Abu Hurayrah)

The distortion of reality by imagination has led people to such inhuman behaviors as looking upon the sick, the crippled, the weak, and the poor in disgust instead of compassion. It makes people feel proud that they are better than others instead of helping them, or provokes them to look at the good things other people have and either attack them or wish that they could take them for themselves. It leads people to look at the skies at night, at the movement of planets and falling stars, and fancy that celestial events show things that will happen to them. It leads people to look at honest covered women and undress them in their minds.

The eye is attracted to everything that moves. Imagination is as quick as the eye, and is capable of changing the shape, color, and meaning of whatever the eye sees. But the faithful should have the will to put a stop to imagination. That is what the Prophet meant when he said:

> O `Ali, do not let what you see first be distorted by what you see later. You will not be responsible for what you see first, but your second impression will be judged. (Abu Dawud, Buraydah)

And:

> If one of you is struck by the beauty of a woman when you catch sight of her, if you protect your eye from lingering, God will consider your act as such a devotion that you will feel it in your heart. (Ahmad ibn Hanbal, `Abdullah ibn Mas`ud)

To stare at a woman with whom one is not acquainted is not permitted in Islam unless there is some necessity, especially if this sight arouses sexual feelings. There is no harm in looking at a woman's face and hands. If the woman is one of those who belong to the category of family members to whom religion forbids marriage, then men can look at them, though without scrutinizing them.

The necessities which permit men to look at the sexual parts of women include: medical examination, or when a medication or operation has to be administered in that area; for assistance during pregnancy and childbirth; during criminal investigations and other such dire cases. In these circumstances, even if they fear to be sexually aroused, men are obliged to look: it is their duty. Other than at the times mentioned above, to look at each others' sexual organs, even during intercourse, is considered shameful.

Hadrat `A'ishah, young wife of the Prophet, said of her husband:

> Neither did he ever see my private parts, nor did I see his. (Tirmidhi)

And the Messenger of God advised us that during love-making:

> Do not tear at each other as if skinning a camel.

The worst of imagination associated with the eye is to peer into the privacy of other people. Peeping through the doors and curtains of other people's homes is as bad as looking through tears and transparencies in the clothing of the opposite sex.

The Messenger of God said:

> When you come to visit someone's home, do not stand in front of the door but stand to the side, so that you cannot see inside when the door is opened. Give greetings and ask permission to enter. If you are permitted, enter; if not, leave without hard feelings. (Tabarani, `Abdullah ibn Busr)

As God says about visiting someone's home:

> But if you find no one therein, enter them not until permission is given to you; and if it is said to you, "Go back," then go back: this is purer for you. And God is the knower of what you do. (*Nur*, 28)

The Messenger of God said:

> If someone looks through the curtains of someone else's window, he has passed the boundaries of a terrain he is forbidden to enter. Therefore he is at fault. If someone pokes his eye out, he has deserved it. But if someone passes in front of an open door and even sees the private parts of the owner, it is not his fault. It is the fault of the one who exposes himself by leaving his door open. (Ahmad, Abu Dharr)

He also said:

> If someone were to look into someone else's home without being permitted, it wouldn't be wrong to blind his eye. (Bukhari and Muslim, Abu Hurayrah)

Anas ibn Malik reported:

> I saw the Messenger of God chase with a stick a man who entered his home secretly and was looking around. (Bukhari)

CHAPTER 23

ON TOUCHING

Many things that our religion forbids us to look at are also forbidden to touch. Our other organs that sense and perceive, see, hear, smell, and taste, are more passive than the hands, and less physically dangerous to others. When we see something desirable that belongs to someone else it may incite us to be envious and even wish to take it for ourselves, but without the engagement of the hand, the thing cannot be taken.

Certainly the hand is granted to human beings in order to give rather than take, to build rather than destroy, to heal rather than hurt. But as in the case of every other tool with which God has blessed us, the human ego distorts the constructive potentials of our hands into means of committing major sins.

Thus God warns us about the proclivities of the hand, which is capable of killing other human beings as well as the owner of the hand himself.

God forbids killing or hurting any living creature, down to the smallest insects, unless they are dangerous to one's own life and property. But when eliminating even a scorpion or any harmful or dangerous creature, one is forbidden to burn or drown it. Even when we burn a log in a fireplace, a believer is asked to be attentive that there are no ants or other living things on it.

To cut off ears, tails, or other parts of any animal, or to hurt creatures by beating them, especially on their faces, is considered blameworthy. To endanger the lives of wild animals, capturing them and imprisoning them in cages, or hunting them not to sustain oneself but for the pleasure of hunting, is forbidden by the religion.

It is reported by Ibn `Abbas that the Prophet said:

Do not make any living thing a target to shoot at. (Muslim)

And according to Jabir ibn `Abdullah, he forbade killing wild animals in captivity and their imprisonment in cages.

He has also forbidden teaching animals to fight each other, as in bullfights, camel wrestling, or cockfights. He discouraged even raising pigeons and birds for pleasure, because the Arabs used pigeons for fortune-telling before Islam.

Abu Hurayrah reported that when the Prophet saw a man chasing a pigeon to make it fly in the direction he hoped would bring him good fortune, he said:

Look, one devil is chasing another devil. (Abu Dawud)

Thus it is clear that all creatures should feel safe from any harm coming to them through the hands of a Muslim.

It is forbidden for a Muslim to take anything that belongs to somebody else unless it is presented or permitted by the owner. We are forbidden to steal, to take any more than our rightful share in a partnership or inheritance, or to try to benefit from other people's inheritances, collected taxes, or public funds that may pass through our hands. It is disgraceful to accept alms, or money someone else has dedicated to fulfill a vow, if one is not in need, even if the giver insists. Need is defined as possessing less than 200 *dirham*s or 880 grams of silver, or without the means to sacrifice a lamb. We should not even touch something that people have lost on the street.

Muslims who belong to the notable Meccan family of Hashim, or descendants of the blessed family of the Prophet, no matter how poor they may be, cannot accept alms. They are only permitted to receive gifts from funds dedicated to maintain pious people who are in need, or funds and goods that have no owners.

There are trusts destined for the maintenance of people of knowledge, the wise and holy who are rich spiritually but without worldly means. But some people are reputed to be wise and holy while they know themselves to be neither, and some people are held to be poor though they are nothing of the kind. It is unlawful for such people to touch funds that others may mistakenly offer to them. Nor is it right even for the very poor to accept alms, either from individuals or from trusts or organizations, when those funds are obtained by suspicious or unlawful means.

It is unlawful to take anything from the property of a minor, a person who is intellectually impaired or in a comatose state, or in one way or another not in a position to make rational decisions, even if one is given legal guardianship. The exception is funds invested with the object of returning with benefit, or at least with no loss.

For a worker to demand payment from an employer that is worth more than his efforts, or for him to take anything from his place of employment, is a grave breach of morals. It is an equal breach for an employer to pay his workers less than they are worth or to delay their payment after the work is done.

To destroy any property, to remove it to a place difficult to reach, or in some way to cause it harm and reduce its value, even if by maligning or belittling it, is considered mischief caused by the hand. Such acts directed toward someone else's property amount to tyranny. Directed toward one's own property they are considered to be immoral acts of thanklessness and squandering of blessings. To throw away leftover food from someone else's table without their permission is equally a fault.

Sometimes people encourage, support, and finance some person or organization to commit sinful acts, helping them to escape from their lawful and moral obligations and responsibilities. For instance, one might encourage people to commit adultery or not to pay what they owe. These are also acts of tyranny. Whoever undertakes them is condemned to reparations and censure, but not to harsher punishments such as paying a fine. To buy, carry, transport, or transfer forbidden items of consumption such as pork, blood, and alcohol is a sin.

To borrow an object belonging to someone without permission, even for a very short time and even if the object will never be harmed nor show any signs of being used, is as unlawful as stealing it, although it is not punishable as such. To do such a thing with the intention of playing a joke on the owner is exactly the same. Once someone in Medina took and hid the shoes of a friend as a joke. When the Prophet became aware of it, he said:

Do not frighten your brother in faith in any way. To cause stress for your Muslim brother incurs serious blame. (Tabarani, Amir ibn Rabi`ah)

Neither, even in jest, should one ever scare a person by brandishing a gun or a knife. The Prophet said:

Whoever pulls a knife on us is not one of us. (Bukhari, Abu Musa).

And according to Jabir ibn `Abdullah, as reported by Tirmidhi, the Prophet forbade his people even to hand one another swords that were out of their sheaths.

To buy, sell, or accept as a gift or as alms any object that has been stolen or taken by force is strictly forbidden, no matter how great or small its value. To give or take bribes is a sin. If you are forced to pay a bribe in order to receive something that rightfully belongs to you then the act is not sinful, but it is still disapproved.

Some things arouse harmful and sinful emotions and states, such as anger, lust, and envy. A Muslim is asked not to look at them. Those things before which we should lower our gaze we should also not touch with our hands. Even to shake hands with an attractive woman is better avoided unless one is sure that the contact will not arouse harmful sexual feelings. Contact with potential to arouse is only permissible when there is a dire necessity, such as saving, helping, or curing a person in need.

To draw, paint, or sculpt any human being is also discouraged as a precaution against creating idols that others may adore. The Prophet said:

On the Day of Judgment, the creators of idols are the ones most chastised. They will be told to give life to the creatures whose images they made, and they won't be able to do it. (Bukhari and Muslim, Ibn Mas`ud)

To write things that our religion forbids us to speak about is another fault of the hand: the written word is more powerful than the spoken word. It is also forbidden to write God's words in the Qur'an, or hold and read the Qur'an, when one is not in a state of ritual ablution.

Hands are tools. We use them frivolously in fun and games. Some games, such as sports, build up strength. Other games a man may play with his wife in order to please her, or parents may play with their children in order to educate them. These are lawful. Outside such moments of recreation, time devoted to senseless activity is considered wrong by our religion. This is especially so when the activities are harmful, when they will cause loss or distress to someone. Examples are gambling, violent competitive matches, and dancing to and playing the kind of music that excites sexual promiscuity and perversity. The Prophet said:

> The one who gambles is revolting against God and His Messenger. It is as if his hands are covered by the guts and blood of swine. (Muslim, Buraydah)

Then there are things one does with one's hand of which it is best to be wary. These include reopening graves and exhuming bodies (unless there is a legal necessity); uprooting trees and plants that grow on top of graves; cutting one's hair short (for women); cutting one's beard shorter than a finger's width (for men); cutting children's hair unevenly; throwing cut hair or fingernails into the toilet. One should take care to use one's left hand when washing one's private parts, blowing one's nose, or holding any dirty object, and to use one's right hand when eating and drinking or holding books and pens or any other object considered clean. When dressing, one should hold the clothes in one's right hand and present them to the left hand, and when one is undressing, one should let the left hand present the clothing to the right hand (taking into consideration whether a person is right-handed).

All these recommendations are intended to hold your attention so that you may be heedful of what your hands are doing.

The sign of people who are unconscious of their acts is that they twiddle or crack their fingers, which the Messenger of God reprimanded, especially at prayer time, when we are expected to be most attentive. He said:

> Do not twiddle or crack your fingers after you make your prayer-ablution, while you are waiting to pray, because the time of waiting to pray is no different from the time of praying. (Imam Ahmad, Ka`b ibn Ujrah)

There are also restrictions on wearing rings. The Prophet wore, and suggested that men should wear nothing other than silver rings, which may contain semiprecious stones.

Buraydah reported:

> Once a man came to see the Messenger of God while wearing rings made of iron on his fingers. The Prophet said, "What a pity! I see on your hands the ornaments of the people of Hell." Next time the man came to see him, he was wearing rings of bronze. The Prophet said, "Mercy! I smell the odor of pagans on your hands." Next time the man was wearing gold rings. The Prophet said, "I see you are presumptuously wearing the ornaments of the people of Paradise." When the man said: "O Messenger of God, tell me what kind of rings should I wear?" he said, "Humble rings of silver, weighing no more than one *midhqal*" [4.4 grams]. (Tirmidhi)

Tirmidhi reported from Anas ibn Malik that the Prophet wore his ring on his left hand and turned the stone upon which his seal was carved inside his hand and used to take it off when he went to the toilet. According to other reports, he used to wear his ring sometimes on his right hand and sometimes on his left hand. According to Imam Bukhari and Shafi`i, it is best to wear a ring on one's left hand.

We have seen some of the trouble our hands may cause us by doing what they ought not to do. They may cause us other trouble by not doing what they are supposed to do. Things that the hands are not permitted to avoid include wiping the tears of those who cry; offering hugs and caresses to relieve the pain of people in distress; giving a helping hand to people in need; attempting to save the innocent from the hands of tyrants; protecting one's own or others' property from loss or damage by fire, flood, burglary, or neglect; trying to prevent people from sinning or doing themselves harm; exercising one's trade; taking care of one's home, children, and business.

Laziness in all its aspects is to be abhorred. The Prophet said:

> The one who masters a craft and abandons it is not one of us. (Muslim, Akaba ibn Amir)

A hand that does not lock the doors of its home and business, put out the fire and the lights, protect its food and water from spoilage, or put its children to bed at night, is indeed remiss and not doing what it was created to do. The Prophet said:

> When the darkness of night comes, have your children at home, because that is the time when evil descends upon earth. An hour after the night falls, close your doors, mentioning the name of your Lord. Put out your fire by the name of your Lord. Cover and close your food and water,

mentioning the name of your Lord: the Devil cannot open something closed in God's name. Do not let your children out at night, for evil covers the world in darkness. See to it that your food and water are not left in the open, for there is a night during the year when a deadly pestilence descends upon earth and enters every sustenance left open. (Muslim, Jabir ibn `Abdullah)

Indeed, the worst sin of the hands is laziness.

CHAPTER 24

ON EATING AND DRINKING

O seeker of Truth, be satiated with the beautiful taste and satisfaction of the intensity of your wish! It is not necessary to eat a lot, nor to be discriminating in the choice of tasty things to eat. Some people live to eat. One should eat just enough to live. Do not eat unless you are hungry, and stop eating before you are full. Less food will give you a healthy body and a sound soul. Your mind will be sharper, your heart kinder, your worldly ambitions will decrease. You will save all the time you spend to satisfy the incessant desires of your stomach. You will be conscious, thankful for your Lord's gifts and ready to accept His trials. You will be heedful. You will be more aware of the unfortunate who are really hungry, and choose to consider their needs above your own. You will leave selfishness and become generous and beneficent. You will remember the inhabitants of Hell who eat poisoned fire, as well as the blessed who relish the fruits and rivers of milk and honey in Paradise. Your worship will be easy and rewarding. Your heart will be light and at peace.

Those who live to eat and fill their stomachs have their hearts hardened. Their eyes, their tongues, their hands, their whole bodies turn against them, leading them to sin, to sickness, to death, and to the punishments of the Hereafter. Their minds are dull: no knowledge worth retaining enters them. They have doubts about God's wishes and are attracted to things God forbids. Their preoccupation is with the world, whose pleasures they seek: they devote their lives to trying to obtain them. All their time and energy is spent upon gaining means to obtain the goods of this world, to consume them, and to excrete them. They have no taste for anything spiritual. Their souls are atrophied. They do not pray. An agonizing death and the terrors of the Hereafter await them. God warns them:

> And on the Day that the unbelievers will be placed before the Fire, it will be said to them, you received your good things in the life of the world and you took your pleasure out of them; but today shall you be recompensed with a penalty of humiliation, for that you were arrogant on earth without just cause, and that you transgressed. (*Ahqaf*, 20)

Hadrat `A'ishah reported that the Prophet said:

> The first deviation of my people from what their Prophet taught will be that they will want to fill their stomachs. And a full stomach will cause their bodies to bloat with fat. Their lust will know no bounds and their hearts will be sick. (Ibn Abi Dunya)

Ibn `Umar reported that a man belched in the presence of the Messenger of God, who said to him:

Be away from us. On the Day of Judgment, those who will suffer from hunger for the longest time will be the ones who fill their stomachs in this life. (Tirmidhi)

Hadrat Nafi` reported that Ibn `Umar never ate unless there was a poor person as a guest at his table. Nafi` one day brought a poor man to eat with him who ate an enormous amount. After he left, Ibn `Umar said:

O Nafi`, don't ever bring him again, because I heard the Messenger of God say that a Muslim eats what one stomach takes, but a hypocrite or a nonbeliever eats enough for seven stomachs. (Bukhari and Muslim)

Miqdad ibn Ma'dikerb related from the Prophet:

In all of time the children of Adam have not filled a pot dirtier than their stomach. It is sufficient to eat enough to enable you to stand on your feet. If you feel obliged to eat more, reserve one third of your stomach for food, one third for water, and one third for air. (Tirmidhi)

Ibn Abi Dunya reports that the Prophet saw a man with a big belly and told him:

That which you fed this belly of yours would have done you more good in the belly of a poor person. (Tabarani)

Umm Bujayr reports that one day when the Prophet was very hungry, he found a flat stone and tied it against his belly and he said:

The intelligent person is the one who opposes the desires of his flesh; because in doing so, he is really doing what is best for himself. (Ibn Abi Dunya)

Jabir ibn `Abdullah reported that the Prophet said:

Food enough for one person can feed two, food enough for two people can feed four, food enough for four people can feed eight. (Muslim)

Abu Umamah reported that the Prophet said:

After me, there will be some among my people who will eat a lot of choice food and drink a lot of choice drinks. They will dress in fancy clothes and their talk will be a false display of words. Woe to them, they will be the wicked among my people. (Tabarani)

It is forbidden to eat pork; animals that have not been butchered but died by themselves; blood; muddied, dirty, or charred food; boiling hot food; any food that has been stolen, taken by force, or bought with money illegally obtained; anything harmful to the body or inclined to change the normal state of one's mind. One may not drink any kind of alcoholic beverage or imbibe any other intoxicating substance. It is also forbidden to sell, to offer, or serve any of these things to other people. Occasionally items from forbidden categories may be recommended as medicine for the cure of certain sicknesses or conditions. If there are no other means of cure, then it is permitted to consume them as medicine in the amount recommended.

In addition to these prohibitions, it is considered socially as well as religiously unsuitable to eat publicly on the street where hungry people may become envious. Muslims are discouraged from joining the meals of non-believers, hypocrites, or anyone who has prepared food to gain fame and feed his own arrogance. We are discouraged from eating in places where there is loud and distracting music. To eat food from gold and silver plates, or to use precious utensils, candlesticks, incense burners, and so forth, is ostentation in the faithful, whose table should be simple and clean.

Anas ibn Malik, who lived in the Prophet's house for many years, said that the Prophet's household ate on a clean sheet on the floor, from a common dish. The Messenger of God did not use a separate plate, even a piece of flat bread, nor did he eat fancy food. (Bukhari)

Hadrat `A'ishah reported that the Prophet asked his household to say *BismiLlah,* "In the Name of God," before they started to eat. If they forgot to do so, but remembered in the middle of the meal, he advised them to say *bismiLlahi li awwalihi wa akhirih*—"In the Name of God for its beginning and its end." He liked people to eat and drink with their right hands, and if they had to give or take anything, always to use the right hand, unless they were physically unable to do so. (Tirmidhi)

`Amr, who grew up as a child in the house of the Prophet, said that when he was a young boy, he used to pick up food from all over the common plate. Then one day the Messenger of God told him to mention the name of God when he started to eat and to pick up with his right hand what was present in front of him, unless there was more than one kind of food on the plate. (Bukhari)

It is recommended that one avoid breathing directly into the cup of water from which one drinks, and to avoid drinking a whole glass of water in a single breath.

Abu Sa`id related that the Prophet said:

Do not breathe out into the glass of water from which you are drinking, nor drink it all in one breath, and do not give the glass on your right side to the person on your left without asking permission from the person on your right. (Abu Dawud)

In another prophetic tradition reported by Ibn `Abbas, the Messenger of God said:

Do not drink water in one breath like a camel. Recite the Name of God, breathe in and out to take three sips, and thank God. (Tirmidhi)

Respect bread. Do not throw crumbs on the floor, and pick up those that happen to fall to the floor so that they are not stepped on. Do not use bread to wipe your knife and fork unless you eat it subsequently.

It should be noted that our religion permits us to partake of forbidden or inadvisable foods in limited quantities if there is nothing else to eat, in order to save our lives and our health.

CHAPTER 25

ON SEX

Two organs between two soft parts of the body are among the most valuable gifts of the Creator of humanity. The tongue between the lips allows us to speak and communicate, to learn from, understand, and live with each other in harmony. The sexual organs between the thighs allow us to taste love and attachment between men and women, and to procreate. But under the influence of our evil-commanding ego, people misuse these blessings and turn them into instruments of affliction. The tongue lies and cheats, and words cause more pain and destruction than the sword. The sexual organs, which seem to have a life of their own, lead people toward the destruction of the family, which is the core of society, and to perdition in this world and the Hereafter. The simplest rule of good behavior for the faithful is to control our tongues, our hands, and our sexual organs as God and His Prophet ordain.

For a believer, sex is an intimate, beautiful, sacred, cherished part of life. It teaches love between opposites and sustains unity in the family. It produces life; a beautiful child. It is God's instrument to sustain the population of human beings upon this earth. That is why a Muslim must abide willingly and lovingly with certain divine rules concerning the activity of his sexual organs, and that is why the misuse of sex is severely controlled and punished.

The only lawful sexual act is between husband and wife, for its purpose is to strengthen love and connection in the sacred institution of marriage, which is the foundation of Muslim society, and with God's will results in the creation of a new life. A child needs a mother and a father who will sustain, protect, and educate him together. Because the purpose of lovemaking is procreation, it is forbidden for a man to have sex with his wife when she is having her period, when he is discouraged from even touching or looking at her body between her belly and her knees; husbands are discouraged from having sex with pregnant wives. And it is forbidden to penetrate one's wife in any way other than her vagina.

Reported by Abu Hurayrah, the Prophet said:

> Any of my people who go to soothsayers and believe in their predictions and those who have sex with their wives during their periods or who have anal intercourse with them are guilty of denying what was revealed to Muhammad. (Tirmidhi)

It is also wrong to take advantage of one's wife when she is sick or too weak and cannot willingly satisfy her husband's desires. On the other hand, it is a marital obligation for both husband and wife to respond to each other's sexual urges if they have no valid excuse.

To have sex where anyone (except a baby who does not understand) may see or hear the couple is strongly discouraged.

Masturbation is also forbidden unless one is not married and is afraid of committing adultery, or for people who are excessively sexual and are obliged to satisfy their urge by this means rather than nonmarital relations.

A Muslim man must be circumcised unless he has a serious excuse. He must marry and have children unless he is physically handicapped. He must share the same bed with his wife and sexually satisfy her whenever she shows the desire. It is a sin for a man to sleep separately unless he is permitted to do so by his wife. Islam permits men to have up to four wives if they have the material, physical, and spiritual means to treat them absolutely equally, and have the permission of their existing wives to marry again. A husband of several wives is obliged to satisfy all of them sexually.

To take sexual advantage of people of the same sex is strictly forbidden in Islam. Reported by Ibn `Abbas, the Messenger of God said:

> If you encounter any persons who do what the people of Lot did, ostracize them and discard them from amongst you. (Tirmidhi)

It is forbidden to castrate or render impotent and infertile any man or woman in Islam.

For a believer to turn his face or his back in the direction of the Ka`bah while going to the bathroom is considered insulting. It is also wrong to throw anything sacred or respected, or any material that man and beast might eat, into the toilet. To urinate in a place where people wash themselves, or into a body of water that does not run, or into a container that is kept in the house, or in exposed places outdoors where people may see or walk, are all discouraged. Abu Hurayrah reported that the Messenger of God said:

> People who defecate or urinate in public places, where people may see or walk by, are accursed. (Muslim)

`Abdullah ibn Yazid reported that he said:

> Do not urinate in a body of water that is not renewing itself, nor in a place where you bathe, nor in a pot that you keep in your house, for angels do not enter a house where urine is stored. (Tabarani)

He also said:

Keep yourself clean of urine, much of the suffering of the grave falls upon people who were unclean. (Ibn `Abbas, Bazzar)

So keep your private parts clean from both material dirt and moral perversity, for the first bothers only you but the second tyrannizes both your partners in sin and the whole of society.

"Paradise is under the feet of mothers."

CHAPTER 26

ON COMING AND GOING

Do not let your feet lead you to places where evil is spoken or listened to, tasted or smelled, seen or touched, thought or felt, especially when your ego invites you to participate in it.

The greater sins—ambition, pride, hypocrisy, the wish to appear better than one is, envy, love of the world—and other maleficent influences constantly urge us to seek the company and help of influential people. In search of a position or an image that will make them arrogant and hypocritical, people humble themselves before rulers, politicians, and famous or influential persons, kiss their feet, and offer their souls for sale.

The Prophet said to Ka`b ibn Ujrah:

O Ka`b, may God protect you from frequenting the rulers who will come to rule after my time. Those who seek favors at their doors, believe in their lies, and support them in their tyranny are not of us, and I am not of them. I will not intercede for them on Judgment Day. But those who may pass through their doors yet do not believe in their lies or support them in their tyranny are of us, and I am with them. I will intercede for them and quench their thirst on Judgment Day, serving water to them from my fountain. (Tirmidhi)

In another tradition, reported by Abu Hurayrah, the Prophet said:

Do not wander in the wilderness, for the desert dweller's heart grows hard. Do not go chasing animals to hunt: it is a sign of unconsciousness. Do not visit rulers, for you will fall into intrigue and mischief. The closer you get to the rulers of the world, the further you will get from your Lord. (Imam Ahmad)

The Prophet cautioned even those who attend on the authorities in order to obtain what is due to them. Ibn `Abbas reported that he said:

Some of my people who practice their religion and read the Qur'an will say, "We visit the rulers to receive what is due to us in worldly things, but our hearts are not with them." I say to them, "This does not work. When you try to pick a fruit from a thorny tree, you are bound to be pricked. Whoever seeks benefit from high authorities is bound to be hurt." (Ibn Maja)

It is also forbidden for believers to risk unnecessary physical danger. You should not take a trip when it is known, even suspected, that a storm, an enemy, or an infectious disease awaits you. `Abdur-Rahman ibn `Awf reported that the Prophet said:

A plague is God's punishment. When it descends upon a place where you are, do not escape and go to some other place. If you are not already in such a place, do not enter it. (Bukhari)

Some interpreters take this interdiction as a matter of faith, implying that one should accept one's fate. Others take it as a practical measure, instructing us to avoid spreading infectious disease. The latter interpretation is supported by the fact that during Hadrat `Umar's rule, news came of pestilence in Damascus and the caliph intended to go there to help. However, after consultation with the people of knowledge, based on the aforementioned tradition, he was convinced not to enter the city.

Our religion also restricts our movements based on consideration for family. If parents object to their sons going to military service during war, even if the parents are not Muslim, their sons are bound to obey them. But if this objection does not grow out of parental compassion and the wish to keep children safe from the horrors of war, but rather aims at preventing the engagement of an enemy of the same religion and nation as the parents, then their sons are not obliged to obey.

If the sole provider for parents or family wishes to go someplace and leave them behind, he is forbidden to do so by the religion, especially if no one can be found to take care of them in his absence.

It is also forbidden to return home after an extended absence without announcing your arrival. Jabir Ibn `Abdullah reported that the Prophet said:

Do not enter your home at night, after a long absence, without announcing your arrival.

And:

When you are returning from a trip, leave enough time before you arrive for your wife to prepare herself, bathe, and dress her hair in order to receive you. Then make love to her, if you wish her to have a child. (Bukhari)

Then there are rules established in consideration of others, of society in general. For instance, we are not permitted to enter any area that does not belong to us without the agreement of the owner. Whether the place in question is someone's home, garden, planted field, or even totally barren land without any walls or indication of boundary, it is out of bounds for any Muslim unless permitted by the owner. If one absolutely has no bad intention and is in dire need of crossing that area to reach someplace else, and if there is no possibility of obtaining the owner's permission; we may hope to be excused, because it is a known custom in Islam that believers allow other believers to cross their property in good faith.

There are exceptions to the interdiction of trespassing on other people's property. For example, if a valuable object worth the equivalent of a thousand *dirhams* of silver [approximately nine pounds] falls into the garden of your neighbor, and if you know that your neighbor will not permit you to enter his property, it is your prerogative to enter without his permission and take back what is yours. But before you do so, you must explain the case to another neighbor who will be your witness.

You are also permitted to enter the property of a thief, whom you know is keeping what he stole, in order to take what belongs to you.

Then there are limitations on going to places toward which one's feet take one based on consideration and respect for the place itself. Thus it is disapproved for women to follow funerals to the graveyard or to enter mosques when they have their periods. Abu Hurayrah reported that the Prophet strongly disapproved of women participating in burials or visiting graveyards; of men stepping or sitting on graves; of crossing a graveyard to shorten one's way to someplace else; of entering a mosque without ritual ablution; of stretching one's feet in the direction of the Ka`bah or toward holy books and books on religion; of stepping on such books or on bread fallen on the ground, even accidentally; of kicking any person, including criminals, or even inanimate objects. (Tirmidhi)

There is agreement among scholars of religious law that to kick a non-Muslim, especially one living in a Muslim society, is a terrible offense punishable on the Day of Judgment unless one begs and obtains that person's pardon. To kick a defenseless animal also deserves certain punishment in the Hereafter. To disturb and trip over people in a crowded mosque because of trying to find a place in the first ranks was detestable to the Prophet who said (reported by Mu`adh ibn Anas):

> In the crowd of Friday congregational prayers, someone who jumps over other people's shoulders in order to get ahead of them has built for himself a bridge to Hell. (Tirmidhi)

Finally, there are duties to which one's feet are obliged, and negligence in performing them is condemned.

You are in default of your duty if your feet do not carry you to schools and places for acquiring knowledge, and if they do not lead you to mosques, to Pilgrimage when required, and to visit your parents, family and friends, and people who are sick or in need of support. Your feet are obliged to take you to the assistance of those suffering from tyranny and from accidents, to bring you to funerals and to the welcome of people who are newcomers to the community. For men to strive to support and protect their families, for women to care for their homes and children, for children to help their parents in their chores, for employers to reward their workers, for employees to fulfill their obligations, and for the whole community to follow its rulers unless they lead their people to sinful acts, are some of a Muslim's duties. It is reprehensible not to perform them unless one has a valid excuse.

Abu Hurayrah reported that the Prophet said:

A Muslim has rights over other Muslims: to be acknowledged and saluted by them; to be visited and cared for when he falls sick; to have them come to his funeral when he dies; and to accept his invitation when he invites them. (Bukhari and Muslim)

Association among Muslims is very important. Inviting and visiting each other and showing hospitality are a requirement. `Abdullah ibn `Umar reported that the Prophet said:

When you are invited by your fellow Muslim to a wedding or on any other occasion, you must go, even if all you will be offered to eat is sheep knuckles. (Muslim)

Abu Hurayrah reported that he said:

The worst food to eat is the food offered at a feast where only the rich are invited and the poor are excluded. (Muslim)

`Abdullah ibn `Umar reported that he said:

The one who refuses an invitation is disobeying both God and His Messenger. And the one who goes to a feast without an invitation enters the place as a thief. (Abu Dawud)

According to Islamic etiquette, the obligation of accepting invitations is satisfied by going into and sitting briefly in the place where one is invited. It is not an obligation to eat what is offered, yet it is recommended to taste it. One sits at a place appropriate to one's importance as a guest and according to one's closeness to the host. If the host is generally known as an undesirable, sinful person, or one knows that during one's visit, one will face certain unpleasantness, one may excuse oneself or stay very briefly and leave politely.

All these rules are necessary for social harmony in an Islamic community.

CHAPTER 27

OTHER PRIVATE AND SOCIAL OFFENSES
TO BE AVOIDED

Your body, the home of your soul, should be kept clean physically and morally. It will be a witness of your deeds on Judgment Day. The body is a sacred gift of God and its appearance should not be changed in any way. Ibn Mas`ud reported that the Prophet said:

> May God's curse fall on the ones who attempt to improve what God has created by having ornaments tattooed on their bodies, by plucking their eyebrows, by wearing other people's hair, by filing their teeth. (Bukhari)

According to reports from Abu Rayhanah ibn Mas`ud and `Amr ibn Shu`ayb, the Prophet said:

> White hair is the trace of divine light on a believer. God's curse falls on the ones who pluck white hairs from their beards or dye their hair. (Tirmidhi)

And Ibn `Abbas reported that he said:

> There will come a time that men will dye their hair as black as the feathers on the chest of pigeons. They will not have even a whiff of the perfumes of Paradise. (Bukhari, Muslim, Tirmidhi)

Under certain circumstances, such as to appear more formidable to the enemy in time of war, it is permissible to dye one's hair and beard with impermanent dyes such as henna.

There are also indications for the proper trimming of one's hair, beard, and mustache. A man's hair should not reach any longer than his earlobes. Mustaches should be trimmed above the upper lip. The proper length of a beard ranges between a pinch that can be grasped by the fingers and the length of a small handful. According to Ibn `Umar, the Prophet trimmed his blessed beard at both lengths and shaped its width on the sides. (Tirmidhi)

Women should let their hair grow and never shave it unless there is a dire necessity or reason. Hadrat `Ali reported that the Prophet forbade having children's hair partly cut and partly left long. (Nasa`i)

A Muslim washes himself many times during the day when he makes his ritual ablution. He bathes, at minimum, when he makes his total ablution after each sexual intercourse. Bodily cleanliness is a sign of faith. Some people may neglect to wash their hands properly after cooking or eating food or having touched something smelly. But we are warned against having any kind of bad smell on ourselves, even if there is no one around to smell us. Especially, we should not go to bed in that state. Abu Hurayrah reported that the Prophet said:

> Whoever passes the night with a smell of meat or any other obnoxious odor on him, and becomes sick, or something else happens to him, it is only his own fault and doing. (Tirmidhi)

As reported by Jabir, he also said:

> Those who eat onions and garlic, leeks and radishes, should stay home and not come to the mosques to irritate people with their bad breath. (Bukhari)

Lying down to sleep, we should arrange ourselves so that the direction of the Ka`bah is to our right, and we should sleep on our right side. The Prophet objected very strongly to sleeping on one's belly. Abu Dharr reported that the Prophet caught him sleeping face down. He woke him up and said:

> O Junaybih! Do not lie down on your face, this is the way that the people in Hell lie down. (Ibn Maja)

And reported by Tihfah, he said:

> God does not approve that the faithful should sleep on their faces. (Abu Dawud)

Your body is a private, sacred property. It should not be exhibited bare to anybody without good reason, such as when one is intimate with one's wife or husband, or when necessary in a medical examination. Even when one is alone, unless on the toilet or bathing or in need of examining oneself, one should hide one's private parts.

We should not touch our own or others' bodies, even without any sexual thought or intention, unless there is a morally and socially acceptable reason. We should clothe ourselves with clean but humble clothing. To wear torn, patched, or old clothes, pretending unworldliness, while one can afford better clothing is hypocritical. To wear expensive clothes in order to show off is arrogance—yet it is well thought of to wear one's best clothing on religious holidays, Fridays, and special occasions such as weddings, celebrations, and invitations. It is not appropriate for men and male children to wear silk and embroidered clothing or bright colors, gold or silver, or accessories such as silk or embroidered handkerchiefs. For children dressed inappropriately the parents are held responsible, because they are educating their children in a sinful behavior that will lead them to luxury and arrogance.

It is reprehensible for men to clothe themselves with clothing appropriate for women and for women to dress themselves like men. During his rule, Hadrat `Umar expelled from the city a man who was dressing as a woman. The Messenger of God expelled from Madinah a woman who was dressing as a man. Ibn `Abbas reported that the Prophet told his people, concerning transvestites:

Send them away from among you. (Bukhari)

The Prophet was very concerned with the physical health and safety of the faithful. Islam indicates that we should sustain ourselves with good and healthy nourishment. Additionally, for instance, to take a trip during which bad weather or other life-threatening conditions may be encountered is religiously unlawful. And it is advised that people should not travel alone. Ibn `Umar reported that the Prophet said:

If you knew what I know, no one would travel alone by night. (Bukhari)

Reported by Sa`id ibn Musayyab, he said:

Satan can mislead one or two people together. But if there are three believers together he cannot harm them. (Tabarani)

Reported by Abu Sa`id, he said:

When three people travel together, let them choose one of them as their leader. (Abu Dawud)

A woman is not supposed to travel unaccompanied by her husband or another male member of her family. Reported by Abu Sa`id al-Khudri, the Prophet said:

For a woman who believes in God and the Judgment Day, it is unlawful to travel to a distance of three days alone, unless she is accompanied by her husband, or her father, or her brother or grown son or another male member of her family. (Bukhari)

In other traditions the amount of three days is reduced to two, or one, or simply to traveling one night alone. To apply these restrictions concerning a woman traveling alone is part of *Hanafi* jurisprudence. The *Shafi`i* tradition permits women to travel accompanied by other women, as long as the routes are safe.

Other dangerous situations, such as sleeping or wandering in elevated places without a banister or a parapet, are disadvised. `Ali ibn Sha`ban reported that the Prophet said:

> Whoever walks or sleeps on a high terrace unguarded with a banister does so at his own risk and peril, and if he falls and dies he is guilty of having wasted his life. (Abu Dawud and Tabarani)

As our souls are housed in our bodies, we and our families are housed in our homes. Home is a sacred, protected place for a Muslim. It is protected by the husband outside, and its harmony and honor are protected by the wife inside. As our clothes are ordained to be proper, clean, and humble, our homes are also advised to be unostentatious, orderly, and clean, their furniture simple and comfortable but not luxurious. Our houses have to be built in such a way that they do not cut off the view and air of our neighbors, nor infringe on their privacy.

To live in a house that belongs to someone else without the owner's consent, especially to occupy or confiscate a house by force or treachery, is considered theft and tyranny and is a grave sin.

There are certain objects that it is objectionable to keep in one's home. Figurative paintings and sculptures representing human images are considered sinful because they are reminiscent of idolatry. In addition, to decorate walls with carpets (unless used as insulation against cold) or ornate silk and satin covers (unless worn by the female members of the family), and to use gold and silver cups and plates for food, are disadvised as ostentation, suggestive of luxury or status. To decorate walls with calligraphy bearing Qur'anic verses, God's names, and prophetic traditions is recommended, yet to have any of these writings on the floor, even on a prayer rug, is forbidden. Playing cards and other instruments used in gambling, even if not used as such, are blameworthy when found in a Muslim's home.

Keeping some animals as pets is also disadvised, out of concern both for the health of the household and for the well-being of the animals, which are imprisoned.

Dogs are considered dirty, for they smell, shed hair, and may transmit sickness. They may nonetheless be kept if they are used as watchdogs to protect the house or herds, or if they are used in hunting. The Prophet said:

> To keep a dog, unless it is intended to serve to guard one's house from intruders or one's livestock from harm or to hunt, is not right. Whoever

315

keeps a dog as a pet in a household loses twice the rewards God would have given for his good deeds. (Bukhari)

It is forbidden to let one's dog loose in public places. If someone does so, people are permitted to reprimand and prevent him, even to take him to court for endangering public safety.

To keep small wild creatures imprisoned in cages for fur or pleasure, including singing birds such as nightingales and canaries, is unkind and not considered right.

A Muslim's family is a sacred institution. Its ways and means are clearly ordained by God. If those rules are broken, it is a major sin. Attachment, love, and obedience to parents are at its foundation. Reported by Amr ibn al-`As, the Prophet said:

To attribute partners to God, to kill a human being, to take a lying oath, and to disobey one's parents are major sins. (Muslim)

And as reported by Thawban, he said:

God may delay the punishment of some major sins until Judgment Day, but not the punishment of one's sins against one's parents. People will suffer for those very quickly, and in this life. (Tabarani)

Jabir ibn `Abdullah reported that the Prophet said:

Some smell the perfumes of Paradise from a distance of a thousand years. The aged adulterers, the ones who oppose their parents, those who abandon their near or far relatives and cut their relations with them, the proud who look down upon others—these will smell not even a whiff of this perfume. For pride belongs only to God, the Lord of the Universe. (Tabarani)

Even if one's parents belong to a religion other than Islam, the care and obedience due them is an obligation. Islamic morals insist that they should be visited, treated kindly, their needs satisfied, unless they attempt to convert their children to their own religion and incite them to sin. In that case the offspring are not required to obey them or even frequent them. For one is forbidden to consider the wishes of the created when they are against the will of God, the Creator.

A strong, unified family is the foundation of society. We are required to be in contact with and take care of even distant relatives. That enlarges the boundaries of the family. Abu Hurayrah related from the Prophet:

When God created the creation and established His dominion in it, the compassion He placed in His creation stood humbly holding onto the skirt of the All-Compassionate One. It begged, saying, "I take refuge in You, I take refuge from the dread that the ties may be broken between us!"

And the All-Compassionate One said, "Would it please you if My compassion falls upon you when you are tied to those who belong to you, and My compassion is withheld from the one who breaks the tie?"

And human compassion said, "Yes indeed!"

Then the Lord said, "Then that will be the rule for you." (Muslim)

After telling this the Prophet recited what God said:

Then is it to be expected of you, if you are put in authority, that you will do mischief in the land and break ties of kith and kin? Such are those whom God will chase away from His Compassion and render them blind and deaf. (*Muhammad*, 22-23)

`Abdullah ibn Abi Awfa reported that the Prophet said:

God's compassion does not descend upon a people among whom there are persons who have cut their connections with their relations. (Tirmidhi)

A`mash reports that Ibn Mas`ud was meditating in a circle with some other believers after they had performed their morning prayers, when he said to them, "Is there anyone among us who has broken his ties with his family? I beg him, for God's sake, to leave our company. Because we want to pray to our Lord to open our eyes to see the Truth. And the gates to the Truth are closed to the ones who have withdrawn from their relations." (Tabarani)

Such withdrawal destroys the unity of the family and is unsociable, but there is more to it than that. To ignore one's relations is usually a clear sign of arrogance: therefore it is disgraceful and sinful.

Family relationships must be kept by visiting, sending gifts, being attentive to the needs of our relatives, and if they live in faraway places, writing to send them good wishes and our news. This closeness is desirable among the members of a family within the circle of those who may not legally marry, but between men and women who are distant relatives but legally marriageable it is not an obligation.

The Prophet recommends that the faithful should marry and have children, which he says will make him proud of his people on Judgment Day. Wives and husbands have clear duties toward each other. The wife is the mistress of the home and the husband is the master of all the affairs concerning the family outside the house. As women are responsible for the home, it is customary that they are charged to have the home clean and the family fed and other chores done in the house. This is not, however, a religious obligation. A woman cannot be pressured to do these things if she chooses not to. Yet she is promised God's rewards in this world and the Hereafter if she assumes her role as a householder, and she may attract divine reprisal if she ignores her responsibilities.

The wife's rights over her husband are mentioned by Abu Layth, an expert in religious law. He said:

A wife has five rights over her husband. While she works in her home, she may not be required to work outside the house, as she may be exposed to conditions harmful to her dignity and humanity. She deserves to be fed, clothed, and taken care of properly. She deserves to be kept safe from any kind of tyranny and adversity coming from her husband or anyone else, and her husband must be supportive and advise her in all matters. She must be educated, especially in religious matters. All the food and necessities of the house must be provided to her with lawfully gained money, and her husband must show patience with her excesses, if any.

Hakim ibn Mu`awiyyah reported that the Prophet was asked about the rights of wives over their husbands. He said:

When you are fed you will feed her, when you are clothed you will clothe her, you will not mistreat her or use vile language. If you get angry at her you will withdraw to another room in your house, but never go out and leave her. (Abu Dawud)

Loyalty between husband and wife is the mortar in the foundation of the family. No married man or woman should be alone with someone of the opposite sex. As reported by Ibn `Abbas, the Prophet said:

Do not be alone with a woman who is a stranger to you unless she has a member of the family with her. (Bukhari)

A wife is not supposed to cause pain, torment, vex, or willfully oppose her husband. She must recognize and abide with his rights over her, which exist principally to provide order and harmony at home and to protect the family's honor and good name. A wife is not supposed to leave home without telling her husband and receiving his permission. If she does so, it is believed that the angels of compassion and mercy will leave her and the angels of wrath follow her, so that the angels of heaven no longer protect her. A wife is bound to respond to her husband's love and desire for her unless she is pregnant or having her period or is ill. As reported by Abu Hurayrah, the Prophet said:

If a husband wants his wife and the wife refuses to sleep with him, and the man passes the night angry at her, the angels in heaven curse her until morning. (Bukhari)

Even in her religious practices the wife is obliged to consider her husband's wishes, unless he is asking her to ignore her religious obligations. For instance, Ibn `Abbas reports that the Prophet said:

It is one of the rights of husbands over their wives that a wife can only fast outside the month of Ramadan with her husband's permission. If she does so in spite of her husband and feels hunger and thirst, her fast is not accepted by God. (Tabarani)

The rights of a man as the head of the family over his wife are so important that Abu Hurayrah reported that the Prophet said:

If it were permitted for a human being to prostrate to another human being, I would have asked women to prostrate in front of their husbands. (Tirmidhi)

Your children are God's sacred trust for you. Parents are fully responsible for the well-being of their children. The father in particular is charged by the religion to protect children against the temptations and dangers of the world, like a shepherd caring for his flock. And it is not only his children: his whole household, all the members of his family dependent on him, and those whose support and sustenance is secured by him even if they live elsewhere, even his domestic animals—all these are a father's responsibility. Their physical, mental, spiritual, and social security, well-being, and improvement are his lawful charge. Any failure in that, especially leaving children on their own, is a grave sin. God warns men to save themselves, their children, and their dependents from Hellfire. And on the Day of Judgment they will be severely punished for any shortcoming in furnishing their children with the best of love, care, attention, food, clothing, home, and education that they are able to offer.

Neither are fathers supposed to spoil children—to clothe them in fancy clothes, to satisfy their every whim and wish. Such treatment makes them feel superior to other children; they run the risk of becoming arrogant and world-bound. Mothers' love for their children is without bounds. If the children are spoiled, it is no excuse for a father to put the blame on the mother. In the case of children the decision of the father counts over that of the mother, for the obligation to prevent the family from doing wrong falls on him.

The most important and longest-lasting education of children is during their early years at home. And the best education parents can give to their children is not by words or books, but by their own example. The best deed a Muslim can perform in his life, the rewards of which are found both in this world and in the Hereafter, is to leave behind offspring with the highest character and morals, devoted to God and His Prophet.

Similar care and attention should be given to people who work for you—your servants, your employees. Abu Bakr reported that the Messenger of God said:

> The one who is bad-tempered and harsh to his employees and those who serve him cannot enter Paradise. (Tirmidhi)

> Ibn `Umar reported that someone complained about his servant and asked the Prophet how often he should forgive him. And the Prophet said: "Seventy times a day if necessary." (Tirmidhi)

Abu Hurayrah reported that the Prophet said:

> Food, clothing, and all the servant's needs are an obligation upon the master, who should not ask in return from his servant more than what the servant is able to do. (Muslim)

And:

> When your servant brings your food to you, eat together with him. If you cannot, at least feed him the same food, because he is the one who suffered the hardship of preparing it for you to serve you. (Bukhari)

On the other hand, Abu Hurayrah reported that the Prophet said:

> The ones who will enter Paradise first are the workers who were loyal and obedient to God and their employers. (Tabarani)

And reported by Jarir ibn `Abdullah:

> An employee who fails his employer has his prayers voided and loses the respect of his religion. (Muslim)

If one has employees under one who are Muslims, it is recommended that they be encouraged to do their obligatory worship. Time and place should be given to them to do their daily prayers, and their load should be diminished while they fast during the month of Ramadan.

One of the worst afflictions people may cause to themselves and to society is to cause pain to their neighbors.

Hadrat `A'ishah reported that the Prophet said:

The angel Gabriel kept bringing me the instructions of my Lord about the treatment of our neighbors, so much so that I thought we would be asked to consider them as members of our family who would inherit our wealth. (Bukhari)

Reported by Anas ibn Malik, he said:

Whoever eats while his neighbor is hungry is not one of us. (Tabarani)

`Amr ibn Shu`ayb related from his grandfather that the Messenger of God said:

Do you know what is the right of your neighbor over you? When he asks you for help, you have to help him. When he asks to borrow money from you, you have to give it to him. When he is impoverished, you must give him alms. When he falls sick, you must visit and serve him. When something good happens to him, you should be happy and congratulate him; when trouble afflicts him, you must suffer and sympathize with him. When he dies, you must carry his coffin and pray for him. You must not let your house cut off his view, light, or air. When you cook something delicious and its smell reaches your neighbors' house, you send a dish of it to them. When they see the fruits you bring to your home, if they do not have the same, you must make some of it a gift to them. When your children eat something in public and their children see it and their appetite is aroused, you must teach your children to share with them.

Abu Hurayrah related that the Prophet said to his Companions one day:

"You are not truly faithful! You are not truly faithful! You are not truly faithful!" When they asked, "Who?" he said, "The one whose neighbor is not truly convinced that no harm can come from him." (Bukhari, Muslim)

And he said:

Whoever believes in God and the Judgment Day cannot cause pain to his neighbor. If your neighbor wants to plant a tree on the wall of your garden, let him. (Bukhari)

Yet another mischief we invite upon ourselves is having bad friends. Reported by Abu Musa al-Ash`ari, the Prophet said:

A good friend is like someone who is carrying a load of musk and a bad friend is like someone who is stoking a fire. If you are close to the one who is carrying musk, he may give you or sell you musk; at least you will smell perfume coming from him. But if you come close to someone who is stoking a fire, you may get burned; at least you will get on you the bad smell of smoke. (Bukhari)

And Abu Hurayrah reported that he said:

Beware of the company you keep, because a person is considered to be of the same belief and religion as the company he keeps. (Abu Dawud)

Reported by Abu Sa`id, the Prophet said:

Do not make your home into a community where the godless live. Neither befriend nor socialize with them. Whoever lives among them and befriends them becomes one of them. (Tirmidhi)

And he said:

Be friends with the faithful, share your food with the ones who love and fear God. (Abu Dawud)

Other breaches of the Islamic code of behavior and morals include:

- creating hostility between the members of one's own and other people's families, between husbands and wives, children and parents, brothers and sisters;
- causing breaches between couples who are about to get married, proposing to a woman who is already promised to another man;
- buying property from someone who does not wish to sell it, but is forced by some other authority to sell, or from someone who is forced to sell his property below its worth at a price forced upon him by a hostile agent.

It is forbidden for somebody who is charged to distribute alms collected from an individual or a community to give them to someone who does not need them or who will spend them on illegal and sinful expenses, or to take any part of them for himself. It is also sinful for people who are not really in desperate need to accept alms, especially when they know that there are others who are in greater need. It is terrible to promise to help someone in need and then change one's mind. Ibn `Abbas related that the Prophet said:

The one who promises to help someone and then changes his mind is like a dog who eats his vomit. (Bukhari)

It is forbidden to charge interest on loans one gives or to pay interest on one's debts. It is also forbidden to cheat others in business, profiteering or exploiting others in one's dealings. Such stratagems include proposing a higher price to a seller who has already agreed to sell his merchandise to someone else at a lower price, as well as receiving something from somebody on credit or consignment and then selling it back to him for a higher price. In fact jurists agree on the undesirability of commerce on credit and consignment in general, even buying things on credit offered without interest.

Do not linger in the streets and public places: be in places where you belong. Abu Sa`id reported:

The Prophet said, "Keep away from public places and wandering in the streets."

Someone said, "O Messenger of God, it will be difficult, as often we meet each other and discuss our affairs and businesses in such places."

Then he said: "In that case, give the places their due."

They said: "What could be due to a public street?"

And he said: "Avoid observing things that are unlawful and immoral, be kind, and do not cause difficulties to other people that use the same place. Greet people who greet you, lead people to do right and prevent them from going astray." (Bukhari)

Reported by Abu Hurayrah, he said:

When you are in public places, help the ones who need help, save the ones who are tyrannized, show the way to the ones who are lost. (Abu Dawud)

Ahmad ibn Hanbal reported that according to an unknown blessed Companion, the Prophet forbade his people to sit half in the shade and half in the sun, and said, "That is the place where the Devil sits." This has both physical and allegorical meaning. Likewise he forbade his people to sit at the center of a circle; to separate two people sitting together and sit between them; or to sit in someone else's place.

Ibn `Umar related that he said:

Do not let any one of you ask someone who is sitting to leave and then take his place. But when you are gathered together and more people come, open up places for them to sit among you. (Bukhari, Muslim)

Someone came to visit the Prophet while his Companions were sitting around him. One of those present got up, offering his place to the visitor, but the Prophet prevented him from doing so. Jabir ibn Samurah related that when his people came to visit the Prophet, they sat where there was an empty space and never tried to squeeze into the front in order to be nearer to him. (Abu Dawud)

Related by `Amr ibn Shu`ayb, the Prophet said:

It is against our faith to separate two people who are sitting together and sit between them, unless you are asked to do so. (Abu Dawud)

When two believers meet they should salute each other, but no matter how important the person whom one salutes, one is asked not to bow in order to show respect or love.

Anas ibn Malik related:

Someone asked the Messenger of God if one should bow when saluting someone one loves. He said no. Then he asked, "Can I put my hand on my heart and kiss him?" He said no. Then he asked, "Can I shake hands with him?" He said yes. (Tirmidhi)

Prostration, bowing down, or bowing the head in humility and reverence as done during the ritual prayers are acts of respect due only to God and never to man or anyone or anything else. Likewise the faith, trust, and dependence we place in God are due to God alone, which is why sorcery, charms, spells, and soothsaying, pretending to predict the future, are sacrilegious. To believe in these things has an effect: they may cause one to lose one's faith.

Abu Hurayrah related that the Prophet said:

The one who ties knots and recites words and blows over them is performing sorcery, and the sorcerer is someone who is attributing partners to the One and Only God. Woe to those who believe in them and give their hearts to them, for they are abandoned by God through what they chose to believe. (Nasa`i)

`Imran ibn Husayn related that the Messenger of God said:

If people believe that certain things are unlucky and bring misfortune, and count on sorcerers, conjurers, fortunetellers, soothsayers to save them, they and the ones on whom they count are denying me and what was revealed to me. (Bazzar)

It is equally wrong to wear charms, amulets, and beads to avert the evil eye, and to believe these kinds of things can cure illness or misfortune caused by such superstitions. As related by Ibn Mas`ud, the Prophet said:

There is no doubt that those who count on magical letters and numbers, beads and amulets, and carry them on their persons to cure their pains and troubles, as well as women who wear knotted ribbons upon which some sorcerer recited some words, hoping their husbands will love them, are guilty of attributing partners to God. (Abu Dawud)

And Abu Ya`la related that the Messenger of God said:

God does not relieve the troubles nor grant the wishes of those who expect relief from magical beads and amulets and other such things. (Ahmad ibn Hanbal)

There is no harm in reciting and carrying on oneself verses from the Qur'an or Names of God, or prayers of prophets and saints, for these are but signs of faith that one hopes for God's mercy in times of trouble.

Finally, the worst affliction one can draw upon oneself is to deliberately abandon one's obligatory worship. All these blessed Companions and great scholars—`Umar ibn al-Khattab, Ibn Mas`ud, Ibn `Abbas, Mu`adh ibn Jabal, Jabir ibn `Abdullah, Abu Darda', Ahmad ibn Hanbal, Abu Dawud, `Abdullah ibn Mubarak, Hakim ibn `Uyaynah, and others—have claimed that a Muslim who deliberately abandons ritual prayers and denies that they were made obligatory by God has committed such a great sin that it is to be feared he may lose his faith totally.

According to the opinion of some Hanafi scholars, to perform one's five daily prayers communally is only recommended. According to Imam Munziri (who quotes the blessed Companions and scholars Ibn Mas`ud, Abu Musa al-Ash`ari, Ahmad ibn Hanbal, Ata', and Abu Thawr), to attempt to do all one's ritual prayers in congregation is obligatory.

Obligations of congregational prayer include keeping the lines straight and following the *imam* who leads the prayers, so that the whole congregation acts as one body.

It is a sign of lack of love and obedience to the Prophet if one totally abandons the supererogatory acts of worship that he practiced. These include the additional cycles in each of the daily prayers, attendance at Friday noon communal prayers, and the special night prayers and the complete reading of the Holy Qur'an practiced during the month of Ramadan.

It is equally maleficent to abandon other obligatory acts of worship. It is dangerous to give up fasting during the month of Ramadan without the accepted excuses of sickness or travel; to avoid paying the prescribed yearly alms or to forego the necessary once-in-a-lifetime Pilgrimage without genuine legal incapacities, to neglect to sacrifice a sheep on the occasion of the festival celebrating the sacrifice of Prophet Abraham on the 10th of the month of *Dhul-Hijjah*, or even to abandon a promised donation for the expiation of a sin or a vow to God that one made with the hope of success in a wished-for thing, or to stop studying and reading the Holy Qur'an. Hadrat `Ali related that the Prophet said:

> Whoever has the means to carry himself to the House of God in Mecca and does not perform the obligatory pilgrimage is indistinguishable from a Jew or a Christian when he leaves this world. (Tirmidhi)

And Anas ibn Malik related that the Prophet said:

> On the night of my ascension, all the rewards due to my people were shown to me—even for the smallest good deeds that you do, such as helping to clean a mosque. But also the sins of my people were shown to me. I have not felt a greater pain than seeing the punishment you draw on yourselves by memorizing a verse from the Qur'an and then forgetting it. (Tirmidhi)

It is also an obligation for a Muslim to fight in defense of his life, religion, and country. A war fought by the whole community is a duty for all. Warding off personal aggression is a duty for whoever is tyrannized. It is also shameful to retreat in battle unless the enemy is much superior in number and power.

Ibn `Umar related that the Messenger of God said:

> When you find excuses to escape from fighting in defense of religion, in the conduct of your business, or gathering your harvest, God will bring upon you such poverty, disgrace, and contempt that you will not be relieved from it until you repent and do what God obliges you to do. (Abu Dawud)

And Abu Hurayrah related that he said:

> Beware of these things that can destroy you: attributing partners to God, killing an innocent person, taking what belongs to an orphan, rendering people destitute with usury, accusing an honest woman of adultery, and running away from the enemy in battle. (Bukhari)

There is a great respect for the written word in Islam, especially texts from the Holy Qur'an or the sayings of the Prophet. We should hold the Qur'an above our waist while reading, and store it on shelves over our heads. To place such holy books, even books on religion or any object upon which there are quotations from religious writings, on the floor—even to write holy phrases on a prayer rug—is considered highly disrespectful. On the other hand, to decorate the walls of our homes with beautifully written calligraphy, quoting the Holy Qur'an, God's names, and the Prophet's advice, is considered to bring blessing to the home and is a reminder of God's and the Prophet's ordinances.

Many of God's orders mentioned in this book have been either forgotten or are ignored by the Muslims of our times. We implore them to learn and practice them. And many other habits of the Muslims during and close to the time of the Prophet have been changed or exaggerated by the influence of contemporary religious scholars, who are overzealous in certain less important things, such as personal appearance, while remaining lax in other more important things, such as social concerns.

For instance, cleanliness is indeed a sign of faith. But as with any other physical concern in a Muslim's life, cleaning and beautifying one's person, one's clothes, and one's environment may become a primary activity, without concern for the time, effort, and expense spent upon them. Then you are likely to use more than your share of water when there is shortage. Time and effort that might have gone toward caring for other people— your family, your neighbors, and your civic duties—is no longer available. You have no time for education to make you a better human being, citizen, and Muslim. You may even become lax in your religious devotions and obligations because you are devoted to ensuring that your person and your environment look better than others'. This is definitely wrong. Such people look down upon other Muslims whose clothes are wrinkled and old, whose hands may not be as clean because of menial work they do, or whose houses are humble. They may be reticent to prostrate in the mosques the poor frequent—unless on their private prayer rugs—and may not take ablution from the same fountains. They may not be dirty, but they do not even realize that they are guilty of a far worse sin: arrogance.

God and His Prophet forbid us to make the practice of our religion difficult. `Abdullah ibn Mughfal related:

> One day I heard my son say in his private prayers, "O Lord! I ask of You to give me the white palace on the right side of Your Paradise."
> I said to him: "My son, take refuge in God from Hellfire and beg Him to let you enter the Garden. Remember this: I heard the Messenger of God say that there will come a time that some of my people will be guilty of excesses in things like looks, cleanliness, and even their devotions." (Abu Dawud)

In their excesses, they will make cleanliness their religion and spend their time enhancing their appearance while their inner selves are in tatters—ugly, dirtied by arrogance, selfishness, hypocrisy, and negativity.

They are haughty and hostile to good Muslims, who are humble both in appearance and in character and actions. They do not associate with them, nor come close to them, nor even pray with them in the same mosque or congregation.

Beware of making a religion out of the details of your religion! Learn the right measure in the practice of your religion and choose moderation over excess. The Prophet said:

I have been sent to teach a religion devoid of all falsehood and difficulties that will lead people to truth with ease. I have not been brought among you to impose on you a severe, difficult asceticism.

Imam Habbazi related that Muhammad Bakir `Ali ibn Husayn ibn Zayn ul-`Abidin used to worry about flies sitting on him in the toilet and had a special cloak made to protect him from the flies. After awhile he abandoned wearing it and prayed to God to forgive him. When he was asked why, he said: "I feel I have sinned. Much better people than I among the Companions of the Prophet did not care to protect their skin from flies."

Dawud ibn Salih related:

My mother brought a dish of meat boiled with wheat to Hadrat `A'ishah, the blessed wife of the Prophet. She placed the dish on the floor while Hadrat `A'ishah was praying. A cat came and ate some of the food. When told, Hadrat `A'ishah said: "It doesn't matter, a cat's mouth is not dirty. I heard the Messenger of God say that a cat is a domestic inhabitant of your house and is not dirty. I also saw the Prophet take ablution with water a cat had drunk from." (Abu Dawud)

There are many Prophetic traditions reported which indicate that during the early days of Islam the devout prayed in mosques with earthen floors, put their faces on dust, prayed with their shoes on, and made ablution with little water, things that in our days might not be considered clean. They ate whatever they could find, as long as it was lawful. As one considers clean a pot made out of dirty clay, which is cleansed by being fired, so the light of faith in a Muslim cleanses that which may appear dirty to the eye.

Imam Ahmad ibn Hanbal reported that a Jew invited the Prophet to join him over a very humble meal of bread and mutton fat, and the Prophet accepted and ate his food. It is also a well-known fact that the Prophet ate poisoned lamb offered to him by a Jewish woman.

God most High says:

This day all good things are made lawful to you. The food of those who have been given the Book is lawful for you and your food is lawful for them... (*Ma'idah*, 5)

Based on this Qur'anic verse, a Muslim may eat food prepared by a Christian or a Jew unless it contains things forbidden by our religion.

It is a fact that during the expansion of Islam, the Muslims ate the food of the non-Muslim countries they had conquered. In one of the wars against Byzantium, the Companions entered a Christian kitchen, where elaborate food was prepared. They inquired if it contained any meat. When they were assured the food was meatless, they ate and sent some to the caliph, Hadrat `Umar, who also ate and offered it to his companions. In yet another incident, reported by Imam Muhammad, when the Caliph Hadrat `Ali was asked if an animal slaughtered by Christians was edible, he said, "Yes, if the name of God was mentioned when it was slaughtered."

Perhaps more concern should be felt about eating the food and accepting the gifts of Muslims who are in positions of power, who may have received what they own through unlawful means. They may have tyrannized, confiscated, stolen from or tricked innocent people in order to build their own wealth and power. Such figures may have control of public funds. It may be questioned whether even their salaries paid out of these funds are religiously lawful. Yet after the time of the Messenger of God, three of the first four blessed caliphs (with the exception of Hadrat `Uthman) drew salaries from the public treasury. Thus as long as their incomes do not exceed the value of their services, for government or public officials to receive compensation from the public funds is lawful and religiously correct.

Alas, in our time it is almost impossible to judge what is lawful and what is not. One can no longer abstain from everything doubtful, as practically everything is doubtful. Imam Kaadihan has offered this formal legal opinion:

> According to the consensus of scholars, our times are no longer times in which we can pay heed to doubtful things, for they have increased so much. Now the obligation of Muslims becomes to shy away from things that they know certainly are wrong.

Abu Layth says, "You may associate with someone whose fortune you know to be mostly gathered legally, even if it is not totally so, and you may accept his gifts." He claims this opinion is based on Imam Abu Hanifah's view that if a property obtained by force is added to legally obtained wealth and becomes separately unidentifiable, it becomes assimilated to the legal property.

To clear the doubts in the minds of those who are suspicious about the lawfulness of the property of the rich and the powerful, and whether receiving any benefit from such people is right, one may consider the following *hadith* related by Hadrat `Umar. The Messenger of God said, "If something is given to someone without his begging for it, let him take it.

It, or part of it, is his due sustenance sent by God." And Hadrat `Ali said, "A ruler may gather his wealth both lawfully and unlawfully. But take what he gives you, it is lawful. For it is only from what he has obtained lawfully that he is able to give anything away."

In our days, when it is not sure even whether the land that grows the wheat in the bread we eat legally belongs to the farmer, or whether the money we use to buy the bread is really worth its value, we cannot spend all our time and effort in being scrupulous. Originally, according to Abu Hanifah and Imam Muhammad, currency's value was that of the weight of the silver and gold it contains. But in our times, silver coins weigh only a quarter of their assessed value.

Under the circumstances, all that the faithful can do is to keep their minds, their hearts, their tongues, and their own actions clean and lawful. We have to be honest, truthful, beneficent, and just to others. We should not accuse others unless firm proof about their dishonesty and injustice is public knowledge.

Remember that everything and everybody is essentially and fundamentally good and clean. Dirt and indecency are accidental. The principle of the good in everything cannot be discounted by a doubt to the contrary. An honest Muslim's prayer is not nullified if he has some dirt on his hands or a spot on his clothing. Neither is a poor man blamable when he eats unlawful food offered by a tyrant. If those who pray should stop, delay, or miss a prayer because they doubt whether they are clean enough, if the poor should suffer hunger because they fear the food offered by the rich may not be lawful enough, they would all be losers. Such people become toys in the hands of the Devil, who fools them with doubt and scruple.

Ubayy ibn Ka`b related that the Messenger of God said:

Truly, there is a devil called *walhan* to fool you when you make your ritual ablution. Beware of the anxiety he inspires about the cleanliness of the water. (Tirmidhi)

Hasan al-Basri said:

Beware of the devil called *walhan* who laughs at your doubt of whether your ablution is valid or not.

Imam Qushayri related that a student came to his master, Shaykh Abu `Abdullah ibn Khafif, and complained that he constantly had doubts in his heart about whether he was doing things wrong or right. His master said, "In our times we used to fool the Devil and make fun of him. I see these days he is laughing at you."

And God says:

Those who cast doubt and dissuade people from the truth are the Devil's brethren. (*Bani Isra'il*, 27)

So cast away your doubts, but learn to correct your convictions. Study Islamic teaching, fear God, and be pious. Above all, fear God: fear to lose His love and care for you. That is sufficient for you.

Most of what God Most High orders human beings to do, what His Messenger showed us and told us during his life, and what the friends of God urge us to do, is nothing more nor less than to organize our lives around the fear and love of God. In that way we will be safe in this world and in the Hereafter from the punishment and wrath of God Almighty. And we will earn His approval, rewards, and love in this life as well as His Paradise later.

Fear of God is manifested not in zealous care for oneself, but in care for others. By caring for and serving God's creation one hopes to obtain the highest state to which a human being can aspire: to be a servant of God.

Abu Hanifah, the Greatest *imam*, one very hot day refused to rest in the shade of a tree. It belonged to someone who owed him money. When asked why, he quoted the Prophet, who said, "If you take advantage of someone to whom you have lent money, you are guilty of usury."

During one of his travels, Abu Yazid al-Bistami had to wash his clothes. When his companions proposed to hang them to dry on the fence of a vineyard, he said, "No, it belongs to someone and we don't have his permission." Then they proposed that he lay the wet clothes on some bushes. He refused, saying that animals might be prevented from eating their leaves. Finally he put the wet clothes on himself and stood in the sun until they dried.

On another occasion he bought some flower seeds in Hamadan. When he came to his home in Bistam, he realized that there were some ants in the seeds. Worrying that he had carried the ants away from their nests, he brought them back to Hamadan.

Ibn al-Mubarak was called to Damascus in Syria to write a book of Prophetic traditions. One day his pen broke and he borrowed one from someone. When he finished the book and came back to his home in Merv in Afghanistan, he realized that he had forgotten to return the pen and thank its owner. He returned to Damascus to do that.

Ibrahim ibn Adham rented a horse to ride to Amman in Jordan. On the way he dropped his whip, and realized it only quite a bit later. He dismounted and walked back to the place where he had dropped his whip. When his companions asked him why he hadn't ridden back, he told them that he'd rented the horse to go forward to Amman, not to go back.

Another pious man who had rented a horse to go someplace was asked by a friend to carry a letter to someone where he was going. He replied that he had to ask the permission of the man who rented him the horse.

Such are the people who wear the invisible crown of true servants of God. They should be our examples, not the ones who wear large turbans and long robes but who teach what they themselves do not practice.

IN THE NAME OF GOD THE BENEFICENT AND THE MERCIFUL
O Lord! We pray that You bestow Your mercy, grace, and blessings upon our master the Prophet Muhammad so that by this prayer You will deliver us from all fears and from all lowliness, that You will cleanse us of all our impurities, and that You will send us the ultimate of all good in this life and in the Hereafter.

O most loving God, the Benefactor of all things, O Unique Creator of the heavens and the earth, O the Ever-Living, Self-Sufficient God, O Master of all greatness, majesty, and graciousness, in the name of Your exalted essence, we beg that You change our nature from mortality and that You raise our state to that of the most elevated of your angels. O Transformer and Keeper of our condition and our power, transform our state into the best of states. Glorified and praised be You, O God.

I bear witness that there is no god beside You. From You do I seek forgiveness, and unto You do I turn repentant. O God, bestow Your blessings and grace upon our master Muhammad and upon his family and companions. *Amin.*

Interpretation ended on `Id al-Adha
10th of *Dhul Hijja*, 1422
22nd of February, 2002

"Actions are judged by their ends."

AFTERWORD

In the Name of God, the Beneficent, the Merciful

O dear friend! Surely your soul now placed in your living heart has seen and known its Creator. When it was in the realm of the souls, before it entered your body it was taught that the reason of its being was to be His servant, to serve His creation.

On the day of the creation of man, our Lord asked the souls of all the descendants of Adam, us, as well as His blessed prophets:

Am I not your Lord!

and our souls said "Yes, indeed." Then your soul was sent from that realm of joyful communion to this land of loneliness, to this house of distress of your physical existence as a test. Your soul has descended from eternal divine realms which is its home, to this temporal land for a little while to survive.

So do not squander the treasure of your essence, know your origin, be heedful, show patience, purify yourself with the flames of love, keep your soul pure. Beware, the body is but your animal of burden which carries your soul. If the desires of its flesh and its lust carry you away and you think you are one and the same as it, you bray instead of pray, you lose your humanity. Do not cover the light of your heart with the dark veils of unconsciousness. Otherwise your soul may forget its communion with its Lord at the beginning and take this temporal life as its end.

Now hear what God says in a divine tradition:

I have a palace greater than My throne and wider than My footstool, more brilliant than the Kingdom of Heaven, richer than all the jewels in My Paradise, the ground upon which it sits is faith, the heavens up above it are knowledge, its sun is yearning for Me, its moon is the love for Me, its stars are thoughts, its clouds are intelligence, its rain is compassion, its rivers are service, its gardens are obedience, the fruits of its trees are gentleness and its rooms are favoring others above oneself. That palace stands on four columns: Trust in God, Patience, Enlightenment and Contentment with what God gives. And it has four doors: Knowledge, Friendship, Gentleness and Remembering God. Know that this palace is the heart of My believing loving servant and I reside in it.

So watch your heart, turn it toward Truth. Keep your heart clean and at peace. Thus you will not drift away from your real self. And if you know yourself, you will find Him in your heart. Woe to the one who left his heart behind. And he who knows his heart, his Lord will find.

*

Now please take heed. There is one thing we must never forget. Even if you forget all but not this, it does not matter much, do not fear. Everything in existence can do anything but this, that only man can do. That is why God said:

Verily We praised man above all else ...

When man does that thing, his heart is cleansed, ignorance is replaced by wisdom and hatred by love. This life is a test. If you do every good deed but not this, you will fail the test. All else is in vain, useless, except Intelligence.

The Mind: pure light, is like the Holy Spirit. It is only in man. It is God's trust given only to you, which makes you high in rank in His view. So seek your origin, where you came from and where you will end. God says:

Surely God has bought from the believers their lives and that which they own, theirs in return are gardens of Paradise. (*al-Bara'at*, 111)

So do not sell yourself cheap to this world for a day's worth of fun and games that your flesh demands. Use your mind, choose eternal life in Paradise.

*

If there is anything to love in this life, it is to love our Lord. What else is there to love but Him? But to believe in this, to be aware of this, we have to feel it, and we have to come to know Him. To know one has to learn, acquire the necessary knowledge. Our Lord says:

Are those who know and those who know not alike? Only man of understanding mind. (*al-Zumar*, 9)

Someone asked our Prophet, the beloved of God: "O Messenger of God, what is the best deed?" Our master, the glory of the world, answered: "To know your Lord." They said: "What kind of knowledge do you speak of, O our master?" And the Prophet said: "To know that your Lord is the One and Unique, exempt from any unworthy things, most beautiful, embellished with all that is perfect." They said: "O the Messenger of God, we asked of the best deed to do; you tell us of thought and knowledge." The Prophet said: "Know that whatever you do while remembering your Lord as you know Him will be the best deed and all will benefit from it; while if you spent your whole life achieving a thing, without knowing and remembering Him it will be in vain."

And listen to the beloved of the Prophet, the blessed `Ali (r.a.), who said:

Knowledge is far better for you than the fortunes you strive to amass, because knowledge is a protection for you, while you will spend your life to protect that fortune you call your own. Knowledge judges, property is always judged and often condemned. As you spend it your fortune is reduced; while when you give your knowledge to others it doubles.

So as our master has asked us to do:

Seek knowledge even if it is as far away as China.

*

God says: "Either you worship Me or you worship your evil commanding ego." This is His divine law; either you take refuge in your beneficent Master, or you are rejected from ever tasting the Truth. The all-Powerful does not negotiate! Man is born noble, he has divine qualities. His superiority to the rest of the creation is not in his physical appearance, but in his essence.

So use your intelligence and seek His treasures hidden in you. But you value your appearance, your body so much, you think you are it. Don't you see that it is only your donkey which you ride? And this world is but its stable and grazing ground. Now that donkey eats the green grass in summer and the dry straw in winter from the fields of this world. Is that food good enough for your soul, which is of divine origin? Who has ever heard of a master who eats the straw of his donkey? So know who you are; where your home is high above.

He who knows himself knows his Lord.

And he will know himself by his Lord; he who keeps this world at a distance, unattached to it, keeping his animal of burden well behaved and well under control, leading it on the straight way, better still, with a whole lot of other riders on the same way. While if you let your donkey wander hither and thither on this world of grazing ground, carried away from home and lost without aim, you will be a slave, like some fool who is carrying his donkey on his back, climbing a hill.

In another way, this world is like a steep mountain which echoes. Whatever you say, whatever you do, whatever you think or feel, good or bad comes back to you louder as an echo. Of course you wish that the echo is melodious and sweet. But alas no! If the mountain could speak, it would say: "I have no will of my own, I am but your shadow, your echo. Whatever you are, I show!"

This world is but the arable field of the Hereafter. Whatever you plant here will be harvested in the Hereafter.

*

Do not dissociate yourself from others. You are neither better nor worse, we are in all this together. All mankind are God's children, one family! God is *Rabb-il Alemiyn*, the Lord of all creation and our prophet is His mercy upon all mankind. And whom God loves most among His children are those who love each other for His sake. But we Muslims are charged to heal, not to hurt as some who call themselves Muslims do. Islam is a hospital for the sick at heart and deranged in their minds. Chief doctor in charge is the Beloved of God, Hadrat Muhammad Mustafa (s.a.w.s), the Holy Qur'an is the pharmacy, and the words and actions of the Prophet in *hadith*s are prescriptions of remedies, assured to cure. Here is a sample:

The Messenger of God said to Hadrat `Ali (r.a.):

O `Ali, if you wish to come closer to your Lord than the angels closest to Him, do not abandon friends who have abandoned you; increase your generosity to the ones who try to deprive you of your daily bread; forgive the ones who tyrannize and try to destroy you.

Our salvation is following the path of the friends and loved ones of our Lord. So serve His creation one and all, prefer the felicity of others above your own. When you attain the truth of Islam, you will see how close the creation is to their Creator and all that they appear to be doing is really done by their Lord. Muslim is he who is clean inside and out. And the clean mirror of your heart reflects all which is beautiful and true, clear under the divine light generating from the beloved of God. May God help us clean our hearts and make our own Muhammad be born in it. He is our guide, our intercessor, our hope.

Now know who is the One who acts
And who points to the facts.
He is the one and only God.
Doomed is the one who Him rejects.

And:

Love the creation for the love of the One who created it.

Many are fooled by the attractions of this world during our short life and forget God and the eternal life, while every moment should be spent in preparation for the Hereafter and in helping others to do the same. But all that we can do to help each other, if we know it, is to tell the Truth and to care for them and advise; but we cannot give them the true faith. Not even the prophets can do it. God says:

Surely you can not guide whom you love to faith, but only God guides whom He pleases and He knows best those who are worthy. (*Qasas*, 56)

And:

And it is not for anyone to believe in God except by His permission. And He casts uncleanness on those who will reject the Truth. (*Yunus*, 100)

For one to be worthy of faith, one has first to confirm with all his heart and declare by his tongue, that our master Hadrat Muhammad is His true messenger. Furthermore, one has to consider the whole of creation to have generated from God's first creation, which was the Light of Muhammad. The only scale of value to judge everything is our beloved Prophet who says:

The first creation of God is my light, my soul, my pen, my mind. I was a prophet when Adam was between earth and water. Whoever sees me sees the truth. Religion is my words, the path to follow is the way I live, the truth is what I am.

And God says to him:

... and We have not sent you but as a mercy to the whole world. (*al-Anbiya'*, 107)

Perhaps you will destroy yourself with grief because they believe not. (*al-Shu'ara'*, 3)

And God says to us:

Certainly a messenger has come to you from amongst yourselves; grievous to him is your falling into distress, most solicitous for you; to believers he is compassionate, merciful. (*al-Bara'at*,128)

*

You live your lives worrying about tomorrow and regretting yesterday.

What about Now? Time is a sharp sword if you do not know how to use it. It cuts the hand that holds it.

The essence of time is the moment, that is the time we are living, not yesterday, or tomorrow, but Now. So use your mind, your effort for that indivisible single moment, for it is the soul of time. It is real reality. Don't you see, what is now is often gone the next moment and you missed it. To throw away one's fortune is sinful; the worst of spendthrifts is the one who throws away time. The reality, all of existence is in Now: that breath which you inhale. From that one moment, one breath, sixty Now's become a minute, from minutes hours, days, centuries, but the reality is in the moment. It is that moment which is divine and belongs to God. The past is lost memory and the future, a vague hope. God says:

Every moment He offers a different affair. (*Rahman*, 29)

And His messenger says:

Do not ever curse time, because time is one of God's names.

And Hadrat `Ali (r.a.) used to address God in his prayers as "O the Enduring Moment!"

So if you honor the moment by living it, God "the Enduring Moment" may stretch it to past eternity and to future eternity, for the moment of Now is like the soul of Time.

As the soul penetrates to all the members of your body, if you are aware of it, so will the Now effect your whole life, if you live it.

Woe to you! The one whose breaths are counted!
Why, living the moment, are you daunted?

*

God is ever-present, yet invisible. Invisible, because no eye can look at Him. If you stare at the sun you will be blinded, while you can view the full moon to your heart's content. And what you see in the moon is but the reflection of sunlight. Like this, the divine light of God is reflected in His beloved prophet. In this life if you wish to see God's light, look at the beauty of His prophet, and his deeds and his words that came from his blessed lips.

Words are the smell of the breath of one's inner self. It is what distinguishes man. A word is a promise. So watch your words. It is said: "To judge a man, make him speak."

Take care to always tell the truth. Speak kindly and positively or keep silent. Do not be suspicious or opinionated about others.

God says:

O you who believe, avoid suspicion, for surely suspicion is sin. And spy not nor let some of you backbite others. Do you like to eat the flesh of your dead brother? (*Hujurat*, 12)

When you give your word, keep it under any circumstances. Do not talk in vain without any meaning or sense. Man is not created in vain. Your breaths are numbered; do not spend them in speaking nonsense. God says:

Good words are heard by God.

And the speaker reaps rewards. So remember God is listening when you speak. And our master, the Prophet said:

God speaks from the lips of His true servants.

So watch your tongue, do not ever insult anyone. Harsh words cut deep wounds, deep down to the heart. But when you are the one so wounded say to your oppressor "peace" and no more. For it is said:

The one who guards his tongue is at peace.

The best of all words are in God's Holy Qur'an and the best way to say them is the way His beloved Prophet did. So study it.

*

Man is small in size, but his inner world is big! So big that God fits in his heart! As God Himself says:

I fit into the loving heart of My believing servant. (*hadith qudsi*)

He is as if a vast city: seven heavens above and seven layers of earth below and all that is in between: God's Throne, His Footstool, the hidden Tablet, the divine Pen, Paradise and Hell, and the universe are all in it. That is the meaning of "Man and Qur'an are two twins." That city is at the crossroad of four roads where all and everything forever travel. And it has four gates called the Eye, the Ear, the Tongue and the Hand. At the center of that city there is a throne called the Heart. That is where God's dominion reigns. Its domain is the soul, its treasures are love and compassion, its law is submission, its government is Intellect. All who enter that city are screened by the

Intellect, and are under the law of submission. Some are let in and some are not. Some enter from the gate of the Eye and go out from the gate of the Hands. And some enter from the gate of the Ear and go out from the gate of the Tongue. But everyone passes through the screen of Intellect where his image is captured and recorded in a file called Memory, which the mind keeps in secrecy.

Now every man, believer and non-believer alike, is like that city, except in the case of the believer the mind screens only that which is beautiful, good and wise; and they are permitted to enter the city, where they multiply:

As the parable of a single grain growing seven ears, in every ear a hundred grains. And God multiplies further for whom He pleases. (*Baqara*, 261)

On the other hand, the perverted mind of the non-believer admits lies, hate, violence into the city where they multiply like rats by the thousands, where they infect the city with plague of rape, murder, destruction and the population can find peace only in their imagination, when their hearts are like those distorting mirrors in fun-fairs, where the thin becomes fat, the short becomes tall and vice versa, etc.

Now let the mirror of your heart be pure and reflect only that which is real and nothing ugly will ever be reflected in it, for the worst of reality is better than the best of imagination.

Guidance and success is but from God and God knows best.

*

It is said that God asks man to spend his life with one thousand kinds of things to do and another thousand kinds of things never to do. How many of us know what those thousand good deeds are, and the other thousand deeds which are forbidden to us?

There are three moral scales where you can weigh your actions: the Holy Qur'an, the *hadiths* (the recorded words and deeds of the Prophet), and your conscience (your own Qur'an inside of you). God says:

Read your book. Your own soul is sufficient as a reckoner against you this day. (*Bani Israil*, 14)

Half of the Holy Qur'an is allegorical, only understandable to very few. And the meaning of the whole of the Qur'an is so vast that if all the oceans were ink and all the heavens paper it would not be sufficient to write it down. Then there are numbers of volumes of the recorded deeds and sayings of the Prophet, but hard to remember, even if one can read them all. But if you are sincere, your conscience is easy to consult, to know if what you do is wrong or right. You are afraid to appear in front of a judge in a human court. Surely soon we will face a divine court on the day of the Last Judgment, where the supreme judge is God, the prosecutors are His angels who have recorded our most minute deeds, our defense lawyers will be the prophets and saints, if we are worthy. The witnesses are our own members: eyes, ears, tongue, hands and feet as well as our deeds who will witness against us. God's messenger says:

> On that day, your deeds will be given material form and shape and they will come one by one and tell you "I am your such and such deed," and the angels will produce records of what you did in life till your last breath, and you will be raised the way you died.

He also said:

> Repent before you are at the point of death, for God does not accept repentance that late. Only up to that moment do both your good deeds and your sins count and are your prayers and repentance accepted.

And God says:

> And repentance is not for those who go on doing evil deeds, until when death comes to one of them, he says: now I repent ... (*Nisa*, 18)

You cannot wait to repent, because repentance takes time, needs certain conditions, and a lot of effort. It suffices not to say *Astagfirullah* ("I ask pardon of God"). First one has to be aware of what one did; then one should know and admit that it was wrong; then one regrets what one did; then sincerely decides not to do it again and asks God's help. But all this still does not help until one has undone the wrong deed. Give back what you took, heal the heart you broke, build what you destroyed. It is said that the sign of the acceptance of one's repentance is that one cannot commit that sin ever again.

Repent and do not ever forget that there is that day when your fortune, your fame, your family and friends on whom you count and depend in this life will be of no help to you. Only your faith in God, service to others for His sake, your submission to Him and your love for Him may obtain His mercy and your love for and obedience to His prophet will secure his intercession for you.

And God's messenger says:

> Do your accounting now, before the time you have to do it on the Judgment Day.

The Creator created the creation and placed His signs everywhere as a reminder to man. From the very beginning He teaches us how to live this life. He has shown us as a lesson what happened to the first man, our father Adam: if you disrupt the divine harmony and eat the forbidden fruit, you are banished and punished. But when you realize your sin of "tyrannizing yourself," and ask pardon you are forgiven.

Over and over again in the history of man, the children of Adam broke the divine law, and over and over again in His mercy the Lord sent His prophets as reminders to teach us anew to follow the divine harmony and to show us that He has created man as His supreme creation. He has given us a mind and made us His deputy and master over all, but also ordered us that "the best of masters is the one who is a servant to his servants." His advice is in this:

> By My oath on the time you will spend in your life. Surely man is in loss; except those who believe and do good; and exhort one another to Truth, and exhort one another to patience. (*Asr,* 103)

O the one who wears the crown of mind, faith, conscience and goodness, do not look upon man as an empty shell of his appearance. Respect all of mankind. The Lord says He has created man in His own image, not that which appears to the eye, a weak, upright creature standing on two feet, but what is in them; their soul, which God breathed unto them from His own soul. Man's supremacy and the respect due to him is neither for his physical beauty nor for his fortune or fame, but for his soul which is divine.

And when he leaves this world, in respect to his soul which has departed, one washes, cleans and wraps the shell which housed the soul and buries it in a hole in the ground. But the soul returns to its home, to its Lord, saying:

> Surely we are God's and to Him we shall return. (*Baqara,* 156)

The temporal body changes day by day; it is born, grows, gets strong, ages, shrinks, weakens and finally falls apart. Like all other material things, it is made of the four primary elements of earth, air, water and fire and like all composed matter it decomposes at the end. Earth to earth, water to water, air to air, but the fire remains.

So the body by its nature burns in fire except those whose souls have been infused into their bodies, and their bodies became souls during this life. Those are the ones who love God and who live for God and who die before dying.

As the Prophet says:

> The faithful do not die. They are moved from here to the hereafter.

He who is with his Lord will never die. God says:

> Everything will perish but He. His is the judgment, and to Him you will be brought back. (*Qasas*, 88)

The real man is ever traveling. He lives in this world like a wandering exile. Hadrat Mawlana says:

> O wander, not to freeze like the running river,
> Leaving home, passing from one place to another.

Now take heed! As the souls wander from one place to another, at some places they gather and they take shape, they assume an identity. The ones who know say, but God knows best, that there are three such places: the first is where God gathered the souls before He created matter and asked them "Am I not your Lord?" and the souls said "indeed, You are!" where the souls took the identity of servanthood. Then with this identity the soul enters the four-month old embryo in the womb of the mother. During man's lifetime, the image of the soul in man is that of the four-month old embryo.

On man's death the soul is transformed to another shape and gathers with the other souls in purgatory: that is the second gathering place. The souls reside there until all matter disappears, no one is left alive in the created universe, and some say another hundred years more. Then it will rain there for forty days and like trees sprouting from the ground all dead will rise from their graves: on that day of last judgment the souls will take the shape of their bodies the day they died and will gather for the third time.

For those who do not recognize the truth of this God says:

> We are the One who created man and We know what misgivings he has in his head and We are closer to him than his jugular vein. (*Qaf*, 16)

> Were We unable to create him first, that they are in doubt that We can recreate? (*Qaf*, 15)

> Surely We give life and cause to die, and to Us is the eventual coming. (*Qaf*, 43)

And:

We know best what they say, you are not one to force them. So remind the ones who fear My threat, by the means of the Qur'an. (*Qaf*, 45)

God's will can never be bent
By no one's powerful arm
The flames Lord has set afire
Will not burn or any one harm.

Believe in destiny. Divine order is such that nothing can change it; it is God's will. Nothing in the created universe is created in vain nor is left unfettered. And man, His supreme creation is certainly not left alone, uncontrolled. Every moment, every breath, every heartbeat is in His hand. Your breath and your heartbeat know it: each time you inhale you say *Hayy!* ("the Ever Living"); each time you exhale you say *Hu*, the name of His essence. Your body also knows the soul which He breathed into you. A hundred thousand times a day your heart, upon which He has written with your veins *la ilaha illa Llah*, repeats His name *Haqq, Haqq, Haqq* ... ("the Ultimate Truth") at each beat over and over again. But you do not understand. Why don't you admit? Can you change the way your heart and lungs are built? In the same way your life is also predestined, whether you believe it or not. Surely this is innate in you, it is your nature, so what is the benefit in denying it? Is it that you think you know better what is best for you, or that you can do better than the One who created you and everything else, while your Lord says "You do not know what is best for you, I do."
And He says:

And whoever is in the heavens and on the earth makes obeisance to God only, willingly and unwillingly. (*Ra'd*, 15)

There is hope in faith for those who obey God and harm and suffering for the disbeliever who imagines he is the master of his own destiny. Peace is in believing that all good and that which seems not so good to our egos are from God. Peace is in being content and showing patience for trials with which our Lord tests our obedience. Peace is in our love for Him and being always thankful to Him. It is not difficult because that is how life is: there are things which are full, half full or empty. Let us not be of the ones who resent when things are "half empty."
When Hadrat `Ali (r.a.) discoursed with someone who disbelieved he said:

I believe in God and eternal life in the Hereafter and I try to live a good and decent life to face my Lord on the day of the Last Judgment, pure and without shame. If, as you believe, there is none of this, what is my loss? But you who believe that there is nothing else but this life on earth, imagine your loss tomorrow when you leave this world and wake up to another life: with what countenance will you face your Lord and will you risk the terrors of Hellfire? What is the benefit in this?

*

We must use our minds to seek where we came from to this temporal life in this world and where we will go at the end. We must learn who we are and why we are here and find our Lord. We cannot live this life without knowing our Lord, nor can we find peace and happiness. For even if we shut our eyes and ears to Him, everything all around us sing His praises. He says:

Seven heavens and the earth and those in them declare His glory. And there is not a single thing but glorifies Him with praise, but you do not understand. (*Bani Israil*, 44)

All that we receive and all that we have are His gifts. At best we sometimes realize and appreciate the good things we receive, but good fortune, happiness and riches become our gods and become veils between us and Him, instead of reminding us of the generosity of our Lord. The only time God's gifts are going to be really ours and benefit us is when we share them with those who need help: alms are the true expression of thankfulness, and praising our Lord the Most Generous. It is said, "The beginning and the end of this life is but gratefulness."

In seeking who you are, what will help you is to be grateful that you are alive. One of the names of God is *Hamid* ("the Praiseworthy"), the only one to be thankful to. During the 40 cycles of our 5 daily prayers we say *al-hamdu li-Llahi rabb-il alemiyn*. What are we offering but empty words? Let your ear hear what you say! Let us be sincere in our prayers to God at least when we say "all thanks and praises to God alone, the Lord of all and everything in the whole universe." God is not only the Lord of the Muslims but of all of mankind. But none of us are truly able to praise and thank Him. No one has the means and capability to truly offer thanks to the Owner of all and everything. But perhaps the only gesture of gratefulness acceptable to Him may be to share the blessings He pours upon us with the ones who are in need: in a way that your left hand does not know what your right hand gives humbly, without expecting any thanks, and for His sake, who really is the One who gives.

May Allah Most High forgive our faults and have mercy on us and help us on the straight path and accord us the intercession of the one whom He has sent as His mercy upon the universe, Hadrat Muhammad Mustafa (s.a.w.s). *Amin.*

Shaykh Tosun Bayrak al-Jerrahi al-Halveti

BIOGRAPHICAL NOTES

IMAM BIRGIVI was an Ottoman Muslim scholar and moralist who lived during the height of the Ottoman Empire, in the 16th century of the common era. He was born Muhammad ibn Pir Ali, later called Birgivi, in Balikesh, Turkey in 1522. His first teacher was his father, Pir Ali, who was a famous professor, admired both for his scholarship and as an example of virtue. In young manhood Muhammad was sent to Istanbul, the capital, to study theology under Ahizade Mehmed Efendi. Later, he studied law under Kazasker Abdurrahman Karamani Efendi, who was the Chief Military Judge of the Ottoman Empire. After the completion of his education, he taught in various schools. During this time he became a dervish, attaching himself to a Sufi master of the order of Bayramiyyah.

Shaykh Abdurrahman Karamani, his teacher in law school and the Chief Military Judge, obtained for him a government position as Judge of Estates Court in the city of Edirne, in the European provinces of the Empire. After briefly serving in this capacity, our author wished to abandon all worldly concerns, dedicate his life to God, and become an ascetic. He resigned from his government post and returned to the treasury all the salary he had received. But his Sufi master, who appreciated both the virtue and the knowledge of his student, directed him to become a teacher of religion, religious jurisprudence, and morals, and to write books as well.

Another one of his admirers and patrons was Ataullah Efendi, the teacher of the sultan of the time, Selim II. This dignitary arranged for a large *madrasah*, a religious institution of higher education, to be specially built in the small town of Birgiv, close to the city of Izmir on the Aegean coast. He sent Muhammad ibn Pir Ali to be master there.

Shortly, through his teaching and the writing of twenty-seven books, Muhammad ibn Pir Ali (now called by the title and name of Imam Birgivi) became very famous.

Imam Birgivi and his followers were very critical of the lack of Islamic morals, both within the Empire and beyond its borders, in the wider Islamic world. Birgivi especially objected to the corruption of rulers and governments, since they were supposed to be examples to the people, as was the case at the origin of Islam. He fought against the distortion of Islamic teachings for the benefit of the ruling classes. And he expressed his opposition publicly: not only were his critiques taught in his school and written in books and articles, but he voiced them directly. Imam Birgivi traveled to the capital of the Empire and reprimanded the Prime Minister, Sokullu Mehmet Pasha, who listened to him, and asked for his advice on curing the degeneration of the Islamic virtues.

The administrative branch of the government at last heard his justified criticisms. The *Shaykh-ul-Islam*, the religious authority of the Empire responsible for all matters connected with canon law and religious teaching, who was second only to the Prime Minister in importance, stood against Birgivi.

Imam Birgivi's ideal was an Islamic society as it was at the time of the Holy Prophet, a model he felt was ageless and valid for all times. He believed that a character distinguished by the qualities of unselfish heedfulness, sincerity, kindness, compassion, generosity, valor, and the other virtues of the Prophet and his Companions was essential equipment for all Muslims. And he claimed that the ruling classes and educators should follow the dictum of the second *caliph*, Hadrat `Umar (r.a.), who said: "A master is he who is a servant to his servants."

Because of his vast influence in his efforts to lead people to the truth of Islam, even his most powerful enemies could not do any more than keep him away from the capital of the Empire. He continued to live in the small distant town of Birgiv until he died of a plague in 1573, at the age of fifty-one.

The influence of Imam Birgivi is felt to this very day: his book *al-Tariqah al-Muhammadiyyah* ("The Path of Muhammad") is still being used as an Arabic text in the most important faculties of theology and in the universities of many Muslim countries.

SHAYKH TOSUN BAYRAK is a Sufi master of the Halveti-Jerrahi order. Born in Istanbul in 1926, he studied Art, Architecture and Art History in the Studios of Bernard Leger and Andre Lhote in Paris. He has also studied at the University of California, Berkley; the Courtauld Institute in London; and Rutgers University. Until the 1970s he was a well-known artist with works in many museums and universities. He was also a Guggenheim fellow.

In 1970 he devoted his life to the study and teaching of Islam and Sufism after he met his teacher Muzaffer Ozak Ashki al-Jerrahi. He became the shaykh of the Halveti-Jerrahi Order in America in 1974. He has also translated, edited, and written numerous books on Islamic spirituality. Among his books are *The Name and the Named: The Divine Attributes of God*, *What the Seeker Needs: Essays on Spiritual Practice, Oneness, Majesty and Beauty* (by Muhyiddin Ibn 'Arabi), *The Secret of Secrets* (by Abdul Qadir al-Jilani), and *Divine Governance of the Human Kingdom* (by Muhyiddin Ibn 'Arabi).

DR. SHAYKH ABDUL MABUD is the Director General of the Islamic Academy in Cambridge, England. A graduate of the University of Cambridge, Dr. Mabud also has a Masters degree from the University of Rajshahi, India. He is the editor of *Muslim Education Quarterly*, and has written several books. He is the director of a major research project on curriculum and textbooks at the primary and secondary levels in Bangladesh and has also worked with other Muslim organizations both in England and abroad. Dr. Mabud lives in Cambridge.

VINCENT J. CORNELL is a *summa cum laude* graduate of the University of California, Berkeley. He received his Ph.D. in Islamic Studies from the University of California, Los Angeles, and has taught at Northwestern University, the University of Georgia, and Duke University. Since 2000 he has been Professor of History and Director of the King Fahd Center for Middle East and Islamic Studies at the University of Arkansas, with interests that cover the entire spectrum of Islamic thought from Sufism to philosophy and Islamic law. His books include the highly acclaimed *Realm of the Saint: Power and Authority in Moroccan Sufism* and *The Way of Abu Madyan*. He has lived and worked in Morocco for nearly six years, and has spent considerable time both teaching and doing research in Egypt, Tunisia, Malaysia, and Indonesia.

Titles in the Spiritual Classics Series by World Wisdom

The Buddha Eye: An Anthology of the Kyoto School and Its Contemporaries, edited by Frederick Franck, 2004

Gospel of the Redman, compiled by Ernest Thompson Seton and Julia M. Seton, 2005

Lamp of Non-Dual Knowledge & Cream of Liberation: Two Jewels of Indian Wisdom by Sri Swami Karapatra and Swami Tandavaraya, translated by Swami Sri Ramanananda Saraswathi, 2003

Light on the Indian World: The Essential Writings of Charles Eastman (Ohiyesa), edited by Michael Oren Fitzgerald, 2002

Music of the Sky: An Anthology of Spiritual Poetry, edited by Patrick Laude and Barry McDonald, 2004

The Mystics of Islam by Reynold A. Nicholson, 2002

Naturalness: A Classic of Shin Buddhism by Kenryo Kanamatsu, 2002

The Path of Muhammad: A Book on Islamic Morals and Ethics by Imam Birgivi, interpreted by Shaykh Tosun Bayrak, 2005

Tripura Rahasya: The Secret of the Supreme Goddess, translated by Swami Sri Ramanananda Saraswathi, 2002

The Way of Sufism by Titus Burckhardt, 2006